Scholarship and

Scholarship and Christian Faith

Enlarging the Conversation

DOUGLAS JACOBSEN AND
RHONDA HUSTEDT JACOBSEN

With essays by
Rodney J. Sawatsky
Crystal L. Downing
Edward B. Davis
David L. Weaver-Zercher
Susanna Bede Caroselli
Kim S. Phipps

UNIVERSITY PRESS

2004

OXFORD
UNIVERSITY PRESS

Oxford   New York

Auckland   Bangkok   Buenos Aires   Cape Town   Chennai
Dar es Salaam   Delhi   Hong Kong   Istanbul   Karachi   Kolkata
Kuala Lumpur   Madrid   Melbourne   Mexico City   Mumbai   Nairobi
São Paulo   Shanghai   Taipei   Tokyo   Toronto

Published by Oxford University Press, Inc.
198 Madison Avenue, New York, New York 10016

www.oup.com

Oxford is a registered trademark of Oxford University Press

Library of Congress Cataloging-in-Publication Data

Scholarship and Christian faith: enlarging the conversation /
Douglas Jacobsen and Rhonda Hustedt Jacobsen.
p. cm.
Includes bibliographical references and index.
ISBN-13 978-0-19-517038-2
ISBN 0-19-517038-5
1. Church and college. 2. Learning and scholarship—Religious
aspects—Christianity. 3. Education (Christian theology) I. Jacobsen,
Douglas G. (Douglas Gordon), 1951– II. Jacobsen, Rhonda Hustedt.
LC383 .S33 2004
378'.071—dc21   2003008369

9 8 7 6 5 4

Printed in the United States of America
on acid-free paper

For Ernest L. Boyer (1928–1995)

Foreword

Martin E. Marty

Right off, many readers will find themselves a bit disoriented as they read this book. Contrary to expectation, the coauthors and essayists are not engaged in whining about what went wrong with Christian scholarship.

Up to now, much if not most of the literature on their subject has been marked by complaints and whimpers:

> In a golden age theology was queen of sciences and now it is not.

> Once higher education in the Western world was Christian and now it is not.

> In the good old days scholars in other disciplines honored Christian learning and today most ignore or disdain it.

> We Christian scholars have much to say but we cannot get a hearing because of the low priority given religious inquiry and teaching in colleges and universities—including those associated with the church.

> And on. And on.

Now, each of these complaints, which sound peevish to those not in "the conversation" but resound consolingly among us happy few in "the community" of Christian scholarship, reflects realities and calls for reaction, response, and responsible setting of new priorities. They should prompt criticism, of which Christian scholars may not receive enough. There is plenty of criticism on these pages, but very little whining.

The case against whining is one to which most parents can relate. "Get out of here until you get over your snit, and as soon as you are ready to state your case in a way that I can grasp it, come back." Let the tantrum, or at least the sour mood, pass—and *then* we can converse. I often ask parents if they can recall taking a constructive action as a consequence of a child's whining, and they characteristically draw a blank. Ask them whether in critical conversation they were confronted with challenges to which they could relate, and most will find plenty of instances.

The Jacobsens' openness to critical learning and teaching may be traceable to the conversation that goes on in lively marriages like theirs, shared classroom and curricular enterprise as durable as theirs, and a willingness to listen to diverse voices before speaking up. Whatever its source, this whine-free critical approach is refreshing, and it must be catching, since the guest authors emulate it, by and large.

A believable foreword should not be a mere puff or hyperbolic endorsement; I don't picture potential buyers standing in a bookstore and reading the up-front material when deciding whether or not to buy the book. Because forewords are called forewords they have to appear in the "fore" parts of books. I often think it would be better if they could always be turned into "afterwords." After readers have become familiar with the contents of the book, they like to compare impressions with others—at least I always do—and an afterword could provide the initial conversation partner. To use the language of the subtitle, a foreword is a first move toward "enlarging the conversation," proposed by an invited intruder to the discourse that is already underway.

On those terms, a foreworder is free to point to some additional directions the conversation might now take. There might be more talk about the Christian scholarship that issues from the private "secular" or public college and university, where countless Christian thinkers pursue learning. More rooting in the inquiries that have long gone on and now intensify on Roman Catholic campuses is also indicated.

But the present work, with its generally Protestant flavor, is both valuable and important in its own right. It is easy to see its relevance to zones not highlighted in this book, on secular campuses. For that matter, there is much here for scholars and lay people who are not currently teaching or studying the collegiate aspects of scholarship with the intensity that this campus-bound roster of writers demonstrates. And the perspectives on Christian scholarship offered will certainly make the future participation of a wider circle of conversation partners easier to bring about.

The accent of several of the essayists and the co-authors on "wholeness" and "integration" of the various components of campus existence and the diverse voices of scholars in the disciplines is actually very Catholic. Father Walter Ong, S.J., who is mentioned in these pages, coached me half a century ago on dimensions of the term and concept of catholicity. Catholic does not only mean "universal"; its etymology reflects *kata+holos,* the attempt to penetrate the whole, to reach all aspects of being. Of course, catholicity is never realized on earth, but Christian scholarship keeps its scope in mind. Read this book, please, as a set of themes and variations on ways to address the whole of human learning.

We speak of the goal of finding elements of community, Christian community, in colleges and universities. But I have been influenced by thinkers— Glen Tinder comes to mind—who caution against too ready resort to the dream of community. Community, given human nature and human interests, is very, very hard to realize. It comes more readily to a family, a congregation, a company of people who have shared profound experience than it does to the college and university, to say nothing of the nation. Community occurs among people who can share each other's secrets and exact profound commitment.

A college or university is more like a republic, a congeries of disciplines, interests, voices, approaches, not all of which mesh or are imbricated—yes, the word is in this book and is properly used! Not everything there will look or be relevant to everything else. Not all controversies and conflicts will be resolved. To belong to a college does not mean the surrender of other belongings and loyalties, however embarrassingly most "Alma Mater" anthems suggest it does and must. Rather a campus is a set of people who form *associations* where less is at risk than in true community, but where the yield therefore may be greater than in places where the conversation has to be guarded, sheltered, muffled. I think that is what most of the authors are speaking about here, and the code word "community" comes naturally to them and to us readers. But to think through the nature of associational commitment can be a way of helping "enlarge the conversation" in fresh ways.

A foreword, I said, dare not simply be a puff, or it will not be credible. A foreword certainly should not shy away from evidencing enthusiasm. The dominant note here is one of enjoyment. Enjoyment because the authors have gathered so much, conversed so well, and tantalized us to pursue what they approach. Enjoyment because they successfully invite us into the conversation and show that they stand ready to keep on learning, even as they teach. I learned much while reading this book in manuscript form and intend to consult it regularly when it lands on my desk in book form. The Jacobsens are aware that the Christian cause advances not only when believers out-act, out-give, or out-commit those around them, as one hopes they sometimes do. But they also have to out-think more of those who pursue human goals, but who are now often unmindful of what the Christian individual, association, and— oops!—community might have to offer.

Preface

This book is about Christian scholarship. It is about individuals who identify themselves as both Christians and scholars and it is about the ways faith and scholarship are intentionally blended and unconsciously embodied in their lives and work. To some degree, this book is also about the colleges and universities in which Christian scholars do their work. Some of those institutions are explicitly Christian in their statements of mission and identity; a number of other schools are church related but are more tangential in the connections they maintain with their founding denominations; and still other institutions of higher learning are intentionally secular in their self-understanding. Our contention is that Christian scholars and Christian scholarship can flourish in all three of those settings.

In recent years a significant number of publications have addressed this general topic, and many of them have had a critical edge to them, telling Christian scholars how they ought to insert faith into their scholarship and often telling the academy as a whole that it ought to show more respect for faith-informed learning. Our goal is more humble and empirical. Rather than propose any new model of what Christian scholarship ought to look like, we seek merely to describe the many different forms that Christian scholarship has taken and can take. Our intention is not to pronounce definitive answers but to enlarge the conversation: to provide a framework that will better enable persons who embody different styles of Christian scholarship to converse respectfully and intelligently with each other and with their other-religious and non-religious peers in the academy.

As for the place of religious faith in the academy as a whole, we view the contemporary situation in a relatively positive light. True, a pall of residual secularism does hang over many of the disciplines, but in recent years more and more scholars in more and more fields of study have begun to acknowledge that faith or spirituality is a factor in the way people see and understand the world, including the way scholars see and understand the world. As the academy becomes more willing to (re)include faith as a factor in scholarship, and as Christian scholars become less defensive about their roles and identity within the academy, the possibility exists for a new and positive engagement between faith and scholarship that can enrich us all.

The calling of scholarship is a calling to pay attention to the world. Scholars pour their lives into the details of what they study with passion and intensity. No one can pay attention to the entire world, of course, so the realm of scholarship has been divided into a wide assortment of fields of study, disciplines, and subdisciplines that mark off separate segments of reality. Scholars often tend to inflate the importance of their own particular foci of study—that is what keeps them going—but on their better days most scholars remember that their own scholarly efforts are only part of the larger human task of paying attention to the world. Every scholar contributes to that larger task, and every scholar simultaneously benefits from the work of others. Scholarship is thus a communal activity. While scholarship is partly driven by simple curiosity and wonder (scholars typically cannot help but pay attention to the things that fascinate them), it is also to some degree undertaken on behalf of and for the benefit of others.

Christian scholars have a special responsibility with regard to this communal dimension of scholarship because the core Christian values of love and reconciliation are communally oriented. This means that while Christian scholarship will often follow the lines of division that exist within the academy as a whole, Christian scholars should feel a special responsibility to frame their work in a way that really does contribute to the overall good of the world and to the benefit of the academy as a whole. Robert Bellah and his associates expressed this sentiment well in the closing words of *The Good Society* (1991), writing: "[I]f we are fortunate enough to have the gift of faith through which we see ourselves as members of the universal community of all being, then we bear a special responsibility to bring whatever insights we have to the common discussion of new problems, not because we have any superior wisdom but because we can be . . . ambassadors of trust in a fearful world."[1]

In the past Christian scholars have perhaps been too defensive, spending too much time trying to prove the validity of Christian faith and perhaps not enough time actually contributing to the good of the world. While not denigrating the work of Christian witness and apologetics within the realm of scholarship, we stress that Christian scholarship can take many valid forms. Christian scholarship can involve listening as much as speaking, service as much as leadership, and simple friendship as much as critical engagement with one's colleagues. And an either/or choice is not required: one can both listen and speak, serve and lead, be a friend and a critic. The goal is to honor all these options and to encourage Christian scholars always to season their work with a concern for love, reconciliation, and the building of trust in the scholarly world.

In a very small way, this book seeks to exemplify what it discusses. It is the product of three years of collaboration—of friendship, conversation, argument, laughter, and revision upon revision of our thinking. We have all grown through the process and have been forced again and again to move beyond mere criticism to constructive dialogue about the nature and character of Christian scholarship. This project began in the fall of 1999 when, funded by a grant from the Christian College Consortium (under a program headed by Harold Heie), Messiah College launched a yearlong faculty "Christian Scholarship Seminar" designed to explore existing models and to discuss our own practices of Christian scholarship. Following that seminar, a group of us continued to refine our thoughts via a series of colloquies, forums, public presentations, and circulated papers reflecting on the nature of scholarship in general and on Christian scholarship in particular. Helpful feedback on an earlier draft of this book was provided by administrators who participated in a "Mission and Vocation Seminar" that met regularly during the 2002–2003 school year and by senior faculty who participated in a "Capstone Course Retreat" held in the summer of 2003, both of which were funded by the Lilly Endowment through its Theological Exploration of Vocation grant program. Insightful suggestions were also provided by Joseph Huffman, Richard Hughes, Nancey Murphy, Mark Schwehn, William Vance Trollinger, Jr., and Valerie Weaver-Zercher. Finally, we have benefitted from the counsel of Cynthia Read and her colleagues at Oxford University Press.

The structure of this book is designed to capture at least some of the flavor of this collaborative, dialogical endeavor. The five chapters, written by Douglas Jacobsen and Rhonda Hustedt Jacobsen, line out the main conclusions we have drawn along the way. The essays (composed by Crystal Downing, Edward B. Davis, Susanna Bede Caroselli, and David Weaver-Zercher) that are paired with the first four of these chapters then exemplify, examine, enliven, or expand the issues and ideas raised in each chapter. The general flow of the argument moves from a critique of the most prominent existing model of Christian scholarship (called "the integration of faith and learning") through a series of chapters exploring the personal dimensions of Christian scholarship, the variety of Christian traditions affecting scholarship, and the multifaceted character of scholarship in general, ending with a map of the complex terrain of Christian scholarship in all its many forms and manifestations. While the book as a whole seeks to address Christian scholarship in the broad context of the academy, the prologue by Rodney Sawatsky and the epilogue by Kim Phipps helpfully situate this larger conversation in the specific arena of Christian higher education. Sawatsky questions the "myth of declension" that has driven so much of the literature on Christian higher education and suggests that hope is a much more fitting ideal for church-related colleges and universities. Phipps reflects on some of the practical ramifications that flow from the book's analysis of Christian scholarship, arguing that Christian colleges and universities need to function as diverse communities of learning where everyone is respected and where all the many different forms of Christian scholarship are honored and supported.

While intelligent readers need no advice about how to read a book, it might be worth pointing out that while the prologue, chapters, essays, and epilogue do follow a logical pattern of progression, the argument of the book is ultimately more configural than linear. Thus it is possible to jump into the argument almost anywhere and then read backward or forward to complete the picture. While a few short sections of the text do become necessarily technical, the book as a whole is written to be read by scholars in all the disciplines and to engage the widest possible number of scholars in the discussion. We hope you find it both helpful and enjoyable.

NOTE

1. Robert N. Bellah, Richard Madsen, William M. Sullivan, Ann Swidler, and Steven M. Tipton, *The Good Society* (New York: Knopf, 1991), 286.

Contents

Contributors

Susanna Bede Caroselli, SSG, received her Ph.D. in art history from Johns Hopkins University. She has served on the curatorial staffs of the Frick Collection, Detroit Institute of Arts, and Los Angeles County Museum of Art and has taught at USC, UCLA, and Yale Divinity School. Her publications include *The Painted Enamels of Limoges* and *Italian Panel Painting of the Early Renaissance*. She is Professor of Art History at Messiah College.

Edward B. Davis earned his Ph.D. in the history and philosophy of science from Indiana University in Bloomington. He has edited the complete *Works of Robert Boyle* (14 volumes; Pickering and Chatto) and prepared a special edition of Boyle's work *A Free Enquiry into the Vulgarly Received Notion of Nature* for Cambridge University Press. He is Distinguished Professor of the History of Science at Messiah College.

Crystal L. Downing has a Ph.D. in English from the University of California at Santa Barbara. She writes on a variety of topics, ranging from Victorian aesthetics to postmodern ethics, and is a film critic. Her book *Writing Performances: The Stages of Dorothy L. Sayers* is forthcoming. She is Associate Professor of English and Film Studies at Messiah College.

Douglas Jacobsen has a Ph.D. from the University of Chicago. His publications include *An Unprov'd Experiment: Religious Pluralism in Colonial New Jersey* and *Thinking in the Spirit: Theologies of the Early*

Pentecostal Movement. He is Distinguished Professor of Church History and Theology at Messiah College.

Rhonda Hustedt Jacobsen has an Ed.D. from Temple University in the social foundations of education. She has been granted several teaching awards and has also received support from the John Templeton Foundation for her work in the area of science and religion. She is Professor of Psychology and Director of Faculty Development at Messiah College.

Kim S. Phipps received a Ph.D. in communication studies from Kent State University. She writes and presents regularly in the field of political and religious rhetoric and is a frequent speaker on themes related to Christian/church-related higher education. She was formerly Academic Dean at Malone College and is currently Provost at Messiah College.

Rodney J. Sawatsky has a Ph.D. in religion from Princeton University. His publications include *The Limits of Perfection* and a host of articles dealing with American religion, Mennonite history, higher education, and interreligious dialogue. He was formerly President of Conrad Grebel College, University of Waterloo in Ontario, and is currently President of Messiah College.

David L. Weaver-Zercher received his Ph.D. in American religious history from the University of North Carolina at Chapel Hill. He is the author of *The Amish in the American Imagination* and editor of *Minding the Church: Scholarship in the Anabaptist Tradition.* He is Associate Professor of American Religious History at Messiah College.

Scholarship and Christian Faith

Prologue: The Virtue of Scholarly Hope

Rodney J. Sawatsky

Scholarship at its best is much more than the pursuit of truth; it is the quest for wisdom. But what is wisdom? Who is wise? For Christian scholars, and for their Jewish and Muslim colleagues, wisdom is grounded in God. Wisdom is the fear of God, says the wisdom literature; it is the love of God and neighbor, the law declares; and it is doing justice, loving kindness, and walking humbly with your God, the prophets clarify. Wisdom requires careful thought, but it is much more than intellectual knowing. It embraces emotions and actions, and indeed our entire being. Such wholeness of heart, soul, and mind lifts wisdom above mere cognitive truth.[1] Christians believe wisdom is defined by the harmony, integrity, and unity of the divine *logos* made flesh in Jesus of Nazareth. Wisdom is truth incarnate. The incarnation is then the alpha and omega of Christian scholarship.[2]

Christian scholarship is a wonderful and even holy calling. The words and metaphors employed to describe the dynamics of being both Christian and scholarly tend also to prescribe. At best our language opens the imagination to ever greater creativity and possibility; at worst it narrows the vision and limits the promise. The task of this book is to enrich Christian scholarship both descriptively and prescriptively by considering existing vocabularies and by exploring expanded metaphors. We hope to enlarge the conversation by hearing more voices and by encouraging the participants to listen to each other and to learn from each other.

The conversation regarding Christian scholarship is between and among countless Christians who deem themselves scholars and scholars who are or would be Christians. These scholars are affiliated with many different denominations or, as is becoming increasingly common today, with no denomination at all. Within the conversation there is a rich diversity of theological voices. Many participants are located in private and public universities and colleges that today have no religious affiliation. Others pursue their scholarship within an intentionally Christian academic community, be it Roman Catholic or Protestant. These institutions are strongly committed to encouraging Christian scholarship, so this conversation often engages entire institutions as well as individual scholars.

The pervasive metaphor of integration cannot help but be central to this conversation, as in "the integration of faith and learning." In the essays that follow, my colleagues reflect on the strengths and limitations of this particular way of shaping the conversation and propose promising complementary formulations. Here I only wish to draw attention to the word "faith" in the foregoing phrase. On the one hand, "faith" is often a simple synonym for being Christian, as in "the Christian faith." On the other hand, faith can be seen as only one dimension of Christian being. The Apostle Paul used three words to describe the full contours of Christian identity: faith, hope, and love. Christian scholars need to pay more attention to that three-part formula—a holistic formula for wisdom—and not limit their metaphors to faith alone.

Too often, Christian scholars have focused too exclusively on faith—not hope or love—and thereby have narrowed their definition of faith to mean religious beliefs about God, the world, and humankind, or a worldview embracing all these ideas. Faith as a verb, faith understood as trust or "seeking and discovering meaning," unfortunately is not usually part of the conversation.[3] When we speak of the integration of faith and learning, the noun form of faith is typically what is meant: how do Christian beliefs about the nature of reality compare, contrast, and integrate with assertions made by the various academic disciplines? This is surely an important question to ask, but it is not the only question.

Christian scholarship also necessarily involves love and hope. We might then speak about the integration of love and learning and of hope and learning. The connection between love and learning is relatively easy to understand. Many Christian scholars undertake their work out of a profound love for God's creation, a deep desire to serve all that God pronounced good. In fact, the concern to apply knowledge morally and ethically must be present in some way for that scholarship, no matter how abstract, to be considered Christian. Parker J. Palmer, a Quaker philosopher of education, even argues that love is the origin of knowledge: "The deepest wellspring of our desire to know is the passion to recreate the organic community in which the world was first created." The goal of this knowledge "arising from love is the reunification and reconstruction of broken selves and worlds." Education shaped by Christian spirituality, says Palmer, has an incarnational understanding of truth and an incarnational purpose.[4]

Hope is equally essential to a definition of Christian scholarship. Hope is the deep-seated confidence that this is God's world and that the future, including the future of scholarship, need not be feared, for God's kingdom will come, and God's will will be done, on earth as it is in heaven. Students and the larger society are often fearful and hopeless, and too often Christian scholarship fails to offer an alternative. Even Christian scholars have been lacking in hope— sometimes to the point of being pathologically pessimistic, almost always to the point of being overly defensive.

Whence comes this defensiveness and lack of hope? The metaphor of integration does not encourage hopelessness. Instead this lack of hope is derived from another dominant theme in Christian higher education, namely a reading of American religious history that says the decline of Christian higher education is virtually inevitable. More than anything else, this myth of declension has cramped our thinking and narrowed our reflection on the nature and character of Christian scholarship. If we truly want to enlarge the conversation, we must first revisit this reigning mythology.

The Limits of Declension

The decline of Christian privilege and power in the American academy is by now well established. The massive transition over the past centuries of America's leading private and even public colleges and universities from their original Christian foundations, affiliations, and vocations to pluralistic and secularized institutions has recently been subject to extensive analysis, especially by George M. Marsden and James T. Burtchaell.[5] Indeed, this metamorphosis of higher education can be seen as one of the clearest examples of secularization in American history.

Nevertheless, the declension thesis must be significantly qualified. A common conclusion and prevailing fear that Christian colleges today continue on an inevitable slippery slope leading them ever further away from their original edenic purity is inaccurate and counterproductive. True, many schools have abandoned and others may well still abandon their Christian heritage. But surely even Father Burtchaell, who exhaustively documented this trend in his *Dying of the Light,* is not a historical determinist, despite his unfortunate use of the term "inexorable" to describe this pattern.[6] In fact, the overwhelming reality today is that both Christian colleges and Christian scholarship are thriving. Intentionally Christian colleges are experiencing rapid growth not only in enrollments and facilities but also in academic quality.[7] And it can be argued that some American colleges and universities are actually becoming more Christian. These success stories have been documented by Richard Hughes and William Adrian in their *Models for Christian Higher Education: Strategies for Success in the Twenty-First Century* (1997) and Robert Benne in his *Quality with Soul: How Six Premier Colleges and Universities Keep Faith with Their Religious Traditions* (2001).[8] Declension is clearly not the whole story!

Even in universities and colleges now thoroughly secularized, religion generally and Christianity specifically have far from declined into oblivion. Secularization has not resulted in unmitigated secularism. A recent study of four such campuses argued, versus the proponents of declension, that the patterns of religious change at these institutions "seem more clearly to add up to the declericalizing, de-denominationalizing, and, in some cases, de-Christianizing of campuses than to their secularization or their marginalization of religion."[9] The authors rightly contend that scholars today are debating the very notion of secularization, recognizing thereby the continuing, and perhaps even increasing, strength of spirituality (if not always institutionalized religion) in America and on the nation's college campuses. Their conclusion "that the ethos of decentered, diverse, religiously tolerant institutions of higher education is a breeding ground for vital religious practice and teaching"[10] rightly qualifies an overanxious version of declension.

Craig Dykstra of the Lilly Endowment has similarly argued that many colleges and universities that seem secular on the surface still possess convictional traits that, properly understood, are supportive of rather than antithetical to religious faith.[11] And Robert Wuthnow, the premier sociologist of religion in America, says much the same. He writes: "I take issue with those who emphasize the inexorable processes of secularization in dealing with church-related higher education." Acknowledging recent tensions between liberal and conservative subcultures in America, Wuthnow says: "Church-related colleges are for the most part a force in the middle. They include not only conservatives, but also liberal—and even secular—tendencies. And public universities are not only secular, or liberal, but contexts in which the sacred is evident as well."[12]

Yet the fundamental fact remains that spirituality on most contemporary college campuses is highly subjectivistic and individualistic. It is often distinguished from and even hostile to "institutionalized" religion. Christian faith, however it might have been engaged as an overt conversation partner with the scholarly essence of the academic enterprise in years past, does so only rarely today. Pursuing connections between faith and scholarship is simply not on the agenda except in overtly faith-based colleges and universities. Indeed in the wake of religion's academic disestablishment, Christian perspectives and interpretations sometimes struggle to gain a place at the academic table. George Marsden has led those Christian scholars who insist that this situation must be rectified, that the postmodern academy of today ought to welcome Christian interpretations of reality into the conversation alongside other alternatives if it is to be true to its own pluralist claims.[13]

But is the problem only one of Christian scholarship not being granted a seat at the academic table? Not so, says Daryl Hart.[14] He argues that Marsden's experience of feeling excluded from the "secular" academy is also a function of his own peculiarly Reformed and Kuyperian definition of what constitutes legitimate Christian scholarship. For Marsden and other like-minded Reformed scholars, Christian scholarship tends to be different from and in some sense necessarily opposed to secular scholarship. Hart paraphrases Marsden to say: "Christian faith causes believers to see things differently, and this difference leads, or at least should lead, to scholarship from believers that is distinct from the learning of non-believers."[15] How could one hold such a view and not feel estranged at least to some degree from the larger academy? Hart says that in order for Christians to enter more constructively into the world of mainstream scholarship, they will need to adopt "an understanding of the university that is less antagonistic and more accommodating." His suggestion is that a more "Lutheran notion of the paradoxical relation between the affairs of man and the ways of God may prove to be a better approach for [Christian] scholars than the Reformed notion of taking every thought captive for Christ."[16]

We do not need to adjudicate between these two academicians and their respective approaches to Christian scholarship. It is sufficient to note that Christian scholars are actively debating how their Christian commitments should inform their scholarship. Certainly different theological traditions and scholarly dispositions will respond differently to this challenge. The declension metaphor, however, tends to slant the conversation toward more defensive and even adversarial perspectives instead of opening the dialogue to include more hopeful and irenic views and voices.

But the language of declension is also problematic for another reason: it implies a questionable moral judgment. Declension is a falling away from an ideal, but from whose ideal or, more accurately, from what mix of ideals and less-than-ideal realities? Individuals will differ in their assessments of these matters. Marsden admits to his own ambivalence in this regard. Thus even while he asserts that "we are not using *secularization* naively as equivalent to *decline*," he adds that "most of us see the change in the role of religion in modern higher education as *in some ways* a loss."[17] Nonetheless he qualifies his remarks by saying that his critique of American education "is far different from arguing that there was a lost golden age to which we should return." Marsden recognizes that correction was needed, even if an overcorrection resulted: "The old colleges and their predecessors were part of a Christian establishment that provided Christianity with an unjustly privileged social and political position and attempted to promote the faith by associating it with power and coercion. Although these institutions had many good features as well, they needed to be disestablished."[18] And disestablished they were. But how is this disestablishment to be evaluated?

The social ethicist Ernst Troeltsch, writing in the early twentieth century, offers a helpful perspective.[19] He argued that Christians tended to organize and function within history in three typical ways. The first mode he called "church." Here the goal was the Christian control of the entire culture, with the state church as its natural expression. He labeled a second type of Christian self-consciousness "sect." Sectarians believed that the ideal form of Christian existence was found in the purity and love of the local community of faith. Any desire to control the larger culture was jettisoned. They celebrated religious freedom, separation of church and state, and voluntarism. Pluralism was assumed, not feared. Troeltsch's third approach to Christian faith and life, the one he rightly predicted would become increasingly significant, he labeled "mysticism," for here the individual, interior experience of God predominates.

In American history, the "church" approach to Christianity flourished most strongly in Puritan New England. This vision surely influenced the founding of Harvard profoundly, as well as many other church-related colleges thereafter. By contrast, sectarian and mystical forms of faith flourished in places like Pennsylvania, where Anabaptists, Quakers, Pietists, and other dissenters found religious freedom and erected their own colleges. Scholars attracted to the declension thesis invariably take their cues from New England; those less troubled by the disestablishment of religion tend to be more oriented toward a Pennsylvanian view of faith and society. Indeed, pietism is often blamed by students of declension as a major force undermining the Christian identity of church-related colleges and universities.[20]

Today Pennsylvanian-style sectarianism, alongside mysticism, defines much of American culture. Religious pluralism is thriving, and educational pluralism is gaining increasing recognition. But New England churchliness, with its passion for a unified Christian culture and worldview shaped by well-formed Christian minds, still has a powerful voice. What we are seeing now is an emerging recognition within the world of Christian higher education of legitimate and valuable alternative visions. Some scholars and schools that historically were more sectarian in orientation are developing a greater sense of public responsibility and cultural engagement, and other scholars and schools that historically were more churchly are recognizing the realities and possibilities of religious and educational pluralism. The time is surely ripe for the conversation that this book seeks to encourage and facilitate.

Learning from the past is a necessary part of our conversation, and those who remind us of that story deserve our gratitude. Yet the past dare not overwhelm the present or the future. A focus on maintaining what theoretically *was* limits the potential of *what yet may be*. Good things have been lost, and some should be recovered, but we must not forget what has been gained. Even though controlled by churches and privileging Christian language, so-called Christian colleges and universities of the past were in many ways profoundly un-Christian. Consider only their attitude toward African Americans. Historically few, if any, explicitly Christian schools led the way in battling racism and championing integration. And without major spiritual renewal that pattern will continue into the future, according to the excellent Christian scholarship of Michael O. Emerson and Christian Smith.[21] If we consider other ethical issues, such as attitudes toward women, the same general pattern prevails. With all due respect for those who champion the declension thesis of Christian higher education, might it not be better to engage the future with hope rather than grieve a questionable past?

The Importance of Hope

A more adequate formulation may be to speak in terms of becoming ever more fully a Christian scholar or a Christian college rather than recovering or preserving an uncertain past. The language then shifts away from defensiveness toward the purpose, the end, the *telos* of Christian scholarship. Christian academicians often view the past as the basis for the present, by grounding their scholarship in a rich theology of creation. Complementing this with an eschatological orientation—a biblical vision of the future in which peace and righteousness will flourish and learning will result in wisdom—might be a helpful, appropriate, and even necessary counterbalance to what can become a nostalgic and anxious fixation on the past.

A hopeful posture toward the future is not uniquely Christian. For example, the Jewish scholar Neil Postman argued that to avoid the *end* of education, education must have an *end*, that is, "a transcendent, spiritual idea that gives purpose and clarity to learning.["22] "Similarly, a Hindu friend of the late Christian missiologist Lesslie Newbigin said: "You cannot have hopeful and responsible action without some vision of a possible future. To put it another way, if there is no point in the story as a whole, there is no point in my own action. If the story is meaningless, any action of mine is meaningless."[23]

Combining *telos* and praxis or, even better, grounding praxis in *telos* is central to all education, but especially to Christian education.[24] Meaningful scholarship must be inspired by a purpose, by an ideal end toward which it strives. Ernest Boyer said it well in *College: The Undergraduate Experience in America*: "Education for what purpose? Competence to what end? At a time in life when values should be shaped and personal priorities sharply probed, what a tragedy it would be if the most deeply felt issues, the most haunting questions, the most creative moments were pushed to the fringes of our institutional life." Boyer concluded: "The undergraduate experience at its best will move the student from competence to commitment."[25]

As for more explicitly theological understandings of hope and *telos* in higher education, certain Roman Catholic scholars seem to be at the forefront. Walter J. Ong, for example, explicitly challenged the declension obsession with the past in his Marianist Award lecture at the University of Dayton, saying:

> The Catholic Church builds on the past, of course, on tradition. But the faith is not retroactive. As I have earlier suggested, there is no

way to recover the past, even if we wanted to. And who would want to? I have never met anyone who knows in scholarly detail any age of the past who would prefer that age to the present, however threatening and dangerous and ugly many things in the present may be. If you know the past in detail, it was in its own ways threatening and dangerous and ugly as well as beautiful and consoling. Tradition builds on the past but it always faces not into the past but into the future.[26]

Rather than seeking to restore the past, Ong suggests we forge into the future. He says that if scholarship is truly Christian,

it will keep itself moving on a quest which is impossible to realize entirely but which is promising always, and often exhilarating. . . . We have a faith that seeks understanding—*fides quaerens intellectum*, as St. Anselm, in his learned humility, put it some 900 years ago. Our quest for understanding lives in Christian hope, a hope in Jesus Christ, who became incarnate in this world. . . . Since all this world is God's creation, all learning not only about God but also directly about this world can further our quest to understand our faith.

Ong is no glassy-eyed optimist. He knows that the path to the future, as in the past, will be laced with "overwhelming human suffering and evil." But he holds fast to hope nonetheless, explaining:

For much evil, there is no human answer at all, but for the Christian, if there is not a simple answer, there is a response, in God's own response. The response is that we must counter evil with good. In the incarnation of the Son, in Jesus Christ, the infinite God responds to evil by entering into the human condition, with its suffering and its subjection to evil, to overcome suffering and evil by good, culminating in the obedience that Jesus expressed on the cross.[27]

Grounded in this spirit of realistic hope, Christian scholarship seeks not only to understand and to celebrate the creation as it is but also to participate in God's work of restoring and transforming the world. Thus Christian scholarship will evoke and provoke creativity, curiosity, and imagination. Like prophecy of old, it dreams dreams and sees visions. Inspired by the biblical promise that some day all things will be made new, Christian scholarship can and should be both deeply optimistic and simultaneously shamelessly realistic. The Apostle Paul admonished: "Do not be conformed to this world, but be transformed by the renewing of your minds, so that you may discern what is the will of God—what is good and acceptable and perfect."[28] Christian scholars will take this advice seriously, identifying with and, by grace, contributing to God's will that all be made new. Christian faithfulness invites us to embrace the future with hope, as well as faith and love, in and through our scholarly work and calling.

The vocation of Christian scholarship, like the mission of the Christian college, is thus situated teleologically, in the context of Christian hope. Christian scholars are a community of pilgrims on a journey into a hope-filled future. On our scholarly journey we are often tempted to stop and settle down, claiming to have arrived at the sum of truth that others still seek, or at least, ought to seek. Such triumphalism is a constant temptation, especially for Christians. But following the model of Jesus, we are called to humility. Certainly as Christian scholars we have unique understandings of reality, important perspectives to bring to the academy, and significant insights to offer the churches. Yet our calling is to undertake our work with a spirit of compassion, kindness, humility, meekness, patience, forbearance, forgiveness, love, peace, and thankfulness, for these are the virtues through which knowledge becomes wisdom.

It is this journey of hope, tempered by genuine humility, that requires us to enlarge the conversation concerning the nature of Christian scholarship. None of us by ourselves sees the world in all its fullness the way it is, much less what it might yet become. Thus we need the insights of others to complement and complete our own. We need to enlarge the conversation about Christian scholarship because scholarship is by definition an ever-enlarging conversation. By bringing the wisdom of the past into creative dialogue with the ever-widening horizons of emerging knowledge, we anticipate the future with hope. The Russian literary critic and Orthodox Christian philosopher Mikhail Bakhtin[29] understood the dialogic character of scholarship and its connection to history and eschatology as well as anyone. He described the human conversation toward truth in the context of "great time" as follows:

> There is neither a first nor a last word and there are no limits to the dialogic context (it extends into the boundless past and the boundless future). Even past meanings, that is, those born in the dialogue of past centuries, can never be stable (finalized, ended once for all)— they will always change (be renewed) in the process of subsequent, future development of the dialogue. At any moment in the development of the dialogue there are immense, boundless masses of forgotten contextual meanings, but at certain moments of the dialogue's subsequent development along the way they are recalled and invigorated in renewed form (in a new context). Nothing is absolutely dead: every meaning will have its homecoming festival.[30]

While time endures, the work of scholarship will never be complete, and neither will the task of Christian scholarship. Let us, then, enlarge the dialogue to embrace all who are called to this wonderful vocation, no matter what their disciplines, denominations, or dispositions. And let us invite others to the table as well. In the great conversation of scholarship, Christians have nothing to fear and much to learn and contribute. Our calling is to seek wisdom at the many points where our faith, hope, and love intersect with our learning and to share that wisdom with all other seekers after truth.

NOTES

1. Ellen T. Charry, in "To Know, Love and Enjoy God," *Theology Today* 59, 2 (July 2002) says: "Modernity created a new understanding of the truth that divorced truth and knowledge from goodness, beauty and wisdom, that is from psychological and moral flourishing" (174).

2. Incarnational theology, in which Jesus as the incarnate God reveals the truth by being the truth, is central to many Roman Catholic as well as Anabaptist approaches to Christian higher education. See George D. O'Brien, *The Idea of a Catholic University* (Chicago: University of Chicago Press, 2002). See also Rodney J. Sawatsky, "What Can the Mennonite Tradition Contribute to Christian Higher Education?" in *Models for Christian Higher Education: Strategies for Success in the Twenty-First Century*, edited by Richard T. Hughes and William B. Adrian (Grand Rapids, Mich.: Eerdmans, 1997), 187–99.

3. See Sharon Daloz Parks, *Big Questions, Worthy Dreams: Mentoring Young Adults in their Search for Meaning, Purpose and Faith* (San Francisco: Jossey-Bass, 2000), 7. Parks writes: "Faith is more adequately recognized as *the activity of seeking and discovering meaning in the most comprehensive dimensions of our experience.* Faith is a broad, generic human phenomenon. To be human is to dwell in faith, to dwell in the sense one makes out of life—what seems ultimately true and dependable about self, world and cosmos (whether that meaning be strong or fragile, expressed in religious or secular terms)."

4. Parker J. Palmer, *To Know As We Are Known: Education As a Spiritual Journey* (San Francisco: Harper, 1993), 8, 14.

5. George M. Marsden, *The Soul of the American University: From Protestant Establishment to Established Nonbelief* (New York: Oxford University Press, 1994); *The Secularization of the Academy*, edited by George M. Marsden and Bradley J. Longfield (New York: Oxford University Press, 1992); and James Tunstead Burtchaell, *The Dying of the Light: The Disengagement of Colleges and Universities from their Christian Churches* (Grand Rapids, Mich.: Eerdmans, 1998). See also Philip Gleason, *Contending with Modernity: Catholic Higher Education in the Twentieth Century* (New York: Oxford University Press, 1995); and Douglas Sloan, *Faith and Knowledge: Mainline Protestantism and American Higher Education* (Louisville, Ky.: Westminster John Knox, 1994).

6. James T. Burtchaell, "The Alienation of Christian Higher Education in America: Diagnosis and Prognosis," in *Schooling Christians: "Holy Experiments" in American Education*, edited by Stanley Hauerwas and John Westerhoff (Grand Rapids, Mich.: Eerdmans, 1992), 132.

7. See *Professing in the Postmodern Academy: Faculty and the Future of Church-Related Colleges* (Waco, Tex.: Baylor University Press, 2002).

8. Robert Benne, *Quality with Soul: How Six Premier Colleges and Universities Keep Faith with Their Religious Traditions* (Grand Rapids, Mich.: Eerdmans, 2001).

9. Conrad Cherry, Betty A. DeBerg, and Amanda Porterfield, *Religion on Campus* (Chapel Hill: University of North Carolina Press, 2001), 4–5.

10. Cherry, DeBerg, and Porterfield, *Religion on Campus*, 295.

11. See Craig Dykstra, *Growing in the Life of Faith: Education and Christian Practice* (Louisville, Ky.: Geneva Press, 1999), esp. chapter 9, "Love's Knowledge and Theological Education."

12. Robert Wuthnow, "Struggling to Manifest the Sacred," in *The University through the Eyes of Faith*, edited by Steve Moore (Indianapolis: Light and Life Communications, 1998), 138.

13. George M. Marsden, *The Outrageous Idea of Christian Scholarship* (New York: Oxford University Press, 1997). See also Warren A. Nord, *Religion and American Education: Rethinking a National Dilemma* (Chapel Hill: University of North Carolina Press, 1995).

14. D. B. Hart, "Christian Scholars, Secular Universities, and the Problem with the Antithesis," *Christian Scholar's Review* 30, 4 (summer 2001), 383–402.

15. Hart, "Christian Scholars," 384.

16. Hart, "Christian Scholars," 385. For another non-Lutheran voice encouraging a more Lutheran understanding of Christian scholarship, see Richard T. Hughes, *How Christian Faith Can Sustain the Life of the Mind* (Grand Rapids, Mich.: Eerdmans, 2001).

17. Marsden, introduction to *Secularization of the Academy*, 5.

18. Marsden, "The Soul of the American University," in *Secularization of the Academy*, 12.

19. Ernst Troeltsch, *The Social Teachings of the Christian Churches*, vols. 1 and 2 (1911; New York: Harper and Row, 1960).

20. See James Turnstead Burtchaell, *The Dying of the Light*, 838–46, and Benne, *Quality with Soul*, 36–38.

21. Michael O. Emerson and Christian Smith, *Divided by Faith: Evangelical Religions and the Problem of Race in America* (New York: Oxford University Press, 2000).

22. Neil Postman, *The End of Education: Redefining the Value of School* (New York: Vintage Books, 1996), 4–5.

23. Lesslie Newbigin, *The Gospel in a Pluralist Society* (Grand Rapids, Mich.: Eerdmans, 1989), 91.

24. For a fine discussion of this dynamic see Steven Garber, *The Fabric of Faithfulness: Weaving Together Belief and Behavior during the University Years* (Downers Grove, Ill.: InterVarsity Press, 1996).

25. Ernest L. Boyer, *College: The Undergraduate Experience in America* (New York: Harper and Row, 1987), 283–84.

26. Walter J. Ong, S.J., "Realizing Catholicism: Faith, Learning and the Future," in *Faith and the Intellectual Life*, edited by James L. Heft (Notre Dame, Ind.: University of Notre Dame Press, 1996), 41.

27. Ong, "Realizing Catholicism," 40.

28. Romans 12:2.

29. See Ruth Coates, *Christianity in Bakhtin: God and the Exiled Author* (Cambridge: Cambridge University Press, 1998).

30. Mikhail Bakhtin, *Speech Genres and Other Late Essays*, translated by Vern W. McGee, edited by Caryl Emerson and Michael Holquist (Austin: University of Texas Press, 1986), 170.

CHAPTER ONE

More Than the "Integration" of Faith and Learning

Our discussion begins with an analysis and critique of the most popular contemporary model of Christian scholarship, an approach called "the integration of faith and learning." This model of Christian scholarship, which has been popular for several decades within evangelical Protestant academic circles, has recently been championed in the larger academy by George Marsden in his book The Outrageous Idea of Christian Scholarship *(1997). The integration model has many strengths, but it is clearly not the only way of defining the task of Christian scholarship. This chapter describes the integration model at its best and then examines its limitations. We suggest that a more pluralistic approach is needed if all the varied expressions of Christian scholarship are to be acknowledged and respected.*

In the second century, the North African theologian Tertullian famously inquired, "What has Athens to do with Jerusalem?" He was asking, of course, just what the world of human learning had to do with the world of Christian faith, and his answer was blunt: the two cities had virtually nothing in common. But he was wrong. His own eloquent writing style, borrowed from the academy of his day, reflects the deep connections of faith and learning that existed unacknowledged in his own life. Despite his profound belief that faith and learning were antithetical, Tertullian's life exemplified something else. He modeled the fact that faith and learning are always intertwined, even in the lives of those who might want to deny that fact.

This book explores those connections, the many ways faith and learning are and have been related to each other in the lives of Christian scholars. Sometimes the relationship has been one of conflict, but just as often faith and scholarship have blended comfortably together, crossfertilizing, overlapping, complementing, sliding temptingly past, or creatively bordering each other. Our goal is to draw that entire range of relations into the conversation about how to understand the nature and character of Christian scholarship.

The question of how faith and learning should be related—the question of how to make sense of the phrase "Christian scholarship"—has been a perennial topic of discussion in Western culture. The "A" section of the index of any standard history of Christianity points to some of the most important participants in that conversation: Abelard, Anselm, Aquinas, Augustine. But those are all medieval names, scholars who lived in a previous age when Christianity dominated the culture and defined the terms of scholarly debate. What are we to make of the notion of Christian scholarship in our post-Christian age, when Christianity no longer rules the academic roost? What does it mean to call oneself a Christian scholar now? What is the nature of the academic work we do? How do we and how should we define Christian scholarship today?

In that task, we are not starting from scratch. Various models of Christian scholarship already exist, and we begin this book by examining one particular model of Christian scholarship that has had far-reaching influence in recent years. That model goes by the name "the integration of faith and learning." For the most part, this understanding of Christian scholarship has flourished in colleges and universities located within the more or less "evangelical" zone of American Protestantism, but it is not limited to that domain. In particular, George Marsden and others have recently championed this understanding of Christian scholarship in the mainstream academy.[1] We begin with the integration model because it has largely defined the terms and delineated the boundaries of the current conversation.

The so-called integration model of Christian scholarship emerged in its present form during the second half of the twentieth century, though its roots go deeper and many trace its ultimate source to the nineteenth-century Dutch thinker Abraham Kuyper.[2] This model has many strengths and for that it should be lauded. In particular, the integrationist vision of Christian scholarship has been an important factor in the renaissance of evangelical scholarship since the mid-1970s. It is not, however, the only option available to evangelical Protestants and it certainly doesn't define the manner in which all Christian scholars ought to approach their work. Our goal is to affirm the many positive contributions of the integration model and also to critique its weaknesses. Having done that, we will move beyond the integration approach to explore the broader world of Christian scholarship which encompasses many different ways of reflecting on faith and learning.

One significant clarification needs to be made before we proceed. A number of scholars have used the term "integration" in a variety of ways that differ from the "integration of faith and learning" model we will be discussing in this chapter. Most notably the philosopher of science Ian Barbour has used the term to describe his own preferred method for relating science and faith. For Barbour, *integration* refers to the process of weaving the insights of faith and science into new, creative, and scientifically contemporary visions of God and the world.[3] In Barbour's model of integration almost every dimension of faith is on the table for negotiation; almost anything potentially can be rethought in the light of scientific advance. The evangelical idea of the integration of faith and learning is rather more conservative when it comes to defending historic Christian beliefs and more critical when it comes to evaluating the strengths and weaknesses of contemporary scholarship. We note this difference of definition simply to avoid confusion over the term "integration." Barbour's view, along with the views of a host of other Protestant and Catholic scholars who may employ the term *integration* from time to time, need to be included in the enlarged conversation about Christian scholarship that we seek to foster. The focus of this chapter, however, is on the notion of integration as it has been promoted by Marsden and other similarly minded Christian scholars.

Historical Origins of the Integration Model

The integration model of Christian scholarship was developed within the world of evangelical Protestantism in the years following World War II. As Americans went back to school after the war, many evangelical Protestants found themselves in a double bind. On the one hand they wanted desperately to show the world that conservatively oriented Christians could think as well as anybody else. The evangelical movement was just emerging from the shadows of early twentieth-century fundamentalism, and one of its greatest challenges was to shuck off the pejorative image of fundamentalist antiintellectualism. Thus Christian scholars of an evangelical bent felt compelled to demonstrate that they could master the details of their academic disciplines on a par with their secular colleagues. With that in mind, they trekked off to Harvard and Yale and to other prestigious universities to get their degrees and to prove once and for all that evangelicals could think.

But even before they had arrived on those campuses, they knew they were different from their peers. Graduate school students from evangelical churches knew in advance that they would not necessarily agree with all the ideas taught by their university professors. In fact, they often assumed that some of the key thinkers in their disciplines had been deeply mistaken about the nature of human life and the makeup of the universe. They slogged on anyway. They learned the dominant theories to the point where they could sometimes recite them with more finesse and detail than their secular friends. However, they never fully believed that university learning could be equated with the pursuit of truth. True truth, as some of them liked to say, came only from God. Rather than being in graduate school to learn truth, they were there to prove their intellectual mettle, to refine their thinking skills, and to be duly certified by the guardians of the American (liberal) academy. Having been credentialed in that way, they felt they had earned the right to be heard when they confronted modern learning with the claims of faith.

That way of putting things may imply a starker contrast between Christian truth and the knowledge claims of the academy than was actually the case for many of these budding young scholars. While most believed the modern academy was tainted to some degree with atheistic opinions, they were also convinced truth could be found through the scholarly disciplines. After all, truth belonged to God wherever it was found, even if it sometimes took a good deal of effort to separate the truthly gold embedded within secular scholarship from the dross of merely human speculation. Thus the task of the Christian scholar was understood to be twofold: (1) to critique the premises of modern learning when and where they directly conflicted with Christian truth, and (2) to discover the ways modern learning at its best might either reinforce or refine the truths of faith. This was and is the foundation of the integration model of Christian scholarship.

This model approaches the larger world of scholarship warily. While it affirms that faith and learning may potentially overlap in a number of positive ways, it recognizes that faith and scholarship may also conflict. Such disagreements arise because knowledge always involves both raw data and interpretation, and interpretation brings the personal worldview of the scholar into play, making the clash of Christian and non-Christian worldviews part and parcel of academic debate. In a certain sense, early proponents of the integration model were ahead of the academic curve on this point. Today it is a commonplace of postmodern insight that who we are affects how we see the world and thus autobiographical self-disclosure needs to be part of most, if not all, scholarship. The integrationist paradigm agrees, but then goes further and stresses that many academicians are not sufficiently self-conscious of the worldviews that shape their work. The hope is that when Christians lay their own value-laden cards on the table and ask others in the academy to do the same, the level of discussion will rise in ways that potentially aid everyone.

That is the ideal. To be honest, however, many Christians are just as unreflective about the ways their faith interacts with their scholarship as anyone else in the academy. A strength of the integration model is that it condemns that kind of unreflective attitude and challenges Christian scholars to be as thoughtful about their faith as they are about their fields of academic specialization. There is a cognitive imbalance in the lives of many scholars who also happen to be Christians: while they have developed detailed and nuanced understandings of their academic disciplines, many have allowed reflection on faith to languish at a Sunday School level of insight. While not denying the value of simple faith, the integration model insists that Christian scholars need to maintain some kind of rough parity between their disciplinary expertise and their ability to think intelligently about their faith. This does not mean that every Christian scholar must become a trained theologian, but it does mean that theological and biblical studies do need to be consulted from time to time, and most proponents of the integration approach would say a little knowledge of philosophy would help, as well.

The Integration Model at Its Best

During the last three decades, the two most articulate proponents of this model have been Arthur Holmes, formerly professor of philosophy at Wheaton College, and Nicholas Wolterstorff, formerly professor of philosophy at Calvin College and the Free University of Amsterdam and later at Yale. They each first put their thoughts into print in the mid-1970s, and those original statements still deserve reading today. In many ways, their early explanations of the integration model remain the best statements of the position. Holmes discussed the subject in fairly general terms, emphasizing the teacherly side of things; Wolterstorff was more research oriented, concentrating on the ways academic theories are created and evaluated.

In *The Idea of a Christian College* (1975), Holmes argued that the integration of faith and learning was "concerned not so much with attack and defense as with the positive contributions of human learning to an understanding of the faith and to the development of a Christian worldview; and with the positive contribution of the Christian faith to all the arts and sciences."[4] He argued that the real goal of Christian scholarship was the development of an "integrating worldview" that would allow reality to be seen as a whole in the light of God's creative and redemptive work in the world, in contrast to "the fragmented view of life" that prevailed in the secular academy.[5] Holmes knew the potential for conflict existed. He said that "the Christian revelation claim puts limitations on the scope of scientific knowledge," and he said that Christians had to be alert to those potential tensions if they were going "to think with integrity" as Christians.[6] But the main thrust of his message was constructive. Believing the issue was primarily philosophical, Holmes argued that each of the academic disciplines, and each of the major schools of thought within those disciplines, was built on a distinct set of historical and philosophical foundations. Those underlying assumptions defined the basic blueprint for how knowledge in that discipline or school of thought would be organized and utilized.

Foundational assumptions of this kind are unavoidable, and choices have to be made. For example, it is impossible to be a Platonist and an Aristotelian at the same time. One will either see knowledge primarily as a function of certain large insights about the nature of the universe applied to particular examples or incidents (Platonism), or one will see knowledge primarily in terms of the slow accumulation of little bits of raw data that can then slowly be fitted together into larger and larger theories of the world (Aristotelianism). Holmes identified these kinds of different approaches to scholarship as divergent worldviews. He also indicated that, as in many other areas of life, the decisions people made about the worldviews they adopted were often unconscious decisions. Most scholars were unaware of their own foundational assumptions about their disciplines. Somewhere along the way they had been nurtured into one way or another of seeing the world that had become second nature to them, but most scholars thought of themselves as simply open-minded searchers for truth. They were utterly unaware of the particularities and/or peculiarities of their own worldviews.[7]

Holmes said Christian scholars could not afford such blissful self-ignorance. It was part of their task as scholars to examine both their own worldviews and the foundational philosophical assumptions of their disciplines. This was part of what Christianity could contribute to the larger human search for truth. Thus every Christian scholar had to be, at least in part, a philosopher. In fact, Holmes suggested that Christian colleges should require students to take, in addition to courses in Bible and theology, one or more courses in philosophy that would provide the skill to examine the similarities and differences of deep worldview perspectives that exist among the academic disciplines and between Christian theology and the disciplines. He argued that this kind of education "would help the next generation of college teachers to do what the present generation has not always been able to accomplish in interpreting scientific and scholarly findings."[8]

Holmes was clear that the work of integration was open-ended. He said it was "but the vision of a possibility, an unfinished symphony barely begun."[9] Holmes was also ahead of his time in asserting that the process of integration did not need to assume a stridently realist epistemological stance. He stressed the softer notion of "perspective," explaining "we start with a confession of faith, with an admixture of beliefs and attitudes and values." In contrast to many of his peers and to the more strident antipostmodern realists of today, Holmes admitted: "We need not proceed deductively from universal and necessary truths, from axioms or scientifically demonstrable propositions. . . . Good and sufficient reasons may be given for what we believe, but ours is still a confessional stance and from the perspective of this confession we look at life." In Holmes's view, it was mere honesty to say "we see things from a Christian point of view."[10] That was the necessary first confession that allowed the task of integration to proceed. He did not believe, however, that scholarship necessarily would leave that initial confession untouched. Quite to the contrary, Holmes said the work of "integration should be seen not as an achievement or a position but as an intellectual activity that goes on as long as we keep learning anything at all."[11]

Nicholas Wolterstorff's understanding of the integration of faith and learning was similar to that of Holmes but took into account more fully the actual practices of the academy. To a greater degree than Holmes, Wolterstorff recognized that the lived practice of scholarship involved constant argument and debate. Individual disciplines were defined and shaped by the shared questions they sought to address much more than they were held together by any similarities of answers or foundational assumptions. Scholarship was about the competition of theories, and intelligent scholars needed constantly to make choices about which theories they would adopt in order to advance their own scholarly work.

The integration of faith and learning took place in the midst of this ongoing struggle of theories versus theories, and in that world Wolterstorff said Christian scholars faced basically the same problem as everyone else: the need to develop some way of intelligently choosing between competing theories. Wolterstorff's *Reason within the Bounds of Religion* (1976) asserted that three kinds of beliefs were necessarily involved in the process: (1) data beliefs, (2) data-background beliefs, and (3) control beliefs.

Data beliefs are minimal, testable assertions about reality with which a theory has to be consistent if it is to be accepted. To illustrate, we might offer the theory that the moon consists of cheese. Either the moon is or is not made of cheese, and the cheese theory of the moon rests on the answer to that simple question of fact. Wolterstorff says *data-background beliefs* have to do with the kinds of evidence one is willing to accept as either supporting or undermining one's data beliefs. Would a light spectrum analysis of moonlight suffice to disprove the cheese theory? Would a look at the moon through a telescope be considered valid evidence? Or would it take an astronaut actually going to the moon and bringing back a noncheese rock to dissuade hard-core believers in the moon-cheese theory? Different scholars might accept different kinds or degrees of evidence depending on their specific data-background beliefs. Finally, Wolterstorff says *control beliefs* are larger or deeper convictions about what might constitute "an acceptable *sort* of theory"[12] in the first place. These include factors such as placing greater or lesser value on logical consistency, finding certain theories more or less aesthetically appealing, being concerned with the practical or moral consequences of different theories, and examining theories to see if they are compatible with the ideas, values, and practices of one's own religious community. For Wolterstorff, control beliefs do not function as external limitations imposed on one's scholarship from the outside; instead they are part of the scholar's own deep value system that naturally attracts him or her toward certain kinds of theories and away from others.

The thrust of Wolterstorff's argument was twofold. On the one hand his description of theory choice situated Christian scholarship more than ever in the mainstream of the academy. All scholars, whether persons of faith or not, had to make decisions about what they considered facts worthy of consideration. All scholars, regardless of their religiosity or secularity, had to reflect on why they accepted certain kinds of evidence and rejected others. And all scholars, not just Christians, had control beliefs that deeply affected their choice of one theory over another. Christians were not that different from other thinkers.

But Wolterstorff also had another somewhat different point to make. Because virtually all scholars possessed control beliefs that functioned in a thought-shaping manner similar to religious faith, Christians should feel free to admit their own control beliefs and take them seriously. Wolterstorff suggested that, in the past, Christians following a path of "conformism with respect to science"[13] had often been too quick to rethink their faith in light of changing views within the academy. His own suggestion was that Christians ought to be more confident, even stubborn, in asserting the privileges of faith over against science. The belief-content of the Christian scholar's authentic commitment ought to "function as a control belief over his theory-weighing."[14]

This did not mean that Wolterstorff thought Christian scholars should never change their views in light of scientific advance. In fact, he said there were times when faith should give way to learning; there were times when new scientific developments should cause Christian scholars to revise their views of Christian faith:

> The scholar never fully knows in advance where his line of thought
> will lead him. For the Christian to undertake scholarship is to un-
> dertake a course of action that may lead him into the painful pro-
> cess of revising his actual Christian commitment, sorting through
> his beliefs, and discarding some from a position where they can any
> longer function as control.[15]

For the most part, however, Wolterstorff thought this kind of reevaluation of religious beliefs should emerge only from new data or new techniques that might alter one's data-background beliefs. When the issue was the clash of control beliefs alone, Christians were more than justified in defending themselves and their views against "theory constraints [that were] alien to Christian convictions."[16]

When Integration Takes a Negative Turn

As formulated by Holmes and Wolterstorff, the integration model is a helpful and insightful approach that still has an important role to play within the overall scope of Christian scholarship.[17] However, the integration model has not always been promoted in the positive manner outlined by these two philosophers.

While Holmes and Wolterstorff describe the integration of faith and learning as a two-way street of open-ended inquiry, many Christian scholars who have adopted the model have acted as if the influence should all flow one way. For them the model has basically meant that faith has the right, and indeed the duty, to critique learning but that learning has no authority to critique faith. Scholarship of this kind often ends up being both derivative and pedantic. It is derivative because it waits for the academy at large to produce new ideas and then critiques them on the basis of Christian faith, and it is pedantic in its pose as the long-suffering teacher who must repeatedly instruct the recalcitrant academy in the folly of its ways. In its worst forms, this attitude can blend into what the Christian scholar Merold Westphal has called the sometimes "criminal arrogance of religion" in the realm of scholarship: the haughty illusion that our views of God, the world, and ourselves are both incontestably true and unquestionably God-blessed. Westphal recommends that a harsh hermeneutic of suspicion be applied to all such claims.[18] While faith may provide Christian scholars with certain important clues concerning the deep nature of the universe that others lack, the ways Christians interpret those revelatory clues are as subject to error as the thinking of anyone else. There is no room for epistemological arrogance in Christian scholarship.

Another related weakness of the integration model is that, despite the deep goal of exploring the connections of faith and learning, the integration approach often promotes conflict rather than conversation. According to Holmes and Wolterstorff, critique of the mainstream academy is part of what Christian scholars must necessarily do, but for some Christian scholars critique becomes virtually their only concern. When that happens, the integration model devolves into a win-lose contest over truth. Instead of bringing insights from the two domains together, the task of Christian scholarship is reconceived as one of conquest: an antisecular crusade for truth.

The temptation for the integration model to degenerate into conflict is so strong that even as superb a scholar as George Marsden can sometimes fall into this trap. For example, at one point in his influential book *The Outrageous Idea of Christian Scholarship*, he identifies Carl Sagan as the model of how the secular academy really thinks. Repeating Sagan's memorable line that "the cosmos is all that is or ever was or ever will be," Marsden comments that while "most scholars are not as blunt as Sagan" they all basically share the same attitude.[19] For Marsden, at least in this passage, the contrast is clear. The secular academy, rooted deeply in the soil of scientific materialism, is fundamentally opposed to Christian faith. That way of describing the context of Christian scholarship reinforces the notion that the real job of Christian scholarship is combat rather than conversation—to wage war for the faith through the means of heavily footnoted books and rapier-like essays. At one point, Marsden says the world of scholarship is much like the battle-strewn world of Middle Earth described in J. R. R. Tolkien's popular trilogy *The Lord of the Rings*. He writes:

"Suppose we scholars thought of our understanding of things as equivalent to that of the Hobbits in Tolkien's world. The most important thing to take into account is that we are involved in a great spiritual struggle between forces of darkness and light."[20] In some sense this is merely standard Christian theology—the world is seen as caught in a battle of good versus evil and Christians are called to side with the good—but when applied too quickly to the realm of scholarship, this imagery can have unfortunate results.[21]

Most scholars would see themselves largely as noncombatants in this kind of Tolkienesque war of scholarship. While aware of the existence of good and evil and of the subtle forms those realities can take, scholars, like most other people, usually do their work in a world colored by shades of gray—a world of people and situations that are partly good and partly not so good. Most secular scholars (and most Christian scholars, as well) find it impossible to separate all the complexities of the world into neat categories of moral darkness and light. This does not make such scholars enemies of Christian faith and moral virtue; in fact, many might make fine allies in the task of nourishing the good. But if Christians approach the academy with too much suspicion and with too much expectation that, underneath it all, most scholars are as ideologically atheistic as Marsden thinks Carl Sagan was, we will probably never strike up the friendships that might lead to mutual respect and cooperation. When speaking of Christian scholars, Marsden is almost always willing to give them the benefit of the doubt. Thus he says it is wrong for the academy to toss out the ideas of good-hearted Christian scholars because of the moral failures of Christians from previous generations or even of Christians in our own age. He argues that Christian scholars and their ideas ought to be judged on their own merits and not be unfairly caricatured so that they can be dismissed. Marsden is right, but Christians need to extend the same spirit of generosity and graciousness to their secular peers. Christians need to be welcoming of others if they want to be welcomed themselves.

Inherent Limitations of the Integration Model

Even if we set aside the way the integration model of Christian scholarship can sometimes be negatively misconstrued, the integration approach still has limitations. First, this model contains the implicit claim that it is the only valid way to bring faith and learning together; it defines the singular path that all Christian scholars must follow regardless of their own particular understandings of faith or their specific fields of disciplinary expertise. The second limitation is its hyper-philosophical approach to Christian scholarship. In essence, the integration model requires that Christians scholars temporarily become philosophers (instead of being biologists, psychologists, engineers, artists, or whatever else they are), whenever they want to engage in the specific activity of doing Christian scholarship. Neither claim seems warranted.

In the past, many of the most vocal proponents of the integration model have spoken as if they were simply setting forth what all Christians should be doing in their work as scholars. They acted (and sometimes still act) as if the integration of faith and learning approach was, if not the one and only valid way to do Christian scholarship, clearly the best and brightest way. That simply is not true. There are many valid and insightful ways of construing the goals and purposes of Christian scholarship. The integration model is one particular vision of Christian scholarship, but it is not a neutral, one-size-fits-all paradigm that applies equally to everyone or to every field of scholarly endeavor.

To be precise, the integration model is at its roots a Reformed (i.e., Calvinistic) vision of Christian scholarship. Virtually all the most articulate spokespersons for this approach to Christian scholarship have been Reformed in both their church affiliations and their views of theology. This includes Holmes, Wolterstorff, Marsden, and numerous others. For the most part, these individuals have not touted their Calvinistic predispositions in their writings on Christian scholarship; in fact, they have typically suggested in good faith that they were trying to speak in the most generically Christian language possible. But their works are informed by a decidedly Reformed view of the world nonetheless, and because of that Christians from other traditions may find this model only marginally beneficial in helping them explore their own deepest instincts about how faith and learning should be connected in their academic work.

Reformed theology posits that the world is fallen in the most radical of ways; the created order has gone wrong at its very roots. At the center of this disorder stands unredeemed humanity, defiant and proud in its resistance to God and God's laws. Despite the effects of sin—and those effects are great—the Reformed tradition says that God is still clearly in control of the world and everything in it. At present God is calling out a people, electing them to salvation, so that through them God's grace can be displayed to the world. One of the tasks of this redeemed community is to model in its own life and practices how God intended humanity to live. Another task assigned to the redeemed is that of resubduing the created order, helping the world to reacknowledge God's dominion and submit to God's will. As they pursue this work, the redeemed discover that God is already at work in the world ahead of them, limiting the effects of the Fall and paving the way for the ultimate restoration of all things. Through the gift of common grace God prevents humanity from declining into total moral oblivion, and through the gift of sustaining grace God maintains the orderly processes of the cosmos. The Reformed tradition says that in the end everything will be set back in its rightful place and sinners will be forced to bow before Jesus Christ, the one and only divine ruler of the world.

Within this scenario, it makes sense for Christian faith to serve as a fulcrum of correction for humanity's sinful thought and action. And the integration model does exactly that, stressing the need to bring a distinctively Christian perspective to bear on all merely human efforts to understand the created order. The assumption is that the academic disciplines are, for the most part, expressions of humanity's sinful revolt against God. They are manifestations of human arrogance, symbols of humanity's prideful claim that it can fully understand the world without any reference to God. But Calvinists know there is always room for surprise. Even the most mature Christians still harbor the seeds of sin within them and thus can be mistaken. What is more, God can, through the gift of common grace, sometimes allow the unregenerate to see truths that the righteous have ignored, overlooked, or miscontrued.[22] Because that is the case, Reformed Christian scholars must be ready to be tutored on occasion by both their non-Reformed fellow believers and by their secular academic peers. This will surely be the case with matters of fact and sometimes even with regard to issues of philosophy and faith. Still, the assumption is that on most matters of scholarship Christians will see things more clearly than their non-Christian colleagues.

This is a powerful vision of faith and scholarship, and it has spawned perhaps more sustained reflection on faith and learning than any other Protestant theological tradition. For this the Reformed tradition is to be complimented—truly and honestly complimented—even as we remember that this is but one way of understanding the task of Christian scholarship. The integration model is powerful precisely because its Calvinistic particularity gives it both clarity and a sense of consistency. Scholars from other traditions can gain insights from the integration model, but other Christian scholars—whether of the Catholic, Wesleyan, Lutheran, Pentecostal, Anabaptist, or any other non-Reformed tradition—will probably feel they are speaking a second language of sorts if they try to adopt the integration model in its entirety. Some of the core theological concerns of non-Reformed Christian traditions simply do not translate into integration-speak. Thus there is a need to acknowledge and nurture the development of other models of Christian scholarship that can stand alongside and complement the Reformed, integrationist approach.

In more recent publications, supporters of the integration model have been increasingly forthcoming about the Reformed character of their approach, but most continue to assert that the integrationist position remains the common ideal for all Christians. Cornelius Plantinga, Jr., provides an example. After confessing, in his recently published book *Engaging God's World: A Christian Vision of Faith, Learning, and Living*, that he writes from a Calvinistic perspective, he immediately suggests that his own relatively moderate understanding of Reformed theology is really nothing more than the kind of "mere Christianity" that he thinks all Christians should affirm.[23] Plantinga has tried to tone down the strongest Calvinistic aspects of the integration model and to incorporate other views, but his book will undoubtedly still feel rather Reformed to most non-Reformed Christians.[24] It is just not that easy to overcome one's own particularities—and that is not necessarily a bad thing. Our particularities allow us to see parts of the world that others may miss. Thus the Reformed view of Christian faith does provide us—all of us—with a powerful vision of the world's fall and redemption and a compelling model of Christian scholarship based on that theological foundation, even if it is not the only way to see things.

The second limitation of the integration model has to do with its fixation on what might be called the philosophical worldview approach to Christian scholarship. In essence, the integration model can be defined as the philosophic task of comparatively analyzing the ideas and theories (i.e., doctrines and theological systems) of Christian faith in relation to the ideas and theories of the various academic disciplines. The goal is to examine the deep philosophical presuppositions of the disciplines (or of different subfields within the disciplines) in order to see whether and to what degree those philosophical presuppositions may overlap, inform, or conflict with the truths of Christian faith expressed in propositional form. There are two problems here. The first comes from the side of the discipline, the second from the side of faith.

Some disciplines are clearly more philosophically driven than others. Thus sociology unquestionably pays more attention to theory than chemistry, and literary criticism is more self-consciously ideological than engineering. Even in those disciplines where philosophy has a significant role to play, however, the potential for critical or creative interaction with faith can vary greatly. Thus theories of education, psychology, and biology typically carry more religious punch than theories of mathematics or music. The integration paradigm can be very helpful in those disciplines that tend to be more theory conscious, and it can be especially helpful when dealing with disciplines that touch on issues that have been of traditional concern to religious faith—that is, questions of human origins, meaning, and moral values. The integration paradigm often flounders, however, when applied either to disciplines that are more neutrally descriptive or pragmatic in orientation or to disciplines in which issues of human meaning rarely enter the mix.

Even within those disciplines where the integration model has worked fairly well in the past, its power has waned in recent years. For the most part, this is the result of an overall shift in the academy away from grand-scale theorizing about the nature of the world toward the analysis of smaller aspects of the world examined eclectically using a range of different theories, techniques, and approaches. This change in the way scholars see their work is rooted, in turn, in the larger cultural transformation that has taken place in the last fifteen years as we have moved away from the clearcut, bilateral, Cold War thinking of the past to the decentered, multilateral, postmodern orientations of today. Contemporary ways of thought and life are less concerned with the norms of logic favored by the worldview approach and much more concerned with the quirky and often unpredictable ways things actually fit together in their local and global environments. This does not mean that the large-scale philosophical questions of the past have simply faded into oblivion. Christian scholars and others still argue about things like sociobiology, evolution, and the strengths and weaknesses of global capitalism—and because of that the integration model still has an important role to play—but many academic discussions now take place closer to the ground in a zone where the worldview radar of the integration model does not necessarily help us find our way. In the years ahead, Christian scholars will probably need to develop a range of new, less grandiose ways of relating faith and learning that are more attuned to contemporary scholarly practices.

Questions about the sufficiency of the integration model's fixation on philosophy and worldview have also been raised within the Christian community. In particular, many non-Reformed Christians, and even some Reformed Christians, are uncomfortable with the notion that faith supplies the believer with a full-blown Christian worldview. The issue for them is not the fact of revelation but the nature of revelation. Is Christian revelation personal or propositional? Does revelation supply us with a complete vision of the world, or is revelation more piecemeal, offering important clues about the origins, meaning, and purpose of the universe but never spelling things out in fine detail? Do Christians possess extrafactual knowledge about the world, or is the addition of Christian revelation primarily a matter of values and attitude?

Virtually all Christians believe that in the person of Jesus, in the text of the Bible, and in the historical experience of the church God has revealed important truths that would otherwise be largely hidden from view, but Christians differ significantly regarding how easily and thoroughly they think that revelation can be translated into the language of philosophical/systematic discourse. The Eastern Orthodox tradition has a long history of apophatic theology—an approach that stresses the fact that the most important truths about God cannot be put into words.[25] In a rather different way, Anabaptists have also tended to marginalize philosophical theology, asserting that faith is best expressed in actions and not in words. Pietists and mystics of all traditions would similarly be suspicious of any overreliance on words and logic because for them the real nub of faith is to be found in the heartfelt experience of God. The emphases of these theological traditions, if they are taken seriously, will produce visions of Christian scholarship that differ from the dominant model of integration. This is not to denigrate the integrationist model—it is an important perspective and a necessary part of the mix—but one of the main goals of this book is to make space for alternative models to develop.

The following essay by Crystal Downing helps open that space. She sees the vocation of Christian scholarship as a calling of creative reflection about God, the world, and ourselves, and there is no one way to do that. The inspiration that faith gives to scholarship can bend and twist in many different directions; faith and learning can overlap—be imbricated—with each other in many different ways. Our point is not to declare one model better than all others and then to fend off rival approaches but to encourage an ongoing conversation that has the potential to help all of us deepen our understanding of both the world and Christian faith.

NOTES

1. See George M. Marsden, *The Outrageous Idea of Christian Scholarship* (New York: Oxford University Press, 1997).

2. See Abraham Kuyper, *Principles of Sacred Theology* (Grand Rapids, Mich.: Baker Book House, 1980).

3. Barbour uses this metaphor in many of his works. Perhaps the fullest discussion of the term is found in his *Religion and Science: Historical and Contemporary Issues* (San Francisco: HarperSanFrancisco, 1997), 98–105.

4. Arthur F. Holmes, *The Idea of a Christian College* (Grand Rapids, Mich.: Eerdmans, 1975), 46.

5. Holmes, *The Idea of a Christian College*, 57.

6. Holmes, *The Idea of a Christian College*, 55.

7. Holmes's understanding of the role of underlying worldviews and nonrational factors in the history of science and the other disciplines parallels the view of his contemporary Thomas Kuhn, who described the nonrational messiness of scientific advance in his famous book *The Structure of Scientific Revolutions*, 2nd ed. (Chicago: University of Chicago Press, 1970).

8. Holmes, *The Idea of a Christian College*, 57.

9. Holmes, *The Idea of a Christian College*, 58.

10. Holmes, *The Idea of a Christian College*, 59.

11. Holmes, *The Idea of a Christian College*, 46.

12. Nicholas Wolterstorff, *Reason within the Bounds of Religion* (Grand Rapids, Mich.: Eerdmans, 1976), 67.

13. Wolterstorff, *Reason within the Bounds of Religion*, 82.

14. Wolterstorff, *Reason within the Bounds of Religion*, 94.

15. Wolterstorff, *Reason within the Bounds of Religion*, 96.

16. Wolterstorff, "Theology and Science: Listening to Each Other," in *Religion and Science: History, Method, Dialogue*, edited by W. Mark Richardson and Wesley J. Wildman (New York: Routledge, 1996), 104.

17. The integration model as outlined by people like Holmes and Wolterstorff has spurred a tremendous amount of scholarship over the years. This literature is too vast to even begin to list representative examples. One relatively easy point of reference, however, is a series of "through the eyes of faith" books published by Harper and Row in the late 1980s and early 1990s. For the most part, these volumes exemplify the integration approach, and they have been widely used in evangelical colleges and universities. See David G. Myers and Malcolm A. Jeeves, *Psychology through the Eyes of Faith*, 1987; Roger Lundin and Susan V. Gallagher, *Literature through the Eyes of Faith*, 1989; Ronald Wells, *History through the Eyes of Faith*, 1989; Richard T. Wright, *Biology through the Eyes of Faith*, 1989; Richard Chewning, John W. Eby, and

Shirley J. Roels, *Business through the Eyes of Faith*, 1990; David A. Fraser and Tony Campolo, *Sociology through the Eyes of Faith*, 1992; Harold M. Best, *Music through the Eyes of Faith*, 1993. The psychology and biology texts in this series were revised, updated, and rereleased by HarperSanFrancisco in 2003.

18.   Merold Westphal, *Suspicion and Faith: The Religious Uses of Modern Atheism* (Grand Rapids, Mich.: Eerdmans, 1993), 5.

19.   Marsden, *The Outrageous Idea of Christian Scholarship*, 74.

20.   Marsden, *The Outrageous Idea of Christian Scholarship*, 95. Marsden goes on to say that even though Christian scholars believe they are involved in a great spiritual battle, they must confess that they "understand these forces only imperfectly. Nonetheless as limited creatures we accept that our role is to do what we can to promote the cause of light and to use our talents where they may be helpful. As scholars, we might think of ourselves as something like map-readers on a mission the dimensions of which we cannot fully comprehend. Even so, we can try to do the best job we can of interpreting some technical down-to-earth matters that may contribute, in ways we do not fully understand, to the larger spiritual mission" (95–96). More than fifteen years earlier, Marsden had said much the same thing in his *Fundamentalism and American Culture: The Shaping of Twentieth-Century Evangelicalism, 1870–1925* (New York: Oxford University Press, 1980), but the tone then was a bit more apocalyptic. After describing Tolkien's good-versus-evil view of the world, Marsden wrote: "Frail as we are, we do play a role in this history, on the side either of the powers of light or of the powers of darkness. It is crucially important then, that by God's grace, we keep our wits about us and discern the vast difference between the real forces for good and the powers of darkness disguised as angels of light" (239–40).

21.   One of the most strident examples of how this kind of warfare thinking has been applied to the world of scholarship can be found in David K. Naugle, *Worldview: The History of a Concept* (Grand Rapids, Mich.: Eerdmans, 2002). Presupposing that the world is engrossed in "a conflict of epic proportions" between God and Satan, Naugle argues that "from the perspective of Christian theism . . . nothing could be of greater final importance than the way human beings understand God, themselves, the cosmos, and their place in it." Because of that, he says "it is not surprising that a worldview warfare is at the heart of the conflict between the powers of good and evil" (xii). His position is that most people, including most scholars, are "under the vice grip of the disenchanted worldview of modern naturalism and scientism" (280), and the most important task of Christian scholarship is to help free people from that diabolical bondage. In note 55 on pages 279–80, Naugle, who teaches at Dallas Baptist University, provides a brief list of some of the literature on "spiritual warfare" that has informed his thinking.

22.   For a recent and generous Calvinist explanation of how common grace operates in the lives and thinking of non-Christians, see Richard J. Mouw, *He Shines in All That's Fair: Culture and Common Grace* (Grand Rapids, Mich.: Eerdmans, 2001).

23.   Cornelius Plantinga, Jr., *Engaging God's World: A Christian Vision of Faith, Learning, and Living* (Grand Rapids, Mich.: Eerdmans, 2002), xv.

24.   A similarly toned-down but still strongly Reformed vision of Christian faith can be found in Mark A. Noll, *The Scandal of the Evangelical Mind* (Grand Rapids, Mich.: Eerdmans, 1994). The scandal of the evangelical mind, as Noll describes it, is

the absence of mind—the movement's persistent antiintellectualism. But from what source does that antiintellectualism arise? Noll says three non-Reformed movements within the larger evangelical world are especially to blame: Holiness Christianity, Pentecostalism, and dispensationalism. By contrast, the corrective he proposes is drawn straight out of the Reformed world, as he argues that "the Dutch Reformed tradition has been the single strongest intellectual resource for the renewal of Christian philosophy" and, by extension, of all other evangelical scholarly endeavors (237).

25. On the apophatic dimension of Orthodox faith and its relation to Christian scholarship, see Alexi V. Nesteruk, *Light from the East: Theology, Science, and the Eastern Orthodox Tradition* (Minneapolis: Fortress Press, 2003).

ESSAY ONE

Imbricating Faith and Learning: The Architectonics of Christian Scholarship

Crystal L. Downing

This essay reflects on the ways communities of faith and communities of knowledge often police the use of language within their ranks to prevent linguistic "allergens" from disturbing established forms of thought and life. Downing prefers a more open-ended understanding of scholarship that welcomes interaction with the new and the other. Her own preferred metaphor for the relationship of faith and learning is "imbrication," meaning a pattern of overlap, and she argues that faith-learning patterns of overlap will differ markedly from scholar to scholar. The ways faith and learning are imbricated in our lives will give rise to different questions and to different provisional answers, and will remind us of the necessary relationality of truth as we converse with others.

Though trained academically as a literary critic, I have an intense passion for architecture that, like my faith, often inflects my scholarship. Even in childhood, architectural paradigms molded my pursuits; indoors I would draft blueprints for fictive houses rather than dress my lonely dolls, while outdoors I would play "Realtor" rather than kickball, showing make-believe houses, configured from the bushes and trees of my backyard, to imaginary clients. In more daring moods, I would ring doorbells up and down my street, ostensibly to ask if anyone wanted to play, but really because I wanted to catch glimpses inside people's homes.

Other than my age and location, things have not changed much. I currently have a goal to run every country road within thirty miles of my college, driving to a new location with each run in order to guarantee that I have seen every historic edifice in the area; and, if a woman is working in the yard of an especially charming house, I will stop to chat until I get an invitation to glimpse inside.

Just as I make bodily connection with architectural space, my mental life is filled with architectural connections, affecting my publications, presentations, and pedagogy. Just as my dissertation and its succeeding journal articles focused on the way Victorian and Edwardian writers employ architecture in their texts, this essay employs architecture to both raise and raze integrationist models of Christian scholarship. With the help of two Christian scholars who have been at the center of much of my recent scholarship—Dorothy L. Sayers and Mikhail Bakhtin—I will argue that faith should operate for the Christian scholar much as architecture functions within my physical and mental life, affecting my habits, disciplines, and affections.

Before I inspect the integrationist scaffolding of Christian scholarship, I want to lay some groundwork by interrogating the very vocabularies we use to talk about faith and scholarship. I will do so by describing a strange architectural form that I encountered while teaching at a famous research university. In the spring of 1992 the chair of the English department at that university asked me to provide a tutorial for a student who experienced "severe" allergic reactions to any enclosed classroom. When the woman arrived for our first session, she carried a huge glass-lidded box enclosing her Shakespeare anthology. As we started discussing *Macbeth*, she stuck her hands through gloved-lined holes in the side, enabling her to turn pages without exposing her skin to the allergen-laden book. As the summer session came to a close, the student invited me to have dinner with her family in gratitude for my tutorial. So on a warm June afternoon I drove into the mountains above the city's smog line to an isolated cabin where the family had taken up residence. As I approached the porch of the old wooden structure, the front door opened just wide enough to show a pair of lips, which articulated the words, "Please go to the shed across the road and change into the clothes we have put there for you." When I returned to the porch, holding up size 10 woolen slacks on my size six frame, the lips once again appeared, this time telling me to go into the woods behind the cabin in order to spit out my gum. After I fulfilled this request, the front door was opened a bit wider, but this time a hand shot out holding a shower cap, and I was instructed to make sure all my hair was safely ensconced underneath the elasticized plastic. Feeling less than lovely, I was finally allowed to enter the cabin, which looked as natural as I did. Each wall was lined with aluminum sheeting, and every bit of wood on the furniture was wrapped with aluminum foil, except for a television, which stood in the fireplace cavity behind bullet-proof glass. After dinner, which consisted of a huge yam sitting next to a piece of chicken with feather shafts still embedded in the skin, I asked my hosts what symptoms necessitated such severe measures. The three women agreed that the primary manifestation of their allergies was "irritability." Hence, in their efforts to avoid getting irritable, they proceeded to eliminate more and more allergens from their life.

I would like to employ this family's obsessive monitoring of any allergen that might infiltrate their house as a metaphor for the monitoring of verbal allergens that often occurs within Christian communities. For example, several years ago I was accused of blasphemy by the mother of one of my first-year students because I said in a Christian college classroom that Jesus, "tempted in every way that we are," was tempted by lust. This mother obviously felt that the big fat allergen of sex should not enter a sentence that contained the name of Jesus. Of course, I was quoting Hebrews 4:15, explaining what I thought the text meant by "tempted in every way"—though, of course, without sin.

My dip into blasphemy was brief in comparison to the dive taken in 1941 by Dorothy L. Sayers, the English creator of the Lord Peter Wimsey detective stories, who had been commissioned by BBC radio to write a series of plays about the life of Jesus. Sayers's scandal went national, with people denouncing her not only to the archbishop of Canterbury but also to Prime Minister Winston Churchill, because she had put slang expressions into the mouths of several of Jesus' disciples. To add insult to injury, the expressions were identified as American slang, a vocabulary to which many Brits are allergic. Because it was in the middle of World War II, one complainer actually suggested that "Singapore fell because these plays were broadcast" and appealed for them to be taken off the air "before a like fate came to Australia."[1]

Here are examples of Sayers's blasphemy: the disciple Matthew says "Fact is, Philip my boy, you've been had for a sucker," and a zealot needles Judas with "And how did Jesus get taken? Somebody squealed then, I fancy."[2] Protestors were appalled by what one called "a spoliation of the beautiful language of the Holy Scriptures which have been given by inspiration of the Holy Spirit," referring of course to the King James Version—as though to say Jesus actually spoke Jacobean English.[3] Ironically, of course, a good portion of the King James Version is based on William Tyndale's translations of the Latin New Testament into vernacular English, which were denounced and burned by the English church in the 1520s. Language reverenced by Christians in Sayers's day had once been declared heretical by equally earnest Christians four hundred years earlier, illustrating how words can become idols impeding our view of the incarnated Word of God. Because she was extremely earnest about the saving work of Christ, Sayers repeatedly eschewed "the general air of stained-glass-window decorum with which the tale [of Jesus] is usually presented to us."[4] Behind her metaphor is the image of a church, which, like the house of my university student, can be treated as a protective space where we keep Christianity safe from the allergens of alternative vocabularies for faith. For example,

I have heard Protestants repudiate Roman Catholicism as the superstitious worship of pieces of the cross, refusing to believe that Catholics can be Christians because they do not use the phrases "born again" or "asking Jesus into their hearts." But how is this language any different from pieces of the cross? Both are human constructions based on biblical material that some people turn into idols by which "authentic" faith is measured. While Catholics can err by excessive mystification of the physical, Protestants err by excessively mystifying the verbal.

Scholars embedded in the Anabaptist tradition (such as Ernest Boyer and Nancey Murphy, who are discussed in the following chapter) might feel especially sensitive to this issue, since the forebears of present-day Anabaptists were tortured by both Catholics and Protestants alike for not using the correct signifiers of faith. Our word "language," of course, comes from the French word *langue* meaning "tongue," which explains why many a sixteenth-century Anabaptist, when insisting on adult-only baptism, had his or her tongue bolted to the roof of the mouth, if not entirely severed from the body. They were not using the right language, the right *langue*. Another famous torture is more architectural; Anabaptists in Münster, Germany, were suspended in cages outside the stained-glass windows of St. Lamberti's Church, making them seem like rabid dogs that, if let inside, might infect the faith.

Significantly, when universities were first established in the Middle Ages, they were modeled after monastery cloisters, and academia has struggled with the same tensions over which vocabularies can be allowed inside the cathedral of learning and which—like allergens and Anabaptists—must be left outside. In England, women were not the only allergen barricaded from the university until the twentieth century. I have been told that some scholars in Shakespeare's day considered mathematics unsuitable for study, since it carried the taint of alchemical equations for turning lead into gold. In the nineteenth century Shakespeare himself was caged outside a curriculum that was largely Latin and Greek literatures, for his language was considered too popularistic, and it was not until the mid-twentieth century that Wordsworth and Coleridge were allowed to be taught inside the Oxbridge cloister.[5] Today, of course, things have flip-flopped, so that mathematics and its related fields of business and computer science are considered more worthy than literatures ancient and modern—for the same reason, ironically, that they were rejected in the sixteenth century: they are associated with turning leaden studies into the gold of a career track. My resentments as a professor of literature aside, I wish to suggest that, just as in the cloister of faith, so with education: what is reverenced by one era is eschewed by the next—and vice versa.

Instructors at Christian colleges, of course, are inheritors of both cloisters, and must fight the temptation to become repositories of rarified vocabularies that leave challenges to both faith and scholarship caged safely outside the walls. Take the issue of evolution, for example. When Dean Kenyon, who has a Ph.D. from Stanford and is coauthor of one of the most respected texts endorsing macroevolution, started changing his mind several years ago, his science colleagues were appalled. An article in *Insight* magazine describes how the dean of the School of Science at San Francisco State, where Kenyon taught,

> insisted that Kenyon "teach the dominant scientific view," not the religious view of "special creation. . . ." Kenyon replied that he taught the dominant view, but he also discussed that some biologists see evidence of intelligent design and have problems with the dominant view. He received no reply. Instead, he was yanked from teaching introductory biology and reassigned to labs.[6]

Caging theories of intelligent design outside of the academic cloister, administrators kept the vision of students stained by the sanctified glass of evolutionary theory. The opposite problem, of course, often occurs at Christian colleges, where administrators get phone calls from parents angry that their instructors do not nail up aluminum siding to protect their students from learning about evolution, as though to say God is not strong enough to withstand human theories that do not include the godhead. Dorothy Sayers recognized this problem when she wrote to a friend about Christians who think "the whole thing will fall to pieces if one starts asking questions." Imagining them in the form of an old-fashioned "grandmama," Sayers mused:

> I see her, deeply reverent in black bombazine, standing protectively between the pushing interviewer and the frail and aged figure of God in a bath-chair, [saying], "Now, don't you speak rough to Him— He's very old and shaky, and I wouldn't answer for the consequences."[7]

We can laugh when the subject is evolution, which most of us can see operating within a Christian worldview, but in many Christian circles, that black-clad grandmama starts shaking her finger when the discussion turns to homosexuality, as though God will fall out of the bath-chair once what has been traditionally caged outside is let in.

As Christian scholars, we want to avoid the end of Philip Gosse, the Victorian Plymouth Brethren pastor who invented the aquarium and wrote a definitive work on sea anemones. He was so well respected as a scholar that Charles Darwin consulted him about his theory of natural selection; Gosse's first reaction to Darwin, however, was to shore up his walls of faith to keep the evolutionary allergen out. In fact, in order to protect the language of the Genesis accounts, Gosse wrote a book of "Christian scholarship," *Omphalos*, which argues that God placed the fossils in the earth at the moment of creation.[8] *Omphalos* is the Greek word for navel, and part of Gosse's argument was that, just as God created Adam with a navel intact, so God created the sedimentary layers of the earth with fossils intact. But how did Gosse know that Adam had an omphalos? Just as Christian scholars in the late Middle Ages had to invent complicated loop-de-loos to explain the movement of the planets in order to protect their worldview that God placed the earth at the center of the universe, so Gosse had to invent a belly-button at the center of Adam. Rather than protecting the gospel, Gosse merely reinforced to scholars of the 1860s that Christianity is a naive, outmoded discourse that must be surmounted if true science is to be pursued.

Gosse anticipated the modernist-fundamentalist debates in the first half of the twentieth century, wherein secular humanists looked on Christians as paranoid people distributing shower caps. Modernists, of course, valorized those "enlightened" ones who were able to transcend the escapism of religious vocabularies, attaining truth either through the intuition of art or the logic of science. Following Ezra Pound's famous dictum "Make it new," avant-garde artists saw themselves as the new ministers of "culture," creating art that, like pillars of cloud by day, fire by night, would lead the masses out of their wilderness of bourgeois values. As prophets of a new dispensation—one that dispensed with God—the high modernists preached that the humanities could save humanity.

Not surprisingly, architecture reflected the displaced religious energy of modernism; Walter Gropius founded the Bauhaus school in 1919 as a "cathedral of the future."[9] Architects committed to the Bauhaus ideology, like Mies van der Rohe, believed that technology could provide the salvation necessary for their contemporaries. They thus designed architecture that foregrounded functionality, repudiating the petty bourgeois need for decorative flourishes. Indeed, the reason we have so much ugly architecture in all the major cities around the world—"row upon Mies van der Rohe" of iron- and cement-framed factoryesque boxes[10]—is that the ideologues of Bauhaus went out into all the world, preaching the modernist gospel.

Modernism's foundational belief in the epistemological supremacy of reason, of course, relegated Christianity to the margins of cultural discourse. Writers who believed or, worse, promoted Christianity were disdained, if not attacked, by the modernist intelligentsia. In a 1953 book entitled *The Emperor's Clothes*, for example, Kathleen Nott contemptuously disparaged poets and critics who were outspoken Christians, saying they were "engaged in the amputation and perversion of knowledge." She is especially hard on C. S. Lewis and Dorothy L. Sayers, calling them "braver and stupider than many of their orthodox literary fellows" because of their "tub-thumping" popularizing of the faith. With modernist condescension, Nott proceeds to contrast Christian dogmatism with the "open-minded inquiry" of science: "If men learn to think consistently in the direction that leads to aeroplanes, they will also think in the direction away from authoritarianism and therefore theology. Moreover they will learn to think in a direction . . . toward psychology and anthropology and away from Sin and the Church."[11] Made irritable by Christian vocabularies,

Nott attempts to protect scholarship from the allergens of faith by lining the academic cloister with the aluminum siding of empiricism. Ironically, in her attempt to silence the tongue of dogma, she dogmatically mystifies science, perpetuating what the postmodern philosopher Richard Rorty calls "a picture of the scientist as a sort of priest, someone who achieved contact with non-human truth by being 'logical,' 'methodical,' and 'objective.'"[12]

In contrast, Dorothy L. Sayers's faith-filled resistance to modernism anticipates Rorty's postmodern recognition that the scientist has no better access to "the real" than does the Christian, for all truths are embedded in language. Indeed, Sayers sounds decades ahead of her time in a view that Nott disparages with the disdainful words "[Sayers] tells us that we must think by analogy or refrain from thinking at all, and that thinking about God is merely no exception to this rule."[13] Today, Nott is the one who looks foolish in light of Rorty's commonly held assumption that "speaking a language . . . is not a trait a man can lose while retaining the power of thought. So there is no chance that someone can take up a vantage point for comparing conceptual schemes by temporarily shedding his own."[14] All thought arises from faith—faith in a conceptual scheme that is limned by language. Sayers says as much in a letter to a skeptic:

> One act of faith must, indeed, be made before one can accept Christianity: one must be prepared to believe that the universe is rational, and that (consequently) human reason is valid so far as it goes. But that is an act of faith which we have to make in order to think about anything at all. . . . Admittedly, we cannot prove that the universe is rational; for the only instrument by which we can prove anything is reason, and we have to assume the rationality of things before we can trust or use our reason.[15]

Because of tensions between Christianity and modernity about the inside and outside of "Truth," it is admirable how Reformed scholars sought to provide another paradigm, calling for the "integration" of faith and learning. Christian colleges across the country picked up their language, encouraging professors to write "integration papers" that might defy the Kathleen Notts of the world. However, some faculty members are hard pressed to conceptualize how to achieve an interpenetration of their disciplinary and their Christian vocabularies in the way that the word "integration" implies. In a 1999 *Christian Scholars Review* article, for example, Larry Lyon and Michael Beaty report that 42 percent of their colleagues at Baylor University believe that faith and learning "are separate tasks and ought not be integrated," with one respondent saying: "Attempts to integrate faith and learning are, at best, treacherous and often lead to dogma and intolerance." And even those scholars who endorsed "integration" were unclear as to how to go about it; as Lyon and Beaty put it, "believing that faith and learning ought to be integrated is one thing; being able to integrate these two areas is quite another." They conclude that Baylor increasingly operates according to a "two-sphere" paradigm, in which "the truths of scientific knowledge and the truths of religious faith are . . . intellectually insulated from one another."[17]

I, however, come to a different conclusion. The very word "integration," employed by Lyon and Beaty in their survey and reiterated dozens of times in their article, might be causing the resistance. "Integration" reflects modernist sensibilities, valorizing the autonomy of the individual, who within himself melds faith and scholarship into a unified, almost monumental, form—like modernist architecture. Indeed, the motto of the Bauhaus movement was "Art and Technology—A New Unity." Significantly, the Baylor scholars who had the most problem with the integration model were assistant-level professors;[18] in other words, those most likely to be trained in postmodern interpretive strategies resisted the modernist paradigm.

The architect Charles Jencks dates the beginning of postmodernism to the demolition in 1972 in St. Louis of worker housing—monolithic "unities," built according to Bauhaus ideals, that the "unenlightened" people who actually had to live in them hated.[19] I want to suggest that we similarly undermine the modernist term "integration." This, of course, is what ethnic minorities have done, valorizing the postmodern concept of multiculturalism over the modernist construct of integration, which often led to a Bauhaus-like, autocratically enforced conglomeration of peoples who were suddenly supposed to share a common vocabulary. Of course this often meant that in the name of integration, minorities were artificially supposed to fit their sensibilities into the dominant white discourse, just as some of our faculty feel that they must force their disciplinary language to fit somehow into the language of their faith—or vice versa.

Instead of integration, I want to offer a paradigm that reflects not only our postmodern times but also the constructs of religious traditions that are different from the Calvinism that generated the integration model. In *Models for Christian Higher Education: Strategies for Success in the Twenty-First Century,* James D. Bratt summarizes scholarship in the Reformed tradition using metaphors that might trouble scholars who operate according to different vocabularies of faith. Bratt writes that "the redeemed [are] to be agents of . . . correction"; they are "commissioned to scout out error"; they are to "use learning to harness the agonizing clash between divine intent and earthly woe, making education the bit and bridle by which to guide the world."[20] To me, this language of coercion echoes the modernist sensibilities whereby Bauhaus architects imposed their aesthetic on what they contemptuously referred to as the "bourgeoisie."

Far more attractive to me is the 1848 description of the River Brethren that identified them as "zealous in maintaining, as all should, what they believe to be truth, they still manifest an unusual degree of kindness and Christian forbearance toward those who differ very essentially from them in matters of faith."[21] This statement of faith-full zealousness is laced with an epistemological humility that results in Christian service rather than intellectual coercion. As Mark Schwehn notes in his essay "Christianity and Postmodernism: Uneasy Allies,"

> all of us . . . must ponder anew the striking fact that those Christians who are most welcome without question or suspicion everywhere in the world are the ones who are short on doctrinal propositions and theological verbiage and long on service to neighbors in need. I am thinking here of those very groups that Luther himself persecuted, like the [Anabaptists].[22]

Significantly, Schwehn begins his essay with an architectural image, describing the library designed by Thomas Jefferson for the University of Virginia. The domed space is so well conceptualized that when one stands at the center of the rotunda floor, the bookcases that radiate out to the walls of the circular room are hidden behind pairs of white pillars that surround the observer. Schwehn compares this visual effect to Enlightenment perspectives, wherein "Reason" is at the center of all knowledge: a reason that is self-sufficient, universal, and totally objective in its ability to see and innocently comment on the pillars of truth. If the observer gets off center, however, she starts to see "tradition"—as represented by the books, situated in the cases, which embed knowledge. Employing this brilliant analogy, Schwehn illustrates how postmodern discourse destabilizes Enlightenment thinking through acts of decentering that reveal the "traditional character of all rationality as well as the rational character of all traditions."[23]

I, then, wish to similarly decenter the "integration of faith and learning," such that it reflects the books behind our pillars of truth, the tradition-based character of our scholarly rationality as well as the rational character of our Christian traditions. In fact, I want to replace the modernist word "integration" with a word postmodern thinkers have appropriated to talk about the various overlapping discourses that make up the self: "imbrication." Used by architects to refer to the overlapping shingles on a house, "imbrication" also describes the scales of a pine cone. For many a postmodernist, just as a pinecone is its scales, so one's subjectivity is the various vocabularies by which one speaks and thinks. Christians, of course, believe in a central core that holds all these discourses together, but just as we would not say the core is the pine cone, we should also be hesitant to say the soul is the self. Indeed, Paul spent a good part of his first letter to the Corinthians combating such an assumption.

Like the imbricated scales of a pine cone, then, the imbrication of faith and learning, in contradistinction to integration, registers awareness that we are made up of multiple vocabularies, some of which overlap, others of which do not, but all of which are manifestations of the self. I want to clarify that I do not see Christianity as just one shingle, for we all have multiple vocabularies to discuss our faith—one to talk about Jesus with an eight-year-old, another to our grandmothers, another to our colleagues or our friends. Furthermore, these different vocabularies overlap differently from scholar to scholar. To imbricate faith and scholarship, then, is to acknowledge that one's Christianity does not always overlap with one's discipline, that many times scholarship will mention nothing of faith issues. But in some venues, a Christian professor might quite self-consciously talk about how her love of Jesus overlaps with the love of engineering, film, history, science, or mathematics; and vice versa: how one's decision to become an artist, accountant, nurse, or teacher is consonant with one's commitment to follow Christ.

My sense of imbrication is quite similar to what the Russian theorist Mikhail Bakhtin calls "heteroglossia"—divergent tongues—wherein the individual is defined by the multiple vocabularies not only of, but also outside, the self, vocabularies that are constantly interrogating and qualifying each other.[24] For Bakhtin, every self is imbricated differently, due to each individual's situatedness not only in time and space but also in relation to others; he calls this the "architectonic" of the self.[25] For Bakhtin, "architectonic privilege" does not lead to the modernist autonomy of the Übermensch; instead it implies that we have a responsibility toward all that is "other" than the self because our individualized imbrications will respond to and hence affect the other uniquely—whether the other is a self or a scholarly topic; and vice versa: other selves and subjects affect each one of us differently. Therefore, rather than the "authentic being" of modernism, Bakhtin advocates the "unfinalizability" of "becoming" as the various imbricated discourses of the self take on new shapes through genuine dialogue with the vocabularies of the "other."[26]

Significantly, well after Bakhtin had been celebrated by postmodernists, it was discovered that he was a Christian, exiled to Siberia by Stalin for his participation with a group of Christian scholars and for writing subversive things like "the cross is the origin of all life, of all becoming."[27] Bakhtin, like Sayers, defied modernism at its height, but because he lived under the most coercive of all modernist ideologies, communism, he got into much more trouble for it. This may explain why, for Bakhtin, "Christ's truth is real, but its authority cannot be known as dogma or as proposition. Genuine truth always involves more work and more risk than dogma or propositions require of us."[28] Dogma—whether for or against evolution, homosexuality, postmodernism, or anything else—can too easily become an aluminum-lined fortress that keeps the risk of alternate perspectives caged outside. Therefore, as one critic explains,

> the term used by Bakhtin to denote the human subject's responsible
> act of transcending his or her own boundaries to engage with the
> world is *iskhozhdenie*, or "going out." Clearly this is closely linked

semantically and axiologically with Christ's act of Incarnation, described by Bakhtin with the term *niskhozhdenie*, or "going down."[29]

It is also implicitly linked to architecture, through the concept of exiting protective spaces of thought. For Bakhtin, "any truth we might achieve in life is available only as a relationship":[30] relationship with Christ, the source of all "going out," relationship with people of faith, relationship with people and issues outside our faith, our ethnicity, our class, and even our sexuality, and, finally, relationship among the imbricated discourses that define the self and that give meaning to all the other relationships of our lives.

So also the imbricated architectonics of Christian scholarship free us to "go out" of protective edifices of thought to enter into relationship with all for whom God, by way of Christ's architectonic self, chose to "go down." The freedom comes not through reconciling dissonant discourses, as the word "integration" implies, but through acknowledging that finality is always a pretense, that unfinalizability, like the cross, is the source of all becoming.

NOTES

1. James Welch, introduction to *The Man Born to Be King* (London: Gallancz, 1946), 15.

2. Sayers, *The Man Born to Be King: A Play Cycle on the Life of our Lord and Saviour Jesus Christ* (Grand Rapids, Mich.: Eerdmans, 1979), 105, 263.

3. Quoted in David Coomes, *Dorothy L. Sayers: A Careless Rage for Life* (Batavia, Ill.: Lion, 1992), 18.

4. Sayers, *The Man Born to Be King*, 6.

5. For a helpful discussion of the Oxbridge resistance to English literature in the curriculum, see Chris Baldick, *The Social Mission of English Criticism: 1848–1932* (Oxford: Clarendon, 1983).

6. Stephen C. Meyer, "Open the Debate on Life's Origins," *Insight*, February 21, 1994, 26.

7. *The Letters of Dorothy L. Sayers: 1937 to 1943, From Novelist to Playwright*, edited by Barbara Reynolds (New York: St. Martin's Press, 1997), 380.

8. Philip Gosse, *Omphalos: An Attempt to Untie the Geological Knot* (1857; Woodbridge, Conn.: Ox Bow Press, 1998).

9. The postmodernist architect Charles Jencks, from whom I quote, describes the Bauhaus movement as "a Protestant Reformation putting faith in the liberating aspects of industrialisation and mass-democracy," in *What Is Post-Modernism?* (New York: St. Martin's Press, 1986), 31.

10. I borrow the pun from Tom Wolfe, *From Bauhaus to Our House* (New York: Farrar Straus Giroux, 1981).

11. Kathleen Nott, *The Emperor's Clothes* (1953; Bloomington: Indiana University Press, 1958), 16, 31, 43, 68, 298.

12. Richard Rorty, *Contingency, Irony, and Solidarity* (Cambridge: Cambridge University Press, 1989), 52.

13. Nott, *The Emperor's Clothes*, 294–95.

14. Rorty, *Contingency, Irony, and Solidarity*, 50.

15. Sayers, *Letters 1937 to 1943*, 401.

16. Larry Lyon and Michael Beaty, "Integration, Secularization, and the Two-Spheres View at Religious Colleges: Comparing Baylor University with the University of Notre Dame and Georgetown College," *Christian Scholar's Review* 29 (fall 1999), 83–84.

17. Lyon and Beaty, "Integration, Secularization, and the Two-Spheres View," 74.

18. Lyon and Beaty, "Integration, Secularization, and the Two-Spheres View," 95.

19. Jencks, *What Is Post-Modernism?*

20. James D. Bratt, "What Can the Reformed Tradition Contribute to Christian Higher Education?" in *Models for Christian Higher Education: Strategies for Success in the Twenty-First Century*, edited by Richard T. Hughes and William B. Adrian (Grand Rapids, Mich.: Eerdmans, 1997), 130.

21. Owen H. Alderfer, "Anabaptism as a 'Burden' for the Brethren in Christ," in *Reflections on a Heritage*, edited by E. Morris Sider (Grantham, Pa.: Brethren in Christ Historical Society, 1999), 145.

22. Mark R. Schwehn, "Christianity and Postmodernism: Uneasy Allies," in *Christianity and Culture in the Crossfire*, edited by David A. Hoekema and Bobby Fong (Grand Rapids, Mich.: Eerdmans, 1997), 166.

23. Schwehn, "Christianity and Postmodernism," 155–56.

24. Mikhail Bakhtin, *The Dialogic Imagination*, translated by Caryl Emerson and Michael Holquist, edited by Michael Holquist (Austin: University of Texas Press, 1981).

25. Mikhail Bakhtin, *Toward a Philosophy of the Act*, edited by Michael Holquist and Vadim Liapunov (Austin: University of Texas Press, 1993), 54.

26. Mikhail Bakhtin, *Problems of Dostoevsky's Poetics*, translated and edited by Caryl Emerson (Minneapolis: University of Minnesota Press, 1984).

27. Quoted in Caryl Emerson, "Russian Orthodoxy and the Early Bakhtin," *Religion and Literature* 22, 2–3 (1990), 112.

28. Emerson, "Russian Orthodoxy and the Early Bakhtin," 113.

29. Ruth Coates, *Christianity in Bakhtin: God and the Exiled Author* (Cambridge: Cambridge University Press, 1998), 34.

30. Emerson, "Russian Orthodoxy and the Early Bakhtin," 113.

CHAPTER TWO

Living the Questions of Learning and Faith

The ways faith and learning are linked in our lives and thinking are complex, with personal factors often playing as important a role as logical argument. The task of Christian scholarship involves the exploration of these already existing connections as much as it involves the forging of new points of contact between faith and the academic disciplines. This kind of reflection requires that we take issues of ethics and aesthetics into account alongside logic. When that happens, Christian scholarship becomes a matter of "living the questions" as much as it is a search for definitive answers.

If we are going to enlarge the conversation about Christian scholarship, we must begin with a frank acknowledgment of the untidy humanness of the endeavor. While Christian scholarship, like all other forms of scholarship, ultimately seeks to express itself in reasonable modes of communication that can be examined and critiqued in the realm of public argument and conversation, the soil in which Christian scholarship typically grows is not the soft loam of ideal logic but the gritty ground of our full personhood. Individuals who become Christian scholars do not usually take up that calling because they suddenly decide they need to build previously nonexistent bridges of rational connection between the isolated parts of themselves, which they identify respectively as faith and learning. Instead, most people who become Christian scholars do so because they know faith and learning are already intimately bound together in their lives, and they feel a need to explore that faith-learning/learning-faith hybridity in an intelligent manner. Because that is the case, the task of Christian scholarship always includes a mapping of one's own soul as well as a mapping of the many more external ways that the interactions of faith and learning can help us understand the world in which we are enmeshed.

The Princeton University sociologist Robert Wuthnow says that virtually all the Christian scholars he knows have ended up becoming Christian scholars for these kinds of reasons. He suggests that the typical scenario runs something like this: a person "learns the basic stories of Christianity as a child, becomes a scholar sometime later, and yet continues to be influenced by the questions those stories asked, even though his or her rational arguments, theological outlooks, and philosophy of life may have undergone much change."[1] Wuthnow says faith does not so much give these scholars ready-made answers about how faith and learning are supposed to relate as it gives them a set of open-ended questions about how they *might* relate. In essence, their life stories impose an extra set of questions on their scholarship—questions of meaning, value, responsibility, and sometimes questions of pain and loss. These questions are not uniquely Christian, nor are they even uniquely religious, but Wuthnow implies that Christian scholars, and undoubtedly scholars who are deeply rooted in other religious traditions, find it harder to push these questions aside than their more secular counterparts. So when Wuthnow asks whether "it is possible to combine a deep personal commitment to the Christian faith with the life of the mind," he answers by saying that, of course, it is possible and that the best way to do it is by "living the questions" of intelligent faith rather than by trying to provide neat and tidy answers to all the quandaries of life.[2]

The foregoing might imply that Christian scholarship is in a certain sense a simple fact of life: if one is raised as a Christian or converts to Christianity one cannot help but produce scholarship that is in some way influenced by Christian ideals and points of view. If you are a Christian the scholarship you produce will be in some sense Christian. On one level, this is undoubtedly true. Faith, because it involves deeply held convictions and values, will naturally flavor almost everything one does. But that is not the whole story. In the same way that people work hard to develop their natural talents through years of practice if they want to become great musicians, athletes, or scholars, individuals who hope to be truly excellent Christian scholars will have to work at developing the natural connections that already exist between their faith and learning. They will need to carefully explore those connections through self-reflection as well as conversation with others.

The end result of this process will not necessarily be the neat and systematic articulation of a fully integrated Christian scholarly worldview. More often than not it will be what the Jesuit political philosopher David Hollenbach has called a "fragile achievement"—a tentative and provisional understanding of the connections of faith and learning that is rooted in one's way of life as much as it is an expression of one's life of the mind.[3] This is a rather different posture than that of the integration model discussed in the previous chapter. The integration model defines the ideal of Christian scholarship in relatively dispassionate terms as the rational, objective examination of academic learning in the light of Christian faith. It is something outside the person, and it is often more argumentative in tone than it is either contemplative or conversational. While rationality and argument clearly have important roles to play within Christian scholarship, self-reflection and nonargumentative dialogue with others must also be part of the picture. Martin Marty helpfully clarifies this distinction between arguments and conversations. He says that the typical situation in an argument is that "one contender knows an answer, turns it into a proposition, and debates it with the intent to convince or defeat an opponent." In dialogue something else is going on. Marty writes: "Conversation partners do not [claim to] know everything. . . . They relish the presence of others, of those who are different; they enjoy the contributions of the many." What is more, unlike arguments that are necessarily oriented toward a clearly defined goal, conversations usually meander along "toward some end, but not always a well-defined one."[4] Conversation is more like a walk through the woods than a race around the track; it is more cooperative than competitive.

Conversation, as opposed to argument, also allows "the real" to penetrate into our discussions of and reflection on Christian scholarship. George Dennis O'Brien, following Jacques Lacan, defines "the real" (he always places the term in quotes) as the mysterious totality of life in all its messy, wonderful, and troubled complexity. O'Brien, a Catholic layperson and past president of both Bucknell University and the University of Rochester, explains that "the real" is elusive and mystical, and "runs beyond the neat orders of 'normal' academic pursuits."[5] But simply because "the real" exceeds the grasp of academic discourse does not mean it can be ignored. "The real" is part of the steady drumbeat of our ordinary lives and emotions, and it can erupt into our thinking at almost any minute without our ability to control it. The University of Chicago philosopher Martha Nussbaum has described such emotional occurrences as "upheavals of thought," and she insists that we take them seriously as "essential elements of human intelligence." In her view, abstract, logical thinking by itself is "too simple to offer us the type of self-understanding we need" because it cannot "grapple with the messy material of grief, love, anger and fear" that so profoundly shapes our lives.[6] O'Brien says the proper response to these kinds of affective experiences is not to distance ourselves from them through objective analysis but to pour ourselves into "the real" through participation in the ebb and flow of life, through love of the people around us, and through commitment to the values, ideals, and practices that make life meaningful. Even if we cannot "integrate" all of that into our scholarship, O'Brien argues that Christians have to try to take it academically into account. He says "life participation" is the "grammar" of Christian scholarship.[7]

This chapter examines what that might mean—how Christian scholarship might look if it was undertaken in a conversational and cooperative style that was open to the claim of "the real" on our lives. Such scholarship would emphasize connections more than differences—connections of one's scholarship to one's life as a whole and connections with other scholars who are seeking to understand the world in that holistic kind of way. In this style of Christian scholarship, even the differences that supposedly separate the secular academy from the realm of Christian faith would be minimized on the basis of shared humility in the face of truth and shared mystery at the wonder of life. As the Christian educator Craig Dykstra explains, Christians believe

> that all fall short of the glory of God and are deeply in need of forgiveness and grace. At the same time, the spiritual foundation of intellectual inquiry may not ultimately be hubris, but humility in the face of realities that do not finally submit to our fantasies and manipulation. These are complementary convictions, and that fact suggests a way in which religious communities and colleges and universities, even secular ones, might fruitfully understand and relate to one another: by searching out as many complementarities as possible and by working to redeem one another where sins are being committed.[8]

This chapter focuses on two people who envision Christian scholarship in just that way.

Ernest L. Boyer's Moral Vision of Faith and Scholarship

Ernest L. Boyer was commissioner of education under President Jimmy Carter and then presided for many years over the Carnegie Foundation for the Advancement of Teaching. He was one of America's greatest twentieth-century educators, and he was also a devout Christian, associated at different times in his life with the Brethren in Christ Church and the Society of Friends. At the core of Boyer's religious faith and at the core of his vision of public education was a profound belief in the underlying connectedness of all things. Boyer was convinced that nothing exists by itself, in itself, for itself. Everything and everyone is related to everything else. He liked to cite his friend the biologist Barbara McClintock as saying "everything is one."[9] He was also fond of quoting Mary Clark, another well-known biologist, to the effect that "social embeddedness is the essence of our nature."[10] Perhaps Boyer's favorite comment on the subject, however, came from the literary figure Mark Van Doren, who once said: "The connectedness of things is what the educator contemplates to the limit of his [or her] capacity."[11] While Boyer believed that connectedness is a fundamental fact of life—part of the warp and woof of how God has put the universe together—he was simultaneously convinced that the connectedness of the world is often underappreciated. The connections within creation have a living quality to them. They are more organic than they are logical or mechanical and, having that lifelike quality to them, the connections of the world are, like life itself, both durable and fragile. They need to be nurtured and cultivated or they might wither and die.

Within the human community, especially, Boyer believed that the connectedness of persons is both a fact and a moral mandate. That is, the fact of mutual connectedness contains within itself a required ethic of mutual care. Because we are all dependent on each other, we have a natural moral obligation—a human obligation that is also a Christian obligation—to act in ways that preserve and improve the webs of connection that sustain us. To undermine those relationships or to sever them intentionally would be both morally wrong and just plain dumb.

Boyer was especially attuned to the ethics of human relatedness because of the way it applied to his own field of disciplinary expertise: communication. Boyer firmly believed that language has the power either to build or to destroy human lives and organizations; humanity lives in a world of language, and the ways people use words can either improve the life they share together or terribly harm it. Thus, for Boyer, the ability to speak and listen is "a sacred trust" that entails a clear moral mandate always to speak truthfully. He said: "Truth is the obligation we assume when we are empowered in the use of words."[12] Human relations are sustained "by the honesty of our words, and by the confidence we have in the words of others."[13] When trust is broken through the use of dishonest words—lies, propaganda, or artful dodges—all of humanity suffers. Boyer's Anabaptist religious roots undoubtedly predisposed him toward this view of language. The Anabaptist movement stressed the importance of plain, direct, honest speech. In fact, Anabaptists took the responsibility of honest communication so seriously that they refused to take any kind of oath for fear it would imply that their normal modes of speech were not fully truthful. For the Anabaptist movement, linguistic honesty was a divine command; for Boyer, it was also a requirement of being human. On this issue, and on many others, his faith and his academic perspectives were perfectly attuned.

Ultimately, however, Boyer believed this ethic of human relatedness found its purest expression not in the fair and honest exchange of words but in a willingness to reach out in tangible ways to meet human needs. Service to others was the foundation of Boyer's philosophy of life and education. Boyer said he had learned this truth from his grandfather, the most important mentor in his life: "When Grandpa was forty, he moved his family into the slums of Dayton, Ohio. He spent the next forty years running a city mission, working for the poor, meeting the needs of those who had been pathetically neglected, teaching them. He taught me as I observed his life, that to be truly human one must serve."[14] Throughout his own distinguished career in education, Boyer never tired of repeating the dictum that "to be truly human, one must serve." Service to others was not a nice moral add-on to the rest of life; service was part and parcel of what it meant to be human. It was the best way existentially to understand the actual connectedness of human life, and it was simultaneously the highest moral expression of humanity's interrelatedness.

Given the great significance Boyer assigned to the connectedness of the world in general, it will come as no surprise that he thought the notion of relationality ought to be at the heart of all scholarship and education, and especially at the core of Christian scholarship and education. At one point he commented:

> We urgently need to shape a curriculum that shows relationships, not fragmentation. Today's students are offered a grab-bag of isolated courses. They complete the required credits, but what they fail to gain is a more coherent view of knowledge and a more integrated, more authentic view of life. To put it simply, their sense of the sacred is diminished. . . . We affirm differences, but fail to capture the commonalities. And in the absence of larger loyalties, we're settling for little loyalties. Students are hunkering down in their separate interests failing to find the relationships that bind.[15]

If that was true of students, it applied even more to the faculties of the nation's colleges and universities. For years budding young scholars had been told that the wisest thing to do if they wanted to advance in their individual fields of study was to find some little niche of knowledge they could know better than everyone else—and then to claim their intellectual property rights over that piece of academic turf. The way of advancement in the world of higher education was through hyperspecialization. Especially in the sciences, any display of serious interest in subjects unrelated to one's focus of research was interpreted as a sign of lost concentration and weakened scholarly resolve; the same basic attitude could be found dispersed throughout the academy, including the humanities. Boyer thought many professors had contentedly become masters of "little loyalties" and were actively passing those minuscule senses of scholarly allegiance down to their students. Boyer was deeply troubled by this state of affairs. Knowledge was fragmenting, and lives were being truncated by the narrowness of education. An appreciation of the whole was being lost: the world was no longer being seen in its complex interrelatedness. As the wonderful relational complexity of creation was parceled off and packaged in neat little unrelated blocks, a sense of the sacred was being lost as well.

On this point, Boyer's thinking was, despite his Anabaptist upbringing and church affiliations, profoundly Catholic. A commitment to the unity of all truth has been a hallmark of virtually every Catholic discussion of scholarship since at least the time of Thomas Aquinas. Boyer agreed. He would also have agreed with the Catholic contention that the unity of the world includes the

sacred. In fact, it would not be wrong to call Boyer's view of the world sacramental. Boyer believed that even the smallest act of care or kindness could
sometimes convey enough grace that it could transform a life from despair to
hope. And it was not just that the world *could be made* sacred by such acts, he
also believed that in many ways the world *is already filled* with the sacred. God
is already sacramentally present in the world. Boyer argued that the sacred is
"inextricably interwoven with the most basic of human impulses."[16] He knew
this sacred dimension of life was often buried under the rubble of the world's
brokenness, but it was there nonetheless, and the task of uncovering it was
not a job for Christians alone. Instead, the process of discovering and nurturing
the sense of the sacred that adhered to human experience was a project in
which all of humanity not only could be but needed to be involved.

While Boyer had an almost mystical appreciation of the world's connectedness, he was also a pragmatist. He knew that in the modern world no one
could know everything. Specialization is, accordingly, a required fact of academic life. This is especially so for those involved in what he called the *scholarship of discovery*,[17] where it usually is necessary to narrow one's focus to only
one isolated part of reality in order to understand its intricate complexity. What
he was unwilling to do, however, was to allow the label "scholarship" to be
restricted to that kind of activity alone. The world itself is not divided up into
the neat categories of analysis that the scholarship of discovery requires.
Rather, the world is a complex, interrelated whole. Therefore, Boyer argued,
the scholarship of discovery, though important, is inadequate by itself to fully
understand either ourselves or the world as a whole.

In addition to the scholarship of discovery, Boyer said we needed other
kinds of scholarship to help us see the world in all its interrelated complexity.
Thus he called for a *scholarship of integration*, which he defined as the attempt
to arrange relevant bits of knowledge and insight from different disciplines
into broader patterns that reflected the actual interconnectedness of the world.
(This notion of "integration" is obviously quite different from and unrelated
to the integration model of Christian scholarship discussed earlier in this
book.) Boyer also called for a *scholarship of application* (which he sometimes
labeled the scholarship of engagement) that would take seriously the moral
mandate of our interconnectedness, seeking to close "the gap between values
in the academy and the needs of the larger world."[18] Finally, he called for a
scholarship of teaching (which he also identified as the scholarship of sharing
knowledge) that would focus on the means and ways of handing down knowledge, faith, wisdom, and wonder across the fragile bonds of connection that
linked different cultures and successive generations to each other. Some have
criticized Boyer's enlarged definition of scholarship for supposedly watering
down the demands of real scholarship (meaning the scholarship of discovery).
Boyer saw his definition as doing the exact opposite. It raised the bar of scholarship, requiring everything that the scholarship of discovery already de-

manded and then asking for more. It imposed on scholarship the requirement that it locate itself within the actual connectedness of the world and not falsely presume it existed outside the connected order of human relations in some independent realm of academic objectivity.

Boyer never explicitly described the role that he thought faith might play in this enlarged taxonomy of scholarship. Undoubtedly he would have presumed that the direct implications of faith are least visible in the scholarship of discovery, where the focused research methods of the disciplines predominate. Even there, however, he would probably have thought faith would play an active role in the selection of research topics. In the other three forms of scholarship, Boyer would surely have believed that the concerns of faith would blend naturally into one's work. According to Boyer, the ultimate purpose of Christian scholarship is to "celebrate the majesty, the integration, and the wholeness of God's creation."[19] In his estimation, the primary task of Christian scholarship is not to defend Christian truth against secular learning. That approach overstresses discontinuity and underestimates the actual connectedness of the world. Nor is it the primary task of Christian scholarship to analyze and critique competing worldviews, another exercise that emphasizes difference much more than connectedness or convergence. Instead, he said, the power of Christian faith is best seen in the way faith motivates scholars to observe the world in all its interconnected wholeness and to offer their skills and insights as a form of intelligent service to humanity and the created order in general.

According to Boyer, that kind of engaged scholarship is not something Christians can do all by themselves. Rather, Christian scholars need constantly to communicate with other scholars and work alongside them in the common human task of seeking to understand, nurture, and where necessary, mend the tough but delicate fabric of the world. Anything less than that—any kind of scholarship that is intentionally segregated from the larger human community—would itself be a denial of the interconnectedness that God had woven into the created order. Christian scholarship, according to Boyer, is at its best when it is humbly and almost invisibly immersed within the larger academy, tincturing the world of scholarship as a whole with a deepened sense of the unity of reality and of our responsibility to serve others, especially those least able to help themselves.

While Boyer thought that Christian scholars need to be active participants in the larger academy, rubbing shoulders with non-Christian academicians on a regular basis, this did not mean that he was critical of the existence of independent Christian or church-related colleges and universities. In fact, Boyer believed such institutions were a needed part of America's ecology of higher education. Private religious colleges and universities could explore certain points of contact between faith, the academic disciplines, and ethics that public universities simply could not address because of the constraints of church-state separation. Boyer was a firm believer in religious freedom and, applied to higher education, that meant he even affirmed the right of Christian colleges and universities to require some kind of faith affirmation from faculty. What he was opposed to were rigid tests of orthodoxy and forms of Christian education that built walls between Christian faith and "secular" scholarship rather than bridges of care and mutual understanding.

Boyer's comments concerning the connections of faith, learning, and life were forged in the full light of public and political inspection. His chief concern—the role he thought he was called to play as a public figure in American society—was to inspire all scholars, and especially all teachers, to see their work as focusing on the task of understanding the world for the purpose of making the world a more caring and humane place for everyone. Given that context, Boyer clearly believed that Christian scholarship should not fixate on the needs of the Christian community itself but should be turned outward toward the needs of society as a whole. When Boyer said that to be truly human one must serve, his assumption was that this maxim is even more true of Christianity: to be truly Christian, one must serve. In his view, true Christian faith would necessarily lead to public service.

Boyer thought that Christians should not isolate their scholarship from the larger academy, nor should they be overly concerned with highlighting the distinctively Christian character of their work; that smacked too much of religious chauvinism. Instead, he suggested that Christian scholarship at its best should identify as much as possible with the constructive work of the academy and then be a leavening influence within that realm, directing the energies of the academy wherever possible in pathways that would more fully address the hopes, dreams, and deepest needs of humankind. Living in an age that had produced more violence and warfare than any other in history, Boyer was acutely attuned to the tragedy of death. As a person of faith, however, he was convinced that the real tragedy is not death itself. Everyone will eventually die; that is unavoidable. What is tragic is that people so often die with "commitments undefined, convictions undeclared, and service unfulfilled."[20] Boyer believed that the role of scholarship, whether Christian or not, is to help people discover a calling and purpose in life that draws them out of themselves and into constructive relationships with others.

What is truly helpful about Boyer's vision of Christian scholarship is not merely that it acknowledges the complex autobiographical and interpersonal dynamics that are involved but that it is so profoundly positive in nature. For too long too many Christian scholars have thought of the work they do either in defensive or aggressively apologetic terms. Boyer's vision is neither of these. Instead, what he presents to us is a model of Christian scholarship that is at once thoroughly confident and utterly humble. Boyer is thoroughly confident that this is God's world and that the core values of Christianity are in perfect agreement with the deep structures of the created order. He is simultaneously utterly humble in that he thinks the same core values require Christians to put the needs of others ahead of their own. Following a Boyeresque approach, Christian scholarship would adopt a generally positive stance toward the academy as a whole. The goal would be neither to erect a hedge against the inroads of secularism nor to launch an attack on secular thinking. Instead, the ideal of Christian scholarship would be to walk alongside the mainstream academy, adding insights as appropriate and helping to make sure no one would ever forget that the deepest calling of the scholar, Christian or not, is to care for those who most need one's help.

Nancey Murphy's Postmodern Vision of Christian Scholarship

Nancey Murphy, professor of Christian philosophy at Fuller Theological Seminary, points in a different direction. For her, the focus of Christian scholarship is not so much ethics (though ethics does play a significant role in her thinking) as epistemology, and the primary focus of her work has been the relationship of science with theology. Murphy calls herself a postmodern philosopher because she rejects the modernist notion that in order for any belief to be deemed "knowledge" it has to be formulated and defended solely on the basis of objective facts and impeccable logic, wholly removed from the personhood of the scholar. By contrast, her own form of postmodern epistemology recognizes the personal factors that saturate all forms of scholarship and acknowledges that the interconnections between faith and learning are rarely purely logical.[21]

Murphy develops her argument historically, tracing the rise of modern epistemology and then the postmodern turn toward epistemological holism. She argues that the modern paradigm of knowledge was linked to the metaphor of knowledge as a building: a large public building constructed on the solid foundation of incontestable, objective facts about the world. The superstructure of this building was erected on that empirical foundation using the crane of sound deductive reasoning. The goal was to produce a dwelling place for universal human knowledge that was absolutely firm and capable of withstanding all the howling gales of skepticism and doubt, a crystalline palace where, pure and untainted by any kind of subjective judgments at all, truth could be preserved for all time.

Modern epistemology found one of its purest expressions in the philosophy of logical positivism, which asserted that scientific claims were meaningful only if they were expressed in ways that could be either confirmed or falsified by empirical observation. Once such claims had been tested and the real facts of the matter had been ascertained, then scientists could construct theories out of those building blocks of pure facts on the basis of rigorous mathematical reasoning. In this scheme of things, the discipline of physics, the hardest of all the supposedly "hard sciences," became the model for human knowledge in general. While logical positivism had little if anything to do with religion, a very similar understanding of knowledge was emerging within Christian academic circles at the same time. In the premodern world, Christian faith had been based largely on tradition understood in the sense of authoritative beliefs handed down carefully, but somewhat flexibly, from generation to generation. But this notion of tradition had been criticized by Protestant reformers in the sixteenth century, pilloried by the *philosophes* of the Enlightenment, and finally cast aside entirely by the end of the nineteenth century. In the resultant vacuum, Christians felt they had to construct a new epistemological foundation for their historic beliefs, and many theologians concluded that faith, like science, needed to be based as much as possible on indisputable facts and sound logic alone. These developments obviously took different trajectories in the Protestant and Catholic worlds, but the overall pattern was similar.

The reconstruction of faith generated by this modern fact-logic definition of knowledge took two rather different forms. Some Christian theologians (i.e., liberals) appealed to the supposedly indubitable facts of Christian experience and built their theologies logically from that foundation; other theologians (i.e., fundamentalists) based their logical restatements of faith on the supposedly absolute and error-free body of propositional truths found in the Bible or church tradition. The divide between these two orientations of theology was never absolute, for many theologians tried to weave these two strands together, but the bipolar divide between modernists and fundamentalists did describe an important tension nonetheless. These contrasting ideals of how Christians could and should reconstruct their faith to be more compatible with modern ways of knowing were in some senses diametrically opposed to each other. In terms of their underlying method, however, they were nearly identical. Modernists and fundamentalists both assumed that truth was a function of facts, logic, and nothing else, and Murphy thinks both approaches were dreadfully wrong in the way they redefined the nature of Christian faith and the task of Christian theology.

Murphy says that as neat and seemingly solid as modern epistemology appeared at first glance, what it actually produced was a shaky house of knowledge positioned on slender stilts of data and logic rather than a durable dwelling situated firmly on the ground of truth. With time, both science and theology had to acknowledge how flimsy modernist epistemology was, and both fields made adjustments. Within science—partly as a result of the development of quantum physics, partly as a result of Thomas Kuhn's analysis of the history of scientific revolutions, and partly as a result of the simple progression of generations—logical positivism was slowly jettisoned. Ludwig Wittgenstein, often taken to be one of the chief architects of the positivist platform, eventually changed his mind as well, turning away from pure logic to the analysis of how language functioned in different contexts. Scientific theories, even in the "hard" sciences, came to be understood as useful, predictive *models* of how the world behaved; they were no longer considered precise blueprints of what was actually going on in reality. Thus contemporary physics actually posits that at least at the subatomic level it is impossible for us ever to know what is "really going on." The very act of observing certain kinds of data changes that data. Contemporary scientists have thus come to believe that the world is stranger and more wonderful than logical positivism could ever understand.

In the religious realm a similar development took place but with perhaps a bit more tension and contention in the process. That is, just as theologians of the right and left were getting comfortable with their new styles of theology based on the supposedly universal structure of human experience or the objective truth of the biblical text, other discoveries in the realm of scholarship began to dissolve that seemingly solid ground out from underneath their feet. On the liberal side of things, the supposedly universal character of human religious experience came under severe attack. The more closely scholars looked at religious experience—indeed, the more closely they looked at human experiences of any kind—the more those experiences seemed like interpretations of reality rather than simple perceptions of experiential fact. At the very same time, the notion that the Bible could be considered a repository of divinely attested propositional truths was coming apart as scholars of both the right and left rediscovered the literary character of the biblical text—it was neither a science textbook nor a philosophical treatise. The understanding of tradition underwent a similar rethinking. The Second Vatican Council, in particular, opened the possibility of seeing tradition in a more lively manner, not as static truth but as evolving insight. As a result of these changes, the nature of theology has been altered in the past few decades as much as science.

Murphy, along with a host of other postmodern thinkers, believes that modern canons of factual indubitability and mathematical rationality never did ring true to how people actually thought, and the dissolution of modern epistemology has accordingly been a good thing. Its passing means we can once again examine the untidy and complicated ways that human beings have always reflected on God, the world, and themselves without embarrassment or apology. In this more realistic understanding of epistemology, it is possible to admit what we all already know: our ideas and values are connected to each other in complicated webs of relation and reference that have as much to do with our autobiographies as with pure logic. Following terminology first developed by Willard Quine, Murphy says we instinctively and unavoidably think holistically. We do not believe any given truth about the world because of its own self-evident facticity; instead we believe certain assertions about the world with differing degrees of intensity based on how well they fit into the total network of other related ideas that we (and the communities in which we live) also hold to be true. We develop and refine our beliefs on the basis of their connection with the broader patterns of belief and practice that characterize our community's life.

In this interrelated understanding of human knowing, Murphy argues, "there are no indubitable (unrevisable) beliefs";[22] instead what we find are complex connections that go in many different directions at once. She says some of these connections do take the form of strict logical implication, but others are more probabilistic in nature. Our webs of belief are complex and to some degree unpredictable, but what holds them together is their general sense of coherence with each other rather than their individual certainty. As Murphy puts it, we test our ideas about the world on the basis of how well "each belief is supported by its ties to its neighboring beliefs, and ultimately, to the whole"[23] and not by the canons of strict logic alone.

This inner dialogue of belief—our own individual musings on what we believe and why—is always situated within a parallel "outer" context of conversation with others. We develop our beliefs on the basis of our interactions with those whom we hold dear, with those whom we value as personal or institutional authorities, with those with whom we routinely disagree, and with a host of strangers who cross our paths at irregular intervals. Our thinking is socially embedded in those overlapping networks of tradition, connection, and contention, and we need constantly to evaluate and reevaluate how our own ideas and beliefs stack up against the views of others with whom we come in contact.

The integration model discussed in the first chapter of this book argues that the best way to engage in this task of evaluating other ideas and views is by comparing the worldviews that underlie those beliefs. But Murphy says that approach, as appealing as it might appear at first glance, is simply not an option. It is impossible to compare worldviews with that kind of objectivity. To do so would require us to step outside our own worldviews onto some kind of neutral viewing platform from which we could see all worldviews in equal detail with no predispositions one way or another. But human beings cannot step outside themselves in that way. Borrowing Quine's image of worldviews as ships on the sea, Murphy says bluntly that "we cannot walk on water; we cannot jump ship to examine [our own worldview] from the outside and compare it to all the other ships at sea. We cannot judge them all from the outside on the basis of some universal standards."[24] Instead, she says, the best we can do is to engage in a series of ad hoc analyses of the potential connections or conflicts that might exist between some of our ideas and some of the ideas of others. Then, if we see something that attracts us or repulses us in the views of the other, the most we can do is make small adjustments to our thinking here and there. Returning to Quine's nautical imagery, Murphy argues that the only way we can alter our beliefs is the same way we would repair a ship at sail: a little at a time. Murphy explains: "We cannot rebuild the whole thing at once—we can only make small repairs here and there, keeping the rest intact in order to keep ourselves afloat."[25] Granted, sometimes more dramatic changes do take place. People "jump ship," as it were, and swim over to board another boat.

These kinds of conversions are relatively rare, however, and often they involve more continuities of thought and conviction than appear at first glance.

What does this mean for our understanding of Christian scholarship? According to Murphy, the interactions between faith and learning will be many, and they will often point in different directions at the same time. Sometimes the views of faith and learning will conflict; sometimes they will confirm each other; and more often than not those interactions will be of an oblique nature that produces neither confirmation nor conflict but something else—curiosity, deepened insight, humility regarding one's claims of knowledge, slight modification, the admission of ambiguity, or just plain wonder. Like Wuthnow, she senses that Christian scholarship may have more to do with the questions one feels compelled to ask than the answers one provides.

But it is not just the interactions of faith and learning that produce these kinds of responses. This also happens within the world of learning itself when people with differing views interact, and it happens within the realm of faith when persons steeped in different theological traditions converse seriously with each other. Complex relations exist between persons who represent different schools of thought within the sciences. Complex relations also exist between persons from different Christian (or other religious) traditions. And very complex relations emerge when people representing different and sometimes conflicting traditions of theology dialogue with people representing different and sometimes conflicting academic schools of thought—especially given the fact that the persons of faith involved in such conversations also possess certain academic convictions and that the academicians almost surely possess certain religious beliefs or spiritual convictions.

In short, interactions between faith and learning are at best complex, convoluted, and unpredictable, already connected with each other in a host of ways. Undoubtedly there are ways that faith and learning might conflict, but the explorations of how faith and learning are related within the realm of Christian scholarship will involve much more than that. Edward B. Davis explores some of that complicated terrain in the accompanying essay, which focuses on the history of science. As for Murphy herself, she says "yes, there are conflicts between religion and science, but they are only a small part of a much more complicated story."[26] In that more complicated story, Murphy argues that the traffic between theology and science—the traffic between faith and learning in general—has to go both ways. "We sometimes have to correct our theology as science advances. . . . But sometimes theology must correct science."[27]

Murphy views all knowledge as essentially communal. Each community, whether theological or disciplinary, moves together toward an articulation of its standpoints. Individuals have a role to play in this process, but scholarship is never a purely individual enterprise. Murphy, for example, has been quite blunt about her own convictions, saying that she works explicitly out of an Anabaptist or radical Reformation perspective, but her work also reflects a host of Catholic convictions she obviously imbibed in the process of growing up Catholic. While affirming particularity, then, Murphy's epistemology allows for and even requires a certain ecumenical sensitivity and commitment. As Christians and as scholars we necessarily work out of our own particular (and sometimes hybrid) traditions, but in another sense we all—at least, at our best—work to benefit the whole church and the whole world.

In making this last assertion, Murphy's vision of Christian scholarship bends toward the Boyeresque. Ethics, understood as concern for the other—as service—becomes a necessary part of the equation. Murphy argues that it has become a commonplace of contemporary thought to assume that one's social location determines one's vision of the world. This position, which derives from Nietzschean philosophy, Marxist political thought, and liberationist theology, was given blunt expression by Michel Foucault when he claimed that "knowledge" was really much more a function of one's ability to impose one's will on others than it was a picture of the way things actually were. Murphy rejects Foucault's description of knowledge as nothing but cognitivized self-interest; however, she accepts that "it would be naive to suppose that knowledge is not subject to the taint of powerful self-interest." Thus she concludes that self-renunciation—the rejection of self-interest and the caring embrace of the other—is "not only the key to ethics . . . [but] it is also the key to knowledge." She writes: "Renunciation of the will to power is a prerequisite for seeking truth."[28]

Murphy is not, of course, unique in making this point. Many Christian writers and theologians have said the same thing. One of the most articulate statements comes from the short commentary on the Nicene Creed entitled *The School of Charity* (1934) by the Anglican scholar Evelyn Underhill, whose scholarly work focused on religious mysticism. She wrote:

> We are Christians; and so we accept, in spite of all appearances to
> the contrary, the Christian account of [God's] character. God is Love,
> or rather Charity; generous, out-flowing, self-giving love. . . . To enter
> the Divine order then, achieve the full life for which we are made,
> means entering an existence which only has meaning as the chan-
> nel and expression of an infinite, self-spending love. This is not pi-
> ety. It is not altruism. It is the clue to our human condition. . . . This
> means that the true demand of religion will never be a demand for
> correct behavior or correct belief; but for generosity, as a controlling
> factor in every relation.[29]

For people like Murphy, Boyer, and Underhill, Christian scholarship can never be reduced to "the life of the mind" alone. Instead knowledge, faith, and morality mingle and cohere in the context of our entire lives as scholars. This is not a normative ideal but a mere fact of life. Epistemology and ethics are inseparably linked. Murphy and Boyer are not saying that Christian scholars ought to be more careful to live up to their own highest values; they are not ranting against hypocrisy. What they are saying is that the way we think and the way we live are intimately connected to each other. In that sense, Christian scholarship is not so much something one does as an expression of who one is. To repeat the words of Robert Wuthnow, Christian scholarship is ultimately a matter of living the questions; it is never a matter of thought alone.

NOTES

1. Robert Wuthnow, *Christianity in the Twenty-First Century: Reflections on the Challenges Ahead* (New York: Oxford University Press, 1993), 203. Wuthnow is a Protestant, but the Catholic sociologist Andrew Greeley says much the same thing. Greeley suggests that religious "worldviews are not propositional paragraphs that can be explicated and critiqued in discursive fashion. Rather they are, in their origins and in their primal power, tenacious and durable narrative symbols that take possession of the imagination early in the socialization process and provide patterns which shape the rest of life." *The Catholic Imagination* (Berkeley: University of California Press, 2000), 133.

2. Wuthnow, *Christianity in the Twenty-First Century*, 209. This insight is not necessarily foreign to those who affirm the integration model, but it is only infrequently incorporated into their theoretical reflections on the nature of Christian scholarship. One exception to this general rule is Nicholas Wolterstorff. His sensitivity to this issue, like that of many other people, is rooted in the experience of personal suffering and loss. See his "The Grace that Shaped My Life," in *Finding God at Harvard*, edited by Kelly Monroe (Grand Rapids, Mich.: Zondervan, 1996), 149–58. Agonizing over the death of his son, Wolterstorff said his Reformed faith "had always encouraged [him] to live with unanswered questions" and had also taught him that "life eternal doesn't depend on getting all the questions answered; God is often as much behind the questions as behind the answers. But never had the unanswered questions been so painful" (157). See also his deeply touching *Lament for a Son* (Grand Rapids, Mich.: Eerdmans, 1987).

3. David Hollenbach, "The Catholic University under the Sign of the Cross: Christian Humanism in a Broken World," in *Finding God in All Things*, edited by Michael J. Himes and Stephen J. Pope (New York: Crossroads, 1996), 283.

4. Martin E. Marty, *The One and the Many: America's Struggle for the Common Good* (Cambridge, Mass.: Harvard University Press, 1997), 22–23.

5. George Dennis O'Brien, *The Idea of a Catholic University* (Chicago: University of Chicago Press, 2002), 59.

6. Martha C. Nussbaum, *Upheavals of Thought: The Intelligence of Emotions* (Cambridge: Cambridge University Press, 2001), 1–3.

7. O'Brien, *The Idea of a Catholic University*, 203.

8. Craig Dykstra, *Growing in the Life of Faith: Education and Christian Practice* (Louisville, Ky.: Geneva Press, 1999), 137.

9. Ernest L. Boyer, "A College of Quality" (originally presented in January 1988), in Ernest L. Boyer, *Selected Speeches 1979–1995* (Princeton: Carnegie Foundation for the Advancement of Teaching, 1997), 60.

10. Boyer, "Lifelong Learning in the Arts" (originally presented in April 1994), in *Selected Speeches*, 134.

11. Boyer, "The Basic School" (originally presented in April 1995), in *Selected Speeches*, 25.

12. Boyer, "Making Connections" (originally presented in March 1993), in *Selected Speeches*, 10.

13. Boyer, "A College of Quality" (originally presented in January 1988), in *Selected Speeches*, 66.

14. Boyer, "Ready to Learn: A Mandate for the Nation" (originally presented in February 1993), in *Selected Speeches*, 12.

15. Boyer, "Teaching about Religion in Public Schools" (originally presented in November 1991), in *Selected Speeches*, 125.

16. Boyer, "Teaching about Religion in Public Schools," in *Selected Speeches*, 119.

17. On Boyer's fourfold analysis of scholarship, including the scholarship of discovery, see Ernest L. Boyer, *Scholarship Reconsidered: Priorities of the Professoriate* (Princeton: Carnegie Foundation for the Advancement of Teaching, 1990). See also Ernest L. Boyer, "The Scholarship of Engagement," *Journal of Public Service and Outreach* 11, 1 (spring 1996), 11–20.

18. Boyer, *Scholarship Reconsidered*, 22.

19. Ernest L. Boyer, "Reflections on a Church-Related Higher Education," *Cresset* (Valparaiso University) 57 (June 1994), 3.

20. Boyer, "Making Connections," 116.

21. See Nancey Murphy, *Theology in the Age of Scientific Reasoning* (Ithaca: Cornell University Press, 1990); *Beyond Liberalism and Fundamentalism: How Modern and Postmodern Philosophy Set the Theological Agenda* (Valley Forge, Pa.: Trinity Press International, 1996); *Reconciling Theology and Science: A Radical Reformation Perspective* (Kitchener, Ontario: Pandora Press, 1997). See also Nancey Murphy and George F. R. Ellis, *On the Moral Nature of the Universe: Theology, Cosmology, and Ethics* (Minneapolis: Fortress Press, 1996) and Nancey Murphy, "Postmodern Apologetics or Why Theologians *Must* Pay Attention to Science," in *Religion and Science: History, Method, Dialogue*, edited by W. Mark Richardson and Wesley J. Wildman (New York: Routledge, 1996).

22. Murphy, "Postmodern Apologetics," 107.

23. Murphy, "Postmodern Apologetics," 108.

24. Murphy, "Postmodern Apologetics," 109.

25. Murphy, "Postmodern Apologetics," 109.

26. Murphy, *Reconciling Theology and Science*, 9.

27. Murphy, *Reconciling Theology and Science*, 4.

28. Murphy and Ellis, *On the Moral Nature of the Universe*, 139.

29. Evelyn Underhill, *The School of Charity* (1934; Harrisburg, Pa.: Morehouse, 1991), 11.

ESSAY TWO

Is There a Christian History of Science?

Edward B. Davis

The preceding chapter argues that scholarship is a decidedly human en-deavor that involves a host of personal factors as well as logical reflection. This essay tests that thesis as it relates to the history of science. An earlier generation of scholars stressed the logical side of scientific advance; more recently, historians of science have given the nonlogical influences of social and cultural development greater due. That shift of focus has paved the way for a reevaluation of the relationship between science and faith. The older notion of "warfare" between science and faith has been replaced with a much more complicated story of mutual influence. The essay con-cludes that historians of science today, whether Christians or not, largely share the same goal: to document the complexity of that relationship without prejudicing the case either for or against faith.

I begin this essay by asking a question that was often raised by an earlier generation of historians of science: The history of science—is it science or is it history? What is at stake in this query is whether scientific development represents the slow victory of rigorous obser-vation and logical thought over the irrationalities of human culture (i.e., the "science" side of the question) or whether the trajectory of scientific development is part and parcel of the larger, often less than rational, story of society (i.e., the "history" side of the question).

In the halcyon days of my discipline, which overlap with the growth of American science after World War II, leading scholars in the field tended to favor the science side of things over the historical. These scholars, who were almost without exception males themselves, invariably focused their attention on the "great men" of the past who had "made" what was then called "modern science"—that is, the natural philosophy of the sixteenth and seventeenth centuries, the age of Galileo and Newton. But a rather intense debate soon broke out as another group of scholars began to champion a new "external" approach to the history of science that questioned the great-men approach. Scholars of the great-men school of thought usually favored an "internal" history of science, one that focused on the conceptual development of a given field of science, say astronomy or physics, emphasizing the almost miraculous work of that handful of geniuses who were the "great men" in that discipline. They typically ignored or at least downplayed possible influences on these "great men" from "outside" science, influences such as theology or alchemy or politics or even personality. (It was not by accident that the eighteen-month period in Newton's early adult years when he was said to have invented the calculus and discovered gravity was called the *annus mirabilis*, the "marvelous year," for it was indeed the functional equivalent of a miracle for scholars whose positivistic sensibilities told them that miracles do not happen.) "External" history of science, on the other hand, dealt with the ways science might be related to the social and cultural context within which it exists. These externalists did not typically suggest that nonscientific concerns such as gender or religious beliefs had any direct impact on the actual *content* of science, but they acknowledged that science was influenced in some way by "external" factors nonetheless. Although the terms "internalist" and "externalist" have passed out of use, the issues they refer to are still being debated and are highly relevant to the question at hand.[1]

It is highly instructive here to read afresh from one of the most influential "externalists" of them all, the sociologist Robert Merton. As a doctoral student at Columbia in the 1930s, Merton wrote what came to be considered a seminal study of the social dimensions of seventeenth-century English science.[2] When his work was reprinted in book form more than three decades later in 1970, Merton added a fascinating preface, contextualizing his own earlier contextualization of science:

> By inquiring into the *reciprocal* relations between science, as an ongoing intellectual activity, and the environing social and cultural structure, the monograph managed to by-pass the then current tendency—one still marked today in some quarters of historical and sociological scholarship—of giving uneven attention to the distinct directions of that reciprocity, with the impact of science (and of science-based technology) upon society eliciting much attention, and the impact of society upon science very little. This study takes seriously the notion of institutional interchange as it abandons the easy assumption of exclusively one-sided impact.[3]

Despite this statement in the new preface, in the text itself Merton had been much more cautious about this very type of interchange. He argued that while the "Puritan ethos," as he called it, "may well have been congenial to the development of science," this did not "imply that the discoveries of Newton, Boyle, or other scientists [could] be directly attributed to the sanction of science by religion. Specific discoveries and inventions," he added, "belong to the internal history of science and are largely independent of factors other than the purely scientific."[4]

Some social constructivists today would go a good deal further, further indeed than I would go with them, as when science is sometimes seen to be *nothing but* a set of socially constructed ideas, as if there were no external world "out there" to impinge on our senses and to move us to think thoughts we would not otherwise think about how the world works, or no internal logic of a scientific discipline that shapes questions and the kinds of answers that can be given.[5] But those scholars who emphasize the way science *is* influenced by other ways of thinking and by broader social practices have done a genuine service to Christian scholars, for they have helped clear away the tentacles of an overbearing positivism that ruled out, a priori, the very possibility of such influence. History of science now looks a great deal more like history and less like science than it used to, and this is on the whole a very good thing, provided we do not forget that its subject remains *both* science *and* the people who do it.

Christian Faith and the History of Science

Given that history of science now resembles history more than science, I am led to ask: Is there such a thing as a Christian approach to history in general? From my perspective, the answer to that question is no. The Christian historians I know all use exactly the same methods, the same sources, and the same concepts as other historians. In other words, Christian historians belong to a scholarly community whose standards and vocabulary they fully share, though they sometimes apply their historical expertise to subjects that other historians might pass by. In short, the Christian scholars I know do not do either history in general or the history of science differently from other historians; there is no distinctively Christian way of conducting a historical inquiry into any particular aspect of the past, including science.

Why not? Why don't Christian historians have different standards for their craft than other historians? One way of answering this would be to ask a similar question of Christian carpenters: do Christian carpenters saw wood, measure walls, and hammer nails differently from non-Christian carpenters? I hope not—good carpentry is good carpentry, whether done by Jews, Christians, Buddhists, or even atheists. Indeed I have an atheist friend, a highly respected philosopher of science, who is also pretty good at making cabinets. I do hope that a Christian carpenter is *more likely* to be honest, fair, and diligent than her unbelieving counterpart, but my unbelieving friend is honest, fair, and diligent, so I would hesitate to push this too far.

Might there be a similar way to view the history of science? Should we expect Christian historians of science to be honest, fair, and diligent? Of course we should—but should we not have the same expectation of other historians of science? In fact, other historians often do meet these expectations, even when writing about topics closely related to religion. A pertinent example would be Ronald Numbers's recent book *The Creationists*, an exhaustive treatment of the history of that movement right down to the present generation, showing in the process the importance of some key ideas derived from the Seventh-Day Adventist prophet Ellen White for the contemporary creationist movement. Now a self-described agnostic, Numbers is himself a former Seventh-Day Adventist, the son of a prominent Seventh-Day Adventist evangelist. Those interested in his personal story can read some of it for themselves in the very revealing introduction to the book. As he reports, his lectures on the history of creationism have led some to castigate him for being a creationist himself, since he does not engage in debunking the ideas he presents. In the final paragraph of the introduction, he writes: "Although I no longer believe in creationism of any kind, I am strongly committed to treating its advocates with the same respect I might accord evolutionists."[6] I know personally several people mentioned in his book, including some of the leading creationists, and none has complained to me of unfair treatment: this is a remarkable thing to say about a book dealing with such a controversial subject. Geoffrey Cantor's wonderful biography of the great physicist Michael Faraday offers another nice example. Although Cantor is Jewish, he treats Faraday's intense Christian spirituality with great sensitivity, so much so that the name of the tiny sect to which Faraday belonged is featured in the title of the book.[7] Numbers and Cantor are prime examples of the fact that it does not take a Christian historian of science to write in a manner that treats Christian themes fairly or even sympathetically.

Still assuming that the religious faith of a historian of science *does* make a difference in his scholarship, where then might that difference be evident, apart from subject matter, apart from simply showing a strong interest in the interface between faith and science? Might there perhaps be differences in the kinds of conclusions that Christian historians of science draw concerning the subjects that tend to interest them? For example, might Christian scholars be *more likely* to see the religious beliefs of scientists as important factors in their thinking as scientists?

To some extent, I think the answer is yes, though the situation is now changing fairly rapidly. A few years ago the Christian historian George Marsden said of historical studies in general:

> There's a tendency of reductionism in history, to reduce something to some essential cause, [an] economic or social factor. I think it's

worth giving religious factors their due. You don't have to be a religious person to do that, but certainly it helps. Most American historians just don't have any antenna for recognizing that.[8]

One could certainly have said something similar about history of science until quite recently.

Some twenty years ago I arrived at that point when a graduate student has to think about passing the examination that qualifies one to advance to doctoral studies. The examination would consist of two parts, one general section on the field as a whole and another section on an area of specialization chosen by me in consultation with the faculty. I clearly remember expressing to my late mentor, Richard S. Westfall, a wonderful person and splendid scholar, my strong desire to declare the history of science and religion as my area of specialization for this purpose. I just as clearly recall his answer: this would be unwise, since it is not a recognized specialty within history of science. Although I would be permitted to do as I wished, I was advised to write my examination on the classic field in which he specialized, the Scientific Revolution, for then I would be a known commodity on the job market. I took his advice, though the irony was not lost on me. Here was a scholar who had published his own dissertation under the title *Science and Religion in Seventeenth-Century England* and who had recently cemented his international reputation with a biography of Isaac Newton that devoted far more space to Newton's theological writings than almost anyone had ever done before.[9]

A short time later I submitted a proposal for my dissertation, in which I outlined a plan to "test" a "bold" historical "conjecture" (the philosophers in my department had introduced me to Karl Popper, whose language I have borrowed here)[10] put forth in the late 1930s by the Oxford philosopher Michael Beresford Foster. Though best known in his own day for work on Hegel and political philosophy, Foster is now usually connected with the controversial claim, developed in three dense articles in the journal *Mind*, that certain distinctly Hebrew elements in Christian theology provided the necessary and sufficient condition for the development of an empirical (vis-à-vis a purely rationalistic) science of nature in the early modern period.[11] I proposed to examine how well this claim compared with what four leading natural philosophers (Galileo Galilei, René Descartes, Robert Boyle, and Isaac Newton) had actually said about God, nature, and the human mind.[12] The initial response from my doctoral committee was not very enthusiastic—my idea might make a good dissertation in religion, but was this really history of science? I then revised the proposal, but not the central idea, by adding carefully chosen quotations, strongly suggestive of the types of connections I wanted to investigate, from Edwin Arthur Burtt and Alexandre Koyré—two intellectual historians of the old school who were deeply respected by the members of my committee. This convinced them that historians of science really could take religious beliefs

seriously in understanding the development of science, even the science produced by the "great men," or at least that one might be allowed to make such
a case.

I doubt I would have a similar experience if I were a graduate student
today. The most recent past president of the History of Science Society (HSS),
Ronald Numbers, is known mainly for his work on the history of religion and
science in America. When Oxford University recently filled a newly endowed
chair in religion and science—the event itself testifying to important changes—
they appointed a past president of the British Society for the History of Science,
John Hedley Brooke, who also gave the HSS Distinguished Lecture in 2001.
A recent issue of the prestigious journal *Osiris* (descended from the journal in
which Merton's study originally appeared) was devoted entirely to the history
of religion and science, and several articles describe interactions in which religious beliefs shaped the content or the presentation of scientific ideas in
important ways. I now find myself immersed in a steadily growing international group of scholars interested in this historical interplay of religion and
science. It is indeed a new world, and Christian scholars are better off in it.

But there is another irony to my story about my mentor Richard Westfall
that deserves mention before I move on. He was a religious person himself,
and he took that part of his life seriously, as his students and colleagues realized. For all of the attention he gave to religion in his scholarship, however, he
never came to believe that a scientist's religious beliefs could positively shape
a scientist's science—at least I am unaware that he ever took such a position,
and I know of several occasions on which he denied it. He failed, ultimately,
to "give religious factors their due," to borrow Marsden's words. Of course,
that kind of evenhandedness can be difficult to embody in practice: to give
religious factors their due, not to overplay them nor underplay them. What the
Dutch historian Floris Cohen has said about the Scientific Revolution can be
applied to the entire history of science: "To find the proper balance between
detachment and involvement seems almost beyond reach when this particular
subject [religion and science] comes up for discussion—partisanship and irrelevance being the Scylla and the Charybdis on which more than one historiographical ship has been wrecked."[13]

One ship that has run aground in the past two decades, to the great delight
of Christian historians, is the "conflict" or "warfare" school of interpretation,
one of the more unfortunate products of the rise of positivism and the research
university in the latter half of the nineteenth century. The two principal American sources of this historiography, John William Draper of New York University and Andrew Dickson White of Cornell, profoundly influenced subsequent
writing and teaching on this subject, fundamentally at the conceptual level but
also influencing the vocabulary of subsequent writers. They chose words deliberately to enhance drama and to create a triumphalistic image of science
winning a mortal combat with theology. The following memorable imagery

introduces White's book; hear exactly how he depicts the relationship between science and theology:

> My book is ready for the printer, and as I begin this preface my eye lights on the crowd of Russian peasants at work on the Neva under my windows. With pick and shovel they are letting the rays of the April sun into the great ice barrier which binds together the modern quays and the old granite fortress where lie the bones of the Romanoff Czars.
>
> This barrier is already weakened; it is widely decayed, in many places thin, and everywhere treacherous; but it is, as a whole, so broad, so crystallized about old boulders, so imbedded in shallows, so wedged into crannies on either shore, that it is a great danger. The waters from thousands of swollen streamlets above are pressing behind it; wreckage and refuse are piling up against it; every one knows that it must yield. But there is danger that it may resist the pressure too long and break suddenly, wrenching even the granite quays from their foundations, bringing desolation to a vast population, and leaving, after the subsidence of the flood, a widespread residue of slime, a fertile breeding-bed for the germs of disease.
>
> But the patient mujiks are doing the right thing. The barrier, exposed more and more to the warmth of spring by the scores of channels they are making, will break away gradually, and the river will flow on beneficent and beautiful.
>
> My work in this book is like that of the Russian mujik on the Neva. I simply try to aid in letting the light of historical truth into that decaying mass of outworn thought which attaches the modern world to mediaeval conceptions of Christianity, and which still lingers among us—a most serious barrier to religion and morals, and a menace to the whole normal evolution of society.[14]

White's colorful title says it all: *A History of the Warfare of Science with Theology in Christendom.* It was theology, the dogmatic content of Christian thinking, rather than Christian moral attitudes and teachings that the positivist propagandists wanted to kill off. Perhaps the greatest irony about the contemporary religion/science dialogue is the fact that, despite their own strongly articulated denials of the "warfare" thesis, a good many liberal Protestant thinkers since the late nineteenth century have implicitly accepted it. They have agreed with Draper and White that traditional theology has proved wholly unable to engage science in fruitful conversation and, therefore, that theology needs to be thoroughly modernized by a complete removal of all references to a transcendent God. Not many contemporary writers—John Polkinghorne would be an outstanding exception—understand just how badly Draper and White misread the history of Christianity and science, and just how much modern theology has been impoverished by its failure to challenge this core assumption of modernity.[15]

The Complexity of Christianity's Relation to Science

While reports of the total demise of the "warfare" school may yet be premature—it remains wildly popular with scientists and journalists, and its implicit acceptance by others has already been noted—at least among historians of science it has begun to disappear in the past two decades. I should add that it has not been replaced by the equally naive view that science and religion have enjoyed a fully harmonious relationship. It has simply not yet been replaced by any alternative scheme whatsoever—and some leading historians doubt that it can be. "We will never find a satisfactory alternative of equal simplicity" to replace it, say David Lindberg and Ronald Numbers.[16] "Serious scholarship in the history of science," notes John Brooke, "has revealed so extraordinarily rich and complex a relationship between science and religion in the past that general theses are difficult to sustain. The real lesson turns out to be the complexity."[17]

This conclusion sometimes frustrates Christian scientists, theologians, and philosophers, who would like the historians to tell them which conceptual models for relating science and faith have the strongest historical support. Although I think history can provide numerous helpful insights for the contemporary situation, various questions about all sorts of historical events are difficult to answer simply, without sacrificing too much of the truth. Historians have a different sense of causality than scientists, and with good reason. Human actions are complex, resulting from diverse motives and reflecting diverse beliefs and perceptions, a situation that is made only more complex for major events by the involvement of more people. Thus we are led to this paradoxical conclusion: the larger the historical target, the harder it is to hit.

Let me apply this to a question that Christian scholars have often raised. Did Christianity "cause" modern science? Obviously the positivist historians would deny this vociferously—their whole argument is for the opposite claim—but even at the height of the positivist hegemony decades ago, several leading scholars advanced the claim that some aspect of the Christian worldview had either "caused" modern science or at least greatly stimulated it. One of the most important examples is the fascinating work on medieval science by the French physicist and philosopher Pierre Duhem. Ironically, Duhem was himself a type of positivist in his *philosophy* of science, in that he adopted a kind of instrumentalist attitude toward theories: like Ernst Mach, he saw them as useful calculating devices that ought not be confused with truth statements that actually *explain* physical reality. Since they lacked status as ultimate truth, the conclusions of science could not threaten or conflict with the claims of theology. His approach to the *history* of science was in sharp contrast to the prevailing positivist view, however. Here Duhem argued quite strongly that Galileo should be seen not as the start of a new, secular, radically modern tradition but rather as the culmination of an older tradition rooted in the High Middle Ages, when Christian thinkers had first begun to question ideas inherited from Aristotle and Greek antiquity. Duhem's overall view is best presented in his own words:

> The only conclusion that these facts impose is that the Catholic
> Church has on many occasions helped powerfully and that it still
> helps energetically to maintain human reason on the right road,
> even when this reason strives for the discovery of truths of a natural
> order. Now, what impartial and enlightened mind would dare to testify falsely against this affirmation?[18]

A similar claim, with an even stronger Roman Catholic flavor and an even more polemical tone, can be found today in the many writings of the Jesuit historian Stanley L. Jaki, who himself has almost canonized Duhem.[19]

A generation later, in the period between the world wars, others worked to turn positivism on its head by showing that religious assumptions about nature and knowledge were deeply embedded in the ideas and practices we associate with the modern scientific worldview. One of these scholars was the English logician Alfred North Whitehead, best described as a theist rather than a Christian, who argued in 1925 that the very *possibility* of modern science depended on the unconsciously held belief, derived from medieval theology, that the created order was indeed intelligible. Although Whitehead's process metaphysics has had a profound influence on some important modern theologians, his claim has thus far inspired little original scholarship in the history of science, and must still be taken as an unestablished, if bold, conjecture.

Two scholars who wrote in the decade after Whitehead, however, have had a major impact on the way the history of science is understood and practiced. I have already outlined the groundbreaking work of Robert Merton on the influence of Puritanism on the *reception* of science in England. (Incidentally, Merton was a Polish Jew from Philadelphia who changed his name to hide his heritage at a time when Jews were subject to academic discrimination. As before with Numbers and Cantor, Merton's work underscores the point that definitions of what counts as Christian scholarship are highly problematic. We might best describe this kind of academic work as "Christian studies" rather than "Christian scholarship," a point that is further discussed in chapter 5 of this book.) The other scholar I have in mind is Michael Beresford Foster, who argued for a direct influence of Christian theology on the epistemic content of early modern natural philosophy. Foster concentrated on the doctrine of creation, particularly on the ways early modern thinkers conceived of God's relationship to the created order, including the human mind as part of that order.

He identified two basic theological attitudes that he labeled "rationalist" and "voluntarist," terms retained by most scholars who have written on this subject (though the suitability of the latter has recently been questioned).[20] Rationalist thinkers, Foster claimed, emphasized the ways God's reason could be understood by the human mind, which God had created. For the rationalists, God's nature was neither mysterious nor inscrutable, and the natural world could therefore be understood by an exercise of pure reason: human reason was sufficient by itself to determine what God must have done in creating it. Voluntarists, on the other hand, did not deny God's reason but emphasized God's freedom to act in ways not entirely conformable to reason. Because the world is a product of free divine activity, its existence and its nature are both contingent; thus the only genuine science must be an empirical science, in which the causes of things are found by observing what God has actually done, not by determining a priori what God must have done.

Because Foster saw this connection between theological assumptions and scientific method as logically necessary rather than historically contingent, his articles (like the books by Duhem and Jaki) do appear at times to be motivated by apologetical concerns. If modern science could be shown to rest on a theological base, then the status of Christianity might be enhanced in a scientific age—and this has made it attractive to Christian scholars. Furthermore, his argument is subtle and carefully developed, the kind of scholarship that Christian scholars ought to emulate. On the other hand, Foster's approach is profoundly unhistorical. Instead of looking extensively at what early modern natural philosophers actually said about God, nature, and the human mind, Foster mainly left his argument in abstract cognitive space. He focused on showing what theological assumptions *should* have meant for natural philosophy, not what real natural philosophers actually thought they meant. As noted at the beginning of chapter 2, "the soil in which Christian scholarship typically grows is not the soft loam of ideal logic but the gritty ground of our full personhood." Foster's study, though undoubtedly linked with his own full personhood, tended to ignore the messy details of the subjects he studied.

Nevertheless, Foster's work suggests that historians might profitably investigate how early modern thinkers actually did construe the relation between God and the creation, and what they thought this implied about the science they constructed. Several leading intellectual historians have indeed looked carefully at early modern science with just such questions in mind, and a more genuinely historical form of Foster's revisionist argument has begun to emerge.[21]

But early modern science is a complex subject, and complexity is the main reason why I believe that Foster's argument has sometimes been pushed too far. Although historians have established a very important role for Christian theology in shaping modern science, we have not "proved" that Christianity "caused" modern science. Any such claim ignores factors other than theology, inappropriately reducing a complex historical situation to a monocausal model. Theological beliefs were certainly important in shaping modern science—and such a conclusion would have been on much shakier ground fifty years ago— but other features of the historical landscape must also be considered. For example, both rationalist and voluntarist arguments about God and nature were heavily influenced by a larger debate about skepticism, originating in antiquity and rediscovered by Renaissance humanists. The skeptical tradition encouraged natural philosophers to challenge rationalism, leading Descartes (ironically) to use skepticism itself to ground his rationalist natural philosophy. On the other hand, Pierre Gassendi used skepticism to ground his voluntarist natural philosophy, and this in turn influenced Boyle and Newton to take a similar attitude toward knowledge. But the crisis of faith that accompanied the Reformation, leading many to question the sources of authority, had already helped to create a skeptical climate—so in that sense it comes back to theology again. My point is that the larger historical picture is more complex than Foster's simple claim. We cannot simply separate science, philosophy, theology, or religious practices from one another without distorting the actual situation. Christianity did not by itself "cause" modern science, any more than the Treaty of Versailles by itself "caused" World War II. It was rather one of several factors, though surely a very important one, in pushing modern science down the road of empiricism.

Let me now return to the original question: Is there a Christian history of science, and if so, what does it look like? Perhaps the broader question is whether Christian scholarship has to be visibly different from scholarship done by persons who are not Christians in order to earn the label "Christian." I cannot answer for scholarship in general, but in the history of science there clearly is no neat way of differentiating Christian scholarship from other scholarship. If we define good historical scholarship in terms of treating your topics and the people about whom you write honestly and fairly, while giving other factors—including religious factors—their due, then we can say that some Christians and some scholars who are not Christians do that well and some others, Christians and non-Christians alike, do that less well. Does that mean Christians have nothing distinctive to contribute? Not at all. Christian historians of science do bring certain sensitivities to their work that others may lack, and they also bring certain apologetic concerns to their work that they may need to keep partly in check if they want to persuade their colleagues. In the wake of the demise of the "warfare" thesis, however, what all scholars in the history of science are called to do is to work with each other, striving with as much care and nuance as they can muster to unravel the complex relations that actually exist between science and faith. If this is not the only role that Christian historians of science can play, it is surely an honorable one.

NOTES

I am grateful to Arie Leegwater and the contributors to this book for helpful comments on earlier drafts of this essay.

1. For further comments on this terminology, see Steven Shapin, "Discipline and Bounding: The History and Sociology of Science as Seen through the Externalism-Internalism Debate," *History of Science* 30 (December 1992), 333–69.

2. Robert K. Merton, "Science, Technology and Society in Seventeenth-Century England," *Osiris* 4 (1938), 360–632. Merton's dissertation was published at the invitation of his teacher, George Sarton, who was also the founding editor of *Osiris*.

3. Robert K. Merton, *Science, Technology, and Society in Seventeenth-Century England* (New York: Harper & Row, 1970), xi, his italics. This preface also contains highly interesting remarks on the dominance of the "conflict" model for thinking about religion and science.

4. Merton, *Science, Technology and Society*, 75. The term "Puritan ethos" does not appear in the sentence quoted but is used elsewhere in the same chapter to refer to the beliefs and attitudes of certain English Protestants. The lack of precision with which Merton used this term has led many to criticize his study.

5. For thorough discussions of the social constructivist approach, see Ian Hacking, *The Social Construction of What?* (Cambridge, Mass.: Harvard University Press, 1999); and the introduction and final chapter in Martin Rudwick, *The Great Devonian Controversy: The Shaping of Scientific Knowledge among Gentlemanly Specialists* (Chicago: University of Chicago Press, 1985).

6. Ronald L. Numbers, *The Creationists: The Evolution of Scientific Creationism* (New York: Knopf, 1992), xvi.

7. Geoffrey N. Cantor, *Michael Faraday: Sandemanian and Scientist, a Study of Science and Religion in the Nineteenth Century* (New York: St. Martin's Press, 1991).

8. George M. Marsden quoted in Tim Stafford, "Whatever Happened to Christian History?" *Christianity Today* 45 (April 2, 2001), 45.

9. Richard S. Westfall, *Science and Religion in Seventeenth-Century England* (New Haven: Yale University Press, 1958); *Never at Rest: A Biography of Isaac Newton* (Cambridge: Cambridge University Press, 1980).

10. Popper held that science advances when scientists make "bold conjectures" (hypotheses) and then try very hard to "refute" them by designing "severe tests." In short, *"we can learn from our mistakes"* (his italics); *Conjectures and Refutations: The Growth of Scientific Knowledge* (New York: Basic Books, 1962), vii.

11. Foster's essays have been reprinted several times. The most useful collection is *Creation, Nature, and Political Order in the Philosophy of Michael Foster (1903–1959): The Classic "Mind" Articles and Others, with Modern Critical Essays*, edited by Cameron Wybrow (Lewiston, N.Y.: Mellen, 1992). For my review of this work see *Isis* 85 (1994), 127–29.

12. The conclusions of my dissertation, "Creation, Contingency, and Early Modern Science: The Impact of Voluntaristic Theology on Seventeenth-Century Natural Philosophy," Indiana University (1984), are found in my essays "Christianity and Early Modern Science: The Foster Thesis Reconsidered," in *Evangelicals and Science in Historical Perspective*, edited by David N. Livingstone, D. G. Hart, and Mark A. Noll

(New York: Oxford University Press, 1999), 75–95; "God, Man, and Nature: The Problem of Creation in Cartesian Thought," *Scottish Journal of Theology* 44 (1991), 325–48; and "Newton's Rejection of the 'Newtonian World View': The Role of Divine Will in Newton's Natural Philosophy," in *Facets of Faith and Science*, vol. 3, *The Role of Beliefs in the Natural Sciences*, edited by Jitse M. van der Meer (Lanham, Md.: University Press of America, 1996), 75–96.

13. H. Floris Cohen, *The Scientific Revolution: A Historiographical Inquiry* (Chicago: University of Chicago Press, 1994), 308.

14. Andrew Dickson White, *A History of the Warfare of Science with Theology in Christendom*, 2 vols. (New York: Appleton's, 1896), v–vi.

15. On this point also see my essay "Appreciating a Scientist-Theologian: Some Remarks on the Work of John Polkinghorne," *Zygon* 35, 4 (December 2000), 971–76.

16. David C. Lindberg and Ronald L. Numbers, "Beyond War and Peace: A Reappraisal of the Encounter between Christianity and Science," *Perspectives on Science and Christian Faith* 39 (1987), 148.

17. John Hedley Brooke, *Science and Religion: Some Historical Perspectives* (Cambridge: Cambridge University Press, 1991), 5.

18. Pierre Duhem, *The Aim and Structure of Physical Theory*, translated by Philip P. Wiener (Princeton: Princeton University Press, 1954), 311.

19. See, for example, Stanley L. Jaki, *Science and Creation: From Eternal Cycles to an Oscillating Universe* (New York: Science History, 1974); *The Road of Science and the Ways to God* (Chicago: University of Chicago Press, 1978); and *The Origin of Science and the Science of Its Origin* (South Bend, Ind.: Regnery/Gateway, 1979).

20. Peter Harrison, "Voluntarism and Early Modern Science," *History of Science* 40 (2002), 1–27. Harrison argues cogently that the important issue was not divine freedom (as the term "voluntarism" suggests) but the limits of human knowledge compared with God's knowledge.

21. These would include John Brooke, John Henry, Reijer Hooykaas, Eugene Klaaren, Ted McGuire, Francis Oakley, and Margaret Osler. These scholars do not share a common ideology—one is a Roman Catholic, two are Reformed, and some are not religious—and cannot be accused as a group of engaging in thinly veiled apologetics.

CHAPTER THREE

Scholarship and the Varieties of Christian Faith

Christian scholars live in a world rich with traditions of both faith and learning. While Christian scholars are not controlled by the religious ways of life they have inherited or by the academic schools of thought with which they have come to align themselves, their work will almost always be shaped to some degree by those commitments. Different traditions of faith and inquiry provide us with different questions to pursue, different hunches about where relevant information may be found, and different sentiments regarding which answers to those questions seem more appropriate than others.

As scholars, and especially as Christian scholars, it is important to be aware of the traditions that have shaped and continue to shape our academic work.[1] On one level, this is a matter of simple self-consciousness. Our scholarship will probably be better if we understand the ways our own tradition-nurtured instincts and perceptions affect our research, analysis of data, and creative efforts. None of us works in a traditionless void; no one does purely neutral scholarship. Even if we decide to set aside some aspects of the traditions of faith we acquired in our youth or if we have cast off approaches to our disciplines that we imbibed from our graduate school mentors, those traditions and approaches often still shape our life and work. Sometimes this takes the form of continuing affirmation; sometimes it takes the form of overt criticism of former ways of thought. Almost invariably the shaping power of the traditions of our youth affect us for the rest of our lives even if and as we fight against them. Thus one of our friends says he will be a Dutch Calvinist until the day he dies, even though he really does not want to be one anymore. Some of our Mennonite and Roman Catholic colleagues have said basically the same thing. It is probably true of us all to some degree.

There is nothing wrong with the fact that our academic work is shaped by the traditions of faith and learning that have shaped us as persons. In fact, the particularities of our traditions can be construed as scholarly assets that allow us to discover or create things that others simply cannot see or do because their traditions are less attuned to those areas. The Russian literary critic Mikhail Bakhtin argued that our experiences, located in the particularities of time and space, enable us to see some things that those around us cannot see but simultaneously block our view of other realities. Bakhtin used that fact to argue for a dialogic approach to knowledge. Take, for example, a room filled with people in conversation. While everyone can see part of the room, no one can see what takes place behind their backs. However, when everyone's vision is brought together—when everyone's "surplus of seeing" (what each individual sees that no one else can see) is added to each other's—the result is a much fuller view of reality. Our traditions, then, become part of our "surplus of seeing," illuminating the blind spots of other scholars, just as our own myopias are clarified through the perspectives of those "other" to ourselves.[2]

When we recognize the traditioned nature of our thinking, we can perhaps engage more fruitfully in discussions and debates with others, fulfilling Bakhtin's call for dialogism. Conversation is a necessary aspect of the academic life, and we learn various things from different kinds of scholarly conversations. Discussions with those with whom we basically agree often have a focusing impact on our academic work, helping us to fine-tune our arguments and perspectives. Conversations with like-minded peers can energize us for the hard work that good scholarship always entails. Knowing that others are chipping away at comparable problems and knowing how their work might dovetail with our own efforts can provide us with a sense of synergy that will make us much more productive in our own projects. Dialogue with those with whom we disagree, or from whom we simply differ, provides something else: a critical assessment of our academic work that, taken seriously, will help keep our scholarship honest, preventing us from mistaking our own views as unalloyed truth. Conversations with "the other," a phrase Bakhtin helped to make fashionable, sometimes give us new clues of understanding that can either augment or rearrange the elements of data and interpretation that make up our own views. Traditions are not impermeable; they can creatively interact with each other. And, of course, when people find another tradition ultimately more compelling than their own, they sometimes convert.

Conversions of this kind—switches of perspective—can take place within the purely academic realm in the same way they can take place in the world of faith. The lore of most disciplines contains the academic equivalent of Saint Paul's Damascus Road experience, when some famous practitioner suddenly "saw the light" and assumed a new theoretical paradigm or, even more shocking, switched disciplinary allegiance. Construing our allegiance to an academic discipline or theoretical perspective as a "tradition" may perhaps be a bit unsettling, but it points toward a reality that we all understand. Within academia, various schools of thought—some old and some brand new—vie with each other for prominence and power. They compete with each other for faculty appointments and research dollars. One of the most astute observers of this phenomenon was Imre Lakatos, who argued that virtually all the disciplines contained within themselves competing research programs oriented around divergent core theories, slightly (or significantly) differing bodies of relevant data, and divergent aesthetic criteria of plausibility and attraction. He argued that it was very hard to predict which of those divergent approaches would ultimately be the most fruitful, so he recommended that competing projects be supported and explored until each finally exhausted its vision or was proven wrong.[3] To the degree that Lakatos's understanding of the academy is accurate, it would clearly be helpful for scholars to be aware of the specific programs of research with which their own work has most resonance. Many such research projects will be discipline specific, but others will cross disciplinary boundaries or combine disciplines in novel ways (just as individual Christians sometimes combine divergent traditions of faith in their own lives). These hybrid projects are often as interesting as, or more interesting than, projects that fall wholly within one or another of the disciplines.

Most academicians are well aware of their scholarly allegiances; graduate school taught them to be methodologically self-aware and cognizant of how they situate their work amid competing schools of thought in the various disciplines. While some Christian scholars have a similar awareness regarding their religious identity, many do not. Granted, most Catholic scholars know they are Catholics and most Lutherans know they are Lutherans, and so forth, but only a relative minority of Christian scholars have any detailed knowledge of how the spiritual and theological resources of their traditions might affect their scholarship.[4] This chapter is designed as a kind of field guide to some of the most common Christian options. A few of these options grow directly out of church traditions and theology; some fall within the domain of spirituality; others are more political or ideological in orientation. It is hoped that this survey of alternatives will help individual scholars understand more accurately where their own inclinations and affinities may lie (regardless of what denominational labels they may or may not presently wear) and simultaneously assist them in their attempts to understand and dialogue with persons from other traditions.

The Catholic Intellectual Tradition

Roman Catholic thinking about faith and learning is both ancient and dynamic. Its roots go back to the earliest centuries of Christian history, yet some of its most dramatic developments have taken place in the last fifty years. While the Catholic tradition is much too diverse and expansive to define in detail, it is possible to highlight certain characteristics or sensibilities present in almost all Catholic discussions of scholarship and faith.[5]

Terrence Tilley, a theologian from the University of Dayton, has argued that the Catholic intellectual tradition has been largely determined by its "analogical imagination" (as opposed to the "digital or dialectical imagination," which is much more prominent in Protestant circles). He explains that analogical thinking "seeks to discern the similarities or the unities that exist among events, entities, or states of affairs that seem different . . . [treating] dilemmas or paired types as 'both/and' in contrast to the 'either/or' of the digital imagination."[6] The University of Chicago sociologist and Catholic priest Andrew Greeley has said much the same thing, arguing that the analogical imagination "stresses the 'like' of any comparison (human passion is like the divine passion), while Protestantism . . . stresses the unlike."[7]

Following the logic of analogical thinking, Catholic models of Christian scholarship have stressed connections, continuities, and paradoxical relationships more than distance, difference, and opposition. For Catholics, nature and grace commingle. The human and divine penetrate each other. The sacred and the secular are not opposites, but complements. In the language of Vatican II, "nothing genuinely human fails to raise an echo" in the Christian heart, and that is why, the document goes on to argue, the Christian "community realizes that it is truly and intimately linked with [all the rest of] mankind and its history."[8] Church and society exist in synergistic relation to each other. Reason, when it is operating properly, leads one to faith, and faith, when it is operating properly, drives one to reason. Viewed through the lens of analogical imagination, the world is a vast web of connections upon connections. Thus faith and learning do not have to be brought together (as if they existed in separate spheres); one needs only to discover the connections that already exist between them.

Analogical thinking taken to its logical conclusion implies the unity of all truth. If everything is in some way connected to everything else, every particular truth is also in some sense linked to all other truths. The nineteenth-century theologian John Henry Newman articulated that hypothesis as clearly as anyone when he wrote in *The Idea of a University* "I lay it down that all knowledge forms one whole, because its subject-matter is one; for the universe in its length and breadth is so intimately knit together, that we cannot separate off portion from portion, and operation from operation, except by a mental abstraction." For Newman, this unity of all knowledge includes assertions about God because God had "so implicated Himself with [the world], and taken it into His very bosom, by His presence in it, His providence over it, His impressions on it, and His influences through it, that we cannot truly or fully contemplate it without in some main aspects contemplating Him."[9] The Apostolic Constitution *Ex Corde Ecclesiae* (1990) says virtually the same thing, arguing that one of the main roles of the Catholic university is "to promote dialogue between faith and reason, so that it can be seen more profoundly how faith and reason bear harmonious witness to the unity of truth."[10] What makes Catholic scholarship Catholic, then, is not merely the integration of some Christian notions with some of the ideas of this or that academic discipline. What makes Catholic scholarship Catholic is that it aims to understand the world whole.

Two corollaries derive from this commitment to the unity of truth. First, any scholarly activity that seeks to break down "the rigid compartmentalization of knowledge within the individual academic disciplines"[11] can be seen as a form of Christian scholarship or, at the very least, it is the necessary foundation of Christian scholarship. Thus a book like *Creating Interdisciplinarity* (2001), by Lisa Lattuca, might be seen by many Catholics as profoundly religious, even though it hardly mentions faith at all.[12] The ultimate goal, of course, is "to work toward a higher synthesis of knowledge" that will locate "each of the various disciplines within the context of a vision of the human person and the world that is enlightened by the Gospel."[13] Even the smallest interdisciplinary steps toward the unity of truth are, however, to be honored as contributing to that goal. The Notre Dame philosopher Mark Roche bluntly says: "Collaborative work across the disciplines is a moral imperative" for Christian scholars.[14]

The second corollary has to do with the limits of individual scholars and the concomitant importance of what might be termed institutions of long duration. It is obviously impossible for any human being to know everything that can be known about everything and to understand all the relations that exist between and among those bits of knowledge. That task would be infinite and could never be completed. Although we each have our work to do, our contributions to the whole will always be merely small parts of the picture. Taking that insight seriously, very few treatments of Catholic scholarship have zeroed in on the work of individual scholars. Instead, the conversation has typically focused on the Catholic university as the locus of Christian scholarship. It is the Catholic university in its entirety that seeks to embody the holistic search for truth. It is in the university that the disciplines are both "studied in a systematic manner" *and* "brought into dialogue for their mutual enhancement."[15] The efforts of individual scholars are crucial, but the task of Christian scholarship is ultimately a communal effort—that is, communities of scholars working together within the structures of enduring institutions that can support the task of Christian scholarship in both its interdisciplinary aspects and its multigenerational continuity.

For Catholics, the scholarship of the present is merely one moment in the long and slow simultaneous discovery/revelation of truth. Thus in his encyclical *Fides et Ratio*, Pope John Paul II links the common human struggle to arrive at reasonable truth with the slow advance of revelation, saying that "for the people of God . . . history becomes a path to be followed to the end" as the Church "constantly progresses toward the fullness of divine truth."[16] This pattern of combining developing new human insight with the revelatory work of the Holy Spirit is paradigmatic for Catholic scholarship.[17] Human knowledge, whether of worldly subjects or divine, is always a work in process. While the Catholic notion of tradition requires that proper respect be shown to what has already been discovered/revealed, tradition also understands that the truth is being pulled into the future by what John Henry Newman called "leading ideas" that broach new questions and seek new answers.[18] The Catholic perspective has been oriented toward the long term instead of the immediate. Catholics know from their centuries-old experience as a church that the path of progress toward truth is slow and can often head off on side tangents or bend back on itself. That is to be expected; that is the way life works. It is the overall direction, averaged out over many years, that matters.[19] Thus Catholic conversations about Christian scholarship have typically been much more paced and patient than their Protestant equivalents, where the discussion has typically focused on the immediate challenges of the present.

The patience of the Catholic tradition is connected to the assumption that the thoroughly human quest for truth, goodness, and beauty will ultimately lead to faith if it is pursued with appropriate vigor and breadth of vision. The goal of Christian scholarship understood from a Catholic perspective is not to judge or evaluate the findings of secular scholarship but to encourage scholars, whether they are people of faith or not, to pursue their studies until they finally and necessarily bump up against the sacred. In somewhat poetic terms, John Paul II speaks about how reason when it is tenaciously followed can "rise beyond what is contingent and set out toward the infinite."[20]

In more prosaic but perhaps also more academically helpful language, the theologian David Tracy uses the concept of "limit situations" to argue basically the same thing. He says that in certain human experiences and at certain points in the scholarly quest we run headlong into questions that rational inquiry cannot by itself address. For example, in the sciences questions of meaning, value, and commitment sometimes present themselves in the midst of one's research. Those questions, which cannot be answered on the basis of science alone, point beyond science to a realm of human concern that can validly be called sacred.[21] And, for the Catholic tradition, the obverse is true as well. Not only does scholarship point toward faith but faith points toward scholarship.

It is a Catholic truism that "faith seeks understanding." Belief alone is not faith; it is mere fideism. True faith weds belief to knowledge. Thus the Jesuit educator Michael Buckley argues that just as learning raises questions that point toward faith, faith raises "questions that lead naturally into the sciences and arts." The end result of this mutual convergence of faith and learning is not that the two blend into each other and lose their separate identities, rather they are combined in a manner that might be called "hypostatic"—a term theologians have traditionally used to describe the connection of the human and divine in Christ. Buckley explains:

> Jesus is the union of God and humanity. So also—similar, but also very dissimilar—the Catholic university is a union of faith and all human culture. . . . Divinity does not become humanity; faith does not become culture. But if they are not identified; neither are they separate. . . . The Catholic university knows that religion does not substitute for the sciences and arts. Physics does not become theology and business is not piety; law remains forever itself and mathematics has its own autonomy. Faith and culture are distinct, but not separate. In the university, they are united but not identified.[22]

It is this open-ended sense of the sacred-secular encounter that defines the core of Catholic scholarship. The questions of faith do not need to be forced on the academic disciplines, but will naturally emerge from the human study of the world. Questions of scholarship do not need to be forced on faith, but will be called forth by faith itself when faith is properly understood and appropriately explored.

This hope-filled articulation of Catholic scholarship is rooted in the conviction that the world as created by God still remains at some level fundamentally good, despite the ravages of sin. Other Catholics have found this hypothesis overly optimistic and insufficient to deal with the horrible violence that has wracked the world during the last century. David Hollenbach, David O'Brien, and John C. Haughey, among others, have repeatedly made the case that a view of Christian scholarship articulated only in terms of a theology of creation is not sufficient to meet the needs of the present day. Their proposal is that "the struggle against injustice and the pursuit of truth cannot be separated, nor can one work for the one independent of the other."[23] They call for a scholarship of the cross, meaning that "the problem of human suffering must be directly confronted in the university."[24] This proposal has not been universally accepted, and some have criticized it as little more than the turning "of Christian spiritual life into ideological politics and activism."[25] But concerns for peace and justice are increasingly prominent in Catholic faith and scholarship and seem likely to remain so in the foreseeable future.[26]

Other Christian Traditions

When we examine the intellectual traditions of churches outside the Catholic orb, it is impossible to formulate a single statement that fits all groups. It seems best, then, to simply survey the options. Our goal is not to be comprehensive but merely to illustrate something of the diversity of approaches that can be found. To that end, we will discuss Lutheranism, Anglicanism, Wesleyanism, Pentecostalism, Anabaptism, and Primitivism as at least partially representative of the wide range of available options.

The Lutheran Tradition

The Lutheran view of Christian faith and scholarship, while somewhat similar to the Reformed perspective, allows for more mystery and ambiguity. Like the Reformed theology described in chapter 1, Lutheranism places significant emphasis on the fallenness of the world, but it is rather less confident than the Reformed tradition that the redeemed can actually overcome their own sinfulness and serve as models or tutors for the rest of humanity. For Lutherans, the world is full of paradox—God is at work in surprising and sometimes hidden ways—and it is hard to predict in advance where truth or grace will suddenly burst forth. Lutherans historically have assumed that truth is as likely to be expressed in great works of art or courageous moral action as through rational discourse.[27] Lutheran approaches to Christian scholarship have tended to show great respect for the independent value of all the disciplines, honoring the arts and social sciences as sources of truth alongside philosophy and theology.

The Lutheran emphasis has been to discover the way the created order actually functions, as opposed to the way we in our limited knowledge think it ought to function. As for who can best understand the world, Lutherans believe that intelligent unredeemed individuals may often possess more insight than less insightful Christians. Mark Edwards, Jr., former president of St. Olaf College, observes that Lutherans claim no special epistemological privilege: "Lutherans and others in this tradition are left with (admittedly fallible) reason, experience and experiment—the sharpest tools of the modern academy." He argues that what makes the enterprise of scholarship Christian is the Christian calling of those involved in it—a calling that ultimately puts more faith in the unseen workings of the Holy Spirit than in the visible efforts of human actors. Because that is the case, Edwards says, "a sense of humility and, yes, an accompanying sense of humor are not out of place."[28] The sense of freedom that runs through this version of the Lutheran view of Christian scholarship stands in marked contrast to the sobriety and discipline that often characterizes Reformed articulations of the nature and character of Christian scholarship.[29]

The Anglican Tradition

One of the things that marks the Anglican tradition as distinctive is its strong commitment to not being distinctive. That is, Anglicans have little if any desire to erect their own battle standard of theology against other Christian traditions. Instead they have typically tried to chart a middle way between or around most church-dividing issues of faith. Anglicanism has valorized the notion of "mere Christianity," and it should never be forgotten that C. S. Lewis, author of the well-known book *Mere Christianity* (written in the 1940s), was himself an Anglican. Lewis's purpose in that book was thoroughly Anglican: "to explain and defend the belief that had been common to nearly all Christians at all times." The danger he sought to avoid was that he "should put forward as common Christianity anything that was peculiar to the Church of England or (worse still) to myself."[30]

More recently the theologian Rowan Williams, who is also the archbishop of Canterbury, has reformulated this Anglican point of view into the principle that theological language, if it is to have integrity, must avoid claiming too much. Theologians do not have complete knowledge of either God or the world; what they possess are a few very important clues about how to reflect on those subjects. Because of that, theologians should not speak as if they possessed "God's point of view." Their task is much more modest, being concerned with repentance and worship more than with explicating a "total perspective" on the world.[31] This humble style of theology is rooted in the Anglican understanding of the incarnation, which accentuates the significance of the ordinary. The fact that God took on ordinary human flesh in the person of Jesus is seen as a valorization of ordinary life with all its frailties and limitations. Because God understands human finitude, human beings themselves can accept their own finitude.

The quandary in this tradition, of course, is to avoid having mere Christianity devolve into simple bland, minimalist Christianity, and the antidote has been a trilogy of interwoven concerns: a vibrant sense of worship, liturgy, and tradition; continual dialogue between faith and reason; and the critical importance of imagination in theology and the religious life in general. Arthur Peacocke, professor of physical biochemistry at Oxford and an Anglican theologian, has tried to strike that balance. He says first that "theology that is not fed by and consummated in prayer and worship is indeed sterile and can deteriorate into a merely intellectual exercise." At the same time he avers that "to pray and worship we need supportable and believable models and images" of God that are consonant with the best and most up-to-date science. Taking those concerns together he argues that Christians must forever be in the business of imaginatively "refurbishing our images of God" so they remain fresh and powerful, fully capable of inspiring both meaningful worship and intelligent faith.[32]

It is this emphasis on the imagination, perhaps more than anything else, that defines Anglicanism's distinctive contribution to Christian scholarship. Dorothy Sayers argued in *The Mind of the Maker* (1941) "that creative mind is . . . the very grain of the spiritual universe."[33] Creativity is what makes us like God; she says it is the *imago Dei* within us. Creativity is also at the heart of the scholarly task. Scholars necessarily reimagine the world in ways others have not seen it. They dismantle the ideas of the past and seek to reconstruct them in better, more attractive, ways in light of advancing knowledge. In the Anglican tradition, creativity and imagination are at the heart of all truly insightful Christian scholarship.[34]

The Wesleyan Tradition

The Wesleyan tradition represents another way of understanding Christian faith and scholarship.[35] John Wesley himself was a priest in the Church of England, so there is an Anglican flavor to most Wesleyan thought. He was generally optimistic in his assessment of the world and, like his Anglican colleagues, he tended to stress the positive power of faith in the world rather than the negative influence of sin. But Wesley was no mere Anglican. In particular, he added a heightened understanding of the work of the Holy Spirit to his vision of faith, and he placed great stress on the idea that all Christians could and should become wholly sanctified during their lives on earth. With these added emphases, Wesleyanism took on a life of its own.

In terms of the intellectual understanding of faith, the key concerns of the Wesleyan tradition can be described as a "quadrilateral" composed of the Bible, experience, reason, and tradition.[36] When the task is theology proper, the usual Wesleyan pattern is for the Bible to take precedence. In terms of Christian scholarship construed more broadly, however, experience has historically played a very significant role. Wesley was an empiricist who believed that if something could not be experientially validated it was not true. Wesley's stress on experience also guaranteed that his followers would internalize a deep respect for our physical embodiedness. Human beings are not merely rational minds; they are also bodies. As embodied selves, persons hurt and hunger, work and play, feel joy and sorrow. Christian scholarship understood in light of this experiential orientation will necessarily incorporate the subjectivity of human existence in a way that other traditions may not.

All dimensions of the quadrilateral, of course, play a part in Wesleyan scholarship. Reason is thus viewed as an invaluable aid in assessing experience and in interpreting both the Bible and tradition. Tradition, in turn, helps moderate the claims of unfettered reason and underscores the fact that all human knowing is situated in larger contexts of relationship and conversation. In fact, Wesleyans see Christian scholarship as a whole as embedded in a never-ending process of traditioning, which receives wisdom from the past and passes it on to future generations in modified and hopefully improved form. Finally, Wesleyans believe that God can reveal new truths through the words of the Bible, but they consider these truths to be characterized by subjectivity as much as by objectivity, focusing on matters of both heart and head.

All of this lends to Wesleyan scholarship, at least in its best expressions, a certain humility and grace rooted in its willingness to admit that knowledge is always partial, never complete, and inescapably mixed with human needs and affections. Thus the Nazarene political scientist Ron Kirkemo has argued:

> Wesleyans are . . . reluctant to draw conclusions too early or too tightly. Rather than drawing up a worldview, they are more willing to leave space for individual differences, which in turn reinforces the grace of human dignity. From this perspective, it is not scandalous that there is no tight intellectual integration of faith and learning. Structures of reality are too dynamic and the rate of our scientific and social discoveries and understandings too rapid to claim much finality. Wesleyans see ambiguity and tension in efforts to understand the two realms [of scholarship and faith] and so are comfortable with differing viewpoints and efforts at reconciliation rather than with the certainties of integration.[37]

The Wesleyan philosopher Samuel M. Powell has proposed much the same thing in his *Participating in God: Creation and Trinity* where he says explicitly that Christian scientists are not called "to create a distinctively Christian form of science," but are rather to demonstrate how scholarship done with sufficient care and rigor can become an act of prayer and adoration offered to the God of creation who both transcends this world and simultaneously participates in each and every aspect of this world.[38]

The Pentecostal Tradition

Pentecostalism represents yet another distinct style of Christian faith with its own implications for scholarship. What distinguishes Pentecostalism from other Christian traditions is its focus on the Holy Spirit, especially as experienced in the baptism of the Holy Spirit. Pentecostals describe the baptism of the Spirit as that event through which the Spirit of God physically enters the believer's body, changing that person forever. The significance of this emphasis on experience is that Pentecostals believe truth necessarily contains an affective dimension. We can learn some things through our emotions that we can learn in no other way. Pentecostals believe that ordinary thinking is valuable and that moral convictions are critical but that raw experience has a pivotal role. Thus Steven Land, a leading Pentecostal theologian, argues that Pentecostal spirituality and Pentecostal scholarship need to pay special attention to the affections alongside beliefs and actions. He says all three—beliefs, affections, and actions—must be blended together to keep them from "fragment[ing] into intellectualism, sentimentalism and activism respectively."[39]

Samuel Solivan has made a similar point, arguing for the importance of pathos in Pentecostal theology in general and Hispanic Pentecostal theology in particular. In making his argument, however, Solivan is more prone than Land to stress the diversity that necessarily accompanies the Pentecostal appeal to the affections. Analyzing the biblical narrative of Pentecost recorded in the second chapter of Acts as an example of "cultural glossolalia," Solivan argues that Pentecostal faith and scholarship should affirm "all people and cultures [as] each having their place and contributions." In his view, "cultural or linguistic arrogance, or the imposition of one language over another" has no place in Christian faith and scholarship.[40] More than most Christian traditions, Pentecostalism affirms the goodness of particularity. Another Pentecostal theologian, Jean-Jacques Suurmond, underscores this point when he writes "the essential contribution of Pentecostal spirituality lies in its playful character . . . [where] everyone has a contribution to make—regardless of race, gender or status."[41]

The person who has perhaps explored the scholarly potential of the Pentecostal vision of Christian faith more than anyone else is the late Princeton Theological Seminary psychologist James Loder. In his book *The Transforming Moment,* Loder argues that the Pentecostal paradigm of knowledge points to a dynamic of insight that exists deep within the self, well "beneath our educated and scholarly ways of knowing." This intuitive sense of knowing, which draws on all the "many splintered ways we are taught to think," has the power "to generate from hidden sources new, sometimes powerful, insights that [can] transform [a person's] horizons of intelligibility." In these moments of transformational knowing, the very personhood of the knower is remolded by the act of knowing; one's very self is deconstructed and reconstructed in a new way. And Loder did not think this was a rare phenomenon, but the normal way that human understanding advances even if the language of the academy tends to obscure it from view. To dramatize his point and to unmask the false objectivity of so much academic discourse, he advocated the following "theory of error":

> Any assertion of truth that does not recognize and accept its primary dependency on some leap of imagination, some insight, intuition, or vision, is guilty of intellectual dissimulation. Reason thinks it secures an objective, airtight case when in fact its processes are open-textured, its sources rooted in "personal knowledge," and its conclusions are laced with human interests.[42]

If nothing else, the Pentecostal vision of scholarship reminds us never to forget the personal factors that are inherent in all forms of faith and learning.

The Anabaptist Tradition

The Anabaptist tradition, which is discussed in more detail in the essay by David Weaver-Zercher that follows, points in yet another direction. The Anabaptist tradition is built around the radical call to obey God in opposition to the coercive powers of the state and to be especially wary of the coercive powers of the Christian state. In the midst of disagreements among persons and conflicts between nations, Anabaptists call on Christians to seek peace and justice without recourse to deadly force. Anabaptists are committed to coexisting in peace with those with whom they disagree and, even more, to actually do good to those who are their enemies. In terms of faith, the main concern becomes, as in the Wesleyan tradition, one of striving for perfection rather than fleeing from sin. But perfection in the Anabaptist tradition is construed in terms that are more publicly visible and ethically defined than is the case with the Wesleyan tradition, which focuses more on the inner character of the believer. In terms of scholarship, the Anabaptist vision is attuned to the corrupting influences of violence, power, and political ideology—including the ways that Christians sometimes lust for hegemony. The positive task of Christian scholarship is framed in terms of reconciliation and service to those in need. Within Anabaptism there is also the implicit understanding that actions come before words and that obedience comes before testimony. This too has profound implications for Christian scholarship, perhaps most notably giving Anabaptist scholarship a decidedly applied edge.

The Primitivist Tradition

An interesting antidote to the other traditions is the primitivist tradition, whose adherents often deny being influenced by any tradition at all. Very few church groups actually use the word "primitivist" to describe themselves, but the term accurately applies to a host of Christians who call themselves pietists, evangelicals, Baptists, or simply nondenominational Christians.[43] The primitivist tradition centers on the Bible alone and on the need always to start afresh in our attempts to understand what God is saying through that holy text. Ideas are not to be handed down from the past but rather to be discovered anew through Bible study. There is something very energizing and important about this kind of biblicism, but it would be a mistake to see it as an untraditioned view of faith. In point of fact, there is a long tradition of antitraditionalism within the history of Christianity.

The notion of Christian scholarship that emerges from the primitivist tradition is, like this tradition's view of faith itself, one that always and ever starts from scratch. For the primitivist, insights from the past may or may not have any current relevance; the goal is to examine the data of the world with fresh eyes in dialogue with our best current reading of the biblical text in order to construct new understandings of reality. An academic application is obvious: so many of the academic disciplines are currently beset by internal ideological squabblings that the notion of just ignoring it all and starting over is mightily attractive. The problem, of course, is that this kind of scholarship can be immature or amateurish. It takes a long time for many scholarly projects to mature—a process that often extends over several generations. The primitivist paradigm simply does not allow for that kind of multigenerational development. While some extraordinary geniuses may be able to flourish within this tradition, it seems likely that most scholars will find the going rough. If the academy does not already have an established niche for one's work, one's scholarship may simply be set aside as idiosyncratic. Such scholarship may be interesting and even insightful, but if it has no ready connections with other ongoing academic conversations, it will probably be ignored regardless of its brilliance.

Traditions of Spiritual Practice

While the churchly theological traditions just described have been central for many Christian scholars, Christian faith transcends churchly affiliation and theological affinity. A person's faith is in some sense a gut-level reaction to the sacred. The early twentieth-century religious philosopher Rudolph Otto described faith as involving the whole person, not just the intellect.[44] In fact, he said nonrational and relational factors often predominate. When we speak of traditions of spirituality, what we have in mind is that holistic experience of the sacred—an experience of faith that involves the entire person: the combined physical, emotional, and intellectual dimensions of who we are as human beings.

Piety or spirituality is almost always complex and multilayered. Our personal response to God pulls us in different directions at the same time: wordless wonder, thankfulness, worship, prayer, joy, sorrow for the pain of the world, desire to serve others. For most of us, however, certain dimensions of spiritual practice ultimately become more important than others. Out of the many and varied impulses of piety, only some seem a natural fit; only some aspects of Christian practice demand our sustained attention. As a result, some Christians pour themselves into the life of prayer. Some devote themselves to the compassionate service of others. Some express their deepest faith through evangelistic outreach. Some seek justice for the poor. Some direct their energy toward worship. Just because our divergent spiritualities push in these different directions—just because we tend to spend more time and effort on one kind of spiritual activity rather than another—does not mean that we thereby dismiss other expressions of piety as inherently less valuable. It simply means that given the time constraints that define our lives, given the need to choose priorities, and given our own natural inclinations, we will find ourselves drawn to certain forms of piety or spirituality more than others. And those different spiritual dispositions can have an influence on the way we understand Christian scholarship.

Although spirituality is a deeply personal response of the individual to God, our expressions of piety are rarely novel. In their book *Spiritual Traditions for the Contemporary Church*, Robin Maas and Gabriel O'Donnell outline fourteen schools of spirituality ranging from monastic and mendicant forms of piety to Marian and modern feminist expressions of spiritual fervor and experience.[45] For our purposes, the simpler cataloging of options developed by Richard J. Foster in his popular book *Streams of Living Water: Celebrating the Great Traditions of Christian Faith* may be more useful. Foster identifies six traditions of spiritual practice that provide a short but helpful taxonomy of the spiritual life.[46]

According to Foster, the *contemplative tradition* of Christian piety emphasizes the mystical experience of God that comes through the life of prayer. It is a deeply personal form of spirituality and one that often draws individuals away from attachments to the world. Saint Antony, the first monk in Christian history, fled the city of Alexandria in the late third century for the deserts of Nitria in northern Egypt to pursue his contemplative calling. In the medieval era Julian of Norwich assumed the life of an anchorite to do the same. Foster lists the twentieth-century figure Henri Nouwen as another exemplar of this tradition of piety. Nouwen did not entirely flee the world, but his contemplative passions eventually led him to leave his teaching post at Harvard for a life of service among the physically and mentally challenged residents of the L'Arche community in Canada. The contemplative tradition of spirituality has the goal of always living in the conscious presence of God.

The *holiness tradition* focuses on the development of Christian character through self-discipline and the cultivation of the virtues. The goal is the restructuring of the inner affections so that right living becomes a natural habit. According to Foster, the rather different sixteenth-century religious leaders Ignatius of Loyola (founder of the Jesuits) and Menno Simons (founder of the Mennonites) both fit this paradigm. What they shared was a sense of Christian faith as a way of life—a way of life that required the cultivation of certain dispositions like humility, a willingness to serve others, nonviolence, and introspective self-criticism. Foster also includes in this category Dietrich Bonhoeffer, the Lutheran pastor put to death by the Nazis, and the nineteenth-century American Holiness leader Phoebe Palmer. In their lives we see a commitment to deny self and to conform fully to the requirements of the gospel, especially as expressed in Jesus' words in the Sermon on the Mount.

The *charismatic tradition* centers on spiritual power. It is supernaturalistic in orientation and seeks to use the gifts of the Spirit, including the more spectacular gifts of healing, prophecy, and speaking in tongues, to recall the church to its miraculous roots. Francis of Assisi and Hildegard of Bingen carried on this tradition in the medieval era; the Pentecostal pioneers William Seymour and Aimee Semple McPherson have done so in the twentieth century. The charismatic tradition embodies a spirituality of divine interruption. God is fundamentally unpredictable and may intrude into our lives and activities at any moment. The Christian's task is constantly to remain open to those inter-ruptions of the Spirit and to be ready to serve as a conduit of God's miraculous grace and power.

The *social justice tradition* stresses the need for Christians to transform the world, to make the earth a more just and peaceable place for all. It is prophetic and often confrontational, demanding that those in power use their positions to aid the poor and oppressed rather than to serve those who are already well off and comfortable. Foster cites Germanus, a sixth-century bishop of Paris who was known for feeding the poor at his own table, as an ancient exemplar of this path of piety. In the modern era he points to Dorothy Day and Martin Luther King, Jr. The social justice tradition of spirituality is more down-to-earth than many other forms of piety, rooted as it is in the belief that no one can claim to love God who does not also visibly love his or her neighbor in need. This style of spirituality demands that the religious life never be separated from moral responsibilities to the poor, the homeless, the sick, and the prisoner. It seeks not merely to comfort those in pain but to change the world so there will be less pain to experience.

The *evangelical tradition* places critical emphasis on conversion and right belief. In fact, it sees these two concerns as necessary corollaries of each other: holding right beliefs about God and ourselves is a necessary part of turning our lives over to God in conversion. Billy Graham obviously comes to mind here, but Foster also lists Augustine, Thomas Aquinas, and Martin Luther as exemplars of evangelical spirituality. The core of this form of spirituality can be defined as submitting to truth. When we understand God properly, our response to God will also be proper, starting with contrition and confession and ending with the submission of our entire lives to God's will. Conversion can take place quickly (the Protestant version) or more slowly and develop-mentally (the Catholic version). Regardless of the speed of the process, this spiritual tradition emphasizes the dramatic way in which conversion totally transforms the believer's life.

Finally, the *incarnational tradition* arises out of the need for Christians to merge faith into the many necessary and unavoidable tasks that are part of human life. A key concept is the idea of vocation: the art of seeing our ordinary work in the world as part of our Christian calling. The enacted rituals of wor-ship—especially the bread and wine of the Eucharist—are important for they model the sacramental manner in which the ordinary can take on spiritual significance. Foster points to Susanna Wesley (the mother of John and Charles Wesley) as one model of this way of life; he cites the writing of Flannery

O'Connor as another expression of this earthy form of Christian piety. In contrast to other forms of spirituality that emphasize the difference between acts of devotion and normal life, this tradition underscores the continuity between those two domains.

The vocation of Christian scholarship is not necessarily central to any of these six traditions of spiritual practice, but each has implications that might apply to the academic life. The contemplative tradition reminds us of the need to make room for divine mystery in our academic interpretations of the world. The holiness tradition points to the fact that the habits we cultivate—either habits of virtue or habits of vice—have the potential to shape our scholarship in subtle ways for good or for ill. The charismatic tradition underscores the fact that reality can surprise us; miracles can happen. It also reminds us that one need not be a scholar in order to be used powerfully by God. The social justice tradition implies that virtually all of our scholarship has ethical implications and asks whether our work truly benefits the poor and needy of the world. The evangelical tradition suggests that scholarship connects with faith most powerfully in the practice of apologetics—explaining the world intelligently in a way that promotes belief and submission to God's will for our lives and for the world as a whole. Finally, the incarnational tradition encourages us to put academic resources to work in the service of ordinary human beings and to find the holy in the ordinary structures of the world.

But while each of these traditions has the potential to influence Christian scholarship in one way or another, it is hard to envision any of them—apart from the incarnational model, perhaps—actively persuading anyone to take up the life of scholarship. This may be because scholarship ultimately is of only secondary concern to most Christians—and perhaps that is the way things ought to be. Perhaps Christian faith should push scholarship into second place well behind love of God and neighbor. (J. R. R. Tolkien enjoyably illustrates this attitude in his short story "Leaf by Niggle," which portrays an artist who can never complete his master painting because he feels compelled to help his grumpy neighbor.)[47] Maybe Christian spirituality predisposes us to regard scholarship as a kind of hobby, albeit a serious one, that often has to be set aside in order to help one's friends, families, and neighbors in more concrete and immediate ways.

Or perhaps Foster has missed something, and a seventh tradition, one that focuses specifically on faith and learning, needs to be added to his list. We might call this the *seeking tradition*. The seeking tradition begins with wonder over creation and the inexhaustible depth of God's being as the ultimate source of all that is. For seekers, that sense of wonder is tantamount to a divine call to explore all the marvelous intricacies of the world in which God has placed us. This is not a Faustian quest, seeking all knowledge—Christians know we "see in a glass darkly," that knowledge will always be limited—but it is a quest nonetheless to know all that God has made us capable of knowing. The exemplars of this tradition of spirituality are, for the most part, entirely missing from Foster's book, but they are not hard to locate in the history of Christianity. Origen, who headed up the famous Christian school in ancient Alexandria, would be an early exemplar. Abelard and Heloise, who loved knowledge as much as each other, would also be included. The great Christian humanists of the Renaissance, with Erasmus of Rotterdam at the fore, would perhaps be the most prominent standard-bearers. In more recent times, Pierre Teilhard de Chardin and Dorothy Sayers might exemplify the seeking model of Christian spiritual practice.

It is likely that almost all Christian scholars would affirm this seventh tradition as their own, even if this form of piety is tempered by a parallel emphasis on one or more of Foster's other six styles of spirituality. Whether that is the case or not, however, is relatively unimportant. What is important is to understand that our personal piety deeply affects our work as Christian scholars. Most of the time Christian scholars might be unaware of how much this is the case, for the influences of spirituality tend to work in largely un-self-conscious ways. Scholarship would surely be enriched, however, if Christian scholars were more self-conscious of their own spirituality and its relationship to the academic work they pursue.

Traditions of Political-Cultural Engagement

A third way of identifying divergent traditions of Christian faith is to look at the different ways Christians have tried to orchestrate their relationship to the larger culture. In one sense, this is the issue of faith and learning writ large because scholarship can be understood as merely one part of culture, but the broader focus on culture and society as a whole lets us see things in a slightly different light. In contrast to our discussions of theological and spiritual traditions, the focus here is not on the inner character of belief but rather on the public profile of Christian faith in society.[48]

In the long history of Christianity, and especially of European Christendom, there has not been much need to debate this topic. From the late fourth century until the eighteenth or nineteenth centuries, Christianity reigned supreme as the formally established, politically enforced religion of the state and society. During this time the relationship of Christianity to culture was clear: Christianity dictated the morals that society was supposed to follow. Compromises had to be made, of course, and Christian leaders occasionally, if not often, bent the rules for political rulers (who were actually sometimes more moral than the leaders of the church). Faith merged with political and cultural power. The church "served" the world by ruling it; the relationship of Christianity to culture was one of dominance.

This pattern of religious power has slowly dissolved in the last two or three centuries. In most countries of the West, church and state are now formally separated, and even where that is not the case, full religious (and irreligious) freedom is for the most part protected by law. In fact, many Christians now feel threatened by their lack of power to shape the public cultures of the countries in which they live. They feel that most Western cultures are so secular—so devoid of Christian values and control—that they have no choice but to withdraw from those cultures and develop alternative lifestyles designed to protect them and their children from corrupting societal influences. This is part of what modern fundamentalism is all about.

But fundamentalism is also about fighting back, and many fundamentalist Christians would like to see Christianity regain the power over society it once possessed. The rise of the religious right in the late 1970s was one expression of that desire, but instead of turning the nation back to its Christian roots, the result was a "culture war" that pitted conservative Christians against liberal secularists. That "war" was never as all-encompassing as the belligerents on either side reported it to be, but the rhetoric of warfare effectively silenced real discussion. What needed to be discussed was not who would win the culture war but rather how Christians should understand their public role in society, given that the option of political power is no longer available. And it is not simply that religious political power is a thing of the past; most contemporary Christians approve of that development and believe in religious freedom as ardently as everyone else. So the question is not merely a matter of tactics, but of principle: How should Christians envision the positive role they can and should play in society?

Despite the criticism he has received, H. Richard Niebuhr undoubtedly remains a helpful guide in this area. His book *Christ and Culture,* published over fifty years ago, has become a classic. Rather than speak in the simplistic bipolar language inherent in any culture-war analysis of society, Niebuhr outlined five different paths Christians had followed in their historical quests to be both faithful followers of Christ and good members of society. He meant for these five models of Christian social ethics to be understood as sociological "ideal types" that have rarely, if ever, been embodied in pure form. But we can also view them as relatively distinct traditions of Christian citizenship that provide us with yet one more conceptual grid to help locate our own views and opinions. Historically, Christians have often drawn on more than one of these traditions to form their own mixed approach to the larger culture and to help them negotiate interactions with various cultural subgroups. Given the increasingly decentered character of contemporary society, this kind of eclectic appropriation of Niebuhr's categories is likely to become even more prominent in the future.[49]

Niebuhr's first ideal type is called the *Christ against culture* model. It stresses the need for Christians to take a firm stand against all that is wrong in their culture, even to the point of actually separating themselves from most cultural activities. Niebuhr says that the Christ-against-culture Christian "uncompromisingly affirms the authority of Christ . . . and resolutely rejects culture's claim to loyalty."⁵⁰ Niebuhr's second model, the *Christ of culture* approach, argues almost the opposite: that Christian faith at its best and the values of human culture at its best are virtually identical. This model calls on Christians to participate fully in all the activities of society as a means of receiving divine grace and of sharing grace with others. Christian citizenship takes the form of being the best artist, teacher, lawyer, businessperson, or farmer that one can possibly be and helping others to do the same. The third model is identified as the *Christ above culture* stance. This approach affirms that while culture is basically good, it still stands in need of being augmented and completed by the grace that comes to the world in and through the church. Seen in this light, Christian citizenship requires believers to honor all that is right in their cultures and then to seek to add the graces of Christian faith, hope, and love to that substrata of human goodness. Niebuhr's fourth style of cultural engagement is called *Christ and culture in paradox*. According to this view, Christians are called to strive to be both loyal to Christ and responsible for their cultures even when those concerns seem to conflict. God is at work in both the church and the culture in surprising and often unexpected ways, and the public task of Christians is to help the world discern that hidden divine presence in all the joys and tragedies of life. The fifth and final model is that of *Christ the transformer of culture*, which argues that human cultures have the potential to embody the values of Christ, but most currently do not. The Christian's task is to enter into the still fallen zones of culture to reorder them so they more fully conform to God's own desire, which is also ultimately best for humankind.

The application of Niebuhr's categories to the practice of Christian scholarship is relatively straightforward. Like the Christ-against-culture model, some Christian scholars see their work as directed primarily against the errors and arrogance of the larger academy. Other Christian scholars are so comfortable within their disciplines, schools, and academic societies that virtually nothing distinguishes their work from that of their peers. A third group of Christian scholars sees their Christian values as subtly but significantly completing their academic undertakings. Still other Christian scholars experience a certain degree of tension between some aspects of their faith and some dimensions of their academic work, but they feel hard pressed to define that tension in clear terms, and they would be troubled by the suggestion that they may need to choose sides between faith and learning. Finally, many Christian scholars hope their academic work will, in some small way, slowly bend their disciplines and their cultures as a whole in directions more compatible with God's overall will for the world.

Beyond any correspondences between Niebuhr's categories and different models of Christian scholarship, however, the real significance of Niebuhr's analysis is to remind us that Christian scholarship is not rooted only in Christian faith but also lives in the world at large. In fact, Christian scholarship always incorporates within itself a disposition toward the larger culture, either of resistance or identity or cooperation or compassion or correction. In short, Christian scholarship has a political edge to it or, at the very least, it always embodies an impulse of desired public influence in one direction or another. If Christians themselves do not recognize this political dimension of their work, others will. Thus this chapter closes with the same point with which it began: Our scholarship as Christians will be better formulated and better received if we are more aware of the subtle ways in which our theological, spiritual, and political dispositions affect our work.

NOTES

1. In the past two decades a large body of scholarship dealing with the issue of tradition has been produced. Alasdair MacIntyre led the way with his groundbreaking work *After Virtue: A Study in Moral Theory* (Notre Dame, Ind.: University of Notre Dame Press, 1981). MacIntyre further developed his views on the role of tradition in a series of other books, perhaps most articulately in *Whose Justice? Which Rationality?* (Notre Dame, Ind.: University of Notre Dame Press, 1988). Two other helpful books are Terrence W. Tilley, *Inventing Catholic Tradition* (Maryknoll, N.Y.: Orbis Books, 2000) and Dale T. Irvin, *Christian Histories, Christian Traditioning: Rendering Accounts* (Maryknoll, N.Y.: Orbis Books, 1998). Irvin describes the notion of tradition in terms that helpfully include more diversity and multidirectionality than is typical in much of the literature in this field. He says traditions are more like "rhizomes: plants with subterranean, horizontal root systems, growing below and above ground in multiple directions at once" than they are "like a tree, organized with a major trunk and smaller (minor) branches, and drawing primarily from a single, dominant taproot that likewise grows in one direction" (47).

2. See Mikhail Bakhtin, *The Dialogic Imagination*, translated by Caryl Emerson and Michael Holquist, edited by Michael Holquist (Austin: University of Texas Press, 1981). See also Michael Holquist, *Dialogism: Bakhtin and His World* (New York: Routledge, 1990).

3. See Imre Lakatos, "Falsification and the Methodology of Scientific Research Programmes," in *Criticism and the Growth of Knowledge*, edited by Imre Lakatos and Alan Musgrave (Cambridge: Cambridge University Press, 1970), 91–196.

4. Richard Hughes has championed the need to recognize the role of church traditions in Christian scholarship and higher education. See *Models for Christian Higher Education: Strategies for Success in the Twenty-First Century*, edited by Richard T. Hughes and William B. Adrian (Grand Rapids, Mich.: Eerdmans, 1997), and Richard T. Hughes, *How Christian Faith Can Sustain the Life of the Mind* (Grand Rapids, Mich.: Eerdmans, 2001). *Models for Christian Higher Education* includes eight thematic chapters on what different Christian traditions (Catholic, Lutheran, Reformed, Mennonite, Evangelical, Wesleyan/Holiness, Baptist, and Church of Christ) can contribute to higher education. These chapters were written by persons who locate themselves within these traditions. In *How Christian Faith Can Sustain the Life of the Mind*,

Hughes provides his own interpretation of Catholic, Reformed, Mennonite, and Lutheran views of Christian scholarship in a chapter entitled "The Power of Christian Traditions."

5. For a helpful introduction to the way Catholic faith has informed Christian scholarship and the practices of higher education see Monika K. Hellwig, "What Can the Roman Catholic Tradition Contribute to Christian Higher Education?" in Hughes and Adrian, *Models for Christian Higher Education*, 13–23.

6. Tilley, *Inventing Catholic Tradition*, 125–126. Tilley derives the notion of analogical imagination from David Tracy, *The Analogical Imagination: Christian Theology and the Culture of Pluralism* (New York: Crossroads, 1981). Tracy develops the difference between analogical and dialectical thinking in chapter 10, "A Christian Systematic Analogical Imagination." See especially the chapter subsection "Classical Theological Languages: Analogy and Dialectic," 405–21.

7. Andrew Greeley, *The Catholic Imagination* (Berkeley: University of California Press, 2000), 9.

8. "Gaudium et Spes," in *The Documents of Vatican II*, edited by W. M. Abbott (New York: Herder and Herder, 1966), 199–200.

9. John Henry Newman, *The Idea of a University* (New Haven: Yale University Press, 1996), 45.

10. John Paul II, "Ex Corde Ecclesiae," in *American Catholic Higher Education: Essential Documents, 1967–1990*, edited by Alice Gallin (Notre Dame, Ind.: University of Notre Dame Press, 1992), 418.

11. John Paul II, "Ex Corde Ecclesiae," 418.

12. Lisa Lattuca, *Creating Interdisciplinarity: Interdisciplinary Research and Teaching among College and University Faculty* (Nashville, Tenn.: Vanderbilt University Press, 2001). It is perhaps not beside the point that Lattuca teaches at a Catholic institution: Loyola University in Chicago.

13. John Paul II, "Ex Corde Ecclesiae," 418.

14. Mark W. Roche, "The Intellectual Appeal of Catholicism and the Idea of a Catholic University," in *The Future of Religious Colleges*, edited by Paul J. Drove (Grand Rapids, Mich.: Eerdmans, 2002), 181.

15. Roche, "The Intellectual Appeal of Catholicism and the Idea of a Catholic University," 181.

16. John Paul II, "Fides et Ratio," *Origins* 28, 19 (October 22, 1998), 321.

17. Catholic scholars who disagree with the way Pope John Paul II has articulated some of these points would still typically agree with his underlying principle, even if they are convinced that Catholic universities need more freedom from the church than the pope wants to allow. See, for example, Catherine Mowery LaCugna, "Some Theological Reflections on *Ex Corde Ecclesiae*," in *The Challenge and Promise of a Catholic University*, edited by Theodore M. Hesburgh (Notre Dame, Ind.: University of Notre Dame Press, 1994), 117–25. LaCugna writes: "To say that the university is born *ex corde ecclesiae* should mean, from the heart of the people of God whose quest for knowledge is genuinely religious. What is the heart of the church? The heart of the church is the Holy Spirit who is leading the church into the fullness of truth. But the institutional church does not control the Spirit, nor does the church control the human need and desire for knowledge, which is why the Catholic university is not simply an extension of the church" (121).

18. Quoted in R. Scott Appleby, *The Ambivalence of the Sacred: Religion, Violence, and Reconciliation* (New York: Rowman and Littlefield, 2000), 32.

19. Newman said: "There are no short cuts to knowledge; nor does the road to it always lie in the direction in which it terminates, nor are we able to see the end on starting. It may often seem to be diverging from a goal into which it will soon run without effort, if we are but patient and resolute in following it out" (*The Idea of a University*, 230). Thomas P. Rausch develops the same point in *Reconciling Faith and Reason: Apologists, Evangelists, and Theologians in a Divided Church* (Collegeville, Minn.: Liturgical Press, 2000). Rausch says that the Catholic historical consciousness "presumes development and change based on new insights, the reinterpretation of traditional positions, and the incorporation of higher viewpoints. Its approach is inductive, not deducing conclusions from some concept of a universal nature, but synthesizing the results of empirical observation, critical, historical evidence, and personal experience. It recognizes that meaning emerges out of a historical process of investigation, that it develops, sometimes becomes frozen, and can change, but is always capable of reinterpretation and arriving at deeper insight" (121).

20. John Paul II, "Fides et Ratio," 325.

21. See David Tracy, *Blessed Rage for Order: The New Pluralism in Theology* (New York: Seabury Press, 1975). See especially chapter 5, "The Religious Dimension of Common Human Experience and Language," 91–118.

22. Michael J. Buckley, *The Catholic University as Promise and Project: Reflections in a Jesuit Idiom* (Washington, D.C.: Georgetown University Press, 1998), 17–18.

23. John C. Haughey, "Catholic Higher Education: A Strategy for Its Identity," in *Enhancing Religious Identity: Best Practices from Catholic Campuses*, edited by John Wilcox and Irene King (Washington, D.C.: Georgetown University Press, 2000), 164.

24. Hollenbach, "The Catholic University under the Sign of the Cross," in *Finding God in All Things*, edited by Michael J. Himes and Stephen J. Pope (New York: Crossroads, 1996), 294.

25. James V. Schall, *Another Sort of Learning* (San Francisco: Ignatius Press, 1988), 263.

26. On these themes in general see David J. O'Brien, *From the Heart of the American Church: Catholic Higher Education and American Culture* (Maryknoll, N.Y.: Orbis Books, 1994), especially chapter 10, "Disciples and Citizens."

27. On this point see Jaroslav Pelikan, *Fools for Christ: Essays on the True, the Good, and the Beautiful* (Philadelphia: Fortress Press, 1955). Pelikan was a Lutheran scholar, but he has recently converted to Eastern Orthodoxy.

28. Mark U. Edwards, Jr., "Christian Colleges: A Dying Light or a New Reformation?" *Christian Century*, April 21–28, 1999, 463.

29. For further reading on the nature of Lutheran scholarship and higher education see Ernest L. Simmons, *Lutheran Higher Education: An Introduction for Faculty* (Minneapolis: Augsburg Fortress, 1998), and *The Lutheran Reader*, edited by Paul J. Contino and David Morgan (Valparaiso, Ind.: Valparaiso University Press, 1999).

30. C. S. Lewis, *Mere Christianity* (San Francisco: HarperSanFrancisco, 2001), viii, xi. Lewis was, on this point, largely in sympathy with Samuel Taylor Coleridge, who once quipped: "He who begins by loving Christianity better than the truth, will proceed by loving his own sect or church better than Christianity, and end in loving

himself better than all." Quoted in A. S. McGrade, "Reason," in *The Study of Anglicanism*, edited by Stephen Sykes, John Booty, and Jonathan Knight, rev. ed. (Minneapolis: Fortress Press, 1998), 125–26.

31. Rowan Williams, *On Christian Theology* (Oxford: Blackwell, 2000), 6, 8–9. Paul Avis, subdean of Exeter Cathedral, makes essentially the same case using a more homely image. Concerning the scope of Christian truth he writes: "The knowledge it gives is not like the noonday sun, but (as Locke used to say) like the light of a candle in a dark room, sufficient to see our way—to make the moral commitment of faith that we are called to exercise as persons in a moral universe." *God and the Creative Imagination: Metaphor, Symbol and Myth in Religion and Theology* (New York: Routledge, 1999), 12.

32. Arthur Peacocke, *Theology for a Scientific Age: Being and Becoming—Natural, Divine, and Human* (Minneapolis: Fortress Press, 1993), 348–49.

33. Dorothy L. Sayers, *The Mind of the Maker* (New York: Harper and Row, 1987), 185.

34. The Anglican theologian and canon of Durham Cathedral, David Brown, defines imagination as the ability "to think laterally" in ways that create new connections between ideas, images, or facets of nature that formerly seemed unrelated. He suggests that skillful imagination is at the heart of both intelligent faith and faithful scholarship. Imagination uses "story, poetry, and the visual arts" to reveal the deepest truths of natural and divine reality in contrast to philosophy which favors "prose as a vehicle for truth." See David Brown, *Discipleship and the Imagination: Christian Tradition and Truth* (New York: Oxford University Press, 2000), 352–53.

35. For a general introduction to the Wesleyan intellectual tradition and its implications for scholarship, see John E. and Susie C. Stanley, "What Can the Wesleyan/ Holiness Tradition Contribute to Christian Higher Education?" in Hughes and Adrian, *Models for Christian Higher Education*, 313–26.

36. For a helpful analysis of the Wesleyan quadrilateral, see W. Stephen Gunter, Scott J. Jones, Ted A. Campbell, Rebekah L. Miles, and Randy L. Maddox, *Wesley and the Quadrilateral: Renewing the Conversation* (Nashville, Tenn.: Abingdon Press, 1997).

37. Ron Kirkemo, "At the Lectern Between Jerusalem and Sarajevo: A Christian Approach to Teaching Political Science" in *Teaching as an Act of Faith: Theory and Practice in Church-Related Higher Education*, edited by Arlin C. Migliazzo (New York: Fordham University Press, 2002), 44.

38. Samuel M. Powell, *Participating in God: Creation and Trinity* (Minneapolis: Fortress Press, 2003), 215–16.

39. Steven J. Land, *Pentecostal Spirituality: A Passion for the Kingdom* (Sheffield, England: Sheffield Academic Press, 1993), 41.

40. Samuel Solivan, *The Spirit, Pathos and Liberation: Toward an Hispanic Pentecostal Theology* (Sheffield, England: Sheffield Academic Press, 1998), 118.

41. Jean-Jacques Suurmond, *Word and Spirit at Play: Towards a Charismatic Theology* (Grand Rapids, Mich.: Eerdmans, 1995), 220.

42. James L. Loder, *The Transforming Moment*, 2nd ed. (Colorado Springs: Helmers and Howard, 1989), 2–3, 26. While Loder was not a member of any Pentecostal church, he explicitly rooted his understanding of Christian faith and scholarship in a charismatic understanding of what he called mainline Christian faith. The charis-

matic tenor of *The Transforming Moment* is evident starting with the preface, and Loder confirmed that understanding of his work in a personal conversation several years before his death.

43. On the idea of primitivism and its influence in American religion see *The American Quest for the Primitive Church*, edited by Richard T. Hughes (Urbana: University of Illinois Press, 1988), and *The Primitive Church in the Modern World*, edited by Richard T. Hughes (Urbana: University of Illinois Press, 1995).

44. Rudolph Otto, *The Idea of the Holy* (Oxford: Oxford University Press, 1923).

45. Robin Maas and Gabriel O'Donnell, *Spirituality for the Contemporary Church* (Nashville, Tenn.: Abingdon Press, 1990).

46. Richard J. Foster, *Streams of Living Water: Celebrating the Great Traditions of Christian Faith* (New York: HarperSanFrancisco, 1998).

47. J. R. R. Tolkien, "Leaf by Niggle," in *Tree and Leaf* (Boston: Houghton Mifflin, 1965).

48. Two alternative perspectives, which we do not explicitly discuss in this book, deserve mention here. One is to view the connections of church and world in terms of evangelism and mission, perhaps best summarized in David J. Bosch, *Transforming Mission: Paradigm Shifts in Theology of Mission* (Maryknoll, N.Y.: Orbis Books, 1991). In addition to outlining all the important debates and developments that have taken place in recent years, Bosch analyzes thirteen emerging paradigms of mission that map the entire range of contemporary opinions. Another helpful perspective is to view the engagement of church and culture as a function of the church's own self-understanding, an approach taken by Avery Dulles in *Models of the Church* (New York: Doubleday, 1974). He develops five different ways of understanding the mission and identity of the church: as institution, mystical communion, sacrament, herald, and servant.

49. H. Richard Niebuhr, *Christ and Culture* (New York: Harper, 1951). For a critique of Niebuhr see Glenn Stassen, D. M. Yeager, and John Howard Yoder, *Authentic Transformation: A New Vision of Christ and Culture* (Nashville, Tenn.: Abingdon, 1996) and Duane K. Friesen, *Artists, Citizens, Philosophers: Seeking the Peace of the City* (Scottdale, Pa.: Herald Press, 2000). A somewhat different way of laying out the political options available to contemporary Christians can be found in J. Philip Wogaman, *Christian Perspectives on Politics*, rev. and expanded ed. (Louisville, Ky.: Westminster John Knox Press, 2000).

50. Niebuhr, *Christ and Culture*, 45.

A Modest (Though Not Particularly Humble) Claim for Scholarship in the Anabaptist Tradition

David L. Weaver-Zercher

This essay both exemplifies and explains the character of Anabaptist scholarship. Rather than focusing on worldview or theology as the key to unlock the distinctiveness of Anabaptist scholarship, David Weaver-Zercher focuses on narrative. Of special concern are the tensions that exist between narratives of American identity and the stories that define Anabaptist identity. Narratives of cultural identity often give rise to competing versions of the group's story. This is true even within the small world of North American Anabaptism. Nonetheless, two elements figure prominently in almost all Anabaptist visions of faith and scholarship: the importance of nonviolence and a commitment to serve the poor and oppressed both at home and around the world.

Shortly after the events of September 11, 2001, the humorist Dave Barry tried his hand at political commentary and U.S. history: "I'm not naive about my country," Barry wrote. "My country has at times been terribly wrong. But I know this about Americans: we don't set out to kill innocent people. We don't cheer when innocent people die."[1]

Barry's comments, echoed by so many others in the aftermath of September 11, should compel us to ponder the state of American historical memory. Consider, for example, March 10, 1945, when the United States Army Air Corps dropped enough bombs on Tokyo to kill one hundred thousand Japanese in a single night, most of them civilians living in working-class sections of the city. The next week *Time* magazine reported on what it breezily called the "Tokyo Bonfire," smugly telling its readers that "properly kindled, Japanese cities will burn like autumn leaves."[2] Five months later, the United States dropped atomic bombs on two other Japanese cities, first Hiroshima and then Nagasaki, incinerating thirty to forty times the number of people who died in the World Trade Center attacks—again, most of them civilians. One New York City daily ran a cartoon the day after the first bomb was dropped; the cartoon was totally blank except for two caustic words at the top: "So Sorry." Another newspaper's cartoon, captioned "Land of the Rising Sons," depicted bodies flying through the air over the Hiroshima landscape.[3]

Americans' poor historical memory is not because Americans are disinterested in war.[4] But many Americans are not particularly interested in exploring the more troubling questions raised by America's warring. Rarely has this historical "disinterest" been more apparent than in the mid-1990s, when the National Air and Space Museum sought to mount a fiftieth-anniversary exhibit commemorating the *Enola Gay*, the plane that dropped the first atomic bomb in 1945.[5] Earlier American exhibits commemorating the bombings of Hiroshima and Nagasaki had been cautious, nondescript, and morally innocuous, but the proposed fiftieth-anniversary exhibit at the National Air and Space Museum, which included melted school lunch boxes and graphic photographs of Hiroshima's burn victims, was intended, at least in part, to focus viewers' attention on the bomb's ground-level effects.[6] Such an exhibit would quite naturally raise questions about the decision to drop the bomb, including the most basic question: Was it justified?[7] In other words, while the National Air and Space Museum exhibit was not intended to instruct viewers about the intricacies of just war theory, it was intended to raise some of the same questions that Christian just war theorists have often thought important, not the least of which pertain to the targeting of civilian populations.

The key word, of course, is "intended." The exhibit was intended to raise such issues, but it never actually did. Due to pressure from various interest groups, heightened by widespread media misinformation, the planned exhibit was eventually canceled, replaced with the plane's fuselage, which, like the fortieth-anniversary exhibit before it, was left largely to speak for itself. And given the historical narrative that's long been dominant in American life, the plane's fuselage, according to historian Marilyn Young, was probably read as follows: "There was a Good War: it ended when Good Men flew a Good Plane and dropped a New Bomb on Bad People. What these bombs did had nothing to do with Us, only with Them: their atrocities, their aggressive war, the horror [of] their resistance." Young continues: "To question this [narrative] is to bring the meaning of the bomb home to us, where it belongs."[8] Or to put it a little differently, to seriously discuss this issue would force Americans to confront the reality of Us—not Them—using weapons of mass destruction on civilian populations in order to achieve military aims.

For many Americans, confronting this reality and others like it is extremely difficult. Indeed, for some Americans, considering these ideas is tantamount to entering the land of heresy, a place where sacred beliefs are examined, challenged, and potentially abandoned. No doubt many Americans, including many American Christians, would object to my associating the word *sacred* with their patriotic proclivities and nationalistic loyalties. But as an Anabaptist Christian trained as a religious historian, I find it impossible to overlook the existence of formative, morally construed narratives out of which Americans (and others, for that matter) make sense of themselves, their communities, their nation, and their world. I would further contend that it is not inappropriate to describe these narratives as sacred—sacred in the sense that they orient people in their universe by constructing their identity, shaping their moral judgments, and fueling their actions.

Because the existence of a sacred counternarrative is so prominent in the Anabaptist tradition, and because Anabaptist scholars are so often cognizant of the contrasts that exist between their particular narrative and other sacred narratives, it seems useful to launch my consideration of Anabaptist scholarship by limning the outlines of two sacred narratives: one largely "American" and one "Anabaptist."[9]

Sacred Narratives, American and Anabaptist

In her oft-cited essay "Culture in Action: Symbols and Strategies," the sociologist Ann Swidler proposes the image of culture as a "tool kit."[10] According to Swidler, every culture possesses a particular set of tools—symbols, stories, and rituals—that persons in that particular culture use to solve problems. Contrasting this understanding of culture to the idea of culture as values (a view of culture that perceives human action as entirely ends-oriented), Swidler contends that most people "do not, indeed cannot, build up a sequence of actions piece by piece, striving with each act to maximize a given outcome." Rather, "they construct chains of actions beginning with at least some pre-fabricated links," that is, the preexisting tools of their culture. Swidler is not simplistic in her cultural analysis, noting for example that all cultures possess diverse and sometimes conflicting symbols, rituals, and stories. But here is where her idea of culture as tool kit is most compelling. Humans are not "cultural dopes," writes Swidler, but are rather "skilled users of culture," selecting the cultural tools that help them construct their lines of action. In all of this Swidler does not dismiss the importance of values, though she does encourage her readers to be realistic about their causal significance. "We can . . . recognize the significance of values," writes Swidler, "if we acknowledge that values do not shape action by defining its ends, but rather fine-tune the regulation of action within established ways of life."[11]

Twenty-first-century Americans no doubt encounter an even more daunting array of symbols, rituals, and stories than existed in 1986, when Swidler's essay was first published. But even as American culture has become increasingly diverse, it is nonetheless true—and especially so after September 11—that most Americans have somewhere in their cultural tool kits a narrative that places America at or near the center of God's purposes.[12] Numerous scholars of American life have probed the power of this particular narrative—few as clearly and concisely as religious historian Catherine Albanese. In her book *America: Religions and Religion*, Albanese rehearses the details of this peculiarly American narrative, highlighting its familiar features: wise Founding Fathers, their passion for liberty, a heroic revolution, and so on.[13] To underscore the sacred quality of this American narrative, Albanese details the Pledge of Allegiance, a ubiquitous ritual that instructs American children about a particular creed (telling them they inhabit "one nation, under God, indivisible," that aims to provide "liberty and justice for all") and reminds them of an uncomplicated ethical code (that, due to what America represents, they must show "allegiance" to). Although Albanese doesn't actually make this point, the visceral power of these cultural tools can be seen in the way certain objects in America's civil religious cultus have been awarded a sacramental quality, most notably the flag itself. Like the bread and the wine in the Roman Catholic mass, which according to Roman thought embodies the real presence of Jesus Christ, so too do red, white, and blue pieces of cloth assume sanctified status in America's civil religion, so much so that some Americans have sought to pass laws against flag "desecration." It's little wonder, says Albanese, that some religious groups have considered the Pledge of Allegiance an act of idolatry.[14]

In addition to limning the contemporary outlines of America's civil religion, Albanese traces how this religion developed over time, often borrowing from Christian sources. Albanese is an astute enough historian to know that the founders of the American republic were not the evangelical Christians that some people have made them out to be. Nonetheless, Albanese grants the seventeenth-century Puritans their due for influencing some of the outlines of America's civil religion, most notably the sense of divine chosenness that Americans have often assumed for themselves and their nation. The "city on a hill" idea in John Winthrop's Arbella sermon—that is, Winthrop's notion that the Puritans were setting out to create a New World community that the rest of the world would view as uniquely connected to God—is deeply embedded in America's civil religion. So even though most contemporary Americans couldn't delineate many differences between a Puritan and an Amishman, many continue to interpret the events that occur on American soil (and September 11 is a good example here) as uniquely important in God's millennial plans.[15]

The Puritans, of course, didn't invent the idea that God might choose a special people and a special land for a special mission. Rather, they tied their sense of themselves to a much older narrative in which God's people were oppressed by God's enemies, escaping that oppression only by making a long, difficult journey through the wilderness and into the Promised Land. Not surprisingly, some Puritan divines talked about the Native Americans in the same cadences as the Hebrew writers talked about the Canaanites, asserting that the heathens needed to be cleansed from the land across the Atlantic Ocean even as the Israelites cleansed the land across the Jordan River.[16] Other Puritan leaders believed that evangelizing their "savage" neighbors was a more humane option than genocide or land dispossession, though even then their means of proselytizing were often less than compassionate. Those who challenged the Puritan party line on Native Americans were given two options: shut up or leave. Roger Williams chose the latter option, setting up camp in Rhode Island, where he became the first great spokesperson for American religious liberty.[17] In sum, Williams decided that being a follower of Jesus Christ and participating in the Puritans' particular brand of Christ-transforming culture were incompatible.

Which brings us to the early Anabaptists, who some hundred years before Roger Williams was banished from Massachusetts Bay decided that if they really wanted to be faithful followers of Jesus, they couldn't be faithful followers of Ulrich Zwingli. Zwingli, the leading minister in Zurich, Switzerland, joined up with the nascent Protestant movement in 1522, just five years after Luther posted his theses on the doors of Wittenberg's cathedral. Concerning himself primarily with moral and ecclesiastical reform, Zwingli soon came to the conclusion that the mass as performed in Zurich's churches was improperly conducted; he also began to hint that infant baptism might be indefensible as well. But rather than vigorously pursue those reforms, Zwingli chose to heed the advice of the Zurich city council, which warned him that implementing such reforms might result in theological confusion at best, social upheaval at worst. In short, Zwingli chose a politically conservative approach, an approach that alienated some of his closest disciples. Following their consciences, these youthful radicals broke with Zwingli and, shortly thereafter, baptized one another, symbolizing with baptismal waters their decision to create a new community based on conscious, adult commitments to Jesus Christ.[18]

The decision of these youthful radicals to become rebaptizers earned them the label "Anabaptists." It also set them at odds with both state and religious authorities. The Anabaptists were deemed outlaws, tracked down, and ordered to recant. Some did, but many did not, resulting in the execution of several thousand of them—not at the hands of Muslims or Hindus but at the hands of their fellow Christians, Catholic, Lutheran, and Reformed. Surprisingly, most of these Anabaptists decided that, to be faithful to Jesus, they could not strike back at their enemies. They were, as one early Anabaptist wrote, like "sheep for the slaughter."[19] Thus the Anabaptist movement was born, somehow surviving until Menno Simons and other second-generation leaders came along to organize, renew, and strengthen the movement.[20]

This particular narrative, which prioritizes Zurich, the first adult baptisms, vigorous persecution, and a nonviolent Christian response, provides an important tool in the cultural tool kit of most Anabaptists. Of course, the *real* story of Anabaptist origins is far more complicated and much less pristine than the one just told. One historian, for instance, has argued that the radicalism of the early Anabaptist leader Conrad Grebel was as much a rebellion against his father (who sat on the Zurich city council) as it was a result of following his Bible-formed conscience.[21] Other Reformation historians have advanced what has come to be known as the polygenesis thesis of Anabaptist origins, noting that there were lots of rebaptizers milling around in the sixteenth century, many of them not pacifists—indeed, many of them rather boorish and unseemly.[22] So again, the historical record is not as tidy as the story I just recounted. But for present purposes, the real historical record is not particularly important. What is important is the fact that most contemporary Anabaptists, including most Anabaptist scholars, embrace the simpler, more pristine narrative as their own. Or to translate this into Swidler's language, this simpler narrative is a much more useful tool for solving the problems that Anabaptists have faced throughout their history and continue to face today.

This formative Anabaptist narrative has been sustained via stories, symbols, and rituals in North America's Anabaptist communities. For instance, membership classes in Anabaptist churches are more likely to instruct new members on the outlines of this narrative than they are to do theologically oriented catechetical instruction. Copies of *Martyrs Mirror*, which provides specific accounts of sixteenth- and seventeenth-century Anabaptist martyrdom, can be found in most Anabaptist church libraries and many church members' homes. The woodcut iconography of Dirk Willems, which illustrates the willingness of an early Anabaptist to lay down his life for his enemy, has gained near iconic status in some Anabaptist quarters; it is, we might say, the Anabaptists' answer to the Iwo Jima memorial in Washington, D.C.[23] And the newest Mennonite and Brethren hymnal, devoid of nationalistic anthems like "The Star-Spangled Banner" and "My Country 'Tis of Thee," contains a thirty-page section of hymns under the heading "Suffering."[24] Far from triumphalistic renderings of the Christian life, these hymns encourage the singing congregation with ideas such as this: "What though my joys and comforts die? The Lord my Savior liveth. What though the darkness gather round? Songs in the night he giveth."[25]

These are only a few of the ways that Anabaptists sustain a historical narrative that orients them in the world. Of course, it's important also to recognize that Anabaptists have traditionally linked the details of this sixteenth-century narrative to a much older narrative in which a lamb was led to slaughter after offending both religious and political authorities. This earlier narrative, expressed most poignantly in the gospels of Matthew, Mark, Luke, and John, features a radical who was encouraged by the authorities to renounce his calling and, when threatened with death, chose not to respond with the sword. For twenty-first-century Anabaptists, these two narratives are not coincidentally connected. Rather, the sixteenth-century story represents a mimetic response to the first-century story, and both narratives offer tools for twenty-first-century Anabaptists, including Anabaptist scholars, to shape their worlds and their work.

An Anabaptist "Perspective" on the World?

Recent discussions of Christian scholarship have awarded the notion of "perspectivalism" a prominent role. This notion, fueled by growing racial, ethnic, and gender diversity in the academy in the 1960s and 1970s, asserts that a person's research is shaped, sometimes radically, by the perspective the person assumes or the social location she occupies.[26] Largely superceding the notion of "objectivity" (at least in the academy), perspectivalism has been warmly and widely embraced by Christian scholars, many of whom see it as a convenient opening to advance "a Christian perspective" on various issues. George Marsden, for example, affirms the notion of perspectivalism in his book *The Outrageous Idea of Christian Scholarship*, noting that "[k]eeping within our intellectual horizons a being who is great enough to create us and the universe . . . ought to change our perspectives on quite a number of things."[27] More central to his book's thesis, Marsden contends there is no compelling reason to silence religious perspectives in the secular academy. Since religious perspectives are as relevant to exploring the world as nonreligious perspectives (Marsden points to Marxism here as a case in point), religiously committed perspectives should not be ruled out of bounds, so long as those who hold them are willing "to support the rules necessary for constructive exchange of ideas in a pluralistic setting."[28]

While it is difficult to deny the reality of perspectivalism, many arguments about doing scholarship "from a Christian perspective" are fraught with problems, often because they claim too much. All too often these arguments neglect the fact that Christianity possesses many disparate theological traditions. Indeed, in their attempts to make a case for Christian scholarship to nonbelieving audiences, some scholars have operated from the naive (or perhaps disingenuous) assumption that Christianity is a monolithic entity, or at least a settled theological conversation. More than being naive, however, this assumption runs the danger of compromising the usefulness of talking about Christian scholarship by reducing Christianity's theological reality to a few abstract, common-denominator beliefs shared by all Christians. More helpful, and ultimately more fruitful, is the nuanced recognition that all Christians participate in particular Christian traditions that, while sharing some things in common with other Christian traditions, nonetheless possess unique emphases and concerns.[29]

Here, then, we arrive at the importance of scholarship in the Anabaptist tradition. More than most North American Christians, Christians in the Anabaptist tradition have long recognized that some of their understandings of the Christian faith clash with those held by other North American Christians. Indeed, Anabaptist theologians, church historians, and church leaders have devoted an extraordinary amount of energy seeking to differentiate Anabaptism and its theology from that of other Christian traditions. One influential book, published in the early 1970s, contended that the early Anabaptist movement was "neither Catholic nor Protestant," a distinction the author deemed applicable to twentieth-century Anabaptists as well.[30] Other writers have cast Anabaptist/Mennonite distinctiveness in a different light, for example, as neither "liberal" nor "evangelical."[31] To be sure, many Anabaptist church members would not be able to articulate the details of their theological distinctiveness, and some have been easily attracted to more predominant (and less particular) theological expressions.[32] Still, the peace tradition that continues to thrive in most Anabaptist churches serves to remind even the least articulate Anabaptist church members that Anabaptists are, in certain respects, different from most North American Christians.

But before I say too much here, I should be careful to avoid the same mistake that others have made in talking about "Christian scholarship," namely, the mistake of assuming there is a monolithic "Anabaptist perspective" that all Anabaptists assume. One needn't spend very much time around Goshen, Indiana, or Lancaster, Pennsylvania, to realize that, just as there are many Christian perspectives, so too are there many Anabaptist perspectives. For instance, the world's most famous Anabaptists—Lancaster County's Old Order Amish—have a perspective on education that essentially forbids the sort of "higher education" advocated in this book. Not only would the kind of scholarship detailed here be of relatively little interest to most Amish people but also many of them would find the suggestion that one's faith might be sharpened by "worldly learning" a dubious idea indeed, perhaps sprouted by the devil himself! But other Anabaptists, who teach at places like Goshen, Bluffton, Penn State, and Harvard, would find the same idea commonsensical, perhaps even spiritually invigorating.

Rather than claiming an Anabaptist *perspective* (or, worse yet, invoking *worldview* language), it makes more sense to speak of the distinctive cultural tools that Anabaptist scholars bring to their work. These scholars cannot and should not be reduced to "Anabaptists," as if being an Anabaptist defined their entire being. For in addition to being Anabaptists, these scholars are Canadians, Americans, Africans, and Asians; they are Mennonites, Brethren, Baptists,

and Anglicans; they are Dutch-Russian Mennonites, Swiss-German Mennonites, ex-Amish Mennonites, Latino Mennonites, and African-American Mennonites; and, of course, they are men and they are women. Like all Christians,
then, Anabaptist scholars occupy a host of social locations and carry an array
of tools in their cultural tool kits. Still, Anabaptists share an overlapping
array of narratives, rituals, and symbols that allow them to fashion their own
form of Christian scholarship. And it should therefore not be surprising that
the scholarship produced by Anabaptists has exhibited distinctive hues and
trumpeted particular themes.

Anabaptist Scholars at Work: A Few Examples

Since I began this chapter by focusing on readings of American history, I'll
continue in that vein, citing an example of historical scholarship presently
being done in the Anabaptist tradition. In their recent book *The Missing Peace:
The Search for Nonviolent Alternatives in United States History*, James Juhnke
and Carol Hunter offer alternate interpretations of various events in U.S. history, highlighting the possibilities of nonviolence to challenge what they call
more traditional, violence-sanctioning interpretations. According to the authors, their nonviolent interpretive bias, which is rooted in their peace-church
commitments, stands in sharp contrast to the prominent bias of "redemptive
violence" that informs much historical writing about the United States, particularly writing at the popular level.[33] For example, when Juhnke and Hunter
look at the American Revolution, they argue that, in addition to having been
unnecessary for Americans to gain greater measures of self-determination, the
war was not at all "revolutionary" in that it did not bring freedom to the people
who needed it most, the African-American slaves.[34] In other words, the war
was not the redeeming event that so many Americans imagine it to be, a
recognition that, while not unique to Anabaptist scholars, is nonetheless an
Anabaptist perspective that finds itself at odds with other prominent interpretations embraced by many American Christians. Indeed, in an insightful essay
in *Fides et Historia*, William Vance Trollinger reminds us that Juhnke and Hunter's historical interpretations are likely to find the coolest welcome in conservative Christian schools that, for various reasons, are deeply committed to the
idea of redemptive American violence.[35]

In my own interactions with American college students, I too have found
the myth of redemptive violence deeply embedded—so deeply embedded that
it is hard for students to recognize it. One of the films I often show when we
discuss the civil rights movement is *Mississippi Burning*. This movie, which
dramatizes the FBI's investigation into the murders of three civil rights workers during Mississippi's Freedom Summer campaign, focuses on the work of
two FBI agents, both of them white. The racial lines in the film are clearly

drawn—and are clearly drawn incorrectly. As the film's African-American characters cower in the background, their white, FBI agent rescuers bravely investigate the murders and, after torturing a white supremacist or two, solve the murder case. The film is a gripping one, and my students seem to enjoy it. But when I ask them afterward what was wrong with the picture it presented (even after we have studied the events of Freedom Summer), they usually do not know. The fact is, the film gets a lot of things wrong. For one, J. Edgar Hoover's FBI was hardly a friend of the civil rights movement. Second, African Americans in the South, while sometimes intimidated into inaction, did not by and large cower in their houses waiting for their white Northern friends to liberate them. But in addition to being a profoundly racist film, *Mississippi Burning* presents a historically indefensible story about the role of violence in the civil rights struggle. Throughout the film, the brutality of white supremacists is countered not by the suffering of nonviolent African Americans but by the "righteous" brutality of the FBI agents, who ride into Mississippi like two gun-slinging sheriffs. In other words, the courageous, largely nonviolent witness of Southern blacks—which I would argue is the real story from Freedom Summer—is itself slaughtered by a filmmaker who embraces and perpetuates the historiographical myth of redemptive violence.

To be sure, challenging the well-worn myth of redemptive violence is not the exclusive domain of Anabaptist scholars (i.e., it doesn't take an Anabaptist to recognize these sorts of shortcomings in *Mississippi Burning*).[36] Still, broadranging historical works like Juhnke and Hunter's, which self-consciously wield the tool of nonviolence, are precious few in the academy-at-large, in part because of a longstanding Anabaptist reticence to participate in discussions deemed relevant by the larger academic community. Indeed, only recently have significant numbers of Anabaptist scholars begun to set their scholarly sights higher than their own confessional (and typically ethnic) communities. These communities, some of which have been places of considerable intellectual ferment over the past fifty years, have nonetheless been relatively insular, and the conversations generated therein correspondingly parochial.[37] But this, I would argue, is undergoing a significant transformation. At the risk of claiming too much for the present generation of Anabaptist scholars, these current scholars have increasingly recognized that their work can contribute something of value not only to their fellow Anabaptists but to the disciplines generally and thereby the larger world.[38]

The growing public-mindedness of Anabaptist scholars is evident at many turns, perhaps most impressively in the realm of peacebuilding and conflict transformation. Eastern Mennonite University, nestled in Virginia's Shenandoah Valley, boasts a well-regarded graduate program in conflict transformation, attracting students from many regions of the world. The credibility of this program is rooted, at least in part, in the ongoing contributions its faculty members are making to real-world conflict transformation. Victim-Offender

Reconciliation Programs (VORP) and related initiatives, which seek to move the justice system beyond "retributive justice" to "restorative justice," have been key concerns, particularly in the work of the VORP pioneer Howard Zehr.[39] Other faculty members have worked internationally, addressing large-scale, deeply rooted conflicts between tribal groups, religious parties, and nation-states. The most renowned individual in this regard is John Paul Lederach, who has worked (among other places) in Northern Ireland, Central America, and Central Africa. Reflecting the practical, ethical concerns that have long characterized the Anabaptist tradition, Lederach, who also holds an appointment at Notre Dame's Kroc Institute for International Peace Studies, is perhaps best known for being a skilled practitioner. But he is also a scholar, reflecting carefully on his craft and contributing frequently to a growing body of literature in the area of peacebuilding.[40]

While scholarly endeavors in the area of peacemaking and conflict transformation reveal the most obvious connections to Anabaptist history and theology, other Anabaptist scholars have wielded other Anabaptist cultural tools. Prioritizing the Anabaptist emphasis on community building and face-to-face relationships, Mennonite economist James Harder argues for an Anabaptist approach to economics that limits "the way in which the market economy is allowed to operate" in order to "preserve space for strong and vibrant local economies that foster a sense of community cooperation." Turning his focus toward caring for the most vulnerable members of American society, Harder contends that America's economists, rather than focusing primarily on economic growth, should devote more of their energy to rethinking policies "that allow the wealthiest 1 percent of households in the United States to control 57 percent of all wealth while leaving 44 million Americans with no health insurance."[41] To be sure, Harder's concern for the poor and oppressed cannot be reduced to his Anabaptist commitments or cultural heritage. In an autobiographical piece describing his scholarly motivations and objectives, Harder recounts his experience of teaching economics in an economically deprived Kenyan province—an experience that, from all indications, affected his thinking as much as the economics courses he took as an undergraduate at a Mennonite-affiliated college.[42] Still, it is arguable that Anabaptist scholarship and, more generally, Anabaptist-related education have demonstrated a keen interest in recognizing, evaluating, and addressing the needs of the world's most vulnerable people, an interest rooted in and sustained by a historical narrative in which Anabaptists are themselves suffering and vulnerable.[43]

Some observers might find it ironic (and perhaps even hypocritical) that wealthy, well-fed, securely employed Anabaptist scholars would claim to identify with the world's marginalized people. Given that most North American Anabaptists are relatively wealthy, and given that the most recent persecution recounted in *Martyrs Mirror* occurred over three hundred years ago, isn't it a little much to claim solidarity with people who suffer today?[44] Similarly, doesn't the Anabaptist emphasis on nonviolence ring hollow in a social context in which Anabaptists are well protected politically, economically, and physically? Such questions, while difficult to address, are certainly not out of bounds. North American Anabaptists, who sometimes overestimate the depth of their own ethical rigor and moral compassion, need humbly to admit that their ability to identify with suffering people, let alone embrace suffering itself, is very limited indeed. At the same time, it is difficult to disparage any cultural tool that compels scholars to tend to the needs of the world's vulnerable people or helps them critique the cultural myths that sanctify American violence, wealth, and power. As long as Anabaptists keep telling their peculiar stories and reenacting their community rituals, those sorts of cultural tools should never be in short supply.

NOTES

1. Dave Barry, "The Power of Goodness Will Prevail," reprinted in *Newsday*, September 17, 2001. Barry's column and the subsequent references to the Tokyo bombing are cited in Perry Bush, "The Lessons of History," *Mennonite*, October 23, 2001, 6.

2. "Firebirds' Flight," *Time*, March 19, 1945, 32.

3. Cartoons cited in Paul Boyer, *By the Bomb's Early Light: American Thought at the Dawn of the Atomic Age* (Chapel Hill: University of North Carolina Press, 1994), 13. My point here is not to argue precise parallels between the events of September 2001 and those of March and August 1945; it *is* to suggest that the historical memory of many Americans is conveniently selective, allowing them to construct a moral universe in which the other is easily demonized and we are easily let off the hook.

4. I was reminded of this recently when I visited a large chain bookstore near my home. Near the store's front entrance sat a table stacked shoulder-high with books, with a sign boasting "U.S. History." Perusing the table, I soon discovered that the only sort of history occupying this table was *military* history, most of it related to the Civil War and World War II.

5. I've placed the word *disinterest* in quotation marks, since disinterest suggests passive noninterest. There was nothing passive about the approach of those who sought to reconfigure and/or cancel the Enola Gay exhibit. Their response to the exhibit was not so much disinterest as an aggressive attempt to quash a morally sensitive mode of historical inquiry.

6. For example, a fortieth-anniversary exhibit, displayed in 1985 at the National Museum of American History, limited itself to displaying replicas of the bombs' casings, along with plaques that, according to historian Marilyn Young, allowed the casings to "speak for themselves." Marilyn B. Young, "Dangerous History: Vietnam and the 'Good War,'" in *History Wars: The Enola Gay and Other Battles for the American Past*, edited by Edward T. Linenthal and Thomas Engelhardt (New York: Holt, 1996), 205.

7. One need not be a pacifist to ponder such questions and come to the conclusion that it was not justified. In his classic *Just and Unjust Wars*, Michael Walzer con-

cluded that America's use of the atomic bomb could not be justified according to standard just war criteria. See Michael Walzer, *Just and Unjust Wars* (New York: Basic Books, 1977), 264–68.

8. Young, "Dangerous History," 208–209.

9. The idea that a particular narrative is central to Anabaptist identity is hardly novel. See, for example, Richard T. Hughes, *How Christian Faith Can Sustain the Life of the Mind* (Grand Rapids, Mich.: Eerdmans, 2001), 82–84. Hughes calls Mennonites/Anabaptists a "story-formed community" and argues that this story compels Anabaptist scholars to honor particular commitments.

10. Ann Swidler, "Culture in Action: Symbols and Strategies," *American Sociological Review* 51 (1986), 273–86.

11. Swidler, "Culture in Action," 276, 277, 282.

12. How else can we explain the surge in interest in apocalyptic literature following the events of September 11? See Nancy Gibbs, "Apocalypse Now," *Time*, July 1, 2002, 40–48.

13. Catherine L. Albanese, *America: Religions and Religion*, 3rd ed. (Belmont, Cal.: Wadsworth, 1999), 438–45.

14. Albanese, *America: Religion and Religions*, 432–33.

15. Albanese, *America: Religion and Religions*, 435.

16. Sacvan Bercovitch, *The American Jeremiad* (Madison: University of Wisconsin Press, 1978), 75; Robert F. Berkhofer, Jr., *The White Man's Indian: Images of the American Indian from Columbus to the Present* (New York: Knopf, 1978), 80–85.

17. Roger Williams's most thorough indictment of Puritan policies toward Native Americans was his treatise *Christenings Make Not Christians*. For a summary of Williams's ideas and influence, see Edwin S. Gaustad, *Liberty of Conscience: Roger Williams in America* (Grand Rapids, Mich.: Eerdmans, 1991).

18. For a more detailed summary of these events, see J. Denny Weaver, *Becoming Anabaptist: The Origin and Significance of Sixteenth-Century Anabaptism* (Scottdale, Pa.: Herald Press, 1987), 25–51.

19. In a letter to Thomas Müntzer in 1524, Michael Sattler wrote: "The gospel and its adherents are not to be protected by the sword, nor are they thus to protect themselves. . . . True Christian believers are sheep among wolves, sheep for the slaughter." See *Spiritual and Anabaptist Writers*, edited by George Huntston Williams (Philadelphia: Westminster Press, 1957), 80.

20. John D. Roth, "The Mennonites' Dirty Little Secret," *Christianity Today*, October 7, 1996, 44–48.

21. Peter Iver Kaufman, "Social History, Psychohistory, and the Prehistory of Swiss Anabaptism," *Journal of Religion* 68 (1988), 527–44.

22. See James M. Stayer, Werner O. Packull, and Klaus Deppermann, "From Monogenesis to Polygenesis: The Historical Discussion of Anabaptist Origins," *Mennonite Quarterly Review* 49 (1975), 83–121.

23. The woodcut image of Dirk Willems can be found in Thieleman J. van Braght, *The Bloody Theater or Martyrs Mirror of the Defenseless Christians*, 5th ed. (Scottdale, Pa.: Herald Press, 1949), 741.

24. *Hymnal: A Worship Book* (Scottdale, Pa.: Herald Press, 1992).

25. From Robert Lowry's 1869 hymn "My Life Flows On."

26. For a consideration of perspectivalism in the discipline of history, see Peter Novick, *That Noble Dream: The "Objectivity Question" and the American Historical Profession* (Cambridge: Cambridge University Press, 1988).

27. George M. Marsden, *The Outrageous Idea of Christian Scholarship* (New York: Oxford University Press, 1997), 4.

28. Marsden, *The Outrageous Idea of Christian Scholarship*, 45.

29. Clearly George Marsden is not so naive as to think that Christianity is monolithic. Nevertheless, in the course of his *Outrageous Idea* argument, he tends to emphasize the commonalities of Christians, underscoring such beliefs as God as creator and the sinfulness of human beings. But as the historian William Vance Trollinger noted in an address before the Conference on Faith and History, such common-denominator beliefs are so abstract that it is difficult to know how they would "mark out a particular sort of historical interpretation," that is, "it is not clear . . . how they will result in a definably Christian interpretation of history." "Faith, History, and the Conference on Faith and History," *Fides et Historia* 23 (2001), 7.

30. Walter Klaassen, *Anabaptism: Neither Catholic nor Protestant* (Waterloo, Ontario: Conrad Press, 1973).

31. See Paul M. Lederach, *A Third Way: Conversations about Anabaptist/Mennonite Faith* (Scottdale, Pa.: Herald Press, 1980), and *Evangelicalism and Anabaptism*, edited by C. Norman Kraus (Scottdale, Pa.: Herald Press, 1979). For more recent (and popular) considerations of these issues, see Thomas Finger, "The Place to Begin Mennonite Theology," *Gospel Herald*, July 30, 1996, 1–3; and J. Nelson Kraybill, "Is Our Future Evangelical?" *Mennonite*, March 5, 2002, 14–16.

32. See J. Denny Weaver, *Keeping Salvation Ethical: Mennonite and Amish Atonement Theology in the Late Nineteenth Century* (Scottdale, Pa.: Herald Press, 1997).

33. James C. Juhnke and Carol M. Hunter, *The Missing Peace: The Search for Nonviolent Alternatives in United States History* (Kitchener, Ontario: Pandora Press, 2001), especially 9–14.

34. Juhnke and Hunter, *The Missing Peace*, 35–51.

35. Trollinger, "Faith, History, and the Conference on Faith and History," 8.

36. Howard Zehr, *Changing Lenses: A New Focus for Crime and Justice* (Scottdale, Pa.: Herald Press, 1990).

37. After Anabaptists had lived in sectarian and antiintellectual isolation for much of their history, some Anabaptists embraced higher education with vigor during the twentieth century, but primarily as a way to shape their own particular culture. When they did engage the larger culture, they mostly did so with the idea that the best way to be "salt and light" was by empowering people in and through small, scattered communities around the world. There's much to be said for this mode of cultural transformation, but whether we frame it positively or negatively, the fact is the vast majority of Anabaptist educator-scholars did little to engage non-Anabaptist minds through much of the twentieth century. See Keith Graber Miller, "Transformative Education," in *Teaching to Transform: Perspectives on Mennonite Higher Education*, edited by Keith Graber Miller (Goshen, Ind.: Pinchpenny Press, 2000), 2–3.

38. The record, of course, is uneven. In the realm of theological ethics, Anabaptists (most prominently, John Howard Yoder) have engaged in larger disciplinary conversations for decades. On the other hand, many Anabaptist historians continue to

focus most of their scholarly energies on tracing the histories of Amish, Mennonite, and Brethren groups. In that sense, Juhnke and Hunter's *Missing Peace* is a welcome exception.

39. Howard Zehr, *Changing Lenses: A New Focus for Crime and Justice* (Scottdale, Pa.: Herald Press, 1990).

40. Lederach's books include: *A Handbook of International Peacebuilding: Into the Eye of the Storm*, with Janice Moomaw Jenner (San Francisco: Jossey-Bass, 2002); *From the Ground Up: Mennonite Contributions to International Peacebuilding*, coedited with Cynthia Sampson (New York: Oxford University Press, 2000); *Building Peace: Sustainable Reconciliation in Divided Societies* (Washington, D.C.: United States Institute of Peace, 1998); and *Preparing for Peace: Conflict Transformation across Cultures* (Syracuse: Syracuse University Press, 1995).

41. James M. Harder, "The 'Anabaptist School' of Economics," in *Minding the Church: Scholarship in the Anabaptist Tradition*, edited by David Weaver-Zercher (Telford, Pa.: Pandora Press U.S., 2002), 137.

42. Harder, "The 'Anabaptist School' of Economics," 127–28.

43. See Miller, "Transformative Education," 7–9. From a curricular standpoint, Goshen College's Study-Service Term (SST) program represents most clearly the Anabaptist concern for the world's most vulnerable people. More than simply an "international" learning experience, Goshen's SST program requires students to spend a trimester in a developing nation, where they learn from and, in small ways, serve their hosts.

44. I should note that some Anabaptist/Mennonite communities have suffered terribly in more recent times, for example, Ukrainian Mennonites during and after the Russian Revolution. For one scholar's reflections on the significance of that, see Alvin C. Dueck, "Anabaptism and Psychology: From Above and Below," in Weaver-Zercher, *Minding the Church*, 114–16.

CHAPTER FOUR

Scholarship Defined and Embodied

Scholarship is a complex practice involving many different kinds of activity and ways of thinking. Often scholarship is (mis)defined in fairly simple terms. As a corrective, we propose a threefold definition of scholarship that includes analytic, strategic, and empathic modes of reflection. In addition to the diversity that exists within the scholarly enterprise itself, a range of other factors surround our work and shape our lives as scholars, including concerns of ethics, academic etiquette, personal motivation, and vocation.

Many discussions of Christian scholarship falter because they presuppose a definition of scholarship that is not complex enough to comprehend all the different kinds of activity that nestle together under the rubric of scholarship. Many scholars seem to assume they know instinctively what scholarship is and what it is not. If they cannot put that definition neatly into words, they would still claim to know scholarship when they see it. But this intuitive approach to scholarship almost always produces a skewed view of what scholarship entails. In this regard, scholars are no different from everybody else. People see the world through the lens of their own experiences and understand best those things with which they are most familiar.

Thus, most scholars are prone to define scholarship in terms that are amenable to their own fields of academic expertise but that are not necessarily equally applicable to other areas of scholarly reflection and activity. Professors in the so-called hard sciences still often continue to believe that the scholarship of their humanities-oriented colleagues is little more than opinionated fluff; humanities professors in turn often wonder if any of their scientific colleagues ever read books and reflect on their meanings. As C. P. Snow pointed out long ago, the humanities and the sciences can be equally oblivious to and dismissive of each other's world of scholarship.[1] Then there is the question of scholarship as it relates to subjects like business, health care, or engineering. Experts in these fields often view their scientific and humanities associates as irredeemably impractical, which may only be fair since the science and humanities professors often view the business, health, and engineering faculty as not genuinely "real" scholars at all. Add to this mix social scientists and visual and performing artists and the picture becomes even more complicated. How does the notion of scholarship apply to all these different forms of academic study?

In recent years, several new definitions have been put forward that allow more kinds of academic activity to appropriately be labeled scholarship. Perhaps the most widely discussed alternative is Ernest Boyer's proposal that posits four different and distinct types of scholarship: discovery, integration, application, and teaching.[2] His model has been widely endorsed as a helpful corrective to past practices. Few in the academy would advocate a return to the pre-Boyer days when the only valued scholarship was original research undertaken in very tightly defined fields of disciplinary expertise and disseminated through publication in scholarly journals or university press monographs.

Boyer's definition does place a high value on the traditional scholarship of discovery, but it also recognizes that other kinds of academic work ought rightly to be counted as scholarship and not be relegated to some supposedly lesser domain. The goal is not to water down the definition of scholarship so that everyone can claim to be a scholar but rather to acknowledge the diversity of tasks that are naturally and legitimately involved in good scholarship. Good scholarship means discovering or creating new bits of truth (discovery scholarship); it means understanding how those new bits of knowledge relate to other fields of academic inquiry (integration scholarship); it means being able to explain how those new items of information apply to situations in the "real world" (applied scholarship); and it means being able to explain your work to others who know relatively little about your field of expertise (the scholarship of teaching). Those are enormous demands, and it is only reasonable to expect that scholars will possess different levels of skill in different areas. However, colleges and universities need people with all four skills, and Boyer wanted to make sure that all four dimensions of scholarship were equally supported and encouraged by institutions of higher learning. To him, it made no sense to force everyone through the sieve of discovery scholarship in order to get tenure if what colleges and universities really needed was a balanced mix of all four aspects of the scholarly task.[3]

Another proposal that has garnered attention in recent years is Howard Gardner's notion of "multiple intelligences."[4] Gardner suggests that human beings have at least seven, and perhaps eight or more, distinct kinds of intelligence. His first listing included linguistic intelligence, logical-mathematical intelligence, spatial intelligence (the ability to perceive things in three-dimensional imagination), bodily-kinesthetic intelligence (the ability to do things with one's body including dance, athletics, and general skill in craftsmanship), musical intelligence, interpersonal intelligence (skills of leadership and effective group interaction), and intrapersonal intelligence (self-awareness and the ability to react adaptively to new environments). Gardner later added the category of naturalist intelligence ("expertise in the recognition and classification of the numerous species—the flora and fauna—of his or her environment") and suggested existential intelligence (intelligence related to "ultimate" concerns) might also qualify.[5] He argues that these separate kinds of intelligence are rooted in different kinds of brain activity, that they evolved on the basis of different evolutionary needs, and that they each possess their own distinct symbol systems. Using this sevenfold categorization of intelligence, it would be possible to develop a corresponding sevenfold definition of scholarship.

Reaction to Gardner's proposal has been mixed. Some have welcomed his expansion of the notion of intelligence, while others have rejected it as simply one more sign of the dumbing-down of the academy. Nevertheless, Gardner's notion of multiple intelligences implies that scholars necessarily bring different insights and abilities to their common tasks. While Boyer's division of the work of scholarship is functional, involving four different kinds of activity, Gardner's division of intelligence is more essential: people perceive, interpret, and interact with the world around them in different ways based on the different configurations of skills and abilities that define them as persons. While these differences may sometimes line up along Boyer's functional lines (e.g., some kinds of intelligence may predispose a person more for the scholarship of discovery than the scholarship of application), Gardner's proposal suggests that scholars with different intelligences will approach similar tasks in different ways. Thus it is a difference in the kind of intelligence (not degree of intelligence) that naturally directs one scholar to become a qualitative researcher and another to become a quantitative researcher. Similarly, one kind of intelligence may lead a person interested in the study of human beings toward psychology, while a different kind of intelligence may lead another person toward sociology.

While both Boyer's and Gardner's views have been validly criticized, their pluralistic definitions of scholarship have helped advance the conversation. Scholarship can and does take many different forms, and new definitions of scholarship must take that diversity into account. At the very least, Boyer and Gardner disabuse us of the notion that any simple definition of scholarship can apply equally to all disciplines or to all fields of research, analysis, and creative expression.

The recognition that scholarship comes in different forms is not only significant for the academy in a general sense but also has immense significance for the notion of Christian scholarship. In many discussions of Christian scholarship the implicit assumption has been that the same approach should be applied everywhere. Historically this has been especially true of the integration model's presupposition that each and every discipline is ultimately defined by the philosophical worldview that underlies it. Those committed to this approach assume that Christian scholars are supposed to root out the foundational worldviews of their disciplines and then subject those philosophical presuppositions to a comparative analysis with Christian faith. However, worldviews are extremely difficult to unearth in many disciplines, and in some cases the search seems like an exercise in futility. Does chemistry really have that kind of underlying worldview? Is music really defined by a foundational epistemology and metaphysics? Do all historians have worldview axes to grind, or are some historians just detail-oriented, pragmatic folks trying to figure out what happened in the past? Does mathematics entail an entire worldview, or is it simply a gorgeously elaborated mental construction that lets us examine the world in a host of fascinating ways we would not otherwise have at our disposal? The integration model has always seemed a bit forced when applied to many of the disciplines.

If we pushed other models of Christian scholarship in a similar way we would probably find that they, too, do not mix equally well with the various disciplines or foci of academic inquiry. The Lutheran view, for example, stresses the independence of the disciplines, but surely this kind of independence has its limitations, especially when moral issues like cloning, economic injustice, or racism come to the fore. The Anabaptist perspective on scholarship has a different kind of unevenness. Anabaptism's suspicious posture vis-à-vis political power and violence predisposes Anabaptists to engage in practice-oriented scholarship, and the same disposition may well divert Anabaptist academic energy away from the constructive exploration of new fields of research, especially in subject areas where the moral relevance of such study is not immediately evident. The Catholic model, for all its strengths, has not always produced the results one would expect. Its ecclesial emphasis may lead Catholic scholars to simply relegate any specifically Catholic reflection on life and learning to the theologians while they pursue their own nontheological disciplines in a manner identical to all their secular peers. Wesleyans and Pentecostals have their limitations, too. Their commitment to the importance of human experience may well make them less naturally prone to reflect on the significance of Christian faith in disciplines that are more abstract and logical in orientation and less directly connected with human nature. Other traditions could be discussed in similar terms, but the general conclusion would remain the same: no tradition of Christian scholarship possesses strengths that apply equally well to all forms of scholarship.

The focus of this chapter, however, is not primarily on Christian faith but on questions related to scholarship itself in all its many varieties. How can we best define the concept of scholarship? Are there significantly different styles or modes of scholarship? In what ways is our academic work shaped by various personal or interpersonal considerations? Only after we have thought about these questions can we discuss the complex ways that faith and different kinds of scholarship overlap and interact in our lives as academicians and persons of faith.

Scholarship Defined

Given the preceding discussion, it may seem foolhardy to propose our own short definition of scholarship, but the task is unavoidable. What is scholarship in the most general sense of the term? How can scholarship be defined in a way that applies, with some degree of fairness, to all the academic disciplines across the board? The need is for a definition of scholarship that makes as much sense to the scientists as it does to humanities faculty, and that is also attuned to the different kinds of scholarly activities undertaken by colleagues in the more practical and professional disciplines and also in the visual and performance arts. Our proposed definition is: *Scholarship is disciplined and creative reflection on the natural and humanly constructed world disseminated for the benefit of others and judged by appropriate standards of excellence.*

Human beings may be curious and creative by nature, but scholarship involves the honing of those natural skills into disciplined excellence. Scholarship involves effort: thought, practice, creative energy, the risk of failure, and the joy of success. Some of this effort is in a sense preparatory, focusing on the development of necessary skills and the acquisition of necessary knowledge for our chosen fields of interest. But on top of that, scholarship requires the hard work of researching one's projects, carefully developing one's own perspective, and then sharing those new, intelligently crafted insights with others. All of this takes time, and it also requires creativity. Sheer work alone does not make one a scholar; scholarship necessarily mixes sustained effort with creative insight. Take away the hard work and all we have is effluent self-expression; take away the creativity and all that is left is the cataloging or repetition of what others already know.

The point at which such reflection on the world crosses the threshold from competent "school work" to real scholarship is fuzzy, but the distinction is crucial. People who teach at colleges and universities know this well. They have all seen some, but only some, of their students progress from being good assignment completers to being scholarly colleagues. Even after a person has become an accomplished scholar, this distinction continues to apply in the sense that only some of our work takes the form of scholarship. We all know that being a member of the local Republican or Democratic county committee is political work, but it is not political scholarship. Performing Beethoven for a university fundraiser is artistic work, but it would not usually be considered artistic scholarship. Preaching a sermon can be theological work, but sermons are not typically examples of theological scholarship. Scholarship is not merely reflecting on the world in an academic manner, it is disseminating that work in a way that is intended to enrich the academic work of others and invite the critique of one's peers.

The primary task of scholarship is to "pay attention" to the world—or, at least, to some part of the world—with a sense of focus, care, and intensity that nonscholars lack. But it is not simply paying attention that matters. Scholars also reflect on the different ways they pay attention to the world; they are methodologically self-conscious. Attention to the world can mean many things. For some, understanding in and of itself is sufficient. For others—artists, poets, musicians—creative response has to be part of the package. For still others paying attention means intervening, encouraging certain outcomes and discouraging others. All of that is part of scholarship.

No one can pay attention to everything; time does not allow it, and limitations of skill and training prevent it. The division of the academy into various disciplines and other focused fields of study is an admission of that fact. Such a division of labor necessitates that scholarship as a whole will always be communal. Because we cannot pay attention to everything—not even everything in our own specialized areas of expertise—we need to rely on the insights and attentive honesty of others. Therefore even though scholarship is often intensely personal, driven by our own need to understand, influence, or creatively interact with the world, the attention we lavish on the world is also always undertaken in relationship with, and in some sense on behalf of, others. The work of scholarship embeds every scholar in a complex web of social relations: some aspects of that web are generational (e.g., the teacher-student relationship), others are collegial (e.g., relations with scholarly peers and friends), and still others are respectful but confrontational (e.g., scholarly relations with those with whom we disagree). And those relations are all necessary to the work of scholarship. Solipsistic reflection that never allows others to react to our work is not scholarship but merely idiosyncratic musing. True scholarship always aims to enrich, expand, critique, correct, and inspire humanity's public and common store of knowledge, wisdom, and creative genius.

Three Styles of Scholarship

While scholarship can take many different forms, three broad categories cover most of the territory, dividing scholarship along the lines of ideas, actions, and feelings. Analytic styles of scholarship are idea-oriented, seeking to construct mental maps or models of the way reality seems to be put together. Strategic styles of scholarship are action-oriented, hoping to understand the world in order to change it in some way. Finally, empathic styles of scholarship are feeling-oriented, focusing on the need to connect with others and the world in ways that are more subjective and aesthetic.

These three modes or styles of academic reflection are not inimical to each other; in fact, they often blend together. Thus, however empathic artists may be, they sometimes need to be analytic in the way they view their own work and the work of others, and invariably they need to be strategic in the way they execute their aesthetic projects. Physicists are perhaps the most quintessentially analytic of all scholars, but they often have strategic reasons for pursuing one project rather than another, and at times they appeal to blatantly aesthetic norms in order to explain their preference for one theory over another, saying the preferred theory is simpler or more symmetrical or more elegant. Engineers, who are first and foremost strategic thinkers, also frequently employ analytic and empathic/aesthetic modes of thought. Similar things could be said about virtually every field of study. Usually one of the three modes of scholarship predominates, but the other two modes are rarely absent from the mix.

Analytic Scholarship

The goal of analytic scholarship is to dissect reality, dividing it into its component parts and then putting it back together again to see how it works. The item under scrutiny might be the ecosystem of a swamp or the sensuous lines of a sculpture. Analytic scholarship has a role to play in virtually every discipline. We analyze plants and poems, historical events and fossil records, the workings of both finely crafted machines and sloppily run societies. Some analytic scholarship is more linguistic (or qualitative) in character, some is more mathematical (or quantitative), and a good deal of analytic scholarship is a mixture of these two. Nevertheless, the goal remains the same: to develop new cognitive models or maps that explain or explore different parts of reality with depth and finesse. Analytic thinking seeks understanding as an end in itself; nothing necessarily has to be done with that information other than to enjoy its well-crafted explication of some aspect of the world.

Scholarship that centers on analysis tends naturally to distance the scholar from the subjects he or she studies. Because of that, much analytic scholarship feels quite "modern"; it has a certain Enlightenment aura to it. Some would also argue that analytic scholarship is decidedly male in its desire to methodologically pry objective knowledge out of the subjective messiness of the world. Feminist and postmodern theorists have accordingly, and perhaps rightly, criticized analytic scholarship for these traits. But it is important to remember that analytic scholarship can claim a heritage that is much older than the Enlightenment—going back at least as far as Aristotle—and that analytic scholarship at its best has no desire to exercise any kind of patriarchal control over the materials it studies. Certain forms of analytic scholarship may border on being hyperobjectivistic or may seem almost immorally neutral on matters that practically cry out for ethical commentary, but this is not necessarily problematic as long as strategic and empathic modes of scholarship are recognized as necessary complements to analytic thinking. The objectivity of analytic scholarship becomes problematic only when the validity of other modes of thinking is minimized or denied.

Analytic thinking as a distinct mode of scholarship is quite easy to identify, and it is almost surely the most common form of scholarship produced by college and university professors. In fact, when something is "academic" in popular parlance, it usually means it is analytic: an explanation of how things work with no plan or desire to apply that knowledge to any particular problem in the real world. Given the pragmatic orientation of American culture, it is no surprise that this kind of scholarship for its own sake—the analysis of literature, history, human consciousness, rocks, and microbes just to understand those items better—has sometimes been pilloried as close to worthless. The pithy phrase "the paralysis of analysis" sums it up. But academicians know that analytic scholarship is far from worthless. In fact, analytic thinking is to some degree the foundation for all other forms of scholarship. Without the ability to analyze something so that one knows how it works, strategic thinking operates in a void. Similarly, without some ability objectively to analyze shapes, sounds, colors, and relations, the arts would collapse into undisciplined expression. Analysis is and always will be a critical component of virtually all scholarship.

Strategic Scholarship

In contrast to analytic thinking, strategic scholarship focuses on understanding the world in order to reshape it. Strategic scholarship is about redirecting developments, rearranging the way things are put together, and realigning the connections that define the fabric of the world. It is a problem-solving mode of reflection. This is the kind of thinking Karl Marx had in mind when he said the goal of philosophy was not to understand the world but to change it. Strategic thinking is not, however, peculiar only to leftists or socialists. Within the academy, numerous applied or professional programs (e.g., engineering, business, teaching, nursing) make this mode of scholarship central, but all disciplines involve strategic thinking to some degree. Artists need to strategize about which techniques will best help them produce the works of art they have already imagined in their minds, and historians need to be able to place themselves imaginatively in the strategic shoes of the people and movements they study from the past. Every discipline involves strategy in some way, if only in the ways we plan to disseminate what we have discovered or created.

Strategic scholarship is often dependent to some degree on analysis. One needs at least minimal knowledge about how something works before trying to reprogram it. But strategic scholarship is never wholly dependent on analysis; it is not merely the application of analysis to the real world. Strategic scholarship embodies a different way of knowing. It is the difference between knowing why a national economy is in decline and understanding how to fix it. It is the difference between being a foreign policy analyst and making foreign policy. It is the difference between knowing how the AIDS virus works and figuring out how to kill it. It is the difference between most sociological scholarship and most scholarship of social work. The point is that some aspects of the world are almost impossible to understand until one has gained some strategic familiarity with them. Strategic scholarship can be the foundation for analytic scholarship, just as things can work the other way around. One recent example of this is found in Stephen Wolfram's book *A New Kind of Science* (2002), in which he explains how his development of the computer program *Mathematica*—an almost purely strategic scholarly project—slowly let him see many aspects of the world (including biology, sociology, art, and philosophy in addition to mathematics, physics, and computer science) in an entirely new analytic light.[6]

Traditional liberal arts schools have sometimes placed "pure" analytic scholarship on a pedestal and have relegated "applied" or strategic scholarship to a lower rank within the academic pecking order. Conversely, strategic scholars have sometimes caricatured liberal arts people as bumbling, absent-minded, ivory-tower intellectuals who could "never make it in the real world." Both stereotypes are wrong. It is a mistake to pit analytic studies against strategic studies; they are naturally complementary and frequently overlapping modes of reflection. Students need both kinds of skills, the world needs both kinds of thinkers, and the academy ought to honor both kinds of scholarship.

Empathic Scholarship

Analytic and strategic forms of scholarship are both predicated on a certain degree of separation between the scholar and the subject matter the scholar studies. A third mode of scholarship, empathic scholarship, adopts an alternative approach, seeking to narrow the gap between the knower and the known as much as possible. Empathic scholarship rejects the objectivization of the things we study, seeking to think with the subject rather than merely about the subject of inquiry. Empathic scholarship seeks to elicit from the world the answers to questions that already exist in the world rather than prodding the world with foreign questions to see how it might react to new stimuli or how it might be redirected into new patterns of behavior. It aims to understand the aesthetic feel of reality without needing to control it. Empathic scholarship seeks to fold itself into the rhythm of a society or an ecosystem, envelop itself in the mood of a work of art, or soak up the character of another human being.

This is Annie Dillard wonder-at-the-world kind of scholarship, rather than the analytic sociology of Peter Berger or the applied economics of Alan Greenspan. Empathic scholarship agrees with Charles Taylor that "an epistemology which privileges disengagement and control isn't self-evidently right."[7] There are other more subtle, more instinctive ways of knowing that provide us with access to certain aspects of reality that would otherwise be unknowable.

Empathic thinkers can often see or make connections between seemingly disparate and unconnected bits and pieces of reality that others cannot see or make. Poets, artists, and musicians tend to have highly developed skills in this area—in a sense, they have to be empathic to do their work—but the giants in many of the disciplines have incorporated some degree of empathic thinking into their work. The Nobel prize–winning biologist and medical researcher Barbara McClintock, whose biography is aptly entitled *A Feeling for the Organism*, made this notion central to her understanding of science. And it is perhaps not inconsequential that McClintock is a woman. Many feminist scholars have suggested that scholarship as a whole needs to pay more attention to empathy, if for no other reason than to serve as an antidote for the so-called "male" desire to control the object one studies. In the end, however, empathic scholarship is not so much linked to gender as it is to being human. More than any other mode of scholarship, empathic thinking acknowledges our creaturely limitations and our dependence on—indeed our essential embeddedness within—the natural and human environments in which we live. It is attention to the empathic that adds human (and humane) depth to our analytic and strategic reflection on the world.

Some might take our use of the term "empathic" to refer not to a different kind of thinking but to a certain moral quality that might or might not be layered on top of our real scholarship as a nice little something extra. It would be good to be polite while also being smart. Others might think immediately of warm and fuzzy classrooms when they hear the word empathic. In their minds empathic scholarship morphs almost instantaneously into empathetic teaching. Empathy can certainly be a boon in the classroom, but that is not what empathic thinking is about. In our perspective, empathic thinking is a form of serious scholarship that allows one to get at certain aspects of reality that could not be understood in any other way. It is subtle and subjective, to be sure, but vast dimensions of reality are subtle and subjective, and we will miss them entirely if we reject the practice of empathic scholarship. The philosopher Alfred North Whitehead understood this principle well when he wrote in the early twentieth century that "subjective ways of feeling are not merely receptive of the data as alien facts; they clothe the dry bones with the flesh of a real being, emotional, purposive, appreciative."[8] The contemporary philosopher Martha Nussbaum would agree and add one further twist: love is often a necessary element. She says some knowledge simply cannot be gained through methodological coercion. Rather than being the result of intellectual grasping, some knowledge can only come through "intellectual vulnerability and recep-tivity." It can only be received as a gift that transcends the solely intellectual and that requires feeling and commitment to be understood. She calls this "love's knowledge."[9]

But perhaps the best way to demonstrate the power of empathic scholar-ship is to illustrate it in various disciplinary contexts. The companion essay to this chapter written by Susanna Bede Caroselli does just this with regard to the field of art, evaluating what one might be able to glean from an empathic or "instinctive response" to art versus the more analytic or "considered re-sponse" that is typical of the trained art historian. An example in the human sciences is found in the work of the Harvard psychologist Robert Coles. One of Coles's main fields of specialization is the moral development of children. Rather than undertaking various quantitative programs of research, however, Coles simply talks to children and seeks to understand their moral visions of the world as they themselves describe them. And his findings are fascinating. Some kids who ought to become paragons of morality end up as troubled adults, while others who have grown up in dysfunctional families and disin-tegrating communities turn out to be saints. No clear, normal, or normative pattern of development emerges. Coles's response is not to reject the value of analytic scholarship but to temper its claims in the light of empathic knowl-edge. He says the role of empathic insight is that it "nudges theory toward human experience, hoping that the latter brings the former to life, and the former helps arrive at a persistent, comprehensible aspect of the human scene."[10] Empathic scholarship rarely if ever exists in pure form—it is almost always mixed with analytic or strategic ways of thinking—but even a little seasoning of empathic thinking can radically alter the tone and flavor of schol-arship in almost any discipline.

Morals, Manners, Motivation, and Vocation

In addition to describing the different kinds of scholarship that exist, it is necessary to also say something about the different ways people embody their work as scholars. Scholarship is not simply a mechanical process; it is under-taken by flesh-and-blood, thinking, feeling, active human beings. Scholarship is also inherently interpersonal; it does not take place in a social vacuum. When scholars do their work they are thus compelled, at least from time to time, to stop and ask themselves what they are doing and why. What moral limits do they or should they put on their work? How do they or how should they interact with other scholars within their own discipline or in other fields of study? What motivates them to pour themselves into the time-consuming and often difficult work of scholarship? What does it mean to understand one's life and work as an expression of scholarly vocation or calling?

With regard to morals, almost all the disciplines have developed specific norms and restrictions that set ethical bounds on scholarship. Some of these guidelines focus on the process of scholarly research (e.g., research protocols); others focus on the final scholarly product (e.g., plagiarism). Less precisely developed ethical norms relate to the dissemination of scholarship, with questions usually focusing on the moral impact that scholarship may have on those influenced by it. The classic example along these lines is the way in which the scholarly examination of the atom led to the development of nuclear weapons technology, but there are moral ramifications to the work we do as scholars in virtually every area of study ranging from art and literature to political theory and engineering.

The ethical codes and moral discussions of the academic disciplines have a major impact on the kind of scholarship that is produced, and the individual scholar's own sense of right and wrong also is deeply influential. This is especially evident in applied scholarship such as medicine. For example, we know a medical researcher in Zambia, where malaria is a massive health problem, who as a matter of moral principle will not test any antimalaria drugs on the Zambian people that they themselves will never be able to afford. Given that Zambia currently spends only six dollars per person per year on health care, this researcher obviously declines to test a number of potentially effective but expensive drugs. Perhaps those drugs would help some Zambians, but he still believes it would be immoral to use the poor villagers around his clinic as guinea pigs to test drugs that will never be available to them. Whether one agrees or disagrees with this particular scholar's sense of research ethics, the principle remains: virtually all scholars place some moral limits or moral requirements on their work. Scholarship is not a value-free enterprise.

The notion of scholarly manners points in a somewhat different direction. Scholarship is a social endeavor—everyone is dependent on each other's work—and because of that the ways scholars treat each other is of significant concern. If the best way to advance thinking on any given subject is through intelligent discussion and argument with others, then scholarship ought to be framed in ways that open dialogue rather than foreclose conversation. Clearly some degree of humility is involved in the practice of good scholarly etiquette, as it requires an acknowledgment that one might learn something from somebody else. But this is not a recipe for mere relativism; it does not require accepting every scholarly opinion. The scholar can remain resolutely convinced of one perspective, even while respecting the differing perspectives of other well-intentioned, intelligent people. Of course, this does not always happen. The theologian and church historian Martin Marty was fond of remarking to his students at the University of Chicago that one of the most important distinctions in the world of scholarship was between people who were mean and those who were not mean—between those who seemed to enjoy tearing their peers apart in person or in print and those scholars who always respected their peers as human beings even when they vehemently disagreed with their views.

In almost any discipline, some people can be found who are truly kind and caring, while others in that field (usually only a few) are mean and nasty. A relevant question is to ask whether faith has any influence on this aspect of scholarship, and the honest if unfortunate answer seems to be that faith has a mixed record. For some scholars, faith prompts modesty in the ways they compose and present their scholarship. For others, faith seems to be the catalyst that turns simple human confidence into mean-spirited arrogance. It is not the certitude of faith that is the problem; cocky confidence is part and parcel of the scholarly world. The problem is when religious certitude (or any other kind of certitude) leads a scholar to discount the humanity of a colleague or to launch a scorched-earth offensive against some viewpoint in a manner intended to destroy both that viewpoint and all who hold it. To be sure, secular ideologies can produce this same kind of meanness, but that does not make religiously motivated nasty academic behavior any less reprehensible. While Christian scholars search to describe how faith can have a positive influence on scholarship, the flip side must never be forgotten: faith can sometimes have a decidedly negative influence on scholarship. Christian scholars need to remember that fact and always be on their guard to keep those negative influences to a minimum. The academy functions best when scholars, regardless of their fields of study and regardless of their commitments of faith or ideology, treat each other with respect.

Motivation is another dimension of any scholar's work. Scholarship requires dedication, effort, and perseverance. One does not decide to become a scholar without some clear motivation to do so. Scholarship also involves personal risk. Every act of scholarship puts the fragile human ego of the scholar— and all human egos are frail to some degree—on the line. Every scholarly undertaking exposes the ego of the scholar to potential bruising. Even the most mature scholars feel some twinge of fear when they release a new work.

Because scholarship is such hard work and so risky, only some college and university faculty take up the challenge. Recent studies have shown that a significant number of college and university professors—around 25 percent— have never published a peer-reviewed essay, book chapter, or monograph.[11] The latest national survey found that 41 percent of full-time faculty had not published a single article in the previous three years and that 54 percent had not authored or edited a scholarly book or research report in that same time period. More than a quarter of full-time faculty reported that they were not currently engaged in any scholarly work that would lead to a publication, exhibit, or performance.[12] While this data is only a rough measure of scholarly activity, these statistics are still revelatory. The work of scholarship demands significant amounts of time and energy, and only some academicians are willing to do it.

To a certain degree this is a simple matter of priorities—we can only do so much in a twenty-four-hour day—but that is not the only factor. The greater hindrance to scholarship may be fear of failure.

Fear of failure can be mitigated to some degree if a scholar is motivated by an explicit sense of vocation. To have a vocation is to live one's life in terms of a calling that is bigger than oneself. It is to view one's life in terms of an overall trajectory (rather than as a series of separate and distinct successes or failures) aimed at goals that transcend any one person's ability ever to achieve them all. One can have a vocation to work for justice, or to produce beauty, or to help those who are in trouble, or to preserve the environment, or to advance human knowledge, or to affect the world for good in any number of other ways. What makes something a vocation is not the specific activity but the way in which that activity is both understood in larger context and carried out in actual practice. Vocation is scholarship embodied in the form of commitment to higher ideals and service to others. The psychologist James Fowler has suggested that having a sense of vocation affects people in several ways.[13] First, it can exempt them from competition with others because they know they are working toward goals they cannot achieve on their own. Cooperation with others is what is required, not competition. Second, it can protect them, at least to some degree, from fear of personal failure because they recognize that the goals they are pursuing are much more important than their mere egos. Third, a sense of vocation can free them from the need to be all things to all people. They know what they are called to do. Finally, having a vocation can liberate them from the tyranny of time since it provides a means of prioritizing their various duties and responsibilities.[14]

Fowler derives his notion of vocation from the realm of faith, but a similar sense of calling can be found in other less religious sources. In this regard, the recently published *Good Work: When Excellence and Ethics Meet* can serve as a model. The authors of this book define good work as skilled activity undertaken in a thoughtful, responsible, and creative manner with the aim of serving social needs (broadly defined), providing personal fulfillment, and somehow making the world a better place. They recognize, perhaps more than many people who write about vocation, that this kind of confluence of ideals is predicated on a range of factors outside any one person's control. Good work never happens naturally, but its chances of flourishing are much greater when the ideals of the individual, the norms of his or her profession, the values of society, and the economic structures that support his or her field of work are all in alignment. But even where that kind of alignment does not exist, individuals can still transform their activity from mere work into good work by locating what they do in a larger moral and meaningful vision of life. The authors argue that "rich lives include continuing internal conversations about who we are, what we want to achieve, where we are successful, and where we are falling short." These internal conversations are to be undertaken in light of what they call "the universal mirror test: 'What would it be like to live in a world if everyone were to behave in the way that I have?' "[15]

Wherever and however this broader view of life as vocation can be brought to bear on our work as scholars, the better our work will be. It will also inevitably make our scholarship more faith-full, whether that fullness of faith is understood in traditional religious terms or as a deep-seated commitment to some other set of values and ideals. Faith, embodied in the motivation of our scholarship and carried out in a manner that respects others, can transform the scholarly task from a mere career path into a lifelong vocation.[16] Vocations of scholarship can and will take different forms: to seek truth and share it with others, to understand the world and nurture it with care, to cultivate a proper sense of wonder and awe at the beauty and complexity of all that is. Christians participate alongside others in all of these modes of scholarly calling, adding their particular values and views to the mix, helping to maximize the academy's overall "surplus of seeing," and hoping to gain new insights for themselves while sharing their points of view with others for their further consideration. The dynamics of the process are not predictable, but the pattern of lively exchange—this cauldron of passionately pursued academic good work—defines the terrain on which both Christian scholars and other scholars live out the sometimes conflicting and sometimes congruent trajectories of their overlapping scholarly vocations.

NOTES

1. C. P. Snow, *The Two Cultures and the Scientific Revolution* (New York: Cambridge University Press, 1959).

2. Ernest L. Boyer, *Scholarship Reconsidered: Priorities of the Professoriate* (Princeton: Carnegie Foundation for the Advancement of Teaching, 1990).

3. On this point see also Jaroslav Pelikan, *The Idea of the University: A Reexamination* (New Haven: Yale University Press, 1992). Pelikan affirms Boyer's definition and especially the value Boyer assigns to undergraduate teaching as a form of scholarship. Pelikan says that it is the scholar's obligation not merely to discover new bits of truth about the world but to draw connections and contrasts and to locate one's work in the broader context and currents of academic discourse. Because that is also precisely what is required in good teaching, Pelikan concludes: "The professor comes to [the] obligation of the scholar far better prepared after having first taken [those tasks] on as an undergraduate teacher" (95).

4. See Howard Gardner, *Frames of Mind: The Theory of Multiple Intelligences* (New York: Basic Books, 1983), and *Multiple Intelligences: The Theory in Practice* (New York: Basic Books, 1993).

5. Howard Gardner, *Intelligence Reframed: Multiple Intelligences for the 21st Century* (New York: Basic Books, 1999), 48, 60. About existential intelligence, in particular, Gardner says: "Despite the attractiveness of a ninth intelligence . . . I am not adding existential intelligence to the list. I find the phenomenon perplexing enough and the

distance from the other intelligences vast enough to dictate prudence—at least for now. At most, I am willing, Fellini-style, to joke about '8^1/$_2$ intelligences' " (66).

6. Stephen Wolfram, *A New Kind of Science* (Champaign, Ill.: Wolfram Media, 2002).

7. Charles Taylor, *Sources of the Self: The Making of the Modern Identity* (Cambridge, Mass.: Harvard University Press, 1989), 164.

8. Alfred North Whitehead, *Process and Reality: An Essay in Cosmology* (New York: Free Press, 1957). 103.

9. Martha C. Nussbaum, *Love's Knowledge: Essays on Philosophy and Literature* (New York: Oxford University Press, 1990), 283. We are largely following Craig Dykstra's interpretation of Nussbaum's views as he explicates them in *Growing in the Life of Faith: Education and Christian Practices* (Louisville, Ky.: Geneva Press, 1999). See especially chapter 10, "Love's Knowledge and Theological Education," 141–42.

10. Robert Coles, *The Moral Life of Children* (Boston: Atlantic Monthly Press, 1986), p. 126.

11. Boyer, *Scholarship Reconsidered*, table A-19, 103.

12. 1997 National Survey of Full-Time Faculty conducted by the Carnegie Foundation for the Advancement of Teaching. Unpublished data obtained via e-mail (July 3, 2002) from Alexander C. McCormick of the Carnegie Foundation for the Advancement of Teaching.

13. James W. Fowler, *Becoming Adult, Becoming Christian: Adult Development and Christian Faith* (San Francisco: Jossey-Bass, 2000), 83–85.

14. The Jesuit scholar John C. Haughey would agree with Fowler but use slightly different language. Instead of using the language of vocation, he speaks of scholarship done from what Bernard Lonergan called "the font of interiority." Haughey writes: "Research chosen from the font of interiority takes seriously the measure of oneself, one's call, idiosyncrasies, interests, talents, and experiences. By contrast, theory is where the discipline itself is at any given time. If theory *solo* dictates research choices, one could be on the way to gaining the whole world (of comprehension, inclusion, recognition, status) and suffering the loss of oneself." John C. Haughey, "Catholic Higher Education: A Strategy for Its Identity," in *Enhancing Religious Identity: Best Practices from Catholic Campuses*, edited by John Wilcox and Irene King (Washington, D.C.: Georgetown University Press, 2000), 160.

15. Howard Gardner, Mihaly Csikszentmihalyi, and William Damon, *Good Work: When Excellence and Ethics Meet* (New York: Basic Books, 2001), 11–12.

16. For an insightful analysis of the vocation of scholarship and teaching see Mark R. Schwehn, *Exiles from Eden: Religion and the Academic Vocation in America* (New York: Oxford University Press, 1993).

Instinctive Response as a Tool for the Scholar

Susanna Bede Caroselli

This essay examines how two different styles of scholarship can be used in a complementary manner to enhance insight and understanding. The disciplinary focus of Susanna Caroselli's essay is the visual arts, and the two styles of scholarship are the "considered response" (corresponding roughly to the "analytic" as described in the preceding chapter) and the "instinctive response" (which corresponds to the "empathic"). The specific work of art that is discussed is the fifteenth-century painting Christ on the Cross with Saints Vincent Ferrer, John the Baptist, Mark, and Antoninus. *Caroselli demonstrates how faith blends naturally into our scholarship through our instinctive responses to what we study, even if we sometimes seek to deny that instinctive element.*

In her book *Image as Insight* the historical theologian Margaret Miles laments that the meaning(s) of a visual image for its creator[1] and its original audience can never be fully recovered.[2] Even supposing the existence of a written record or other documentation of the creation of the image, scholars are bound, as is frequently observed, to filter such evidence through their chosen critical structure and their culturally conditioned perception.

The precise reconstruction of original meaning is unlikely—and, indeed, how could we know if we were successful? Certain bodies of contemporary critical thought maintain that the very concept of "original meaning" is spurious and bankrupt, but even those who posit the death of the author/artist cannot deny the expression of a culture.[3] Image has immediate impact. Even visual images intended by their creators to have primarily intellectual appeal—the late fifteenth-century Neoplatonic arcana of Marsilio Ficino interpreted by Sandro Botticelli in *The Birth of Venus* and the *Primavera*, for example, or the cerebral seventeenth-century "modes" of the *peintre-philosophe* Nicolas Poussin—were intended first to delight the eye and the heart. Why then have scholars largely abandoned the means through which the impact of an image was chiefly conveyed? Is there nothing to be gained by allowing an image to address us as it would have addressed its original viewers: personally, emotionally, psychologically, viscerally, spiritually—call it what you will?

In the last decade there has been some excellent scholarship in the field of art history, especially with the discipline's absorption of reception theory, which acknowledges an interest in the identification and experience of the original, ideal, or present viewer.[4] There has been little or no suggestion, however, that art historians themselves might engage their own instinctive response as a scholarly tool. The academy has long been suspicious of such nonintellectual (read "antiintellectual") activity: approaches that suggest an emotional connection to the subject of scholarly work are often perceived as polluting the crystal stream of intellectual discourse.

Some contemporary scholars have noted and lamented this "psychic distance"[5] between scholars and their objects of study, but they limit themselves to the observation of this phenomenon and not to its alteration. Others advise the acknowledgment and employment of instinctive response. Nelson Goodman, writing of "the domineering dichotomy between the cognitive and the emotive," says:

> The work of art is apprehended through the feelings as well as through the senses. Emotional numbness disables here as definitely if not as completely as blindness or deafness. . . . I am not resting anything on the distinction between emotion and other elements of knowing, but rather insisting that *emotion belongs with them*. . . . In aesthetic experience, emotion positive or negative is a mode of sensitivity to a work.[6]

David Freedberg ends his book *The Power of Images* with the following plea:

> All I claim is the need to integrate the experience of reality into our experience of imagery in general, and into the terms of critical discourse about imagery and about art. If we do not do so, we lapse into the categorical preconceptions and the ideological narrowness against which this book has set itself.[7]

An ally appears in Roland Barthes, who points out that in order to see a photograph in depth, he consents "to combine two voices: the voice of banality (to say what everyone sees and knows) and the voice of singularity (to replenish such banality with all the élan of an emotion that belongs only to myself)."[8]

From this advocacy of the incorporation of instinctive response, we should proceed to examples of art historians who have done so. But there are few who will admit to personal reactions, far fewer to employing them as part of their scholarly approach.

One of the most striking examples of instinctive response is provided by Leo Steinberg as he discusses the art of Jasper Johns. He engages, not with his usual intellectual intensity and assurance, but with the confusion of his "own first reaction":

> I disliked the show, and would gladly have thought it a bore. Yet it
> depressed me and I wasn't sure why. . . . I was angry at the artist, as
> if he had invited me to a meal, only to serve something uneatable,
> like tow and paraffin. I was irritated at some of my friends for pre-
> tending to like it—but with an uneasy suspicion that perhaps they
> did like it, so that I was really mad at myself for being so dull, and
> at the whole situation for showing me up.[9]

In the following pages Steinberg works through his hostility, forcing himself to confront his feelings about these works over and over again, and as he does he provides one of the most moving and at the same time trenchant assess- ments of the work of any modern artist, reaching conclusions that no art his- torian or critic could have attained without the honest examination of a per- sonal response. Even his conclusions continue to emphasize the depth of his engagement:

> In the end, these pictures by Jasper Johns came to impress me as a
> dead city might—but a dead city of terrible familiarity. Only some
> objects are left—man-made signs which, in the absence of men,
> have become objects. And Johns has anticipated their dereliction. . . .
> I am left in a state of anxious uncertainty by the painting, about
> painting, about myself.[10]

I do not advocate that scholars utilize instinctive response as an alternative to intellectual engagement (considered response) but that they both acknowledge and employ it to lead to a richer understanding of the work being studied. To be sure, a scholar's instinctive response is usually freighted with considerable intellectual baggage, but, once acknowledged, the accretion may well enhance the instinctive response and increase its scholarly value. The reaction of a present viewer grounded in Renaissance history and Neoplatonic philosophy to Botticelli's *Birth of Venus* will arguably be more conducive to the reconstruc- tion of perception than the reaction of a casual viewer.

What has this to do with Christian scholarship? If instinctive response is not unique to the contemporary Christian scholar, then it should be more natural and less suspect. We ought not to be afraid of spiritual and emotional engagement. We accept that there are different ways of knowing and that knowledge comes through the soul and the heart as well as through the mind. We are even comfortable with *not* knowing—we call it mystery. No matter how we define and practice Christian scholarship, we have the qualifications to investigate the results of combining more traditional scholarship with the insights of our instinctive engagement. We thus have the opportunity to demonstrate that such a melding of scholarly styles may produce a richer result. We have the challenge, perhaps even the obligation, to advocate the use of instinctive response as a scholarly tool for all scholars, in all fields.

Instinctive Response to Art in Christian Contexts

There is a great deal of evidence for the engagement of instinctive response throughout the history of Christian art. Most Greeks and Romans who became Christians were already conditioned by *ekphrasis*, a literary genre devoted to the description of works of art, not only to re-create visual form for the readers but also to communicate to them the sensation of viewing the work, even to the point of attempting a literary reconstruction of the artistic style for greater effect and affect. In the words of Hermogenes of Tarsus:

> Ekphrasis is an account with detail; it is visible, so to speak, and brings before the eyes that which is to be shown. . . . The special virtues of ekphrasis are clarity and visibility; the style must contrive to bring about seeing through hearing. However, it is equally important that expression should fit the subject: if the subject is florid, let the style be florid too, and if the subject is dry, let the style be the same.[11]

In *ekphrasis*, art was most often praised for its ability to move and astonish—to cause an instinctive response to imagery. These responses may, in fact, explain the early Christian appropriation of pagan imagery considered inspiring or reassuring, such as the Good Shepherd or the powerful Zeus/Jupiter figure transformed into God the Father.[12] Indeed, despite periodic outbreaks of iconoclasm, particularly in the East, Christianity has a long history of encouraging instinctive response to religious art, not only in the unlettered and uneducated but also in the great scholars of the faith, who themselves advocated and celebrated personally engaged response, fully admitting the value of images for their power to move and to encourage devotion. The fourth-century Bishop Evodius of Uzala in North Africa described his experiential sequence before a work of religious art as "astonishment . . . love, admiration, and gratitude."[13] Two prelates from Asia Minor illustrate such response: Bishop Gregory of Nyssa (d. c. 395) reported that he could not walk by a painting of the Sacrifice of Isaac "without shedding tears, so clearly did art present the story to one's eyes,"[14] and Asterius, bishop of Amaseia (d. c. 410), usually assumed to be an iconophobe for his denunciation of Christian images on articles of clothing, confessed to delight in looking at a painting when he was weary of studying philosophy. He described minutely a depiction of the martyrdom of Saint Euphemia, concluding: "But now tears come to my eyes and sadness interrupts my speech: for the artist has so clearly painted the drops of blood that you might think them to be trickling down in very truth from her lips, and so you might depart weeping."[15]

The medieval and early modern periods in the West offer many examples of both sacred and secular art and architecture whose form and content evoked intense personal response regardless of the degree of literacy or intellectual accomplishment of the viewer. Surely one of the most cited observers is Abbot Suger (1081–1151) of Saint-Denis, whose minute descriptions of his architec-tural and decorative projects at the venerable abbey church convey an infectious enthusiasm and assurance that, through his "delight in the beauty of the house of God," he could be "transported from this inferior to that higher world in an anagogical manner."[16] That an instinctive response might be negative rather than positive is demonstrated by Suger's contemporary, Bernard of Clairvaux (1091–1153), whose anger at what he considered the idolatry encouraged by the rich decoration of churches and at the distraction fostered by the imaginative sculpture in monastic cloisters suggests that his own response to such stimuli was uncomfortably strong.[17]

Many of the great Christian mystics continued the tradition of *ekphrasis* by describing their visions and their ensuing emotions in such detail that their readers were moved to see and to respond in kind. Visions of the Nativity and Crucifixion described by Bridget of Sweden (1303–1373) were so affecting that they transformed those scenes in European art, altering the traditional iconog-raphy that had originated in the Christian East.[18] In the age of the Reforma-tions, when both Catholic and Protestant authorities understood and exploited instinctive response to imagery, one of the most influential voices was Ignatius of Loyola (1491–1556), who recommended in his *Spiritual Exercises* the use of all five senses to heighten this response. Most eloquent is his meditation on hell, in which he guides the instinctive response of the devout in a vivid image so that they might experience the "deep sense of the pain which the lost suffer." He writes:

This will be to see in imagination the vast fires, and the souls en-closed, as it were, in bodies of fire. . . . To hear the wailing, the howl-ing, cries, and blasphemies against Christ our Lord and against His saints. . . . With the sense of smell to perceive the smoke, the sul-phur, the filth, and corruption. . . . To taste the bitterness of tears, sadness, and remorse of conscience. . . . With the sense of touch to feel the flames which envelop and burn the souls.[19]

At this time, however, we also encounter an incipient distrust of instinctive response. While the prolific Florentine architect, painter, sculptor, and theoretician Leonbattista Alberti (1404–1472) wrote in his treatise on painting that a well-produced image should affect its viewers ("it will capture the eye of whatever *learned or unlearned person* is looking at it and will move his soul. . . . we weep with the weeping, laugh with the laughing, and grieve with the grieving"),[20] other humanist scholars were pulling back from this type of personal engagement to a position of intellectual hauteur that has continued to the present day.

Our academic training is partly to blame, since in most fields it has stressed immediate intellectual engagement before all else. In fact, most people who would characterize themselves as educated or cultured, academics or not, quickly suppress a purely instinctive (the so-called "gut") reaction in order to engage intellectually with what they encounter, as if the emotional and physical impact of a visual image were a less important, inferior, or even embarrassing manifestation.[21] But it is this very instinctive reaction that connects us to the original viewer(s) of the image, providing us with a precious opportunity to perceive the image as it was first received. As David Freedberg has said,

> however much we intellectualize, even if that motion is spontaneous, there still remains a basic level of reaction that cuts across historical, social, and other contextual boundaries. It is precisely at this level—which pertains to our psychological, biological, and neurological status as members of the same species—that our cognition of images is allied with that of all men and women.[22]

Considered and Instinctive Readings of a Renaissance Altarpiece

If the use of instinctive response as a scholarly tool is to be encouraged, the advocate must be able to demonstrate that its employment enhances the results that can be obtained purely by considered response, in this case, to a work of art.

Straightforward art historical examination yields much information about a work's form, content, and context. The figure shows the altarpiece that will serve as an example, *Christ on the Cross with Saints Vincent Ferrer, John the Baptist, Mark, and Antoninus.*[23] It was commissioned by the silk weavers' guild of the city of Florence to be placed on their altar in the monastery church of San Marco in the late fifteenth century.[24] Judging by the style of the unsigned panel, it should be dated around 1490–95 and is probably the work of Gherardo di Giovanni del Fora (1445–1497), a skilled miniaturist who also executed large paintings and who was known to have worked with his brother for the Dominican community of San Marco.[25]

Master of the Fiesole, *Epiphany, Christ on the Cross with Saints Vincent Ferrer, John the Baptist, Mark, and Antoninus*, c. 1491/95. Los Angeles County Museum of Art, Gift of the Ahmanson Foundation (M.91.242). Photograph ©2003 Museum Associates/ LACMA.

The image is not a depiction of the Crucifixion: Christ seems to hover in front of the cross with outspread arms, wearing a jeweled purple robe and an imperial crown. On each side of the cross are kneeling figures who may be identified by their appearance and attributes: on Christ's right is the patron saint of Florence, John the Baptist, recognizable from his unkempt hair, camel-skin tunic, red robe of martyrdom, reed cross, and a scroll bearing the words "Ecce agnus dei ecce qui . . ." (John 1:29: "Behold the Lamb of God, behold [him] who . . ."). On Christ's left is Mark the Evangelist, patron saint of the church of San Marco, identifiable from his act of writing in an open codex and from the lion glaring from behind his right leg.[26]

The form and presence of these three figures are easily explained. The inclusion of the patron saints of the city and the church for which the painting was intended was very common in European altarpieces from the thirteenth century onward.[27] As for the unusual representation of Christ as a regally dressed figure oddly balanced on a chalice, he is shown in the form of a famous acheiropoietic image known as the *Volto Santo* ("holy face"), a wooden statue believed to have been carved by the Pharisee Nicodemus with divine assistance.[28] The *Volto Santo* was particularly precious to the silk weavers of Florence because it was kept in the cathedral of the nearby city of Lucca, the guild's original home. Their devotion to the statue is suggested by the name of their guild confraternity, the Compagnia della Santa Croce (Company of the Holy Cross).[29]

The painting depicts the *Volto Santo* as it would have been (and still is) dressed for special feast days in jewels and silk garments (no doubt donated by the guild). The presence and placement of the chalice are additional evidence: in manuscripts, paintings, and drawings of the fourteenth through sixteenth centuries the *Volto Santo* is always depicted with a chalice immediately beneath its right foot, ostensibly to secure a golden shoe that kept falling off (a legend tells of the statue dropping the shoe into the lap of poor supplicants) but more probably to refer to the flow of blood and water from the spear wound in the side of the crucified Christ.[30]

There exists in the collection of the Galleria degli Uffizi, Florence, a highly finished drawing for the framed altarpiece depicting only the three central figures,[31] which is probably the formal presentation sketch that accompanied the silk guild's first proposal for the altarpiece, for no image could be put into a church without the approval, if not the more active participation, of the church's authorities.[32]

The two additional figures in the altarpiece may be identified by their monastic dress and attributes as relatively recently deceased Dominicans, the celebrated preacher Saint Vincent Ferrer (1350–1419), to the viewer's left, and the Blessed (later Saint) Antoninus Pierozzi (1389–1459), former archbishop of Florence and prior of the monastery of San Marco.[33] Vincent may be identified by the open book displaying a truncation of Revelation 14:7 ("fear God, for the hour of his judgment is come") and an image of the Christ of the Last Judgment, reflecting Vincent's favorite admonitory sermon topic. Antoninus, a much-loved local figure, wears the white pallium of an archbishop. His face would have been recognizable, either from life (he died within the memory of some of those who would have first seen this altarpiece) or from his death mask, from which the artist probably worked.

These men had no significance for the silk weavers' guild, so their presence in the painting cannot be explained if we do not look beyond the guild's commission. It is most probable that the Dominicans of San Marco took an active role in the content of the altarpiece by stipulating the addition to the panel of two of the most revered figures of their order.

An art historian could certainly stop at this point, having creditably identified the major elements and characteristics of the altarpiece. An art historian with a deeper interest in theology would go further, exploring the transformation of the painting, by the addition of the monks, from a typical guild altarpiece of purely local significance into a powerful didactic image incorporating the expression of political corporate identity, Dominican spirituality, and a visual exegesis of the Sacrament of Penance, all without recourse to instinctive response.

Normally, instinctive response would happen behind the scenes, in the way scholars initially confront a work of art and in the way the product of that confrontation determines the questions asked and the routes taken to answer those questions. To demonstrate the usefulness of instinctive response in this case, however, I publicly present my own response to this work,[34] since it prompted my further progress.

There is literally an "attractive" quality to the figure of Christ. With his open, benign expression,[35] his direct gaze, and his extended arms, which seem an invitation to an embrace, he encourages me to draw near. I am puzzled, however, by several things: Christ's rich clothes, the vanishing shaft of the ornamental cross, the chalice nestled in a tiny bank of clouds, and the aureole of multiwinged angels.[36] These argue for a visionary rather than narrative character and create a barrier between my world and his, keeping me from his presence.

I notice that someone else is looking at me far more intently, the monk at the far left, who holds up a book so clearly lettered that I am obviously meant to read it. It speaks of fear and judgment, and the accompanying image of Christ as final judge, borne up by trumpeting angels, is clear enough: I am being warned that some action on my part is needful in order to experience Christ's embrace, otherwise I will be kept away for eternity. I recognize John the Baptist next to the monk, gesturing toward Christ, and I am reminded of his message of repentance. I instinctively understand that when I have repented I will be welcomed by Christ—on this earth, in the form of the Sacrament represented by the chalice under his foot and, in the age to come, face to face.

In order to test the legitimacy of this reading generated by instinctive response, we must try to recapture by means of considered response how the altarpiece would have been read at the end of the fifteenth century by the citizens of Florence.

The altar of the silk weavers' guild in the church of San Marco was well situated for conveying a message, since it was located on a low transverse wall built across the nave, where it would be on prominent view to everyone who entered by the main portals.[37] During the long sermons that were a tradition in Dominican churches, this part of the nave was reserved for women and children, who were assumed by their culture to be less literate than men and therefore more in need of clear visual imagery.[38]

Our reconstruction of the original reading is vastly aided by a practice employed by artists of late medieval and Renaissance Europe, particularly in Italy. They relied on *festaiuoli*—figures who attract our attention by glance or gesture, point us in the appropriate direction, and indicate how we should respond or behave. The concept of the *festaiuolo* was taken by artists from the Italian theatrical and celebratory conventions. On stage, he or she was usually a secondary character who served as an intermediary between the audience and the main action, explaining, commenting, and modeling the appropriate reaction or response.[39] The meaning of the word itself, literally "feast-maker," suggests the role of master or mistress of ceremonies, who would perform introductions and direct guests, and so the *festaiuolo* functioned in a work of art.

In his treatise on painting, Alberti provided an excellent job description of the *festaiuolo*: "I like to see someone who admonishes and points out to us what is happening there; or beckons with his hand to see; or menaces with an angry face and flashing eyes, so that no one should come near; or shows some danger or marvelous thing there; or invites us to weep or laugh together with them."[40]

In a work of art, the *festaiuolo* usually establishes eye contact with us and, with an expression, gesture, or prop, encourages our gaze to move on to what is most important. The direct gaze was a far more active connection than it is in the modern world: in various ancient theories of vision, there was assumed to be a physical connection between the beholder and the beheld, involving an exchange of some kind. In the altarpiece, therefore, the direct gazes of Christ and Vincent Ferrer were not just devices to gain the viewers' attention but were meant to communicate something of substance. The face of Christ, radiating love, was meant to attract, but the main character is never the *festaiuolo*. So it is the gaze of Vincent Ferrer and the gesture of Antoninus that are our guides.

The inclusion of Dominican monks is not unusual in an altarpiece destined for a Dominican church, but the monks most often depicted are Dominic himself, the theologian Thomas Aquinas, and the inquisitor Peter Martyr. Therefore the appearance of the rarely depicted Vincent Ferrer communicated a specific message, emphasized by the actual message displayed in his book. A gifted preacher, particularly revered in northern Italy, Vincent chose as the topic of his fiery sermons the Last Judgment and the need for repentance, and he identified himself to many as the Angel of the Revelation (Revelation 10:1–7).

Vincent's counterpart, born Antonio Pierozzi, was well known for three influential works on the Sacrament of Penance: *Curam illius habe* (1472) and *Defecerunt* (1473), two manuals for priests, and *Omnium mortalium cura* (1475), a guide to penance for the laity. These three were often bound together as the *Confessionale*, one of the earliest printed books, which appeared in more than one hundred Latin or Italian editions in thirty-two cities before 1501, and his work was cited by many other authors.[41] In this context, the curious gesture of his right hand, with its slightly curled fingers, at his breast, may be read as the "mea culpa" ("through my own fault . . ."), a gesture made three times in the corporate confession of sin in the Mass.

The figures of John the Baptist and Mark the Evangelist now take on another layer of meaning beyond their patronage of city and church: the continuing call to repentance by John the Baptist and the emphasis on John's ministry that begins the Gospel of Mark, with the voice of the Forerunner crying in the wilderness.

Penitence is at the very core of Dominican spirituality and was the chief concern of the prior of the monastery of San Marco in the 1490s, the man whose permission was necessary for the altarpiece to be installed in the church, who would have dictated the iconography, and who would have demanded changes and additions: the reformer Girolamo Savonarola. The ultimate message of the altarpiece is the same as that of many of Savonarola's sermons: that Christ waits to embrace us, but we must approach him in as pure a state as possible.[42] For the Church this meant that in order to be united with Christ in the Eucharist, the Christian must prepare by confession, absolution, and atonement—the process of the sacrament of penance. And there stood this altar, in a prominent location in a prominent church, to communicate this message to the laity of Florence, to instruct them in the proper attention to be given to a holy sacrament for the salvation of their souls.

Thus, it may be argued that considered and instinctive response to the altarpiece meld successfully. And the clarity with which its message was conveyed in its time, when the figures and their significance(s) were easily identifiable, is proven by the clarity with which it may still be read by those who no longer recognize the individual players.[43]

Conclusion

A general conclusion about the didactic, penitential nature of this image might be reached through disinterested scholarship (considered response); it is also accessible through instinctive response alone. But a synthesis of the two approaches yields a richer and more resonant result, and one that allows the scholar to comprehend better, if not experience, the intended effect of this image on its original viewers in the church of San Marco in 1495. By knowing its placement in the church, we know who was meant to read it. By identifying the figures and experiencing the work for ourselves, we know what they were meant to read. One approach reinforces and builds on the other—at a certain point they merge into an inseparable methodological process. The considered response has confirmed the instinctive response and has enriched it with factual and explanatory material. At the same time, the instinctive response has aided in making connections where facts were missing and choices were many.

Reading an image through instinctive response is not limited to Christians even if the image is Christian in its iconography. Any scholar willing to engage personally will respond more deeply and fully and will thus come that much closer to the minds and hearts of those who have gone before. It can only enrich the art-historical mix, and its potential in other scholarly fields is waiting to be explored.

It is legitimate to mention a negative aspect to this: will scholars unconsciously use instinctive response to force the reading they personally advocate, when considered response presents contradictory findings? The answer to that is: they already do. I think it unlikely that there exists any scholar who does not experience instinctive response, no matter how quickly it is suppressed or transformed into intellectual engagement. The damage is done when we do not know or acknowledge that our instinctive response is operating under layers of "rational" processes. This is another reason why I encourage the recognition, utilization, and even celebration of it in scholarship, so that we can be aware of our personal agendas, inclinations, and biases and hold ourselves and each other accountable for the honesty we owe to the academy and, more, to the glory of God.

NOTES

1. Within the concept of "creator" I include the patron or commissioner of the work of art, who until the nineteenth century would most likely have been the primary arbiter of its theme, specific content, and, often, its form.

2. Margaret R. Miles, *Image as Insight: Visual Understanding in Western Christianity and Secular Culture* (Boston: Beacon Press, 1985), 6–7, 9–10.

3. In the interest of full disclosure, I admit to the following personal assumptions about a work of art: it is both form and idea; it is the creation of a distinct, unique individual or group of individuals, not of an unmediated culture; it can contain meaning intended by its creator; and it can communicate meaning to a viewer.

4. See, for example, David Freedberg, *The Power of Images: Studies in the History and Theory of Response* (Chicago: University of Chicago Press, 1989), Michael Ann Holly, *Past Looking: Historical Imagination and the Rhetoric of the Image* (Ithaca: Cornell University Press, 1996); and the more focused studies by John Shearman, *Only Connect . . . : Art and the Spectator in the Italian Renaissance* (Princeton: Princeton University Press, 1992), and William Hood, *Fra Angelico at San Marco* (New Haven: Yale University Press, 1993).

5. Miles, *Image as Insight*, 74.

6. Nelson Goodman, *Languages of Art: An Approach to a Theory of Symbols*, 2nd ed. (Indianapolis: Hackett Art Books, 1976), 247–50; italics added.

7. Freedberg, *The Power of Images*, 434.

8. Roland Barthes, *Camera Lucida: Reflections on Photography* (New York: Hill and Wang, 1981), 76.

9. Leo Steinberg, *Other Criteria: Confrontations with Modern Art* (New York: Oxford University Press, 1972), 12.

10. Steinberg, *Other Criteria*, 14–15.

11. Hermogenes of Tarsus, *Progymnasmata*, second century C.E.; cited in Michael Baxandall, *Giotto and the Orators: Humanist Observers of Painting in Italy and the Discovery of Pictorial Composition, 1350–1450* (Oxford: Clarendon Press, 1988), 85.

12. See, among other sources, André Grabar, *Christian Iconography: A Study of Its Origins* (Princeton: Princeton University Press, 1968), and *The Clash of Gods: A Reinterpretation of Early Christian Art*, rev. ed., edited by Thomas F. Mathews (Princeton: Princeton University Press, 1999).

13. Miles, *Image as Insight*, 44–45.

14. Gregory of Nyssa, *De Deitate Filii e Spiritus Sancti;* cited in *The Art of the Byzantine Empire 213–1453: Sources and Documents*, edited and translated by Cyril Mango, Medieval Academy Reprints for Teaching 16 (Toronto: University of Toronto Press, 1986), 34.

15. Mango, *The Art of the Byzantine Empire*, 39.

16. Suger, *Liber de Rebus in Administratione Sua Gestis*, translated by Erwin Panofsky, cited in *A Documentary History of Art*, vol. 2, *The Middle Ages and the Renaissance*, edited by Elizabeth Gilmore Holt (Princeton: Princeton University Press, 1981), 30.

17. Bernard's opinions are expressed in a letter to the Abbot of Saint-Thierry, translated by G. G. Coulton, cited in Holt, *A Documentary History of Art*, 19–22.

18. Erwin Panofsky, *Early Netherlandish Painting: Its Origins and Character* (Cambridge, Mass.: Harvard University Press, 1958), 125–26.

19. Ignatius Loyola, *The Spiritual Exercises* (Chicago: Loyola University Press, 1951), 32–33.

20. Leonbattista Alberti, *On Painting*, rev. ed. (New Haven: Yale University Press, 1966), 75, 77; italics added.

21. In James Elkins's delightful book *Pictures and Tears: A History of People Who Have Cried in Front of Paintings* (New York: Routledge, 2001), in which he presents numerous accounts of emotional reactions, he found very few art historians who admitted to being moved to tears by a work of art, and even fewer who would admit it for publication.

22. Freedberg, *The Power of Images*, 22–23.

23. Master of the Fiesole *Epiphany*, active Florence, c. 1480–1500; *Christ on the Cross with Saints Vincent Ferrer, John the Baptist, Mark, and Antoninus*, c. 1491/95; tempera and oil on panel, 186.1 × 203.8 cm (73 1/2 × 80 1/4 in.); Los Angeles County Museum of Art, Gift of the Ahmanson Foundation (M.91.242).

24. Giorgio Vasari identified the patrons of the altarpiece in the 1568 edition of the life of the painter Cosimo Rosselli, although for stylistic reasons it is highly unlikely that Rosselli was the artist; see Vasari, *Le vite de' più eccellenti pittori scultori e architettori*, edited by Rosanna Bettarini and Paola Barocchi (Florence: Sansoni, 1966–84), vol. 3 (1971), 444.

25. For a discussion of the reasons for this attribution, see Susan L. Caroselli, *Italian Panel Painting of the Early Renaissance* (Los Angeles: Los Angeles County Museum of Art, 1994), 69–72.

26. Early in the fifth century, in the apse mosaic of the church of Santa Pudenziana and a relief panel from the doors of the church of Santa Sabina, both in Rome,

the four evangelists were first represented as the four aspects of the tetramorph (Eze-kiel 1:5–13; 10:9–14; Revelation 4:6b–8), an interpretation introduced by Jerome in his commentary on Ezekiel. Mark was allied with the lion because his Gospel begins with John the Baptist preaching in the wilderness, the traditional haunt of the lion; see Homily 75(1) on Mark 1:1–12 in *The Homilies of Saint Jerome,* translated by Marie Liguori Erwald (Washington, D.C.: Catholic University of America Press, 1966), 121.

27. References for the content, practices, and materials of medieval and Renais-sance painting are David Bomford, Jill Dunkerton, Dillian Gordon, and Ashok Roy, *Art in the Making: Italian Painting before 1400* (London: National Gallery, 1989); Caro-selli, *Italian Panel Painting of the Early Renaissance;* Jill Dunkerton, Susan Foister, Dil-lian Gordon, and Nicholas Penny, *Giotto to Dürer: Early Renaissance Painting in the National Gallery* (New Haven: Yale University Press, 1991); and *The Altarpiece in the Renaissance,* edited by Peter Humfrey and Martin Kemp (Cambridge: Cambridge University Press, 1990).

28. When the altarpiece first appeared on the art market in England in the mid–nineteenth century, this identification was not made; however, by 1893 the source of the imagery had been recognized; see the 1893–94 exhibition catalogue of the New Gallery, London, *Exhibition of Early Italian Art from 1330 to 1550,* 71.

29. Perhaps the appropriation of the *Volto Santo* imagery for this altarpiece was an assertive act of remembrance: the ancestors of the Florentine guild members had been forced to emigrate from Lucca in the early fourteenth century by the conquering Florentines, who wished to relocate the lucrative silk industry to their own city; see Edgcumbe Staley, *The Guilds of Florence* (London: Methuen, 1906), 216.

30. In many medieval and later images the chalice is held by an angel under the spurting wound in Christ's side. In addition, the *Volto Santo* was a reliquary once supposedly containing a vial of the blood of Christ; for the history of the statue and a discussion of the imagery of the chalice, see Caroselli, *Italian Panel Painting of the Early Renaissance,* 64–65.

31. The drawing is usually attributed to Filippino Lippi; see George Goldner and Carmen C. Bambach, *The Drawings of Filippino Lippi and His Circle* (New York: Metro-politan Museum of Art, 1997), cat. 69. Lippi may have been the artist first ap-proached by the silk weavers' guild; we cannot, however, rule out the possibility that the drawing style is simply similar to Lippi's.

32. An excellent collection of the types of contracts under which artists of this time worked may be found in D. S. Chambers, *Patrons and Artists in the Italian Re-naissance* (Columbia: University of South Carolina, 1971).

33. Antoninus was originally depicted with the rayed halo of the beatified; at some point after his canonization (1523) a solid halo was painted over the rays—repainting details in religious works was a common occurrence—but it has gradually worn away, revealing the original radiance beneath.

34. My present response to this altarpiece is not "fresh," since I first saw it in 1991, but one of the hallmarks of instinctive response is that it does not necessarily lose its intensity over time. I also fall back on the written reactions of people to whom I have shown it for the last eight years, from academic theologians to first-year college students. It is clear that even without recognizing any figures except Christ (and, some-

times, John the Baptist) most viewers have the same instinctive response and reach the same conclusions about the imagery.

35. In all the works attributed to this artist the expressions of Christ and the Virgin Mary are noticeably more beatific and accessible than those of the surrounding figures, who are far more individualized and austere.

36. An art historian familiar with the iconography of angels should recognize these as six-winged seraphim and four-winged cherubim, whose purpose is the ceaseless praise of God in heaven, emphasizing that the viewer is presented with a celestial vision and not an earthly apparition. The arrangement of the heavenly hierarchy was first set out around 500 by Pseudo-Dionysius the Areopagite and became the standard work on the topic of angels after its translation into Latin in the ninth century; see chapters 6–9 of *The Celestial Hierarchy* in *Pseudo-Dionysius: The Complete Works* (New York: Paulist Press, 1987), 160–73.

37. Caroselli, *Italian Panel Painting of the Early Renaissance*, 67; my reconstruction of the original location of the altarpiece (the transverse wall was removed in the sixteenth century and the altars moved) was based on primary documents published in Hans Teubner, "San Marco in Florenz: Umbauten vor 1500. Ein Betrag zum Werk des Michelozzo," *Mitteilungen des Kunsthistorisches Institutes in Florenz* 23, 3 (1979), 239–72.

38. In one of his sermons the Dominican reformer Girolamo Savonarola, who was prior of San Marco at the time this painting was executed, declared that pictures in churches should be for the instruction of children and women; see Martin Wackernagel, *The World of the Florentine Renaissance Artist: Projects and Patrons, Workshop and Art Market* (Princeton: Princeton University Press, 1981; German ed. 1938), 112.

39. See Michael Baxandall, *Painting and Experience in Fifteenth-Century Italy: A Primer in the Social History of Pictorial Style*, 2nd ed. (Oxford: Oxford University Press, 1988), 72–76.

40. Alberti, *On Painting*, 78.

41. Thomas N. Tentler, *Sin and Confession on the Eve of the Reformation* (Princeton: Princeton University Press, 1977), 39. The *Defecerunt* alone saw seventy-two printings in Latin, Italian, and Spanish.

42. The "fire and brimstone" aspect of Savonarola's preaching has been exaggerated by many historians. In fact, his calls to repentance always included "the promise of reconciliation and a life freed from the burden of guilt and sin"; see Marcia B. Hall, "Savonarola's Preaching and the Patronage of Art," in *Christianity and the Renaissance: Image and Religious Imagination in the Quattrocento*, edited by Timothy Verdon and John Henderson (Syracuse: Syracuse University Press, 1990), 494.

43. My Messiah College students in a spring 2001 art history class took twenty minutes to follow the "reading" process I described and to interpret the message, with no prompting from me and no information about the iconography; they did recognize Christ, and several of them guessed correctly that one of the other figures was John the Baptist.

CHAPTER FIVE

Contours and Contexts of Christian Scholarship

The intermingling of faith and learning that takes place in Christian scholarship is often unpredictable, usually multidirectional, and always complex. A mapping of that terrain reveals several broad distinctions that can help Christian scholars better define their own work. Even with a clear understanding of what they are doing, however, Christian scholars will often find their task daunting. In particular, Christian scholars will sometimes find themselves caught between the differing expectations of the academy and the church. But done well, Christian scholarship can be a great boon to both the churches and the academy as a whole. Faith is a part of life, and the struggle to understand faith in the light of scholarship and scholarship in the light of faith is ultimately both unavoidable and potentially deeply rewarding.

Every year, thousands of scholars gather for an academic extravaganza called the Annual Meeting of the American Academy of Religion. One of the major sessions at a recent meeting was a panel of experts responding to George Marsden's book *The Outrageous Idea of Christian Scholarship.* The very fact that a book with such a title could be a focus for serious discussion at the American Academy of Religion meeting might have been cause for celebration among Christian scholars, but what made the panel interesting was that it included voices from a wide variety of perspectives.

One respondent thought that the term "Christian scholarship" was itself "ambiguous and unfortunate" and "freighted, fairly or not, with particularistic, exclusivistic, and triumphalistic overtones."[1] This respondent noted that the term "Christian studies" would be far less outrageous, as anyone, Christian or not, could do scholarship about Christians and Christianity. Christian studies is the scholarly examination of Christian faith and practice: the study of what Christians believe, how they behave in groups, how their beliefs and practices have changed over time. Anyone can answer these kinds of investigative questions. Anyone can engage in the historical, sociological, psychological, literary, or philosophical examination of Christian faith. Anyone can do Christian studies because its aim is to be simply descriptive.

But, of course, Christian studies is not the subject of Marsden's book. His topic is Christian scholarship, and it is far different. The purpose of Christian scholarship is not description but reflection—to reflect on the world from the perspective of faith and to reflect on one's own faith from the perspective of scholarship. This is an insider's task. The questions are existential, and the answers need in some sense to be vetted by one's religious colleagues as well as by one's scholarly peers. Thus it is the faith orientation of the scholar that makes the work Christian. As Paul Griffiths has rightly noted: "One is a Christian scholar if one understands one's work to be based upon and framed by and always in the service of one's identity as a Christian."[2] The Christian scholar does not speak merely *about* Christian faith (i.e., the stance of Christian studies) but *out of* and *on behalf of* his or her own community of faith.

While Christian studies and Christian scholarship have different goals and purposes, the two tasks are not necessarily antagonistic to each other and may even function in a complementary way. At the very least, good Christian scholarship requires some sensitivity to the concerns of Christian studies. Good Christian scholarship is never merely evangelistic or apologetic; it always involves some degree of self-criticism, requiring the scholar to look at faith and life from the perspective of the other. We are all highly limited in this kind of endeavor. It takes a tremendous act of imagination to examine one's own life as if looking at it from the outside, and none of us truly succeeds. Therefore mature Christian scholars will necessarily engage in dialogue with others— with Christians who hold views that differ from their own and with persons from other religious traditions or no religious tradition—who can provide them with external points of reference to maintain the honesty and fairness of their Christian scholarship.

In a similar manner, those who undertake Christian studies will sometimes need to trespass onto the turf of Christian scholarship. They will, that is, if they want to make sure that their outsider descriptions of Christian faith and practice ring at least partly true to the ways Christians understand their own religious faith and practice. The quality of Christian studies is not dependent on the fact that members of the group being studied fully accept an outsider's scholarly description of their faith, but it is a positive sign if members of the group being investigated can recognize themselves in the final scholarly product. In that sense, the self-consciousness of the Christian community (including self-consciousness that takes the form of Christian scholarship) has a role to play in Christian studies. But having said that, we would still maintain that in their primary impulses Christian studies and Christian scholarship are fundamentally different undertakings, and the focus of this book is and has been unambiguously on the latter. Our concern is not with Christian studies but with Christian scholarship: the exploration of the diverse ways in which Christians as individuals and as members of their communities of faith understand their faith to be connected with their scholarship and their scholarship with their Christian faith.

The Contours of Christian Scholarship

Christian scholarship is always a two-way street: faith influences learning and learning influences faith. In most instances, however, either faith will have the predominant role or scholarship will. When the faith side of the equation is most prominent the result will be *faith-informed scholarship*. In instances where the opposite takes place—where the primary flow of influence is from the scholarly realm to the religious—the result will be *academically shaped faith*.

Every act of scholarship involves both questioning and affirmation, two actions that are often intimately related. We assume certain things to be true so we can question other things; we designate certain items or aspects of reality as given, so we can arrange other parts of reality around those points of orientation in new and creative ways. It is impossible to question everything at once, so scholarship tends to question one thing at a time against a background of other items that are deemed, at least for the duration of one's academic project, to be relatively fixed points of reference. A Marxist analysis of history, for example, assumes the truth of Marxism, at least while it is being used as a tool to pry open new questions about history. Later the same historian might turn critical attention to Marxism itself. In a similar way, most composers in Western cultures accept without criticism the standard Western eight-note scale when writing music scores, even though they know other scales are available. The givenness of the scale provides them with a fixed framework for creative expression. The same pattern of affirmation and questioning is evident in Christian scholarship.

In faith-informed scholarship, Christian faith is the fixed point of reference—at least temporarily, the unquestioned background of one's thinking—while some aspect of disciplinary knowledge or expertise is examined and then critiqued or tweaked in light of Christian beliefs or values. Sometimes this kind of faith-informed scholarship can be quite critical of existing ideas and norms within the academy; sometimes it can play a more corroborative role, adding depth or nuance to existing paradigms and ways of thought. Often, as is the case with scholarship in general, Christian scholarship will include both critique of and support for different aspects of the current academic scene. In fact, there is a tremendous variety of potential relations between faith and learning that might emerge, many more than we can document here. Our point is merely to indicate that if the subject is faith-informed scholarship, the faith side of the relationship will by definition remain relatively unaffected by the encounter. This does not mean that Christian scholars are necessarily asserting that Christian beliefs and values can never be questioned (though some Christian scholars would make that claim); instead, Christian scholars are assuming the basic truth of Christian faith in much the same way that a Marxist historian might assume the basic truth of Marxism as a method of economic analysis. Christian scholars, like all other scholars, are asking how our understanding of the world might change if we began our inquiry with a set of assumptions different from that which currently serves as the common standard. In that sense, Christian scholarship is a form of exploratory study seeking to test the explanatory power of Christian faith insofar as Christian faith can be converted into a tool for academic inquiry.

In academically shaped faith the opposite process is at work: Christian scholars turn the issues around and use their disciplinary knowledge as a fixed point of reference to critique or tweak their own Christian faith. Biblical scholars do this all the time. As new archaeological evidence is uncovered, Christian scholars modify their understanding of the biblical text. And so do Christian scientists. Thus as a result of the nearly universal acceptance of evolution as an accurate description of the history of life on the planet, most Christian biologists have adjusted their understanding of the biblical account of creation to square with that scientific theory, even though many still want to argue vigorously (along with many of their colleagues who are not Christians) about the precise details of evolutionary history and the mechanics of evolution. Physicists have done the same, with people like John Polkinghorne (an ordained Anglican priest and president of Queen's College of Cambridge University) leading the way.[3] Christian sociologists similarly use social theory as a fixed point of reference to analyze and criticize the ways churches organize themselves and relate to the larger society. This kind of faith-reformulating scholarship is not necessarily antagonistic to faith. In fact, the academic critique of Christian faith can actually help make Christian faith more Christian. For example, Michael Emerson and Christian Smith's book *Divided by Faith: Evangelical Religion and the Problem of Race in America* can be seen as a form of academically shaped faith. It asks American evangelical Christians to rethink some of their most deeply cherished beliefs and values in light of a scholarly examination of racial realities.[4] In the world of the arts, a good example of how learning can influence faith is found in Jeremy S. Begbie's *Theology, Music and Time* which argues that music can illuminate the meaning of certain doctrines in a way that the traditional language of systematic theology simply cannot.[5] Christian academicians like Polkinghorne, Emerson and Smith, and Begbie are not saying that faith should bend to every new theory or idea developed within the academy, but rather that faith should be open to change in the light of genuine advances that emerge from the academy. Further, they argue that this is not only a matter of keeping up with the academy, it can also be a way of refining and improving the ideas and practices of faith.

While we have emphasized the differences, there is actually no such thing as purely faith-informed scholarship or purely academically shaped faith. Even in those cases where a gushing river of influence goes one way, there will always be at least a trickle of influence going the other. Christian scholarship as a whole would be improved if Christian scholars would more readily admit that fact. In the past, the tendency in more conservative Christian circles, whether Catholic or Protestant, has been to stress faith-informed scholarship as the norm and to discredit the importance or even the validity of academically shaped faith. In more liberal Christian circles, the tendency historically has been almost the opposite: to stress the need to reformulate Christian beliefs and practices in the light of emerging scholarly trends and to be very cautious about imposing any norms of faith on the work of scholarship. Numerous scholars have, of course, always sought to avoid these extremes, and in recent years that tendency seems to be increasing. From our perspective, it is this middle ground, where influence flows both ways at once, that holds the most promise for the future of Christian scholarship.

Another distinction in mapping the terrain of Christian scholarship has to do with the issue of how visible the dimension of faith is or ought to be in that scholarship. In some forms of Christian scholarship the influence of faith will be quite intentionally *explicit*. In other examples of Christian scholarship the role of faith will be protrude much less visibly, being only *implicit* in the motivation, assumptions, and message of the work rather than being explicitly flaunted. The decision to be more or less explicit about matters of faith is often a function of audience. When Christian scholars are aiming their work at predominantly Christian audiences, they may speak of faith in a manner that would not be appropriate if they were addressing a broader public. In fact, it is sometimes said that Christian scholars need to be "bilingual" in the ways they relate faith to their academic work, speaking explicitly to their Christian colleagues but adopting a much more implicit style when addressing the larger academy.

A related issue is the degree to which Christian scholarship is or should be different and distinct from other scholarship produced in any given disciplinary domain. Some Christian scholars stress difference; others do not. Scholars who emphasize the fact that Christian faith either forces them or allows them to look at the world in a manner different from other scholars often think of Christian scholarship as a separate school of thought or practice within their disciplines (e.g., Christian psychology in contradistinction to cognitive psychology or behaviorism). The more one adopts this kind of stance, the more likely one is to feel it necessary to be explicit about the faith dimension of one's work. Other Christians, however, are much less prone to stress difference. For them, Christian faith does not so much change the way they think within their academic fields of study as it adds depth or breadth or seriousness to the work they do as scholars. Persons of this ilk will normally be attracted to forms of scholarship in which the dimension of faith is implicit in the tone and orientation of what they do, but they will not necessarily discuss faith as something that sets their work apart from the work of other scholars.

The factors that draw scholars toward different styles of Christian scholarship are multiple and overlapping. Personality often plays a role. Some people are naturally blunt or brash while others are cautious or tentative. Theology also has an effect. Thus Protestants often speak more explicitly about these matters—even confrontationally (after all, the word "Protestant" is historically derived from "protest")—than Catholics who tend to favor a more implicit approach (which is very much in keeping with how they see God's grace sacramentally infused into all of creation). The disciplines themselves play a role. In some fields of study—especially in the human sciences—issues of faith and values naturally arise. In other disciplines—calculus or chemistry, for example—the insertion of religious themes into the discussion will almost always feel a bit awkward, if not out of place. None of this can be easily systematized. In fact, most Christian scholars would find it hard to predict which style of Christian scholarship they will adopt with regard to any given project. In this regard, Christian scholarship is just like scholarship in general. As scholars we are engaged in an open-ended enterprise of learning—a process of exploration, creativity, and insight—that is larger than we are. The subjects we examine and the questions we ask lure us forward into areas of reflection where our previous experience eventually exhausts itself and where we do not know the answers in advance. But of course, that is the point of scholarship—that is the way learning works—and in their scholarly endeavors, Christians necessarily follow the same path as everyone else.

Christian Scholarship in the Context of the Academy

The task of Christian scholarship within the academy, when the academy is functioning at its best and when Christian scholars are performing at their best, is basically the same as the task of scholarship in general: to ask well-crafted questions about the world, to formulate creative and well-reasoned answers to those questions, and then to assist in the work of vetting those answers so as to identify which show the most promise for further exploration. That is the way the academy is supposed to work, and Christian scholars obviously have an important and valid role to play in that ongoing process of intelligent reflection.

There is, of course, a great deal of overlap in what different scholars can contribute to the process of asking good questions, proposing interesting answers, and evaluating options, and the contributions made by Christian scholars often have nothing directly to do with their faith. Much of what Christian scholars do is what everyone else in the academy tries to do: to think clearly about the world and to reflect critically on our varying interpretations of the world. Christian scholars, like all other scholars, seek to pay attention to the details of what they are studying. They seek to understand their subjects of study in a larger context and to make connections with other related facts and theories. Then they propose their own ways of fitting things together that they hope will prove to be more insightful and dynamic than other available alternatives. None of that takes religious faith, only good sense and a keen mind.

But having said that, there are a number of areas where Christian scholars may have a naturally greater propensity to contribute something. In particular, Christian scholars should bring a commitment to antireductionism to their work. Reductionism is defined as the attempt to explain—and, indeed, sometimes to explain away—the complexity of the world by claiming that everything can ultimately be reduced to only one or a very few underlying mechanisms of cause and effect. The key phrase is often "nothing but." Thus some Marxist scholarship can be seen as reductionistic because it asserts that human life is really "nothing but" economic struggle. Similarly, biology would be reductionistic if it asserted that the history of life is "nothing but" the competition of selfish genes. Christians can also be reductionistic at times, seeming to claim that every subject can and should be viewed through "nothing but" religious categories of thought. However, the more common role for Christian scholars is to be reductionism detectors. The Catholic commentator Margaret Steinfels says "it is a characteristic of [the Christian] tradition, at its best, to resist reductionism; it does not collapse categories." With regard to the human sciences in particular, she argues: "Empirical findings are not solely determinative of who we are and what we do. Yes, absolutely: Findings in psychology, sociology, anthropology, history, neurobiology enrich our understanding of the human person and the human project, but they do not exhaust that meaning or determine that trajectory."[6] There is no question that scholars often do have to lop off one part of reality in order to examine it for a time in isolation from everything else, and there is no doubt that it is sometimes helpful to describe complex systems in drastically simplified terms, but Christian faith precludes stopping at that point. Simplification for the purposes of research and analysis is fine, but when reductionistic scholarship is presented as an accurate description of all that really matters about the world or when scholars simply refuse to consider the fact that information that falls outside their narrow areas of expertise can have any relevance for their own work, Christian scholars invariably protest. They are convinced that the world is an interrelated whole.[7]

As seen through the eyes of Christian faith, the world comprises many complex layers of organisms, entities, interrelations, and levels of meaning. Thus any study of any particular item in the world is naturally connected to a host of other realms or dimensions of existence. It is impossible to study economics without simultaneously dipping into the concerns of culture, health, geography, education, and the arts. It is impossible to be a good engineer without occasionally considering the economic, aesthetic, historic, and "human factor" aspects of what is involved in that discipline. Especially in the study of persons, Christians stress that we are dealing with whole persons who possess emotional, moral, and spiritual dimensions as well as physical and physiological attributes. This type of concern for and awareness of the seamless fabric of the world is surely not a uniquely Christian contribution to the larger academy, but it is a concern that Christian scholars tend to promote with vigor.

Another area in which Christians may make a contribution, even if here again their actions are not unique, might be called the scholarship of compassion. Like many individuals from other faith traditions and like many other persons who profess no religious faith at all, Christians often include in their scholarship a deep sense of empathy for those who are poor, sick, oppressed, or suffering from violence at the hands of others. What marks the Christian contribution in this area, if it is distinctive at all, is not so much the concern itself as the way it has been so clearly articulated in relation to the scholarly task. Thus David Hollenbach of Boston College has argued that

> the intellectual solidarity that is required if religion and the academic are to be brought into a higher unity must be accompanied by a social solidarity that links the Catholic university [and, by implication, all Christian scholarship] to the struggles of a world marred by . . . the long history of human beings' sinful propensity to treat one another in inhuman ways.[8]

Hollenbach is not saying Christians do this better than anyone else; he is merely arguing that this is a necessary ideal for Christian scholars and institutions of higher learning. Other commentators on the American higher educational scene who are not Christians have said much the same thing, and some have even recognized the importance of religiously affiliated colleges and universities in this regard. For example, Martha Nussbaum, in her influential defense of liberal education, Cultivating Humanity, argues that while

> all universities can and should contribute to the development of citizens who are capable of love of the neighbor . . . the religious universities have this mission at their heart in a special way; and it is precisely for reasons such as these that the major religions have founded universities, believing that love at its best is intelligent and that higher education can enhance its discrimination.[9]

She says it well. In many ways, the ultimate goal of Christian scholarship and the reason why Christian colleges and universities exist is not merely to seek truth; the goal is to seek truth in order to more intelligently love the world and every person in it.

Christian scholars also have something special to share with the larger academy when it comes to the subject of religion itself. Here again, the issue is not so much that Christian scholars are naturally better equipped to understand the religious dimensions of the world as that they are naturally more likely, because of their own faith, to pay more attention to the religious aspects of human life and experience. The backdrop of this matter is the issue of secularization. An older generation of scholars assumed that secularization was simply a fact of history; religion was in the process of slowly but inexorably evaporating from the public realm of society and from the academy as well. They assumed human consciousness was inevitably moving away from religious ways of thought toward scientific ways of thought, away from a focus on the metaphorical to a focus on the real, away from the lofty poetry of faith to the blunt prose of logical deduction. As such, scholarship in general and college and university education in particular came to be seen as helping students develop new nonreligious ways of talking about reality that could replace the worn-out language of the churches. True scholarship, then, had to be expressed in language and concepts that had no necessary recourse to the ideas or insights of faith. Religion was seen as a hindrance to understanding, a leftover way of thinking that could not possibly aid in the modern task of understanding how the world was actually put together.

In retrospect, this was not the academy functioning at its best. Many scholars rejected religious interpretations of the world without examining them simply because those interpretations were religious and hence, by definition, anachronistic. But more recent developments have shown that religion is not necessarily disappearing from the world after all—not from among the masses of ordinary believers and not from the ranks of the academy. A recent study of religion on college and university campuses concluded that religious practice was so "vital and inviting" it made the researchers "wonder if it had ever been more so in the past." They even went so far as to muse that it was "possible that young people in American culture have never been more enthusiastically engaged in religious practice or with religious ideas."[10] Richard Light of the Graduate School of Education at Harvard University has noted that religion is a significant factor in the lives of many college and university students and that religious diversity on the campus can be a source of enrichment rather than an obstacle to learning or an irritation in the classroom.[11] Christianity will never again be able to position itself as the one "sacred canopy"[12] under which the entire American academy is supposed to reside—the new world of the nation's colleges and universities is for the most part pluralistic—but it seems increasingly strange to hold religious faith or spirituality entirely at bay.[13] If the best teaching and learning helps students connect new skills and knowledge with who they are as whole persons, religion can no longer be kept out of the mix even on the most secular campuses. Consequently, many professors are struggling with the issue of how to let faith and spirituality back into their classrooms in a manner that enhances learning without undermining critical thinking.[14]

Christian scholars can be of immense help to their scholarly peers in the task of developing new ways to allow faith appropriately into the academic context, but unfortunately not all Christian scholars are in a position to play a constructive role in this process. A number of Christian scholars, embittered by what they have sensed is an unfair prejudice against religion in the academy, have adopted the mirror image of their opponents, condemning the entire academy as irredeemably opposed to faith at least in its Christian forms. Michael L. Peterson is one of the most articulate popularizers of this view. In his *With All Your Mind: A Christian Philosophy of Education* (2001), he bluntly declares that

> the deep structures of modern intellectual life are essentially unaffected by any ideas that could be labeled Christian; instead they are almost completely influenced by the works of non-Christian and anti-Christian thinkers. . . . The set of assumptions that are commonly taken for granted in cultural debate simply rule out the tenets of Christianity.

Peterson also assumes that this is a more or less permanent situation, arguing that "the secularizing influences in contemporary culture will almost certainly keep Christian thinking from ever being a dominant force again." Hence, the only reasonable response is for Christian scholars to become "roaring lambs" within the academy—humble but bold critics of the "serious distortions of reality that have become entrenched in various academic disciplines."[15]

A more nuanced approach is offered by Stephen H. Webb in his book *Taking Religion to School: Christian Theology and Secular Education.* While Webb is, like Peterson, critical of many aspects of the secular academy, his proposal is that religious faith not be privileged but that it simply be allowed a seat at the table. He suggests that reactions to the scholarly discussion of religion "will range from rejection and critique to defense and reconstruction," which is fine with him. He insists, however, that the tone of the academy, and of the college classroom in particular, should be one that allows a positive evaluation of religious faith as readily as it promotes a negative or critical response. Thus he argues that college lectures and other campus discussions of religion should keep alive all the options and that the academy should "not foreclose . . . the possibility that students and teachers alike will draw closer to God" as a result of their interactions in the classroom.[16]

Webb's argument is framed within the context of the discipline of religious studies. However, the question of whether to include religious faith in academic discussions is pertinent far beyond the borders of religious studies. There are a host of other disciplines in which the subject of religious faith might be a required component. Political science is an obvious case in point. How can anyone understand global political developments without some sensitivity to matters of faith? Political scientists and politicians alike need to understand the deep-seated hopes and fears that drive religious persons, and they need to reflect on how their own religious, nonreligious, or antireligious views might affect the way they see things.[17] In other academic disciplines, especially those that focus on the person (psychology, sociology, history, anthropology, literature), the same issues apply. Since faith is part of the reality that these disciplines seek to study, matters of faith ought not be banned from the academic discussion of those subjects.

The doors of the academy seem perhaps more open to the inclusion of religion than they have been for some time, but the reinfusion of faith into the language of the academy is far from certain. This is partly because doubts remain about the willingness of religious believers to genuinely accept the pluralism of views that are present in the academic world. From the Protestant world, George Marsden has sought to assuage these fears by arguing that "traditional religious viewpoints . . . can be just as hospitable to scientifically sound investigation as many other viewpoints" and that, given the pervasive reality of democratic pluralism in American culture, Christians "have little choice but to accept pragmatic standards in public life."[18] But at some church-related institutions it is hard to tell if this kind of acceptance is based on principled conviction or grudging acquiescence.

Catholic scholars have generally taken a less ambiguous and more positive stance toward the academy, arguing, as early as the Land O'Lakes Statement (1967) that "all recognized university areas of study are frankly and fully accepted and their internal autonomy affirmed and guaranteed." The Statement further declared that "all scientific and disciplinary methods, and methodologies, must be given due honor and respect" and that it was inappropriate for theology to try to assert any kind of "imperialism" over the other disciplines.[19] The strength of this position was its genuine respect for freedom of inquiry. The weakness was that many faculty members at Catholic colleges and universities felt free to simply pursue their own disciplinary studies with no reference to faith whatsoever. Colleagues in the theology department were supposed to handle any and all religious questions. As a result, the potential for creative interaction between faith and learning was sometimes undercut. Recently the pope and many other Catholic leaders have stressed the interrelatedness of all truth as a corrective to this fragmented situation. If truth ultimately is all of one piece, then the proper academic goal is both to support the autonomy of the disciplines and to strongly encourage them to explore the connections that exist with both other disciplines (including theology) and all of life (including faith).

Trying to negotiate that kind of balance will never be easy on any college or university campus, nor will it be easy in the academy at large. There should and undoubtedly always will be room for feisty argument and debate. Like everyone else in the scholarly world, Christian academicians have the right, indeed the responsibility, to argue their points as strongly as they can. At the same time, however, Christian scholars who participate in the larger academy would be well advised to avoid any trace of triumphalism and, if they truly want to be heard, they may want to monitor the vehemence of their rhetoric as well. The obverse is that the academy itself, if it is truly interested in expanding the range of discussion so that religious faith and modes of thought are included, will need actively and self-consciously to create spaces and places where that can happen. We are convinced that the world of scholarship as a whole would be stronger if religious faith was more readily allowed into the discussion, but the pathway to that enlarged conversation is still being constructed.

Christian Scholarship in the Context of the Church

The role of Christian scholarship within the community of faith is as delicate and tricky as it is within the academy. On the one hand, Christian scholars are simply part of the community of believers. Like other Christians they look to the church to supply an outlet for their desire to worship God, a place of instruction for their children, a source of comfort in times of trouble, and a means of outreach and service to others. It is not at all surprising then that one of the main goals of Christian scholarship is to make the best thinking of the academy available to the church. Christian scholars serve as the church's allies and supporters. They defend the church when it is attacked and cheer it on in its successes. They assist the church in articulating the gospel in language and symbols appropriate to today's cultures. They share their knowledge and insights with the church about how to be more effective in the ministries of care that the church offers to the world. They provide technical and philosophical expertise to help the church reflect intelligently on the complicated moral issues of our day. Christian scholars also often serve the Christian community in ways that transcend the boundaries of any given church or institution by engaging in scholarly, practical, or artistic projects that help make Christian faith more academically respected and accepted. For many people, C. S. Lewis and G. K. Chesterton skill exemplify the ideal of what Christian scholars should be. These mid-twentieth-century apologists used their quick wits and logical minds to undercut a host of clever secular arguments against Christianity, demonstrating in the process that faith, even if it was not fully provable, was most certainly a reasonable interpretation of reality.

Relations between Christian scholars and their churches have not, however, always been that smooth and easy, and it is helpful to examine some of the reasons why churches occasionally look askance at Christian scholarship. Clearly one major reason for the distrust that sometimes flares up between Christian scholars and their churches is the pervasive antiintellectualism apparent in American culture in general. Most Americans, including most American Christians, have a simple, or even simplistic, notion of truth. What they believe is what they believe, and they do not need any highfalutin scholars telling them what they are supposed to think. They feel they can make those judgments for themselves, thank you very much. The mere fact of being a scholar, unless one adopts an "Aw shucks, I'm just one of the folks" kind of attitude, can sometimes create resentment from people in the pews.

It is discouraging that some scholars seem more than willing to accommodate antiintellectualism, and even to encourage it, for the sake of their own popularity or to assuage the fears of ordinary believers. Some Christian academicians use scholarship against scholarship to reinforce popular prejudice and to validate the dismissal of scholarly questions as esoteric, effete, and of little real value. Such antischolarship is unhelpful to both the church and the academy. Christian scholars are called to help raise the level of scholarly discussion in the churches as much as they are called to raise the consciousness of the academy with regard to faith. When Christian scholars act in ways that encourage the disrespect of scholarship in general, they show that they have already to some degree deserted their calling to hold faith and learning together.

Other tensions exist apart from this generalized antiintellectualism. They occur whenever Christian scholars ask questions that most church leaders and lay people would prefer to ignore. Tensions are also created when the work of Christian scholars—regardless of whether it is in the area of analytic, strategic, or empathic scholarship—smudges the lines of demarcation between the church and the world that many church leaders, parishioners, and theologians would like to keep clear and precise. When Christian scholars raise these questions or produce these boundary-fuzzing works, they usually do so out of a deep sense of loyalty to the church, hoping their efforts will prod the church toward a deeper and more nuanced understanding of both the faith and the world; the result, however, often leaves them frustrated. This pattern of question, rebuff, and frustration is unfortunately almost as old as the church itself. As early as the third century, the well-known Christian scholar Origen of Alexandria was at odds with his bishop, Demetrius, over precisely these issues. Recent debates within the world of Catholic higher education over the Apostolic Constitution "Ex Corde Ecclesiae" are only the latest chapter in this long history of tension between the church and the Christian academy. The nature of Christian scholarship makes it almost certain that similar tensions will emerge in every age.

The corporate role of Christian scholars within the Christian community is to constitute themselves as the church's intelligentsia. They are called to be askers of questions and, to some degree, troublers of the water. Christian scholars are intellectuals who serve the church by exploring the ever-expanding boundary where faith and human learning meet and by seeking to share their insights as much as possible with their fellow believers. In the person of the Christian scholar, faith and learning merge into one, but socially the Christian scholar inhabits two worlds—the church and the academy—and serves as a translator between them. With a foot in each camp and loyalty shared, Christian scholars will inevitably find themselves alternately supportive and critical of the church and academy at different points along the way. Christian scholars live at that intersection. In fact, that liminal identity is a critical element in Christian scholarship and higher education. Theodore Hesburgh, the outspoken former president of Notre Dame, described that state of existence by saying: "The Catholic university is not the Catholic church. It might be said to be of the church as it serves the church and the people of God, but it is certainly not the magisterium, although it does respect it." What the Catholic university is, according to Hesburgh, is "a place—the only place—in which Catholics and others, on the highest level of intellectual inquiry, seek out the relevance of the Christian message to all of the problems and opportunities that face us in our complex world."[20]

From the perspective of the churches, however, some scholars seem much too willing, much too quickly, to set aside older forms of belief and to reconstruct Christian faith anew in the light of contemporary scholarly developments. And, even more troubling, scholars sometimes seem to do that even before those scholarly developments have been fully tested within the academy or have been subjected to critical analysis from the perspective of faith. In the current academic environment, value is placed on being both up-to-date in one's field and creatively different from others. In the best scenario, this emphasis on newness and contemporaneity can lead to leaps of insight that truly advance our understanding of the world; in the worst-case scenario, we end up with trendy tripe. The more typical result is usually in the middle, but the churches often fear the worst more than they hope for the best. They do not want the historic faith of Christendom subjected to repetitive reconceptualization at the hands of Christian scholars who might be more concerned with being on the cutting edge than they are with being faithful to the long tradition(s) of Christian belief and practice.

This perspective, while understandable, is problematic for the Christian scholar. Christian scholars know that the academy does indeed produce wave on wave of new ideas, methodologies, and theories, and only some of them are really worth exploring in relation to Christian faith, but they also know it is not always easy to discern which new insights will last and which will fade. It is hard to tell which new perspectives are truly significant and which are not. The natural impulse of churches is to move slowly in these matters. If some new idea or insight develops within the academy that seems to require a significant rethinking of certain long-held Christian beliefs (e.g., the way Galileo's heliocentric view of the solar system eventually forced the church to change its reading of the Bible), the churches are prone to wait and see if that idea truly has any staying power before using it to reconfigure Christian faith. But Christian scholars do not necessarily have that option; they have to deal with developments at the scholarly edge of progress. What's more, many Christian scholars would argue that too often their churches have not only held back too long from adopting new insights offered to them by the academy but frequently have been openly hostile to new academic ideas that they would later have to accept as true. That is not only an embarrassment but a travesty— especially when the churches sometimes use the language of loyalty to Christ to condemn or reject new points of view even before those ideas have been given a fair examination.

The default position of many Christian scholars is to search for truth even if, at times, that search seems to conflict with some traditional interpretation of Christian faith. Their deep conviction is that ultimately scholarly truth and Christian truth will converge, even if the path to that convergence takes some uncomfortable twists and turns that sometimes seem to pit learning against faith. In this regard, Simone Weil would be their spokesperson when she said that "Christ likes us to prefer truth to him because, before being Christ, he is truth. If one turns aside from him to go toward the truth, one will not go far before falling into his arms."[21]

Scholars who are also devout Christians typically have no desire to weaken the churches that have nurtured them into faith and that continue to support them in their ongoing pilgrimages of faith. Instead, their constant hope is that their scholarly reflections on the world and on their faith will ultimately aid the Christian community in its corporate commitment to the gospel. That assistance can sometimes take an uncomfortable form, as in cases when scholars feel a responsibility to help their churches remember that the religious folkways and commonplaces that shape their own churchly practices are not necessarily identical with the gospel itself. This should come as no shock. The Bible warns over and over again of the dangers of idolatry, that is, the danger of mistaking some lesser good for the divine itself. One of the tasks of Christian scholarship within the churches is to combat this tendency to imprison God in the limited perspectives of our own particular traditions.

Richard Hughes makes this point forcefully in his recent book *How Christian Faith Can Sustain the Life of the Mind*, which argues that one of the main goals of Christian scholarship should be to help Christian churches and individuals "break through the particularities of their own traditions."[22] His purpose is not to deny particularity; we can never overcome particularity. Rather his notion is that Christian scholars need to help their own churches and Christians in general remember that even though the gospel can be cradled in many different forms of thought and practice, the gospel itself transcends those particular expressions. Thus Christian scholarship is both affirmative of Christian faith and iconoclastic at the same time. Christian scholarship seeks to defend the faith, but it also works to keep the language of faith fresh and alive through crossfertilization with new insights that are constantly emerging from the academy. The Notre Dame historian James Turner says the church-friendly, but critical goal of Christian scholarship is to help the thinking of the church become slowly "more nuanced, more supple, [and] more in touch with the culture it hopes to influence."[23]

Establishing a healthy balance between this kind of affirmation and critique is not easy. If the churches would trust their scholars a bit more, that would surely help ease tensions. If Christian scholars would take a bit more time to converse with their churches and with ordinary believers, that would help as well. Richard Mouw's little book *Consulting the Faithful: What Christian Intellectuals Can Learn from Popular Religion* offers some good advice in this regard.[24] While Mouw would agree that Christian scholars have a responsibility to critique popular religiosity, he also argues that academic disdain for the beliefs of ordinary believers is highly inappropriate on grounds that are both moral and scholarly. On moral grounds, academic disdain for ordinary faith is simple hubris: being smarter or better educated than other people does not mean one is morally or spiritually superior to them. But disdain for the views of ordinary folks also runs the risk of being a scholarly sin, for it involves (mis)reading the intentions of others in the worst light possible. Good scholarship will always give the other at least some benefit of the doubt, and when the other is a fellow Christian that need for a hermeneutic of charity seems even greater.

All in all, being a Christian scholar within the context of the church means that one constantly has to be attuned to both what one says and how one says it. The etiquette of the academy allows for the blunt criticism of others and for the brash presentation of new views, but the etiquette of the church is different. Despite a few glaring counterexamples, such as Luther's bombastic rhetoric of the Reformation era, typical churchgoers usually expect Christian scholars to choose their words with care and caution so as to minimize offense to other believers. The task of Christian scholarship within the academy is obviously complex, but the terrain Christian scholars must negotiate within the churches is perhaps even more challenging.

Conclusion

Christian scholarship occurs whenever Christians are wrestling with academic issues, whether they do that as independent scholars, as faculty members of church-related institutions of higher learning, or as professors at secular colleges or universities in America or beyond. The key element is not the place where scholarship occurs but the Christian commitment of the scholar. James Mannoia, the president of Greenville College in Illinois, has used the phrase "critical commitment" to describe mature Christian faith. Mannoia explains that critical commitment goes "beyond dogmatism in applying the best critical tools available to the real questions of life."[25] Christian scholarship at its best will be critically committed both to faith and to the world of scholarship—loyal to both but unbound by dogmatism in either context.

Mature faith—self-critical but committed faith—provides the Christian with an attitude toward the world and others that allows him or her to be a helpful and contributing member of both the church and the academy. The critically committed Christian scholar is not locked into the need to defend every idea he or she has about how the world is put together. Instead, the goal of Christian scholarship, like the goal of all genuine scholarship, is to contribute to the human quest for truth, goodness, and beauty, and to be willing constantly to correct and revise its understanding of the world as new information emerges. The goal for Christian scholars is to use their minds each day to discover a bit more about how the world is put together, to ascertain what roles and responsibilities they might be called to play in the world because of their scholarly expertise, and to infuse all their scholarly efforts with a sense of generous care for the world that parallels God's own deep love for creation.

NOTES

1. Remarks by Robert Sarna at the Annual Meeting of the American Academy of Religion, November 20, 2000, Nashville, Tenn., Evangelical Theology Group (session A196), "The 'Christian Scholar' in Secular America: The Work of George M. Marsden."

2. Quoted in Richard T. Hughes, *How Christian Faith Can Sustain the Life of the Mind* (Grand Rapids, Mich.: Eerdmans, 2001), 138.

3. See John Polkinghorne, *The Faith of a Physicist* (Princeton: Princeton University Press, 1994).

4. Michael O. Emerson and Christian Smith, *Divided by Faith: Evangelical Religion and the Problem of Race in America* (New York: Oxford University Press, 2000).

5. Jeremy S. Begbie, *Theology, Music and Time* (New York: Cambridge University Press, 2000).

6. Margaret Steinfels, "The Catholic Intellectual Tradition," *Origins* 25, 11 (August 24, 1995), 173.

7. See, for example, David Hollenbach, "The Catholic University under the Sign of the Cross: Christian Humanism in a Broken World," in *Finding God in All Things*, edited by Michael J. Himes and Stephen J. Pope (New York: Crossroads, 1996). Hollenbach writes: "Intellectual specialization can easily close academic disciplines, including theology, to insights that arise beyond the boundaries of their field of inquiry. This situation has led a number of contemporary thinkers to conclude that all we can aspire to in intellectual life are fragments of meaning that are not really the meaning *of* anything external to those who find them meaningful. . . . As with the Sophists and nominalists in the past, this can lead to the reduction of intellectual undertakings to matters of power and will." He goes on to argue that "though the presence of these currents in the university is often exaggerated, it would be a mistake to underestimate their influence . . . they both threaten the academic project itself and undercut any attempt to uncover the connections between the religious and the academic" (285–86).

8. David Hollenbach, "Comment [on Michael J. Buckley, "The Catholic University and the Promise Inherent in Its Identity]," in *Catholic Higher Education at the Turn of the New Century*, edited by Joseph M. O'Keefe (Chestnut Hill, Mass.: Boston College, 1997), 227.

9. Martha Nussbaum, *Cultivating Humanity: A Classical Defense of Reform in Liberal Education* (Cambridge, Mass.: Harvard University Press, 1997), 292. The Catholic ethicist John C. Haughey writes that while not all scholarly research can or should be designed and undertaken in a manner that benefits people directly—there is room for the study of crystals, salamanders, differential equations, and medieval plays simply because those things exist—none of our scholarship should ever be undertaken in a manner that is "neighbor-numb." We are all, whether Christians or not, members of the humanity first and scholars second. See John C. Haughey, "Catholic Higher Education: A Strategy for Its Identity," in *Enhancing Religious Identity: Best Practices from Catholic Campuses*, edited by John Wilcox and Irene King (Washington, D.C.: Georgetown University Press, 2000), 161.

10. Conrad Cherry, Betty DeBerg, and Amanda Porterfield, *Religion on Campus* (Chapel Hill: University of North Carolina Press, 2001), 294–95.

11. Richard J. Light, *Making the Most of College: Students Speak Their Minds* (Cambridge, Mass.: Harvard University Press, 2001). See especially chapter 8, "Learning from Differences," 160–89.

12. See Peter Berger, *The Sacred Canopy* (New York: Anchor Books, 1969).

13. See Sophie Gilliat-Ray, *Religion in Higher Education: The Politics of the Multi-Faith Campus* (Burlington, Vt.: Ashgate, 2000). While this book focuses mainly on higher education in Great Britain, the parallels to America are numerous and instructive.

14. A number of scholars have addressed this point, including Martin E. Marty, *Education, Religion, and the Common Good: Advancing a Distinctly American Conversation about Religion's Role in Our Shared Life* (San Francisco: Jossey-Bass, 2000); Robert J. Nash, *Faith, Hype, and Clarity: Teaching about Religion in American Schools and Colleges* (New York: Teachers College Press, 1999) and *Religious Pluralism in the Academy: Opening the Dialogue* (New York: Peter Lang, 2001); and Nel Noddings, *Educating for Intelligent Belief or Unbelief* (New York: Teachers College Press, 1993). For an interesting case study of how religious faith can be allowed into the classroom see Susan

Handelman, " 'Stopping the Heart': The Spiritual Search of Students and the Challenge to a Professor in an Undergraduate Literature Class," in *Religion, Scholarship, and Higher Education*, edited by Andrea Sterk (Notre Dame, Ind.: University of Notre Dame, 2002), 202–29.

15. Michael L. Peterson, *With All Your Mind: A Christian Philosophy of Education* (Notre Dame, Ind.: University of Notre Dame, 2001), 204, 207, 216, 219.

16. Stephen H. Webb, *Taking Religion to School: Christian Theology and Secular Education* (Grand Rapids, Mich.: Brazos Press, 2000), 17.

17. A good example of such scholarship is R. Scott Appleby, *The Ambivalence of the Sacred: Religion, Violence, and Reconciliation* (New York: Rowman and Littlefield, 2000).

18. George M. Marsden, *The Outrageous Idea of Christian Scholarship* (New York: Oxford University Press, 1997), 45–46.

19. "The Land O'Lakes Statement: The Nature of the Contemporary Catholic University," in *American Catholic Higher Education: Essential Documents, 1967–1900*, edited by Alice Gallin (Notre Dame, Ind.: University of Notre Dame Press, 1992), 8.

20. Theodore M. Hesburgh, "The Challenge and Promise of a Catholic University," in *The Challenge and Promise of a Catholic University*, edited by Theodore M. Hesburgh (Notre Dame, Ind.: University of Notre Dame Press, 1994), 4.

21. Simone Weil, *Waiting for God* (New York: Harper and Row, 1973), 69.

22. Hughes, *How Christian Faith Can Sustain the Life of the Mind*, 28.

23. James Turner, "Does Religion Have Anything Worth Saying to Scholars?" in *Religion, Scholarship, and Higher Education*, edited by Andrea Sterk, 21.

24. Richard J. Mouw, *Consulting the Faithful: What Christian Intellectuals Can Learn from Popular Religion* (Grand Rapids, Mich.: Eerdmans, 1994).

25. V. James Mannoia, Jr., *Christian Liberal Arts: An Education that Goes Beyond* (Lanham, Md.: Rowman and Littlefield, 2000), 42–43.

Epilogue: Campus Climate and Christian Scholarship

Kim S. Phipps

This book's use of the term "conversation" is, for the most part, metaphorical. Conversation is used as a symbol for the broad discussion of Christian scholarship we would like to encourage within the academy as a whole. This epilogue seeks to move from that relatively abstract use of the term toward a focus on the real conversations—face-to-face dialogues and institutional conversations—that actually take place on college and university campuses. The goal is to explore how to promote open dialogue and "enlarge the conversation" in our own academic communities.

Virtually every college and university with which I am familiar refers to itself from time to time as a community—a community of scholars, a community of learners, a community of people living and working together. Community is, however, a notoriously fuzzy term. What does it mean? What is its importance for the scholarly quest? How does it relate to "conversation"?

At its core, community is the acknowledgment of our unavoidable interrelatedness; it is the admission that we are dependent on each other. Philip Slater has bluntly said that "the notion that people begin as separate individuals, who then march out and connect themselves with others, is one of the most dazzling bits of self-mystification in the history of the species."[1] Perhaps the most famous expression of this sentiment comes from the seventeenth-century English poet John Donne, who wrote in his *Devotions upon Emergent Occasions*:

> No man is an *Iland*, intire of it selfe; every man is a peece
> of the *Continent*, a part of the *maine*; if a *Clod* bee washed

away by the *Sea, Europe* is the lesse, as well as if a *Promontorie* were, as well as if a *Mannor* of thy *friends* or of *thine owne* were; any mans *death* diminishes *me*, because I an involved in *Mankinde*; And therefore never send to know for whom the *bell* tolls; It tolls for *thee*.[2]

Ernest Boyer, the educator to whom this book is dedicated, often noted that "we are all inextricably connected" to each other.[3] These three commentators on the human condition agree that individualism is a dangerous myth—a myth in the popular sense of the term, meaning something that is simply not true—but they also acknowledge that it is an amazingly powerful myth and one to which the academic world is not immune.[4]

The work of scholarship is, however, not an enterprise that can subsist on individualism. Scholarship is rooted in connectedness—in mutual assistance, conversation, encouragement, support, and evaluation. Scholarship proceeds by building on what others have done, and it makes sense only in the context of what others are doing. Scholarship is inherently and unavoidably communal. As the literary critic Wayne Booth explains: "We depend upon appraising the testimony and authority and general ethos of other people as they appraise the testimony and authority of still others, who in turn depend on others . . . and no one can say where these circles of mutual trust [within the academy] end."[5] This structure of mutual trust is evident within the individual disciplines where specialists share their insights with others and hold each other accountable. Booth argues that a similar structure of trust, assistance, and evaluation can and should operate across the disciplines, and he suggests that in healthy colleges and universities this kind of crosscampus dialogue will be an important aspect of the overall culture.

This campus-wide conversation will sometimes be formally interdisciplinary in nature—that is, the multidisciplinary exploration of some academic topic—but more often it will focus on concerns that transcend the standard academic divisions of knowledge and on issues that have become matters of special attention and importance for a particular college or university. The common threads that emerge and repeat themselves within this kind of campus-wide conversation tend, over time, to become the living identity of the institution. As communities of learning, we are the content of what we communicate. But colleges and universities are also deeply shaped by *how* we talk to each other, and here the ideals of community become even more important. Well-functioning communities nurture people through the conversations they maintain. Well-functioning communities give people the personal and emotional resources they need to flourish both as individuals *and* as persons who can help other members of the community flourish. And well-functioning educational communities produce scholarship because their members are in the business of supporting and encouraging each other in their scholarly work.

While this should be true of all colleges and universities, it is particularly important for Christian and church-related institutions of higher learning. To define community in terms of mutual care and flourishing is after all a distinctively Christian, if not necessarily uniquely Christian, way of understanding the nature of community. In fact, the theologian Rowan Williams has argued that this is the point of the church as an institution: to provide evidence that mutually self-giving human community is possible.[6] Applying that ideal of Christian community to higher education, Monika Hellwig has argued that Catholic colleges and universities (and by implication all other Christian institutions of higher learning) ought to be defined by their

> concern for the whole person of the student and all who are involved in the institution. Genuine human bonds of friendship and mutual respect and support are envisaged as the core of the educational enterprise, because not only book learning but human formation for leadership and responsibility in all walks of life are sought through the community experience of higher education.[7]

My approach will accordingly be to focus on the world of Christian higher education as that realm where Christian scholarship rooted in Christian community ought to be visible in an exemplary way. In doing this, I will concentrate on three specific areas of campus life: the climate of the campus as a place of intellectual hospitality; the practices of the campus as they encourage inclusive conversation; and the role of administrative leadership in nurturing campus cultures that embrace scholarship rooted in community.

An Ethos of Intellectual Hospitality

Hospitality can only be learned by experiencing its wonderful gifts. Hospitality is the gracious welcoming of the other into one's domain—into one's home or office or community, and into one's heart and soul. The term *hospitality* connotes genuine respect and concern both for an individual's needs and for her perspectives. Hospitality is a welcoming of the person in all of his or her uniqueness and fullness as a human being.

My husband and I experienced true hospitality early in our married life when we were interviewed for a staff position at a Midwestern church. A member of the congregation named Numa welcomed us into her home and into her heart during that stressful candidacy weekend. The food she prepared was delicious and the conversation was characterized by laughter and goodwill, but the most important aspect of Numa's hospitality was the way she carefully listened to two naive twenty-two-year-olds who had much to learn and experience (but didn't know it). We received the invitation to serve that congregation, and throughout the ensuing years, Numa repeatedly invited us for dinner, provided us with many tangible gifts, and even included us in family holiday celebrations. But her hospitality was most clearly communicated by her consistent, nonjudgmental, empathetic listening. Although she could have "set us straight" on numerous occasions, she chose instead to carefully listen, gently suggest, and enthusiastically support our initiatives and our dreams. She communicated love and respect to us in every conversation and action. Whenever I encounter the word *hospitality* I am immediately reminded of Numa and the gift of her presence in our lives.

Intellectual hospitality is, of course, not exactly the same as ordinary (which is actually not so ordinary) hospitality, but many traits are shared. Intellectual hospitality involves care and concern for the person, and it also necessitates inviting others into conversation, listening without prejudging, and affirming the value of others and their perspectives even when legitimate disagreement exists. Most important, intellectual hospitality involves the virtue of epistemological humility, which roots our openness to the views of others in the recognition that our own mental powers are limited and that the cognitive, experiential, and affective insights of others, especially when they are different from our own, can truly deepen and extend our understanding of others and the world that surrounds us. Intellectual hospitality is not just a matter of being civil to other people in an academic setting; it is a methodology of inquiry that humbly assumes that we can learn as much (or more) from those with whom we disagree as we can from our like-minded colleagues.

In addition to this academic rationale, there are a host of other reasons for Christian scholars to be intellectually hospitable. The first reason is rooted in the *imago dei*, which implies the infinite worth and value of all human beings because they are uniquely created in God's image. A second reason for Christians to be intellectually hospitable is that it is a concrete manifestation of being obedient to the New Testament commandment to love one's neighbor. Third, Christians are called to be intellectually hospitable because it is reflective of the kind, gentle, and compassionate ways of the Holy Spirit. The ideal of hospitality can undoubtedly be amply supported from scripture and Christian tradition. It is perhaps less clear how to apply intellectual hospitality to Christian scholars' roles as faculty in the classroom, colleagues in academic societies, and administrators at church-related colleges and universities.

Somewhat counterintuitively, applying hospitality to the scholarly realm requires an acknowledgment of legitimate conflict. In his article "The Academic Life as Christian Vocation," Charles J. Matthewes argues that Christian scholars *should* and *could* model for the academy the value of ideational conflict as a context for learning. He argues that "acknowledging conflict is a critical element in the Christian vision of the world."[8] The goal, of course, is not to stop with conflict but ultimately to move toward reconciliation. Without the recognition of conflict, reconciliation is impossible. Matthewes suggests that the work of reconciliation in the realm of intellectual inquiry and dispute should go beyond mere discussion and be expressed in reconciled relation-ships. That is appropriate Christian advice, for the essence of the gospel is reconciliation with both God and others. It is also appropriate scholarly coun-sel: when we are estranged from someone we invariably discount their ideas, and when that happens in the realm of scholarship, we may unthinkingly close ourselves off to any insights the other person might offer, which in turn limits our own reflective analysis of the world.

Intellectual hospitality also requires avoiding the cavalier or judgmental labeling of new or different points of view. Labeling is a necessary function of academic life. We all employ labels to help reduce the complexity of the world to manageable proportions. Intellectual life is rife with metaphors, taxonomies, typologies, and a host of other interpretive frameworks that sort people and ideas into helpful categories. But labels can also be used negatively, as rhetor-ical devices that deter the development of an intellectually hospitable climate by preventing individuals from perceiving people, ideas, and events as they truly exist. Terms such as "secular," "conservative," "liberal," "feminist," and "fundamentalist" often obfuscate more than they elucidate. This is true even when we are using these terms solely as mental categories that are never ver-bally expressed. If we allow ourselves to think in terms of glib or biased cate-gories, those thoughts will affect the social worlds in which we live even if they are never given voice. Intellectual hospitality requires us to use labels sparingly and generously rather than critically and suspiciously.

When scholars fulfill their roles as teachers, intellectual hospitality takes on even greater significance. Diana Chapman Walsh, president of Wellesley College, has argued that taking learning seriously necessitates the creation of campus cultures that engender honest, spirited dialogue about significant is-sues. An open, affirming classroom climate is essential for students to feel empowered to pursue "coherence, connection, meaning, purpose, hope, [and] love" in their lives and thinking. She adds that "these qualities of mind and spirit . . . are the very stuff of what faculty, when they are at their best, are inculcating in their students and passing on to future generations."[9] Christian scholars should possess a particular affinity for these spiritual elements of the educational process and for the ways intellectual hospitality can contribute to a meaningful learning experience.

There is, however, a caveat to this discussion of intellectual hospitality as it relates to church-related institutions of higher education. These institutions sometimes face challenges of intellectual hospitality that other colleges and universities do not encounter. Often the challenge emanates not from the cam-pus itself but from its external constituency. Friends and supporters of the college sometimes ask how much diversity can be allowed before the core identity and mission of the college will be harmed. How embracing can and should a church-related college be? Isn't there a place in American higher education for schools that provide a respite from the unchecked pluralism of the culture as a whole? Those are valid questions, especially when Christian colleges and universities are committed to the nurturing of Christian values in students as well as to the exploration of intellectual issues. But the critical factor is not one of limiting what issues can be discussed or who can be welcomed to the campus; rather this issue is more a matter of learning how to think and live as Christians in the midst of a very complex world. Leaders of church-related colleges need to communicate to their constituents that the particular missions and identities of their institutions can be cultivated even as intellectual hospitality is practiced.

The Practice of Inclusive Conversation

In the quest to create an intellectually hospitable campus climate that supports and encourages quality Christian scholarship, no practice is more important than inclusive conversation. The goal of inclusive conversation is civil dialogue rather than political posturing or the supercilious placating of others. It is the cultivation of true dialogue, rather than dueling monologues. Reuel Howe's little book *The Miracle of Dialogue* (1963) still says it well. He writes:

> At some moment, in the monologue, one participant may give up
> his pretenses and lay aside the masks by which he seeks the ap-
> proval and good will of the other, dare to be what he is in relation to
> the other, invite the other to be a partner in dialogue and be fully
> present to him as he really is. At that moment each of the partici-
> pants must accept the resulting address and response as the disci-
> pline and task of communication. Any relationship less than this
> would not be dialogue and, therefore, not communication.[10]

Creating a space for dialogue, for true conversation, is a core defining characteristic of educational institutions. In fact, John Bennett has suggested that conversation can serve as a metaphor for the entire educational process:

> Conversation points toward the cultural importance of individual
> participation in engagement with the voices that constitute our hu-
> man inheritance; it highlights the importance of the active engage-
> ment of those participating—faculty and students alike—as well as
> the significance of elements of self-involvement and reflexivity. It
> also reminds us of the need for hospitable openness to the other, be
> the other multicultural, global, near or far. And it illustrates the im-
> portance of observing a covenant with the other in mutual learning,
> not simply a contract of mutual convenience.[11]

College or university campuses are places where individuals learn how to hear the voices of others and to enter into scholarly conversations about ideas, images, issues, and ideologies. The campus as a whole, not just the classroom, is a place where students and faculty not only *learn indirectly about* what others think but also a place where we *learn directly from* each other about what each of us thinks.

In a healthy conversation, participants listen in order to deepen their understanding of a subject and to better appreciate one another. The importance of the conversation metaphor for scholarship in general and for Christian scholarship in particular is that it acknowledges the fact that our views on various topics are often derived from our own autobiographies as much as they result from logical reflection. Although reason and logic are central to understanding faith and scholarship, narrative also fulfills an important role. Martha Nussbaum has articulated the way personal narratives positively influence academic conversations in contrast to logic. She argues that narratives—personal and interpersonal stories—inspire creative wonderment and foster a sense of awe about humanity.[12] Narratives elicit empathy and camaraderie. Narratives require listeners to open their hearts and minds to the ideas, struggles, and experiences of others. Narratives often serve to create shared meaning and promote community. Scholarship that precludes consideration of the autobiographical perspectives of individual scholars will be severely limited, lacking creative imagination and insights into human nature.

The conversations we need to facilitate on our campuses regarding the nature and character of Christian scholarship must embrace both personal narrative and rational argument. The academy is slowly coming to understand the value of personal narratives as they relate to critical reflection and analysis, but many discussions surrounding Christian scholarship focus solely on logic and reason. This response may well be a reaction against the past when some Christian scholars used the language of testimony as a means of avoiding serious engagement with intellectual issues. While recognizing that potential danger, contemporary Christian scholarship needs to include both personal narrative and dispassionate reflection on faith, life, and the academic disciplines.

It is not sufficient to only improve our conversational skills; we also need to enlarge the subject of the conversation itself. As has already been suggested in this book, one way to expand Christian scholarship is to include perspectives from a variety of Christian traditions. Every tradition has strengths and weaknesses to bring to the conversation, and all traditions will be enriched by the mutual affirmation and critique of dialogue. This book engages in some criticism of the Reformed integration model of Christian scholarship because, as the current dominant model, it has sometimes tended to squeeze out other voices. Critique of the integration model opens space for other perspectives to be heard and valued. (Similar critical analyses could and should be brought to bear on all the other traditions of Christian scholarship.) The dynamic of conversation at different church-related colleges and universities will be distinctive since each institution ought rightly to give special attention and nurture to the specific tradition(s) that have informed the historic mission and identity of that school. At the same time, we all recognize that individual Christian traditions exist within a much larger matrix of Christian diversity, and we need to be very careful not to assume that our form of faith represents the best or the most authentic expression of Christianity.

Enlarging our campus conversations also means expanding the conversation socially to include voices that have been previously absent or marginalized. There is much to be gained from including the voices of both women and men and those of persons from other cultures, ethnic and racial groups, and religious traditions. The inclusion of these voices will offer new insights into the theoretical and practical assumptions that are foundational to discussions of both academic and faith issues. Of course, this view of inclusivity is now commonly articulated in official institutional rhetoric. Who would disagree? But the sad truth is that most of the participants in the discussions of Christian scholarship on college and university campuses across the nation are white males. We need to devise new ways of framing questions and structuring conversations so others will be attracted to and affirmed for participation in the discussion. Constructive practices that result in inclusive conversation do not happen without intention, commitment, planning, and foresight.

Finally, enlarging our campus conversations about Christian scholarship will require us to understand and value different forms of scholarship. As suggested earlier in this book, Ernest Boyer's categorization of scholarship as discovery, integration, application, and teaching might assist this understanding, and so might Gardner's idea of multiple intelligences. This book distinguishes among analytic, strategic, and empathic scholarship, while recognizing that most scholarship incorporates all three styles to some degree. What happens on many of our campuses is that conversation breaks down along the lines of the more applied versus the more theoretical disciplines (often taking the specific form of the traditional liberal arts juxtaposed against more career-oriented departments like business, engineering, education, and nursing), with the artists located on the periphery.

If we can help faculty members communicate in ways that acknowledge the practical side of the liberal arts and the empathic side of the professional disciplines and the strategic side of art, theater, and music (along with all the other possible existing combinations), we might be able to begin to undermine the ostracizing language of "us versus them" that now comes so readily to faculty conversations. Current discussions of Christian scholarship tend to follow patterns that are most amenable to those in the traditional liberal arts, especially the humanities. While sound historical and practical reasons for this tendency exist, and while the concerns of the liberal arts most emphatically do enrich conversations dealing with more applied fields of study, we cannot be content to leave the discussion in its current state. New models of Christian scholarship must respect all of the academic disciplines and must encourage all scholars to reflect on faith and learning in ways that fit naturally with their specific areas of expertise. Campus conversations that nurture and promote broader, stronger, and more direct connections between scholarship and faith will benefit both students and faculty.

Administrative Leadership

While many aspects of campus culture are shaped by the faculty as they seek to realize the identity and mission of the college, administrative leadership fulfills a critical role in creating a healthy climate of learning and scholarship at any college or university. Christian colleges and universities accordingly have much to learn from the national discussion that has focused attention on the emerging need for college and university administrators (in addition to being simple managers of the institution) to perceive themselves as leaders of a learning community. In fact, this is their first and most important task. Administrators ought to see themselves—and faculty and students ought to perceive them—as scholars with a unique role within the community, a role that often defines the nature of the institution.

The rhetoric that administrators choose to describe their schools, faculty, and students is fundamental. Perhaps the worst mistake an administrator can make is to speak of the college or university as simply a business, where student-consumers purchase various educational services from the institution and where faculty are seen as more or less replaceable assembly-line workers in a knowledge factory. This type of rhetoric demeans the meaning and purpose of education. But it is not just avoiding bad rhetoric that is required; administrators need to provide the campus community with language that inspires faculty and students alike to the highest levels of scholarly aspiration. Church-related colleges may have something special to model in this regard. At a recent gathering at a major research university, the highest purpose for education articulated by the leaders was "to help keep America strong and ahead of the rest of the world." While that may be a worthy goal (even if it is more than a bit ethnocentric), it does not compare to the Christian ideal of education as a means of knowing, loving, and serving God, our neighbors (meaning humanity as a whole), and all of creation.

Beyond language usage, however, administrators have a responsibility to establish and maintain policies that will aid and encourage—rather than undermine and discourage—the nurturing of scholarship and community on campus. Administrators need to work with faculty colleagues to create reward systems, including policies regarding promotion, tenure, and internal grants, that recognize excellence and elicit the best scholarship from many faculty members and departments within their institutions. One means of accomplishing this goal is to negotiate individual professional growth contracts with faculty members that encourage them to explore their unique interests, passions, gifts, and abilities. These contracts could be structured so that the particular stage of a faculty member's career (early, midterm, and late) might be considered a variable in the contract. Growth contracts are not the only way to motivate faculty members to scholarly excellence, but they represent one example of creative options that need to be considered.

Currently, however, institutional policies and practices frequently reflect very wooden, rigid definitions of scholarship. Most campuses have promotion and tenure processes based on the tripartite system of teaching, scholarship, and service; the reality is that scholarly productivity is the essential component at many institutions. Furthermore, there is often an informal caste system that assigns differential worth to different kinds of scholarly activity. At some schools, traditional "discovery" research (to use Boyer's terminology) rules the roost, and alternate forms of scholarship are viewed as deficient or unimportant. At other schools, especially those that pride themselves on being "teaching institutions," discovery research is demeaned as something pursued only by self-aggrandizing and uncollegial faculty. We need to develop policies and processes that recognize all of the various forms of scholarship.

Administrators also need to create mechanisms that demonstrate flexibility and fairness in our approach to faculty evaluation. The notion of flexibility does not imply a lessening of standards but the broadening of categories to include various forms and styles of teaching, scholarship, and service. It also means allowing faculty members to participate in determining how they will divide up their limited time and energy. Promotion and tenure policies that consider faculty interests and strengths in this way affirm the scholar in his or her calling and will undoubtedly result in greater self-understanding, higher levels of intrinsic motivation, and increased levels of performance. Honoring of individual differences among faculty members coupled with the equal valuing of all the scholarly domains, including humanities, arts, social sciences, natural sciences, and the professions will result in a transformed campus climate. No one in the campus conversation should ever be regarded as a second-class academic citizen.

I recently spoke to a national gathering of chief academic officers about the idea of educational community. In the discussion that followed, it became apparent that the term "community" was met with a significant amount of cynicism. Perhaps skepticism about community results from the hyperspecialization in the academy that has led to a divisive process of labeling and organizing according to disciplines, subdisciplines, methodologies, and institutional types. Campus cultures have often been shaped according to those divisions, and it will require courageous and creative commitment to challenge the seemingly impenetrable nature of those labels and boundaries.

But despite those problems, the ideal of community remains foundational to the academic life. The root of the word "community"—to communicate or to make common—is at the core of the academy's sharing of knowledge, wisdom, and understanding. Church-related colleges and universities and Christian scholars on other collegiate campuses have an opportunity to model what it means to fully participate in a community of learning. David Morgan of Valparaiso University suggests that building a Christian community of learning depends on much more than the rhetoric of official published statements, noting that "we must not restrict ourselves to creedal documents and mission statements, but focus with great interest on the things we do, the stories we tell, the rites we preserve, the memories of play, the music we perform, the buildings we build and those we raze."[13] The challenge for the administrator is to sponsor opportunities that enable faculty to tell stories (even their own), to create spaces for the kind of authentic conversation that includes honest questioning about faith, religion, and the academy, and to develop campus rituals and celebrations that focus on what human beings hold in common rather than what divides them. When community is actively preserved and nurtured on a campus, scholars will be empowered to share their questions along with their conclusions. Community makes it possible for colleagues and students to experience the joy of articulating the best of thinking, feeling, and practice.

The benefits of this kind of learning community extend to students and also to the larger contemporary society. As noted by Diana Chapman Walsh,

> inspired faculty—faculty who are not dispirited and whose morale is high—are indispensable in meaning making. They can build the relationships, forge the connections, bind together the pluralistic global learning communities that will provide undergraduates with models to carry throughout their lives, models that inspire lives of purpose and commitment to causes larger than themselves.[14]

Faculty will become inspired when campus structures and policies are designed to nurture rather than obstruct the development of their own interests and vocational calling.

Early in Gail Godwin's novel *Evensong*, the main character, Margaret, writes an angry letter to her friend (and future husband) Adrian Bonner. As a young seminarian Margaret has just experienced an emotionally exhausting, faith-challenging week working in an urban hospital ward. She wonders if ministry is truly her vocational calling. Adrian responds with these words of conjecture: "Something's your vocation if it keeps making more of you."[15] The vocation of the Christian scholar is to remain faithful while pursuing questions, reconsidering paradigms, proposing solutions, and creating artistic works. Christian scholars pursue scholarship because they are called to do so and because their scholarly pursuits make more of them as human beings—more of them intellectually, artistically, professionally, personally, and spiritually. Indeed, scholarship adds depth and breadth not only to the scholar's life and to the educational community in which he or she lives and works but also to the academy, the church, and society. Quality scholarship overflows: it produces passion, curiosity, synergy, and community that cannot be fenced in by the boundaries of any particular institution or organization.

The challenge for administrative leaders at church-related colleges and universities is to nurture and maintain campus cultures that acknowledge, affirm, and celebrate the many varieties of Christian scholarly vocation. Administrators must possess the courage and vision to create campuses that are characterized by "*inhabitable* truth . . . humble confidence . . . [and] relational trust" where students, administrators, and faculty alike can join together in a process of "communal knowing and being known."[16] And that, after all, is what the grand conversation of scholarship and Christian faith is all about: not simply knowing things but also being known. Not claiming the truth as if we owned it but living in truth and toward truth as a style of life. Not holding on to our current views as if they defined knowledge for all time but sharing our ideas and ideals with others in the confidence that they will come back to us in improved form. It is precisely that spirit of hope and trust that both undergirds us and beckons us forward in the ongoing conversation of Christian scholarship.

NOTES

1. Quoted in Rodney Clapp, *A Peculiar People* (Downers Grove, Ill.: InterVarsity Press, 1996), 91.

2. *The Complete Poetry and Selected Prose of John Donne*, edited by Charles M. Coffin (New York: Random House, 1952), 441.

3. Ernest L. Boyer, "Making Connections," in Ernest L. Boyer, *Selected Speeches 1979–1995* (Princeton: Carnegie Foundation for the Advancement of Teaching, 1997), 117.

4. In *Dependent Rational Animals* (Chicago: Open Court, 1999), the philosopher Alasdair MacIntyre argues: "We human beings are vulnerable to many kinds of afflictions and most of us are at some time afflicted by serious ills. How we cope is only in small part up to us. It is most often to others that we owe our survival, let alone our flourishing" (1). Despite that bedrock fact of our existence, he says that in the long history of the West philosophers have given only glancing attention to afflictions of the human condition. For the most part, persons are discussed as if they were "continuously rational, healthy, and untroubled" (2), as if they were powerful, independent agents capable of making their way in the world without assistance from anyone. MacIntyre says it is only recently that feminist philosophers have finally begun to deconstruct the enduring myth of antiinterdependence.

5. Quoted in Dykstra, *Growing in the Life of Faith*, 136.

6. Rowan Williams, *On Christian Theology* (Oxford: Blackwell, 2000), 236.

7. Monika K. Hellwig, "What Can the Roman Catholic Tradition Contribute to Christian Higher Education?" in *Models for Christian Higher Education: Strategies for*

Success in the Twenty-First Century, edited by Richard T. Hughes and William B. Adrian (Grand Rapids, Mich.: Eerdmans, 1997), 21. Hellwig's reference is to Catholic higher education, and, while I have expanded the scope of her remarks to include all Christian college and universities, the particularity of her focus on Catholic schools may be worth noting. Several recent studies have indicated that Catholic faith, social philosophy, and educational practices do tend to nurture and embody the ideals of community better than most forms of Protestantism. See Andrew Greeley, *The Catholic Imagination* (Berkeley: University of California Press, 2000), especially chapter 4, entitled "Community." See also John E. Tropman, *The Catholic Ethic and the Spirit of Community* (Washington, D.C.: Georgetown University Press, 2002). An exception to this rule is found in the Anabaptist tradition which, though Protestant, places great importance on community. See, for example, Sara Wenger Shenk, *Anabaptist Ways of Knowing: A Conversation about Tradition-Based Critical Education* (Telford, Pa.: Cascadia Publishing House, 2003).

8. Charles T. Matthewes, "The Academic Life as Christian Vocation." *Journal of Religion* 79, 1 (January 1999), 110–121.

9. Diana Chapman Walsh, "Taking Learning Seriously," *Change* 22, 4 (July/August 1990), 18–23.

10. Reuel L. Howe, *The Miracle of Dialogue* (New York: Seabury Press, 1963), 37.

11. John B. Bennett, "Liberal Learning as Conversation," *Liberal Education* 87.2 (2001), 32–39.

12. Martha Nussbaum, *Cultivating Humanity: A Classical Defense of Reform in Liberal Education* (Cambridge, Mass.: Harvard University Press, 1997).

13. David Morgan, "Scholarship, Teaching Practices: Reflections on Lutheran Identity," in *The Lutheran Reader,* edited by Paul Contino and David Morgan (Valparaiso, Ind.: Valparaiso University Press, 1999), 93–108.

14. Walsh, "Taking Learning Seriously," 18–23.

15. Gail Godwin, *Evensong* (New York: Ballantine Books, 2002).

16. Clapp, *A Peculiar People,* 186.

Index

THE

EW

EN

INSIDE THE VATICAN'S ELITE
SCHOOL FOR AMERICAN
PRIESTS

BRIAN MURPHY

GROSSET/PUTNAM
a member of Penguin Putnam Inc.
NEW YORK

GROSSET/PUTNAM
a member of
Penguin Putnam Inc.
200 Madison Avenue
New York, NY 10016

Copyright © 1997 by Brian Murphy

Library of Congress Cataloging-in-Publication Data

Murphy, Brian.
The new men : inside the Vatican's elite school for American
priests / by Brian Murphy
p. cm.
ISBN 0-399-14328-9
1. Pontifical North American College (Rome, Italy)—Students—Case
studies.   2. Catholic Church—United States—Clergy—Case studies.
3. Seminarians—Italy—Rome—Case studies.   I. Title.
BX920.I8M87   1997
230'.07'3245632—dc21   97-19620 CIP

Printed in the United States of America

1   3   5   7   9   10   8   6   4   2

This book is printed on acid-free paper. ∞

BOOK DESIGN BY GRETCHEN ACHILLES

ACKNOWLEDGMENTS

The gratitude I owe to others is far too great to fit in this small space.

Above all, I wish to pay my deepest respect and appreciation to the six seminarians who allowed me to intrude in their lives. Their patience and sincerity are the lifeblood of this book. They are exceptional men and, if their calling brings them to ordination, they will be exceptional priests.

An equal recognition of thanks goes to Monsignor Timothy Dolan, who granted me the access to the seminary that made the project possible. His laughter and kindness will never be forgotten.

Thanks also to the seminary faculty and, particularly, to Rev. Cornelius McRae, Lory Mondaini, and Angela Bonilla, who graciously put up with my incessant telephone calls and requests.

No amount of praise could do justice to the work of my exceedingly wise editor, Jane Isay. She took a chance when the project was just a few outline pages and helped it mature into something far richer than I originally conceived. Her stamp is on every page. Her colleagues, Kate Murphy and Clara Baker, were always cheerful during the ups and downs. Thank you, as well, to Wendy Carlton and Timothy Meyer for applying the final polish.

Robert Shepard is an agent, collaborator, and friend. From our first phone conversation until we finally met in Tuscany, he was a beacon that helped keep the project on course.

And to all the others who helped in countless ways: Susan Petersen; Victor Simpson; Vania Grandi; Benedict and Irene Benz and everyone in New England, North Dakota; Stefan Fatsis; Bruce DeSilva; Rev. Robert Panke; Nadine and John Kearns; Rev. Tom Richter; Beth Duff-Brown and Chris Brown; my parents and grandmother; the monks at Assumption Abbey; Missy Daniel at Harvard Divinity School; and the friendly crew at the Center for Applied Research in the Apostolate at Georgetown University.

Most of all, I must thank my wife, Toula Vlahou. Without her, there would be nothing.

FOR TOULA,
MY LOVE AND CONSTANT INSPIRATION,
AND ZOE,
BORN THE SAME DAY AS THIS PROJECT

CONTENTS

PART THREE
SPRING

This is a work of nonfiction. All the events occurred and the seminarians and clergy are real. The names of a few people outside the seminary have been changed to protect their privacy. Dialogue and descriptions from events not personally witnessed were recreated to the best of my ability through interviews with those who were there. Some minor changes were made in settings and chronology to try to avoid confusion on the part of the reader. These changes caused no important revisions or embellishments to the contents or context of the statements and opinions.

I lost my wife.

—NOTE BY SEMINARIAN LOOKING FOR HIS BREVIARY

A stout little book is the seminarians' everyday companion. The text of the Liturgy of the Hours draws on the earliest Christian traditions of celebrating the evolution of the day: morning, midday, evening, and night. The book, called a breviary or the Divine Office, contains psalms, readings, prayers, and other special offerings for each phase of each day as the Christian year draws toward and flows from Easter.

The breviary shapes and guides the seminarians' own meditations—on the faith or their own calling. The passages in their own way tend to reflect the time it should be read: the morning prayers are often full of hope and appeals for stronger faith; daytime passages frequently remind how much faith and religion can be infused with routine tasks; night prayers stress self-examination and intercessions for divine mercy.

Relatively few Roman Catholics dutifully keep up with the breviary readings. But it becomes an intense part of the seminary experience. Seminarians are expected to follow—alone or in groups—the passages in the breviary. At their ordination as deacons, they make the promise to pray daily the Divine Office.

"I love that word," the first-year seminarians at the North American College were told by the rector, Monsignor Timothy Dolan. "That's why we sometimes call it 'the Office.' Because it's our job. It's our office to pray daily."

He adds a warning. "The first thing to go when a priest is in trouble is the Office."

It began at a table with delicious pasta and a seminarian missing a thumb.

The lunch was pleasant and unhurried—in the languid fashion Italians long ago mastered. The fields and woods spilling away from Assisi were still a mosaic of deep summer greens joined together in random patterns like pieces of colored paper tossed to the winds. A big dark bird—some kind of hawk, maybe—coasted on the air currents. Up and down it went, its wings as rigid as a crucifix. But its head flicked from side to side as it scanned the ground below. The bird swooped suddenly, then pulled up just as abruptly. Its prey had escaped.

I watched the bird bank hard and disappear from my view. I was glad I came.

At first, I had resisted. But my sister and her husband, old friends of one of the seminarians at the Pontifical North American College in Rome, pleaded with me to come along. They didn't want to be the only simple tourists on the day-trip pilgrimage of seminarians to the birthplace of St. Francis. We were prepared—as most born-and-fled Catholics would be—for a heavy dose of browbeating and religious dogma.

Then the nine-fingered seminarian started telling his story. He told us how his left thumb was torn off when his bulky mitten wrapped around a spinning iron shaft on the back of an old John Deere tractor. He described how, two years later, he was 1986 North Dakota State wrestling champion at 167 pounds. And he confessed how he was utterly and profoundly surprised to end up in a seminary. "I thought," Tom Richter said, "I was just too normal to be a priest. I fought my calling. I mean, I fought it hard."

I stopped in mid-bite. "You mean," I mumbled, then swallowed quickly, "you mean, you didn't always just know? It wasn't some childhood dream to be a priest? I thought it was like that. That you always sort of knew."

"Are you kidding?" Tom laughed. "I wouldn't have guessed it in a million years. I used to ask myself, 'Why me? Why do I feel this tug to do something I never dreamed of doing?' I used to ask myself that a lot."

"And now?" I said.

"Now I accept it."

"Accept what?"

"That I'm where I should be. But that doesn't mean I stopped asking questions. Did God pick me? I don't know. Or did He just make me able to recognize my calling, which was always there but I couldn't see it? I don't know that either. I just know that now I feel at home. Finally, I feel at home."

So went my introduction to the Americans being shaped into priests at the North American College on the Janiculum Hill, rising near the edge of St. Peter's Square. They are just a small segment of the approximately 3,300 men at American post-university seminaries. But, using the past as a guide, the voices coming out of the North American College will be heard as a force far stronger than their numbers. Some will rise—perhaps reluctantly—to be bishops, archbishops, and possibly even a cardinal. Others will be called to work on Vatican commissions, its diplomatic corps, or study to become canon law experts.

And even a once-inconceivable scenario—the election of an American pope by the College of Cardinals—could grow ever more plausible in their lifetimes, considering the ever-expanding size and strength of the Catholic Church in the United States. When a priest named Karol Wojtyla was ordained in 1946 in Poland, the idea of a pope from Eastern Europe seemed just as remote. Thirty-two years later, he stood on a balcony overlooking St. Peter's Square and announced that he took the name John Paul II.

All the seminarians of the 1990s, from the most unassuming to the voraciously ambitious, will be tested in ways their predecessors were not. The comfortable middle ground is being pried apart.

One side is streaming away from the faith in greater numbers. Their gripes come in all shapes and sizes: disgust with sexually abusive priests, disenchantment with the Vatican's rigid codes, disdain for the seeming anachronism of a male-only hierarchy in a time and culture when inclusion and sharing are among the highest ideals. There are many who have turned their back on the Church but spin around often to glare back at the clergy—hoping that maybe, just maybe, they'll find a reason to move back a little closer.

On the other side are those yearning. They are no longer satisfied with an aloof priest or lazy platitudes from the pulpit. They demand a higher standard: a pastor excited and engaged with his faith. Shortcuts are not appreciated.

"People want to know that there is something there," said Rev. J. Bryan Hehir, senior chaplain at the Harvard Catholic Student Center. "This is fundamental, undeniable."

The 1990s have been conveniently broad-brushed by some as a period of spiritual renewal and self-discovery—a contemplative stroll after the hard-charging eighties. Small events suggest there is truth to this characterization. On a blustery January day in 1997, I watched two men in expensive suits and elegant overcoats race up the stairs of St. Patrick's Cathedral in New York. I thought at first they were just trying to escape the bitter wind. But they put their briefcases down and sat side by side in the last pew. I asked why they were there. "It's my daily ten-minute vacation," one of them said. "I crave the peace."

I often heard the same thing from the American seminarians in Rome.

At the very beginning of their time in the seminary, years before any stumble or rise in the Church, comes the essential confrontation for these men who want to become priests. They must decide if the commitment and faith that brought them to the seminary is enough to sustain them in the priesthood. Can they handle the diverging demands of reaching out to the cynics while appealing to the rising spiritual hunger among others? Can they handle the chores to keep the parish financially afloat? Can they cope with the isolation and temptations of being assigned to run a parish alone because of the declining ranks in the priesthood? Can they find peace?

This is a book about those days.

A year after my lunch with Tom Richter, I began chronicling the first year of six men at the preeminent seminary for Americans. Richter's candid descriptions about his vocation—his sincerity, his humanity—had made me curious. Was he just a joyous anomaly; a four-leaf clover surrounded by clerical conformity? Or was the farmboy with a crew cut inadvertently offering me a clearer look at a religion I thought I knew?

I wanted to ask the same question Tom Richter had posed to himself: Why is this happening? What continues to draw men to the seminary, a place so singular in its ancient—or, some would say, outdated and misguided—mission? Who still hears the call?

The diversity at the North American College shows that this ancient call still, somehow, filters through. The seminarians I followed offer a panorama of backgrounds: a lawyer, a former Air Force pilot, a Vietnamese immigrant, a farmer's son, and, lastly, twins from Lowell, Massachusetts, who went separate ways after graduating from Harvard and were reunited in Rome. They represent as good a cross-section of American Catholics as possible with a half-dozen men. The North American College has few blacks—as does, relatively, the American Church. The issue of gay seminarians did not apply with these six, although it certainly is a dynamic in many American seminaries.

All six men were brought together by the Roman Catholic Church, but this is not a book that attempts to dissect the Vatican or poke for scandals behind the velvet curtains. Theologians and insiders have done this—and will continue to do this—far better than I can. Few institutions evoke such strong opinions as the Catholic Church and, inevitably, any work on the subject is destined to be branded as too apologetic or too critical or "too" any number of things. If anything, I hope this book is called too narrow. I tried as best I could to keep riveted to the seminarians and the seminary. It's their voices and feelings I want to convey: the depths of their faith, fears, and doubts. In other words, what it means and what it takes to seek the priesthood today.

To place them in the context of some sweeping analysis of the Vatican would be, in my opinion, a terrible mistake. These are highly personal stories. The truth—or as close as any observer can get—rests in the subtleties: a quiet conversation or a tear shed in a little chapel. This would be lost on a bigger stage.

Above all, this is a book about change. It's men trying to reinvent themselves under new codes, new demands, new expectations. They are New Men, as first-year seminarians are called at the North American College. It's a year when many notions are destroyed and others take their place. They taste the dry panic of loneliness and the relief of sharing their fears. They learn how to pray and also, for them, the sheer power of those prayers.

The year of the New Men is rarely easy, often painful, and sometimes too much for them to bear. Transformation always exacts a price. But it can also bestow rewards.

I, too, evolved along with the New Men I followed. I began the project with a slushy conception of seminary formation and seminarians. I expected something like Vatican boot camp: squashing individuality and critical thinking. The priesthood, of course, requires a conformity to tenets such as celibacy and the ban on ordination of women. But I quickly learned that today's seminary actually nurtures, even encourages, questioning. These New Men are told to examine their commitment to the priesthood very closely for any imperfections. Later on, sometimes long after ordination, these small flaws, left untended, can cause the whole fabric of their lives to unravel.

Many things about the New Men impressed me. Honesty would be high on the list. The seminarians I grew to know approached their vocations with refreshing frankness. Very little was taken for granted—least of all their calling to the priesthood. They pushed, at different speeds and intensities, to discern where they really belonged. I believe they understood what a special opportunity this was. Few of us ever have the time or latitude for such contemplation.

I left the New Men with a redefined view of the Catholic clergy. Obviously, it would be foolish to project the stories of a handful of American seminarians onto the entire priesthood. But now—and perhaps always—I will look at the priesthood and think about the sincerity and honesty in which the New Men faced their vocations rather than only the stories of priestly abuses and corruption that all journalists, myself included, instantly dive into.

I'll think of the New Men walking wide-eyed over to St. Peter's Basilica for the first time. I'll think of them gathering together to pray each Saturday in front of the little grotto on the edge of the seminary parking lot. I'll think of them leaving Rome so different from when they arrived. But mostly I'll think of the small steps. I'll remember a seminarian walking along the Janiculum Hill in a moment of self-doubt. I'll recall two New Men talking late into the night about how hard it is to let go of the secular world where they both thrived. I'll think about a seminarian so confused he cried. And months later, wept again because he was so content.

"If you excuse the demonic imagery, it's definitely trial by fire," said the rector, Monsignor Timothy Dolan. He watches over it all, reminding me a bit of the bird I watched circling around Assisi. Dolan glides through the seminary, a gregarious and reassuring presence seemingly too preoccupied with other affairs to know about the individual struggles of the seminarians. But his perception is laser sharp. The New Men are especially under his watch. Without Dolan, my own understanding of the seminarians and the seminary would be sorely incomplete.

"Good, holy, happy, healthy, learned, zealous, selfless, committed priests," he told the New Men in one of his many pep talks. He sets the bar high.

"On a purely numerical scale one would say, 'How can you be optimistic?' " Dolan told me. "I'm talking about the numbers of vocations to the priesthood and religious life. About the best thing we can say is at least it seems we've bottomed out. There doesn't seem to be more dramatic drops.

"But if you're in the Church, hope is your business."

Tom Richter keeps a lot of things from the days before the seminary. There's a bulging scrapbook, stacks of photos. And his disembodied thumb. He asked the doctors to preserve it in formaldehyde. Now it's dried out—a creepy black and wizened digit with a purple-tinged fingernail.

How much is the Church—or religious commitment in general—like Richter's old thumb, still around but lacking any pulse? Or, to look at it another way, something so precious it cannot be discarded? After my time with the New Men, I would go even further. Could it be that, as Rector Dolan says, the security and certainty of religion beckons even more as the world speeds ahead on fast-forward? It certainly appears so.

In a March 1996 letter on religious vocations, John Paul II rhetorically chided: "Is the consecrated life not a 'waste' of human energies that might be used more efficiently for a greater good, for the benefit of humanity and the Church?

"These questions," he continued, "are asked more frequently in our day as a consequence of a utilitarian and technocratic culture that is inclined to assess the importance of things and even of people in relation to their immediate usefulness."

Stop lying to one another. What you have done is put aside your old self with its past deeds and put on a new man, one that grows in knowledge as he is formed anew in the image of his creator.

—READING FOR THE CHRISTMAS SEASON (COLOSSIANS 3:9–10)

THE NEW MEN

PART ONE

ALL

CHAPTER I

THE TOMB

Test everything; retain what is good.

—EVENING READING FOR THE FIRST SUNDAY OF ADVENT
(I THESSALONIANS 5:21)

They were so new.

His black leather shoes were as creaseless as polished ebony. He swept each foot back and forth over the patio to scratch a few scars in the unblemished soles. Dew made the stones slick and he didn't want any embarrassing slips. Especially not on this morning. Not in front of all these strangers. He scraped the soles again on the brick trim like he was grinding out a cigarette. He stopped quickly. It seemed obnoxiously loud. Only a few people were talking, and that was in whispers. On the other side of the wall—it was hard to tell how far away—a few motorbikes whined past. Then it was quiet once more.

Strangers. He thought about that word. It seemed a bit odd under the circumstances. Strangers, yes, in the obvious sense. He knew only a few of the others' names and hometowns. Not much more. There hadn't been much time yet to get acquainted. But stranger also implies something separate, something different, doesn't it? That certainly doesn't seem the right way to describe a bunch of American seminarians huddled at dawn in a foreign place. What could be a better way? he wondered. Brothers? Maybe. It was just too early to tell.

He glanced quickly around at some of the others. He liked to study faces. They gave away a lot if you knew the right way to look. It was easy back home on the Dakota plains rising toward the Badlands and the Montana line. A little squint or a tight smile usually meant tragedy; a foreclosure or crops wiped away by pests or storm. Cheeks chapped by sun and dry wind was a good sign. You don't spend a lot of time outdoors if there's nothing to harvest. But these faces around him now were harder to discern: affected by stories and circumstances he didn't know.

What did he expect? A type of instant bond among seminarians coming from every part of America; some who rode the seesaw of indulgence and others who trod the straight and narrow? He wasn't used to this. Back home in his Catholic corner of North Dakota, a place of straight roads and strong-necked children of Bavarian and German-Russian homesteaders, everyone and everything was instinctively understood. Not here, though. It's so much more complicated here. He sensed that right away. Yet, somehow, like the jigsaw of the Catholic Church in America, the complexity fits together. The first thing he noticed was that he wasn't sweaty-palmed nervous like he often was in cities. When he was in third grade, he wrote that the only thing he hated was chickens because of his coop-cleaning duties on the farm. He never really hated much, but he surely hated big cities. But, strangely enough, not here. At least not in this precise place, at this precise moment, waiting to go to this one mass. He looked over his shoulder at the dome of St. Peter's Basilica.

Then he turned back to the seminary. It's a solid building, built in tan stone in the elegant symmetry of a Renaissance palazzo: arched walkways that bend the shadows and sunlight into gentle waves that sweep forward as the sun rises. The central courtyard, following traditional style, is dominated by a fountain and rows of orange trees. But the present seminary compound is not yet even fifty years old— younger than probably any building visible from its ridge on the Janiculum Hill, which rises like a big arm pushing buildings and streets toward the Tiber River from the Vatican to the old neighborhood of Trastevere.

The picture windows of the seminary reflected the blue-green pines and perfectly clipped lawn. Gary Benz shifted a bit in his new shoes. From the proper angle, St. Peter's dome was framed in the glass, clean and streakless after the summer cleaning while the seminary was empty.

Gary felt that electric rush when amazement and anticipation converge. He took a deep breath to try to relax. It only helped a little. Do the others feel it, too? he wondered. They must. Why would everyone be so silent if they weren't also a bit boggled? But soon he'd know. He'd know all about them. These men—these New Men as the rector calls them—would have to become his confidants and, in a way he was just coming to realize on a soggy morning, fellow travelers. That's it, he thought. That's exactly how it felt: different people moving in the same direction.

It was fitting they all looked the same, dressed according to the rector's memo: full clerics. To anyone who could peer over the walls, they would appear no different from a group of young priests. Details, though, gave them away. The creases on the trousers were just too sharp; the prayer book binders were without cracks and still looked like presents fresh from home. Some tugged at their collars and the white band—no bigger than a bandage—that changes everything.

Wearing the Roman collar means donning the full weight of the faith. It means becoming a target for those declaring the Church spiritually bankrupt. It means being a champion for the faithful who are expecting—even desperate for—piety and purity from their clergy. These men, still years away from ordination, felt it instantly. The little white tab demands attention. The rector had given the new seminarians the most startling of orders. "You have one task," he says. "That is to configure yourself to Jesus Christ." The New Men gawked. To some the message seemed medieval in its simplicity; a holy grail in a time when legends don't work anymore. A remnant cry drowned out by the ever-louder Vatican ministering and marketing and the clamor from American Catholics and others pressing special agendas. And this is all the rector can offer? It seemed meager preparation to joining the front lines of the faith's skirmishes.

"Patience," the rector had urged. "You'll see what I'm talking about."

The New Men passed their breviaries—the prayer books of the daily Liturgy of the Hours—nervously from hand to hand as they waited by the back gate. They checked all the buttons and gave their shoes one last buff on the back of their calves. It reminded some of them of their first date.

Gary Benz, slim enough that his Adam's apple poked out, felt instead like he was back on the first day of school, all spiffy and holding nicely sharpened pencils and, if the harvest was good that year, wearing some new clothes. He had picked out a classic model shoe to bring to Rome: wingtips with a military-style gloss. Good for walking, the clerk said. He figured he'd be doing a lot of that in Rome. But now, the first day really wearing them, they pinched. He knew what his dad would say: they pinched like the devil.

He tried to stand still and forget about the blisters he surely would have by the time he returned to the seminary for breakfast. He concentrated on watching other New Men come up the path, past the three-story California redwood the pope planted as a sapling in 1980. Was he early or were they late? He couldn't remember exactly what time the rector had said to meet. It was tough to keep it all straight in the forty-eight head-spinning hours since they arrived. There had been masses, orientations, room assignments, unpacking. He had almost fallen asleep nose-first into his strawberry gelato the night before.

The New Men yawned and fidgeted and waited for the rector at the top of the steps. A cat ran from under a bush, dodged the Americans, and darted away in the direction of the Vatican. Facing downhill from the back of the Pontifical North American College, the white dome of St. Peter's Basilica swells above everything else—over the red-tile roofs, the forest of television antennas. The seminarians kept looking it over the way mountaineers study their next peak. A bit awed, a bit anxious.

"First time?" one of the New Men asked another.

"Yeah. This is actually my first time out of the States. Can you believe it? We're sitting here staring at St. Peter's."

"No, I mean is it your first time wearing clerics?"

"Oh. Yeah, that too. You too? I don't know, I feel kind of like I'm part of the place now."

"Rome, you mean?"

"Sure. Don't you?"

"Makes me feel serious."

"Serious? Really? Like how?"

"Like, you know, it's time to get serious."

"Guess so. What do you think it will be like the first time someone calls you 'Father'?"

"Like I said," the New Man answered. "Serious."

Gary Benz listened to the conversation but didn't add anything. He hadn't really given it much thought. But, no doubt, the other New Man was right. The North American College is a serious place. The rector makes it clear before their pew seats are even warm on arrival day. I'm not interested in halfway seminarians looking to become bend-the-rule priests, he says. Not these days with the Roman Catholic Church being routinely bashed as a haven for maladjusted pastors and retrograde thinking. Not with the congregations back home shriveling up. You got a problem? Let's talk about it, the rector demands. You have unshakable doubts about the priesthood? Here's a ticket home—no recriminations, no accusations.

The rector was one of the last to arrive at the gate. The day hadn't yet turned sultry, but his cheeks already had a spidery blush that looked even more pronounced against his black cassock, adorned with the purple sash of monsignor. He had vowed to lose some weight this year. Less beer, fewer good Italian *dolci* and—the Lord willing—some real exercise. One of his standard jokes is that his contract was for five years or fifty pounds. "Then I'm outta here by Christmas," laughs Monsignor Timothy Dolan.

"Ready, fellas?" he said without breaking stride.

A metal door at the bottom of the steps was pulled back in a little puff of rust and city grit that fell from the hinges and the upper ledge. The narrow exit—just wide enough for one—is rarely used and reserved for special events that merit a shortcut to the Vatican. The New

Men's first trip together to St. Peter's is one of those times. One by one, forty-one seminarians filed through the passageway cut in the ninth-century brick escarpment. All dressed in black, all carrying their breviaries, they walked down the Janiculum, first a gentle descent before the road takes a sharp turn and swings down to the flats that, from time to time over the centuries, were flooded by the dirty Tiber. Markers on some buildings show how high the water rose.

The New Men easily crossed the usually perilous Piazza Sant'Uffizio, where the headquarters of the infamous Inquisition was established after Pope Paul III began his reign in 1539. Now, the piazza is mostly known as a place for traffic bottlenecks at the mouth of a roadway tunnel under the Janiculum. Although the New Men walked across the piazza on the first day of September—always a busy month in Rome—it was still mostly deserted. The August holiday month generally spills over a couple of days. They had the narrow sidewalk to themselves as they neared the colonnades around St. Peter's Square. Just before the first souvenir stand—pope espresso cups and Vatican shake-and-snow domes—they crossed Via Paolo VI.

Pigeons scattered. A bag lady, a skinny figure who is always hanging around, watched the New Men step from Rome's slate-black cobblestones to the bone-white travertine stone of Vatican City.

She didn't bother sticking out her hand and went back to savoring what was left of her cigarette. Clergymen rarely fish out any lire. Anyway, she could tell this group wasn't about to break stride. She blew out a line of smoke that was whisked away in a rush of black cloth—down two wide steps and into the piazza, where the only sound this early was the cascading water in the two huge fountains. Most people coming for the first time stop to take in the expanse of St. Peter's Square and the graceful basilica dome. Some try to figure out which windows look out from the papal apartments that jut out to the side. Others gather around the 135-foot Egyptian obelisk looted by Emperor Caligula—and now topped by a cross. It once loomed over the orgies and chariot races in Nero's Circus and may have been the last thing Peter saw before falling unconscious as blood flooded his head after being crucified upside down.

The New Men just kept going.

With a practiced flick, the beggar launched the cigarette back toward the morning traffic on the road ringing the square. She settled back against one of the thick columns at a spot right at the line between the clean half facing the square and the sooty side looking toward the street. She pulled the hem of her dress tight around her ankles. Two teddy bears, their fur dirty and matted, poked out of her satchels. The basilica was just about to open. The tourists and their spare change would be back any minute. Vatican bells rang seven times for the hour.

The inner oak doors—behind the massive bronze ones—were just being secured open when the group crossed the portico. The door farthest to the right—the Holy Door—stayed closed. It is only opened on papally declared Jubilee years. The next one is 2000: what would be the New Men's first full year as priests.

They brushed back the stiff leather curtains at the end of the doorway and entered the basilica, passing near the disk of red porphyry stone marking the spot where Charlemagne was crowned defender of the Holy Roman Empire nearly 1,200 years ago. Janitors took their dust mops on one last circuit around the papal altar at the other end. Each one of the New Men dipped his fingers into an ornate basin of holy water and crossed himself. With no one else around, they began to walk up the center aisle. They genuflected as they crossed in front of the Chapel of the Blessed Sacrament halfway up the nave. They listened to their own footsteps.

It was exactly as New Men have done since before the Civil War started; just as countless other pilgrims have done. Suddenly, the New Men felt very small, swallowed whole by the leviathan of time and the infinite hungers of the millions who walked this course before them and will do the same in eras to come. Each was thinking, with different degrees of anxiety, about what they were trying to become: Roman Catholic priests in an age when many of their contemporaries are suspicious, if not contemptuous, of this type of devotion.

"Seems like a church for once, doesn't it? I mean, quiet like this. Without all the visitors," whispered Rev. Daniel Kampschneider, walking behind the group.

Eighteen years before, he had made the same first visit to St. Peter's as a lanky seminarian whose family farm near Omaha—hogs, soybean fields, a little corn—could have been easily tucked under its roof. He was now part of the faculty in charge of grooming a new generation of priests at the seminary up the hill. The West Point of the American Catholic congregation, it's been called. Bishop school. The hub of an old boys' network in which the old boys comprise the elite of the Church. Rector Dolan hears this all the time. In part because of the seminary's mythology; in part because of fact. If his seminarians rise to become Church leaders—and certainly many will—that's wonderful, Dolan says. But he whittles his own mission to the fine point: create sound parish priests. Create pastors whose lives are shaped around zeal, compassion, and, above all, respect for the minds and bodies of those who trust them. "And, God knows, we need priests like that," says Dolan.

"A lot of things may happen, but you never forget the first time you walk through St. Peter's," said Kampschneider. "This is powerful stuff."

One of the New Men tugged at another's sleeve. "Look, look," he said, pointing down an alcove to the glass-protected Pietà, carved by Michelangelo when he was twenty-five—younger than about half the New Men. Farther up the aisle, they stopped before a statue of St. Peter and rubbed its bronze foot, worn smooth from hands and lips since 1857 when Pope Pius IX granted a fifty-day indulgence to anyone who kissed it after going to confession. Two years later, the North American College was founded and Pius told the first New Men they were now under the Vatican's paternal eyes. America of that day was maturing quickly and discovering its self-confidence. The country was still very much a Protestant autocracy, but down in the trenches a different class was beginning to rise. The Catholic community in America was growing as fast as steamers could bring over new immigrants. From the Vatican's perspective, it was also growing a bit too feisty. More and more American-born bishops felt greater allegiance to their flock than to the distant Curia. If the Holy See could no longer rein in this new brand of pioneer Catholicism with edicts, it could at least try to steer it its way. When American bishops asked for a seminary in Rome, the answer was a swift yes. The Vatican's view: the more priests it could bring to Rome to train, the better.

The New Men walked to their left from the St. Peter statue to the marble railing around the steps leading to the tomb of the saint. The stairs curve down like ram's horns just in front of the papal altar, covered by the bronze baldachino which rises on Bernini's twisting columns.

After his death, Peter was wrapped in cloth and placed in a simple dirt grave in a public cemetery. The Romans allowed the Christians, this strange new sect, to take the body. Peter was an old man who had suffered in prison. There was no point in putting him to the final indignity that befell other Christians. At his most wicked, Nero was said to coat Christians with resin and use them as long-burning torches. They also granted Peter's final request: to be strapped to the cross with his head facing the ground. Peter thought himself unworthy to be martyred the same way as Jesus approximately thirty-one years before. Word of Peter's burial quickly spread, and soon a simple six-foot-high temple marked the spot for pilgrims. Walls and embellishments were made until the fourth-century reign of Emperor Constantine, who favored the Christians since, as legend says, he had a vision to paint crosses on his soldiers' shields on the eve of an important battle in which his troops defeated superior forces. There are debates whether Constantine actually converted, but he marked his appreciation of the faith in tangible terms. He ordered a huge church—the biggest of the ancient world—built over the spot of Peter's grave. The plan required hundreds of workers and slaves to level the hillside cemetery. The first church was finished in 349. It stood for almost 1,200 years until Pope Julius II ordered a new basilica. Work began in 1506 and the facade was finally finished 108 years—and seventeen popes—later.

The New Men looked down at the steps, which lead to a doorway that gives special access to the tomb. Below that, in the subterranean vaults and passageways below the basilica, is the altar built by the twelfth-century Pope Callistus II. This covers the altar, built around 600, of Constantine's old church. It covers a box of marble and porphyry surrounding the remains of the crude columns and arch built over Peter's grave. And at the bottom of it all, in the dark brown soil, are the remains venerated as Peter's.

Seventy-four tiny flames sparkled from thick gold branches fashioned like palm trunks around the railing. The New Men studied a little chest in the sanctuary halfway down the stairs. It holds the lamb's wool that will be spun into the white cloth adorned with a black cross worn by archbishops, the Church leaders of the world's most important cities.

When Rector Dolan was a New Man, such things seemed a bit arcane. Seminarians seldom wore their Roman collars. It was hard to think about symbols such as consecrated wool when the big picture was growing fuzzy. These were the years after the 1962–65 Second Vatican Council, which sought a religious evolution but instead touched off a revolution. At its core—away from the many ideological and theological clashes it spawned—it tried to reorient the Church back to its followers. By scrubbing away at the residue of centuries of Church paternalism and overinflated majesty, part of the council's message to Catholics was that they are the sum total of the faith and not just an audience for the clergy. A revitalized, modernized Church was what the council was after.

In the States, which adopted the Vatican II principles with typical American zeal, the consequence was the opposite in many quarters. Loyalists to the old ways were disenchanted. Christmas-and-Easter Catholics leaned toward following their conscience rather than the Vatican. Lots of others just cashed it in completely.

Priests, especially young ones, were left groping. Their faith seemed to be in a free fall and many priests could just cringe and watch the Church career from one scandal to the other. On national television in 1992, the Irish singer Sinead O'Connor tore up a photograph of Pope John Paul II. And something even more startling happened. She was mercilessly skewered in the media. Letters to the editor used words like blasphemy and heretic, and commentators slammed her insolence. Some priests heard something else. Could it be the thump of things finally hitting bottom?

The New Men resolutely believe they are part of some sort of rebound. The steep decline in ordinations in the United States began to flatten out in the early 1990s, about the same time trend-spotters believed they could make out the faint horizon line of the next important frontier: spirituality, a quest for meaning in a nation growing ever more frenetic and neurotic.

Everyone in the seminary has a story about the moment he decided to seek the priesthood. Chris Nalty's is as tangy as his Cajun-spiced accent. "It was in the Alabama woods at a hunting camp at my family's tree farm," he said. "It was January. January ninety-three."

Somehow he lost a cherished pinky ring with his family crest: a griffin rising from a castle tower. Maybe it got caught on his rifle? Or maybe a branch? He had become so caught up in a strange preoccupation—an incomprehensible attraction to the priesthood—that the ring could have slipped off and he didn't notice. He prayed long hours to St. Anthony to help him find the ring, but as the months passed, so did his hopes. Then, eleven months after losing the ring, he was back and walking down a timber road toward a deer blind—a hidden wooden perch. Slung over his shoulder was his .270 Browning A-bolt with a stainless steel barrel and 50-mm scope that can pick up a "gnat's eyelash." The sandy soil was packed down and pockmarked after a night of rain.

The mugs of coffee for breakfast finally caught up with him. He couldn't relieve himself near the deer path because the animals can pick up the urine scent. He turned off the road and unzipped his camouflage pants. He sighed and said a short prayer for the ring. He turned around and there it was: a gold circle sticking out from the soaked ground.

"I looked up, and I had tears rolling down my face, and I said, 'All right, I'll deny you nothing. You got me. You've been knocking me. You've been giving me signals and I've been ignoring them and I've not been thinking about them.' I've been kicking this priesthood thing around. I've thought about this thing for eight years. I can think about it for another eight or I can give it a shot."

He began methodically to cut away what he had once coveted: a big house just outside New Orleans with a nice yard for his black Labrador, his legal work and offers from top-money law firms, white BMW, Rolex, his New Year's party when he'd slick his hair back, put on a tuxedo, and light up a smuggled Cuban cigar.

Everything about Nalty is big: his laugh, the way he tells a story with his arms churning every which way, his appetite for life. His hair-line is rapidly receding, as it often does with guys in their thirties. Chris doesn't worry about it, though. But his husky frame was beginning to show just a hint of middle-age sag and, like the rector, Nalty vowed to do something about it. However, there are so many tasty diversions in Rome. After just a few days at the seminary, he already had made plans to collect pine nuts from the grounds to add to his fresh pesto sauce.

"I was pretty wild in college. I was pretty wild in law school. I was pretty wild when I was practicing law because there's the attitude: work hard, play hard."

Now, he was in St. Peter's, wondering how to be a seminarian at thirty-three years old after all the high living and down-and-dirty fun. "For me, there was no harm in giving it a shot. I can always go back to New Orleans and practice law."

Nalty was one of the few seminarians not gawking at the basilica. He had been there before—with VIP treatment. His father was presi-dent of the Louisiana chapter of the Patrons of the Vatican Museum and took the family for the unveiling of the restored Last Judgment fresco by Michelangelo in the Sistine Chapel in 1994.

He made a prayer at the Vatican during that visit that he has re-peated every day since deciding to seek the priesthood. It's simple and direct. Nalty asks: give me the strength to remain celibate. "Celibacy is, in a lot of ways, very foreign to me," he said.

In some ways, Nalty and the "delayed vocations"—as they are called—are beneficiaries of Vatican II. When the council tried to plunge the faith into the modern age, the priesthood itself was rede-fined. With seminaries emptying, bishops cast a wider net. Anyone who felt he had a vocation now had a receptive audience, where before he might have been rebuffed as too tainted or just plain too old. Men started to leave careers and love affairs behind as the seminary ranks became smaller but, in some sense, richer and more diverse. A newly ordained priest who spent five years at the North American College used to carry the nickname "Drench" for his cocktail-soaked lifestyle. He's now considered one of his archdiocese's most earnest young priests. "Without Vatican II," he observed, "most of us wouldn't be here at all."

Even Pope John Paul II, who has little tolerance for Church renegades, speaks often about the need to make the priesthood accessible to all and proudly recalls his days as a quarry worker and aspiring actor. "Mine was an adult vocation," he said at one of the Vatican galas in 1996 for the fiftieth anniversary of his ordination.

Eighteen of the forty-one New Men came directly from college. The rest ranged from blue chip to blue collar: four lawyers, truck driver, furniture salesman, molecular biology researcher, political campaign worker, construction hand. And one set of twenty-five-year-old twins: Scot and Roger Landry.

In St. Peter's—up the main aisle and over to the papal altar—the Landry twins walked side by side, counting on each other as they have since street fights and ball games in the old clapboard neighborhoods in Lowell, Massachusetts.

"So, Rog, we did it," said Scot. "We're in St. Pete's together."

"Yeah. Wish our folks were here. Wouldn't Mom love to see this."

"Imagine if she were here?" Scot said. "Dad, too. It would just blow 'em away."

They walked a little more.

Scot turned to his brother. "You remember our first day at Harvard, when everything seemed exciting but, you know, kind of intimidating?" he asked.

"Yeah. I figured you were going to mention that. In my opinion, though, this is much, much bigger. Don't you think?"

Scot nodded. He had always envisioned Roger as a future priest. Until recently, however, the picture had never included himself walking alongside in a Roman collar, too. Scot always thought he'd be the family benefactor. He'd make enough money to make everyone comfortable.

None of the New Men had yet picked up on the cues to tell the Landrys apart. They each cropped their hair—the color of milk-and-sugar coffee—into bristly crew cuts. Their Merrimack River accent rolled out exactly the same way. The Landrys are classic New England Quebecois stock: built compact, but hard and lean; a good sense of humor, but quick to recognize if someone is feeding them bullshit. When they were kids, if anyone picked on a Landry boy they would have four fists to deal with. But, mostly, they just outwitted everyone else with a potent combination of intelligence, cunning, and young arrogance. Roger was valedictorian of his high-school class and Scot was number three. They went to Harvard, then after graduation they went their separate ways for the first time.

Scot headed to Cincinnati and was making good money in the products division helping keep Comet in its niche in the cleanser world. Procter & Gamble had big plans for him. Then another offer came along in Connecticut that he couldn't turn down. He was going to be an associate product manager at a smaller company. It was more responsibility, something that never intimidated Scot. He made just one personal promise: do at least one thing for someone else. Corporate life was so comfortable and he was so good at it. He was worried about easing in and never coming up for air.

His first day in Norwalk—the first day of October 1993—he stopped at his neighborhood church and picked up the bulletin. An announcement in fat letters begged for religious-instruction teachers for the public-school kids. Why not? he thought. He went looking for the church office.

"And so the secretary looks stunned and says to me, 'It's a miracle. I'm spooked. I'm spooked a little bit.'"

"What's going on?" he asked.

"Two minutes ago we were praying for someone for CCD," she stammered and dialed the phone. The nun who ran the program answered. "Sister," the secretary shouted, "do you believe in miracles?"

The nun rushed up to Landry and smothered him in a bear hug. Her thin arms wrapped around his fire-plug frame.

"She's saying stuff like, 'You're sent from God,'" said Scot.

That night, he thought about the priesthood for the first time. By Thanksgiving, he was giving it serious consideration. The decision was sealed around Christmas.

Scot was grilled by friends—and friends of friends—about his decision to enter the seminary. Colleagues crowded around Scot Landry's desk day after day wanting to know where the religious spark comes from.

"A lot of people who came up to me were fallen-away Catholics. You know, they'd say, 'Hey, you're a normal guy and you're going to be a priest!' I found that there was so much hope in them that there was a future to this Church. Because I think a lot of people look at the Church and say, 'They're all seventy-five years old, all the priests, and the Church is dead once they are dead.' That type of thing."

Scot waited with the other New Men in St. Peter's. There was another mass being celebrated at the tomb. They would have to wait a while on the basilica's main floor before going down to the passageways underneath.

"I don't know if contemporary society in America was lacking something. Maybe I was lacking something? Is this God's will I'm here? What is going on?" Scot marveled. "I'm open for answers."

Roger didn't say much. Usually, he's a monologue waiting to happen. From Red Sox pitching to cutting-edge research into biological rhythms to Washington politics—just about any topic has been at least brushed over by his vacuum-cleaner intellect. Faith, however, had always been his favorite. He had it. There was no doubt about his devotion to Christ. It was clear to him as far back as the daily mass he would attend with his mother before elementary school. Could he, though, pledge the same bond to the Vatican and a contradictory system of advancement: you need ambition and important backers to rise in the Church, but at the same time believe—or pretend to believe—in the meekness and patience that Christ taught. Roger knew he'd already snatched a brass ring with his appointment to study at the North American College. There would likely be others, many others, that would come within reach after his time in Rome. Guys like Roger always seem to get the chances.

Roger walked slower. His brother was back by the altar talking with some of the other New Men. Roger tried to take in every sound, every feeling, as he walked away—one slow, silent step at a time—from the papal altar and toward a place to pray.

In the simple wooden pews in the basilica's apse—with light just starting to push through the golden-stained glass starburst above the elevated throne of Peter—Roger closed his eyes. He tried to contemplate the virtues of the ideal seminarian. He kept returning to humility. It had all come so easily so far: the academic honors at high school, then at Harvard, getting an early taste of Washington power as a student coordinator, and now the assignment to study for the priesthood in Rome. He had always been on the A list and now everyone, from the rector on down, is saying: don't have expectations and don't strive for rewards. That type of thinking can mislead a seminarian and destroy a priest, the rector says. Roger Landry understood the warning clearly, perhaps better than most. But there's got to be a balance there, he thought. Excessive humility is just as dangerous to a seminarian, isn't it? The faith, he knew, was not built by cowards. Roger thought about all the books he had read about the early priests and martyrs, especially the one whose tomb rested just below.

"They were ordained to spit their guts out twenty-four hours a day for the faith," Roger said. "Christ wants people who can take risks."

St. Peter's began to fill. Tour groups trailed behind guides waving umbrellas and flags. A group of altar boys from Naples wearing white robes walked in single file across the geometric marble floor. They had been giggling and shoving each other. A stern look from the chaperon and they straightened up and marched in a practiced row. A choir in one of the side chapels began to sing: Hosanna, Hos-an-na.

Gary Benz rubbed the back of his neck. He did it slowly, deliberately. That's Gary's way. He goes about things quietly without drawing notice: the type of person you remember more for his thoughts than his looks. His hair and eyes are a neutral chestnut. Neither dark enough to be exotic nor distinctively light like the color of pine wood or the spring prairie grass around his home. His looks are neither striking nor homely. Always average. He speaks softly—almost so faint it makes you strain—but his thoughts are often precise and sharply expressed. He knows what he wants to say.

In St. Peter's, however, Gary felt a little light-headed. He couldn't tell if it was jet lag or the setting. "I mean, think about it," he said to another New Man as his eyes trailed up the baldachino. "We're standing here in St. Peter's."

"Centuries!" he gasped, thinking about how the tracks of pioneers' covered wagons still mark the grasslands back home. "They've been coming here for centuries."

A German couple with matching black denim jackets stopped just behind Benz. For a few moments, they all gaped silently at the cupola of the dome 440 feet above. People—no bigger than a matchhead to Benz—looked down at them from the mezzanine halfway up.

"Amazing," Benz said, trying hard to keep his emotions from boiling over in front of the other seminarians. He was twenty-four and farther from home than ever before.

Three days before with two fat suitcases and his new black wingtips, Benz left his hometown of New England, North Dakota— where the sign on Main Street reads "661 Happy People and 2 Old Grumps." It's out in the wheat belt of southwestern North Dakota, where the land is too wide open to hide the sadness. The train spur into town shut down in 1982 and weeds now grow between the wooden ties. Family farms started to become shuttered fast, leaving behind just rings of windbreak trees like the stone circles left by the ancients in other parts of the world. They cry out: someone was once here. The big families, too, started drying up. The Benz clan was one of the last ones—six sisters and four brothers, including Gary. His parents, livestock and wheat farmers, finally called it quits a few years ago. They stayed in the white farmhouse at the base of West Rainy Butte, where as a boy Gary thought you could climb and see the edge of the world.

The homesickness hit hard when he arrived in New York for the TWA flight carrying the other New Men. He thinks often of how it will feel when he can return to his town for the first time and take in the view from the top of West Rainy.

"When you're in a rural area, the land becomes sacred," he said in his thoughtful, almost laconic, manner. His eyes trailed over and over all the corners of the basilica, trying to take in the endless details all at once. "Not only the people and homes, but the land become sacred. I never thought I could leave it, you know. It almost becomes part of your being."

Then he closed his eyes, blacking out the basilica's man-made grandeur. He thought about the sky back home. He imagined the wet snow falling before Christmas. He saw the icy clouds spilling down the prairie from Canada during Lent. Then he tried to recall the first whiff of thawing farmland around Easter.

"It seems the land and Church go so well together," he said, opening his eyes again.

Rome, of course, can never be home. He wonders, though, if he can bear to make it even a temporary stop. He felt something near contentment for a while back at the seminary while waiting for the rector to lead them down to the Vatican. But it was only for a while. The pull of North Dakota—and a monastery where his grandparents are buried—was not getting any weaker.

"Have you ever heard wind whistle over prairie grass?" Gary asked. "It's beautiful. It reminds me of an orchestra."

Perhaps the journey of Tam Tran Xuan to St. Peter's was the most remarkable of all. He had been through something like hell in those last hours before the end came. People were literally crawling over each other to try to escape Saigon. Babies wailing because they didn't understand what was going on; adults crying because they did. The air smelled of fire and bitter fumes. It was so hot.

Tran, a bone-thin boy in shorts, raced with his family around the city—sometimes in a cab, sometimes running. Was there room in an American helicopter? Was the South Vietnamese government providing a way out for members of the police force? Tran's father waved his credentials at anyone who seemed to have connections. "Help us, help us," he pleaded. No one had time for charity, especially for a man who refused to be separated from his wife and three children. Tran spotted a bowl of rice on a restaurant table. He grabbed as much as his small hands could hold and wondered—just for a moment—whether he should take the bowl. He sensed he might need it later.

When the North Vietnamese soldiers raised their flag, Tran and his family were still in the city. Tran was eight, old enough to know that it was time to think about survival.

They tried to hide, to fade into the mayhem of the fallen city, but the Communists were relentless inquisitors. It was only a matter of time before they bore down on families like Tran's. His father, who had thrown away his police officer's uniform, was taken away at night to a work camp to be fed propaganda and little else. Tran was sent back to Da Nang with the rest of his family. He heard the whispers about the starvation in the re-education camps and tried to convince himself they were not true.

School was horrible. The teachers ridiculed Tran and other students whose families were part of the old government. They called him a friend of the Americans even though the closest he ever came to one were the few times his father brought a U.S. military officer home for dinner. The one escape was the church, which the Communists allowed to remain open but with orders to keep activities inside its walls. Tran often visited his uncle, a priest under house arrest. "We talked about faith," Tran said. "It kept him going. It kept me going."

By the time Tran's father was released in 1980, Tran had just turned thirteen and had given the priesthood serious thought. His father told him to think of nothing else but getting out of the country. But how? The family decided they would not take the risk aboard the refugee boats setting off for Hong Kong or Thailand. Tran's father wrote to his brother who had left for Maryland just before Saigon fell, but there was not enough money for plane tickets, and the Vietnamese government was not about to give them an exit visa. Tran's father, meanwhile, scraped by doing a bit of carpentry work and basket weaving learned in the camps. "About the only good thing to come out of his experience," said Tran, who was kept out of university in 1986 because of his family's past even though he aced the entrance exam. He was allowed in the following year under the first bending of strict Communist rule. Tran enrolled but had already decided to enter a seminary. Then the news came: people with ties to the old government could leave under a special pact with the United States if they could come up with the money. Tran begged to stay in Vietnam.

"I didn't have expectations about America," he said in an accent thick with the jumpy cadences of his mother tongue. "I wanted to stay in my country and become a priest. I didn't have any dreams about a beautiful life in America."

But he had to defer to his father, as any proper Vietnamese child would. They sold their house and drove into Gaithersburg, Maryland, just as the last autumn leaves turned in 1990. Tran knew a bit of English—enough to get a job as a busboy and then a clerk at a convenience store.

"The culture shock and, I would say, very secularized society shocked me. But it did not shake my desire to become a priest. In fact, it strengthened more.

"I saw the Church persecuted under Communism. It was sad. I see now Americans have all this freedom but no center, no base. This is sad, too. Maybe even a little more sad."

Father Kampschneider rounded up the seminarians in the basilica. "Let's go," he whispered, "it's almost time."

They descended to the lower level from a set of eighteen narrow steps off to the side of the altar. The grand stairs at the foot of the altar are rarely used except by popes: when they go to pray at the tomb or when they are carried into the grottoes to be entombed. The New Men went down single file on the steps curling underneath the huge statue of St. Longinus, the Roman centurion who pierced Christ's side with his lance and later converted.

The corridor to St. Peter's tomb curves gently to the left, with glass protecting the wall frescoes. The ceiling panels of angels and cherubs are left to chip and fade. Other passages lead to wider tunnels watched over by the crypts of later popes, their death masks chiseled in marble. Someone had left a single rose for Pope John Paul I, whose month-long reign in 1978 was too long ago for some of the youngest New Men to remember.

Brian Christensen remembers. He was a month into his new school run by Franciscan brothers on Long Island. The students were brought in to chapel to pray for John Paul's soul and that God give the cardinals wisdom in picking his successor. For an eighth-grader steeped in public school pluralism, this was all very astonishing. The only reason he transferred to the Catholic school at all was because they had a good hockey team.

Brian had always sort of glided along—friendly, competent, reliable but somehow lacking the passion that comes from full commitment. The right thing is coming, he told himself. The right job, the right relationship. It will come. He shrugged and applied to the Air Force Academy. "I didn't even know where the place was," he said. He gave flight school a shot and ended up co-pilot of a B-1 bomber crew. "I had good vision."

Girlfriends came, girlfriends went. He once thought he'd get married to a woman with two young children whom he treated like his own. He was a handsome guy women could brag about: tall, blond, trim but not skinny and, above all, a sincere listener. He looks you straight in the eye. He draws your words out and nods gently at all the right times. When he was in the Air Force, he never boasted in a macho-pilot way. He didn't think he had anything really important to crow about. The right fit hadn't arrived yet.

Then came the absolute last thing he expected: a vision of himself as a priest. He had only started going to daily mass to escape the morning marches and abuse from upperclassmen at the academy. But it became a necessity—that quiet time of prayer every day. Eventually, he became more intertwined in the faith until someone suggested he consider the priesthood. He laughed about it at first. Then, almost grudgingly, he started to take it seriously. This oddball idea just took root and wouldn't let go.

"Finally, I told myself, 'You need to settle this and you're not going to settle this here.'" He asked the Rapid City diocese to take him as a seminarian. He was just short of his thirtieth birthday and feared the diocese would consider him too old. They eagerly took him.

Brian leaned against the cool stone outside St. Peter's tomb, marked by a gold rope and guarded by the marble statues of two growling lions. Was this finally the right fit he'd been anticipating for so long? It seemed so. Except for one thing left unresolved: his feelings for a pious woman with beautiful green eyes he met just before coming to Rome.

A group of German pilgrims were running late in the small chapel before the tomb—a glass-covered shrine built many feet above the grave. Tourists began to descend into the chambers, forcing Brian back against the wall each time they passed.

"Busy place," he said to the New Man behind him. "I was expecting something a little more, I don't know, remote."

Rector Dolan kept checking his watch. "Come on," he sighed.

The Germans finally filed out and the New Men went in. One seminarian's collar wagged freely from one side before he managed to tuck it in. Dolan waited until they had assembled in the pews. This had to be one of his favorite moments of the year. He loved to watch the reactions of the New Men on the first visit to St. Peter's. "Reminds me," he said, "of the first time a kid goes to the ball park. So many things just hit you all at once."

The pope sometimes comes to this very spot to meditate. Each All Souls' Day—the second day of November—he prays at the tomb for his predecessors in a grotto just a few yards away.

The New Men's clerics reflected off the heavily varnished pews. Arching shadows formed undulating patterns on the low, white ceiling. They sang the ancient Christian chant: *"Kyrie eleison."* "Lord, have mercy."

Dolan's voice echoed loudly. He didn't try to tone it down.

"In a real way, New Men, this is the goal of your journey," he said from behind a small carved stone lectern, "the reason we are here. For over nineteen hundred years our forefathers in the faith have done what we are now doing—gathering in prayer before the tomb of Peter to learn from him and seek his intercession. This spot is surpassed only by the Holy Sepulchre in Jerusalem in the hearts of Christians. Never in your years here will you tire of visiting this basilica; never will the meaning of this spot lose its awe and ability to inspire.

"Forty-eight hours ago, I welcomed you to the Chapel of the Immaculate Conception and I spoke to you of what you had just lost, what you had left behind. This morning, I invite you not to look back but look ahead. I ask you not what you have left or where you have come from, but where are you going? And I suggest that the fisherman buried here can give us the response.

"You have all heard the ancient Christian legend that says when Nero began his vicious persecution of the nascent Church here in Rome, the leader of that community, Simon Peter, reverting to old ways, fled, no, ran, out of town scared. As he was sneaking out the Appian Way, who does he meet but the Master.

"'*Domine, quo vadis?* Lord, where are you going?' he asks.

"'Peter, I am going to Rome to suffer and die with my people.'

"Peter turns around, returns to Rome to be arrested, crucified upside down on a hill across the Tiber and is buried on the side of the same hill we gather on right now.

"My brothers, *quo vadis?* Where are you going?

"Will we falter and begin to sink like Peter? Yes!

"Will we even at times deny knowing Jesus in the way we act or what we do?" asked Dolan. "Probably, like Peter.

"Will we be tempted to sneak out the Appian Way to avoid the challenge and sacrifice that is before us? Like Peter, yes.

"Will we learn the answer to that most pivotal of questions: *quo vadis?*

"Where are you going?"

CHAPTER II

RETREAT

Let us pray that we, too, may listen carefully for His voice.

—INTERCESSION FOR EVENING PRAYER,
FEAST OF ARCHANGELS MICHAEL, GABRIEL, AND RAPHAEL,
SEPTEMBER 29

Sister tried to be very quiet that night.

Her rubber soles squeaked a bit on the freshly waxed convent corridors, but she did her best to make each step come down lightly like someone trying not to wake the baby. She looked over the arrangement of calla lilies and ferns in the foyer, then went down a dark hall to make sure the windows were locked. The front door was also bolted tight. She wiped away a smudge on the brass door handle and looked out into the dusk just as it passed into night.

She had watched more than one hundred seasons come and go from this spot, the nub of a gentle hill where Rome's western fringe meshes with the rocky pastures and artichoke fields on the flatlands heading to the sea. She tugged the sleeves of her old blue sweater over her wrists. She always put it back on around now—the end of September—and wore it every day until spring. The wind smelled faintly of chimney smoke somewhere off in the farmland downhill. Summer was definitely ending.

Each year, the New Men arrive about this time for their retreat—one week of silent contemplation and prayer. The nun, as she also does every year, watched these New Men file in. They looked to her very much the same as all the others: eager, excited, maybe just a little too loud for her tastes. But that's the way of Americans, no? she told herself. She liked the easy smiles of the American seminarians. Some of the European and South American seminarians she knew could be so pompous and unnecessarily serious. The Americans generally treated the nuns with respect and courtesy. Someday she wanted to visit their country and, first on her list, would be a trip to see the Grand Canyon.

The retreat marks the first distinct transition for the New Men, a turning point from getting acquainted to getting down to the business of studying for the priesthood. If they hadn't yet realized what was expected of them, they would now.

Their initial few weeks in Rome are occupied with the unavoidable routines of settling in and meeting the other seminarians from upper classes as they trickled back. The education of the New Men in the mechanics of the seminary is swift and comprehensive—from learning the system of making an anonymous appointment with the staff psychiatrist to getting assigned a cubbyhole for the white cloth napkin they use at every meal in the common dining hall with wall-size picture windows looking out toward the Vatican side of the Janiculum. Afternoons are spent in classes trying to pack in as much Italian as possible before the theology courses begin. The daily schedule is dense. What free time is left is often spent sleeping or slouching in front of the television watching a selection from the video collection, which includes two copies of *Home Alone* and the seminal slasher flick *Nightmare on Elm Street.*

Everyone by this time is growing a bit edgy.

This checklist dash of the first few weeks in Rome was certainly not part of their vision of seminary study. Some, of course, handle it better than others. It's the older New Men like Brian Christensen or Chris Nalty who, surprisingly, seem to fare the worst. They are terribly anxious to move ahead. They've become accustomed to the adrenaline-soaked momentum of discovering their religious vocation and making the life-changing decision to follow it all the way to the seminary. All this organizing and practical planning in Rome comes as a distinct let-down—like the obligations of setting up house after a whirlwind honeymoon.

Many New Men felt something coming apart. For some, it was a separation from the soul; a crack, still ever so thin, in whatever they had built to protect and nurture their vocations. Being so busy was like returning to the old static. They knew the sound well: all the things that can drown out the inner voice that told them to seek the priesthood. The noise comes in many frequencies. Friends scoffing at the Church and its priests; the rattle of a culture that tends to measure success on how much you have rather than how much you understand yourself. Now, in Rome, they had expected some reprieve, some sanctuary. Instead, they were busier than ever. Where was the time for prayer and simple meditation? How, many New Men asked, can we think about our vocations when we're just trying to keep up with the daily program?

The retreat comes just in time. A third-year seminarian, who knew what the New Men were grappling with perhaps better than they did, pasted a sign on his door: Hangeth in There.

"I know what they are going through," said Rector Tim Dolan, sitting at his desk covered with stacks of memos and letters a few days before the retreat. "They are thinking: 'What have I got myself into? They are trying to kill me.' I wish, I wish there was an easier way to get them oriented here. But I don't think there is. Look, they are in a new country, new culture, new way of life. Of course it's all going to seem overwhelming."

Monsignor Dolan, too, counts the retreat as an important milestone. This crop of New Men, thankfully, made it through the first few weeks better than some of the others. There were no serious quarrels and no one had quit in disappointment or frustration. They had elected one of the twins, Scot Landry, as class president in a near-unanimous acclamation. That was good, Dolan thought. He liked Scot's energy and enthusiasm. It tends to rub off on the rest of the New Men. So far so good, Dolan congratulated himself. The mass at St. Peter's tomb was powerful as always, and the New Men already had a chance to see the pope in a visit to the papal country villa outside Rome. A typically hectic, but unusually successful, first month.

Finally, Dolan said, a time for everyone to decompress.

"Good night, sister. Take good care of my guys," Dolan nodded to the nun as he left to go back to the seminary.

"I certainly will," she said.

Dolan felt good—better perhaps than at any time since the New Men arrived. He had just delivered his first long lecture to the New Men. It was part pep talk, part elaboration on his expectations. He reminded them of what he said on the first day: configure yourself to Christ. His legacy and his teachings, Dolan says, are your guide. Understand this and you understand what the seminary hopes to achieve. This was Dolan's first step in trying to explain this most simple yet elusive centerpiece of the seminary. Priests, Dolan tells them, do not spring from some holy font. They are shaped, carefully and meticulously. That's why they call it seminary formation. Don't be arrogant. And especially don't think you, as New Men, fully grasp what being a priest is all about.

"I noticed only a few yawns," he chuckled. "I always consider that a mark of success at one of my talks, don't you, sister?"

The nun politely smiled and locked the door after Dolan left in his private car, driving down the twisting road to the convent's big iron gates. She'd never get used to American humor.

Down the hall behind her, the chapel lights still burned. It was late but the nun decided to take one last peek around the corner before going to bed. The Americans never knew she was there. A few of them were reading the Bible. Others were kneeling in prayer or just sitting alone.

Brian Christensen sat back in the pew and rubbed his blue eyes, now ringed with a little red. It felt such a luxury just to do absolutely nothing. At last, time to himself. He tried to let his mind run blank. Yet he couldn't help thinking about another time very much like this: back when he was a cadet at the Air Force Academy. It had come full circle. In the academy, it was the breakneck schedule and relentless harassment from upperclassmen that drove him to seek a few minutes' refuge at the chapel in the first place. Somehow from those daily visits, a vocation grew. He thought about it often. Was he predestined to be a priest? Is this destiny? If it is, then why isn't it easier? "Shouldn't it feel like, I don't know, the way you feel when you hold a sleeping baby?" he said. "You know what that's like? It just feels right. Right now it feels like I'm trying to hold down a tiger."

Patience, he told himself. Just let things happen. That was always his biggest trouble: analyzing too much and constantly sifting for perfection. Brian is a searcher. He believes in a flawless love, something pure and unconditional. It could be for a woman or the faith—perhaps even both at the same time. It's almost chivalrous in its idealism. He broke his old girlfriend's heart—and their dreams of marriage—to look for it.

"It's out there," he said. "As soon as you say otherwise, then you're giving up."

But maybe only a few are meant to find real contentment? How many lives are spent like this: restless, nomadic, tragically unfulfilled. He thought about it this way—coming to a door and being too timid to knock and find out what's inside. Is this me? Brian asked himself. Am I going to spend my life always looking and looking for something? It scared him, like he had never been scared before, to think that it could be so.

When he decided to join the seminary, he felt he was finally setting the right course. This was the type of bold step he liked. Now, sitting in the chapel on the first night of a retreat with his long legs crammed uncomfortably in the small pew, he was struck by another feeling. The search did not feel like it was over.

Above all, he couldn't shake the sense of incompleteness from his two goodbyes: one to the woman he once adored and thought he would marry; the other to a woman he met just before coming to Rome and felt he could truly love.

Brian ran his hands through his yellow-blond hair, which he let grow a few inches after leaving the Air Force. He sighed.

"The Academy was nuts," he said. "I thought I had put that type of stuff behind me. But, man, we are busy here. I think we're way too busy."

He could keep up. He had always been organized and the military honed it to precision. No, staying afloat wasn't the worry. But this can't be what the seminary is about, shooting from one task to the other? Somewhere in the first bleary weeks, Brian's spiritual director had given him the best advice of all so far: learn how to pray.

"Pray?" Brian asked. "But I pray every day. I spent at least a half hour a day in the chapel."

"What do you pray about?"

"To understand Christ, the scriptures, for the health of my family."

"But," the spiritual director said, "do you try to develop your own relationship with God? A personal relationship?"

He frowned. "I'm not sure what you mean."

"OK," said Rev. Cornelius McRae, one of the North American College's three spiritual directors. "Talk to me about God."

Brian inhaled sharply. It was a question he didn't expect. McRae smiled. "The New Men," the priest said later, "are always floored by the God thing."

The most important decision taken so far by the New Men was picking a spiritual director: their personal confessor and inquisitor. Perhaps no single person has such a profound imprint on the seminarians. The spiritual director hears it all—the most persistent doubts, the nagging troubles, the gnawing urges. And it never leaves the small quarters where they meet. The confidentiality is airtight. Seminaries call this the internal forum, where the real battles are waged. The external forum—tests and evaluations—is what everyone else sees. Already, the New Men have heard the mantra of getting by: six will get you ten. A minimum grade of 6.0 on the oral exams will keep you going for a full half-decade at the seminary, up until the ten fingers of the bishop rest on your head for ordination. The spiritual directors deal in a less-defined world. Classes will teach the New Men about the faith and the rituals of the priesthood. Spiritual directors try to sort out whether they really grasp what lies ahead.

"Don't worry," McRae told Brian. "Just give me your impressions of God."

"Comfort, compassion, wisdom," said Brian. "Perfection."

"And these are—with the obvious exception of perfection—all human qualities as well," said McRae. "God is obtainable. He's accessible."

"But how do you get there?" Brian asked. "I mean, I feel sometimes so separated from my soul, like I'm trying and trying to get there, but I'm being held back. How do I move forward spiritually? Is it God or myself that's holding me back? You got to ask yourself that, right?"

"I think I can answer that," said McRae. "Only you can hold yourself back. Try it this way: don't go into prayer with a full agenda like, I want to get this point across to God today or make this intercession or say this many prayers. Try to just sit peacefully, no prayers, no slate of things to say, and try just to feel God."

"Feel?"

"Sense what it is that makes God speak to you. Try it. Once you discover this, you'll discover how to start building your own relationship with Him. It's addictive. You can count on that."

"So you are saying to pray without prayer?"

"Exactly, Brian. You've got it."

"I'll try."

"That's all we can ever do, Brian."

In the first hours of the retreat, Brian tried to do what McRae suggested. He sat quietly in the chapel and listened to his breathing, feeling his chest gently pulsing. He started to relax. But not completely. Brian wanted to feel something—anything—that would match his desire to hear, really listen to, this inner voice McRae described as part of God Himself. Brian was so good at empathizing with others. Why was it so difficult to slow down and pay attention to what his own soul was saying? Was it happy in Rome? Was it pleading for something else? Brian wanted a sign. Even a glimmer. A faint caress. Anything that would make him feel like a personal relationship with God was possible. Anything to make him feel connected to what was going on inside.

But he just felt like he had for the past few weeks. Tired. Bone tired.

The Landrys walked together. Most of the New Men had gone to their rooms. Night sounds came from the dark corridor: doors closing, taps running, bed springs creaking. There were few voices. The silence of the retreat was settling over the New Men.

Scot held Roger back for moment. This would be their last time to have a conversation before returning to the seminary. Scot needed reassurance—the type only his twin could offer.

Scot was in a sort of secular withdrawal. Work, responsibilities, getting things done: all a powerful high for him. "Workaholic? Some people may call me that," he said before the retreat. "I would just say I enjoy—really enjoy—being in control of what's around me." It was that way from as far back as he could remember. He was the doer, the planner. His twin brother, Roger, the thinker, the scholar. If anything significant separated them it would be these simple but accurate descriptions. Scot's work ethic had been always unshakable. When he focused on a project—from high school to Harvard to the office—it was accomplished. Now it was the seminary studying for the Bridgeport, Connecticut, diocese.

"Finally," Scot told his brother as they walked through the convent to their rooms, "a breather."

"No kidding." Roger nodded. "It's been a lot to absorb the last couple weeks. How you holding up? You said you wanted to talk."

"I do. I mean, after the retreat."

"Sure. Anything in particular?"

"Prayer, the seminary, just everything," said Scot. "This is all still kind of new to me. It's hard to switch gears so quickly. That's all."

"You're not having second thoughts, are you? If you are, we better talk about things now."

"No, Rog. It's OK. Really. I think this retreat will be a good chance to get myself settled. You know, a time to do some thinking."

"You know you can talk to me any time," said Roger.

"I know."

"Any time," Roger repeated.

Probably none of the New Men exuded more commitment than the Landrys. Roger's was the deep, serene type that comes from a boyhood vocation following its natural course. Scot, as he always did, played tornado to his brother's steady breeze. Scot decided to go to the Pontifical Gregorian University—the Greg—where the classes were taught in Italian. Roger enrolled in the English-speaking Pontifical University of Saint Thomas, usually called the Angelicum or the Ang. Whenever a New Man wanted to talk—from the serious to the frivolous—he knew he'd find Scot willing to listen. When an article would attack the Church—or describe priesthood seminarians only in political terms—Scot would stew. "They never talk about our prayer life, our striving to be holy, do they?" he complained. "There are guys here who, for them, the whole pursuit of holiness is so intense it almost makes me want to cry." It was quite easy to imagine him as patient but hard-working Father Scot. He even daydreamed about the type of parish he'd like to run and the type of sermons he would deliver. He'd run a special program for kids. "There's probably nothing more important we can do as priests," he said.

But Scot didn't hide his nostalgia for what he left behind. His last six months of work, after deciding to join the seminary, were near perfect. He was focused, in control—sometimes working later than the janitors at James River Corp. in Norwalk. His bosses nicknamed him "pit bull"—as much for his work habits as his tightly packed physique. "I felt like I hit a home run every day during those last months before coming to the seminary," he said. "I was totally juiced on work." He figured it would be much the same in Rome: just replace sales reports with religion.

"Only it wasn't so easy," Scot said. He didn't envision it would be so hard to follow the Church's command and let go. Of what? he constantly asked himself. His drive? The control, the self-generated energy he loved? In essence, he felt he was being asked to let go of what had always defined him. It's unnerving to think about erasing those lines. You can spill out a shallow and diluted version of what you were before. The Vatican paradox that Roger instantly grasped was also be-coming clear to Scot: be ambitious with your spiritual life and docile with everything else. The Church tells its clergy to surrender to its wis-dom. It will decide where you preach, what you study, and how far you advance along the concentric rings radiating from the Holy See.

Scot wasn't afraid of change. This, however, struck uncomfortably close to home. "My whole life has been geared to being in control and in charge. School, sports, everything," said Scot. "Giving that up is one of the hardest things I'll ever be asked to do."

This struggle he keeps generally hidden. His spiritual director, and, of course, his brother knew. Scot reasoned if Roger could learn humility, then he could, too. The Landry twins had been reunited in Rome after several years apart. Scot was determined they would re-main together.

Roger told him once about his theory of why they both have reli-gious vocations. Assume, Roger says, that the soul is formed at concep-tion. Then identical twins, who split from a single egg four days after conception, just might have identical souls.

In Dolan's estimation, his speech to open the retreat is the most signif-icant he will likely deliver to the New Men. He gives them three weeks or so to begin understanding the workings of the seminary, explore Rome a bit. He holds back during that time. Dolan figures it's disori-enting enough without any added pressure from him. He wants the New Men to try to sketch out the seminary's spiritual topography on their own for a while—what to climb for and what to avoid. He gave them a hint at St. Peter's tomb: how temptations will probably block their way on occasion. Now it was time to hit them straight on with his full expectations. This is the talk that New Men tape or scribble down. It's the compilation of everything they will be told to dig into during the years to come.

The New Men sat on metal folding chairs in the convent's small auditorium. It was already dark out. The bright ceiling lights gave everything a bleached feel, a bit like a stage or an operating room. It made the gathering seem expectant and important. Brian Christensen thought about the crewmen's briefings before Air Force training missions. His squadron was not called to the Gulf War, and he often wondered how his life—and maybe his vocation—would have changed if he had gone into battle. Gary Benz remembered how his parents' farmhouse felt on winter mornings before sunrise with all the lights ablaze and coffee on the stove for a cup before chores and more with breakfast afterward.

The New Men wore the outfits that peg them as Americans anywhere in Italy: sweatshirts, jeans, sneakers.

Dolan took his place behind the mahogany lectern. He gripped the sides and leaned forward a bit—just enough to cast a shadow over his handwritten notes. He rarely looked down. Good orators know their material.

"Not long ago I received a letter from a priest—not out too long—who was criticizing his seminary formation." Then with comic timing: "He did not go to the North American College.

"Well, he says something that at first I thought was silly. Then I thought he had a point. He said, 'You know, all through my years of seminary formation, my spiritual directors, my rector, my formation advisers, they asked me a bunch of questions. They would say, Are you happy? Are you ready for the diaconate? Are you ready for the priesthood? How was your summer?' He said, 'Never once did anyone say to me: Do you believe in God? Now one would like to think that you can take some things for granted.'"

The New Men laughed.

"But," Dolan cut them off, "maybe he had a point. And that is the utter necessity of faith. Daily we are called to die to such things as doubt, cynicism, relativism, and the aimless existence we see all around us—the things that come from lack of faith."

Death. Letting the old ways perish so more holy ways can take their place. This analogy is one of Dolan's favorites. It's the core of Christianity: the death and resurrection of Christ. Dolan's quest is to make the New Men feel this type of metamorphosis—casting off their old lives and rising in a new, priestly identity.

The New Men will hear this rebirth theme over and over. What we ask can be frightening, Dolan acknowledges, but it's almost essential. The life before the seminary cannot compete for the attention of the seminarian. If it does, then Dolan sees trouble. He insists: there must be a definite, irreversible cut in order to let the seminary formation work; to develop what the Church calls a "priestly identity." There are hundreds of little deaths on the way to ordination. The New Men, however, have already experienced one of the most monumental: joining the seminary. Yet Dolan warns there are so many more. "Giving up," he says, "in order to gain a closeness, a connection with Christ." The list of deaths goes on: celibacy, loss of control over your time and money, no longer being able to turn your back on someone in need. This, of course, is the ideal. Priests can be as selfish, greedy, and sexually aggressive as anyone. But Dolan has raw material with the New Men. Why not push for perfection?

"Remember just a couple of days ago?" Dolan asks. "Those men preparing for the diaconate publicly took that oath of fidelity. Remember that? That is the last-gasp effort of the Church to make sure they are going to ordain men of faith. This is the Church's way of ensuring that its deacons and priests have a strong faith in God. Sometimes it's good to examine our consciences to see if we can really take that oath sincerely.

"Hope," Dolan continued, "a firm reliance on the utter dependability of God's promise and a rejection of the despair, gloom, and cynicism we see all around us.

"Simplicity of life. Seeking to live plainly and justly and gratefully and not succumbing to the accumulation and stinginess that seems to be endemic in Western society. You know, fellas, you've seen enough priests to know that luxurious living probably has been a source of greater scandal to the faithful than succumbing to the weakness of the flesh or excessive drinking.

"Another virtue we struggle with daily?" Dolan continued. "Chastity. You must embrace celibate chastity deliberately, maturely . . . freely surrendering all genital activity in thought, word, or deed—

alone or with others, hetero or homo—honestly confronting any inclinations, drives, or fantasies that threaten the wholesome, healthy, realistic purity expected by the Church and its priests."

Chris Nalty didn't move. After years as a lawyer, he knew how
much can be said by just a little flinch or twitch. No one outside his
spiritual director had any idea just how much celibacy weighed on
him. His routine of making a holy hour in front of the eucharist each
morning before prayers and mass helped a great deal—something to
stoke his willpower each day. But then sometimes he dwelled—maybe
a little too much, he wondered—on the consequences of the commitment he was being asked to make. "Look, I'm not going to lie to you
and say it's easy, but you never expected it would be," he said before the
retreat. "I mean, giving up sex is a pretty serious thing. I mean, a serious, serious thing."

Like every New Man, Nalty was free to leave at any time. If he
quit, though, he wanted it to be based on logic, not lust. There was definitely a pull to the religious life. He was upset some friends thought it
was just a temporary backlash from his pressure-cooker world back in
New Orleans. He truly loved the Church and admired its clergy—failings and all. Nalty also knew he could serve his faith in many other
ways than being in the sanctuary. Yet nothing he could imagine, at this
moment, seemed so obviously right. Celibacy was his trial. His only
fear was that he would be too weak to make it a fair fight. His spiritual
director told him to pray for strength. He did. Some days he felt invincible.

"Other times? Well, I joke with my spiritual director that I wear
my sunglasses to class all the time so people don't see my eyes wander-
ing on the way," he told me.

"I also say, 'You know, look, my problem isn't fantasy as much as
memory.' I mean, I don't have to make up something, I just have to
think about a couple of years ago and a woman who wanted to date
me."

The Church needs Nalty—at least those like him. Without the
older seminarians, the priesthood would be even thinner and certainly
less diverse. But there's always a special red flag hanging over the be-

latedly devout. Dolan keeps a close watch on the older New Men. He worries a little about the slingshot effect. The pull to the seminary could just as quickly lose its hold and fire them back to their old lives. "The more sudden the vocation, the greater the possibility that it hasn't really taken root," Dolan said. "A good gust or a few tremors could sweep it away."

But Dolan has a good feeling about Nalty. He's heard that he makes a holy hour every day at the basement chapel before morning mass. And he knows what the prayers are for. It's often so much harder for the New Men who had girlfriends, said Dolan shortly after they arrived in Rome. Few people honestly believe that many Catholics—even prospective seminarians—follow the teaching of abstinence from premarital sex. "And our society orbits so much around sex. It's such a defining thing. Take it away, and many people would lose a big part of their identity," said Dolan. He tries with all the New Men to show that celibacy does not mean an end to sexuality. "We're not eunuchs," said Dolan. "You don't stop being a man because you stopped sleeping around." But these lessons will come later in the year. Dolan wants to lay out his broad rules to the New Men before getting into the subtler points.

Dolan, however, has been watching Nalty. He thinks he'll understand. Some in the seminary were put off by Nalty's flamboyance. Not Dolan. He liked the New Men to talk openly about their past. That's the first step in moving ahead. Plus Nalty loves cigars. "A sign of real class," laughed Dolan as he took a deep drag on one of his beloved Jamaican-made Macanudos.

Dolan was near the end of his pre-retreat speech to the New Men. It was long—nearly forty-five minutes—and he didn't want the New Men's attention to drift. He rapped the lectern once with his right hand. He wanted them to remember this part during the retreat.

"The spiritual life that we talk about isn't some tidy, isolated part of our existence. In some ways, the spiritual life is life itself. The seminary, says Pope John Paul II, should be experienced not as something external and superficial or simply as a place to live and study. But, in an interior and profound way, it should be experienced as the community that relives the experience of the group of twelve who were united with Jesus. New Men, we are trying to recapture in you the experience of Jesus' twelve apostles."

He looked around the room. He paused just enough to let the silence speak.

"We battle against the dark side, brothers," he said. "That dark side from which emerges hate, selfishness and petty resentment, and just plain meanness.

"I urge a commitment to a way of life. This is not just one more avocation, ministry, or job that can be set aside when frustration or temptation or something—or someone—more attractive comes along. The priesthood is an identity, not a profession.

"This means ongoing discernment to guard against drifting toward ordination. Rolling to ordination simply because there is nothing better to do. All of a sudden we find ourselves going to buy our chalices and you say, 'Oh, looks like I'm going to be a priest simply because nothing better has come along.'"

Doubt and desire sway together in a strange dance at the seminary.

It's somewhat like a serious romance reaching a critical stage—emotions are exposed and the prospect of monumental decisions lies ahead. The cozy limbo of the seminarian—shielded from the demands of bills and jobs while still safe from the responsibilities of the clergy—is a temporary grace period. The Catholic priest-making system demands advancement or abandonment. From the first day, seminarians are hit with this dual task. Start hammering yourself into the mold of the priesthood, the faculty says. But at the same time, they are told: be careful not to stash away unresolved problems about who and what you are trying to become.

Dolan snaps his fingers. This is the abrupt tempo now shaping the American Church. It's the sharp moment of conversion that brought many of the men to the seminary. Chris Nalty's tears in the Alabama woods. The old nun wrapping her arms around Scot Landry. Brian Christensen breaking off with the woman he expected to marry. Other seminarians talk about being spun around toward the faith after visiting the shrines to apparitions of Mary at Lourdes or Medjugorje.

Whatever the root, fewer seminarians say they grew up with the calling like Dolan. "I'm what they call a lifer," he said. "I'm a museum piece today." What the snap-conversions bring is intensity. They have infused many listless seminaries with a fervor and spiritual hunger. From Dolan's perspective, however, there are hidden dangers among the most zealous.

"Some of them came in dark periods," he said. "Some of them came in light periods. One of the challenges we face today deals with making sure the vocation's interiorized." He snaps his fingers again.

"When you have religious conversions, sometimes it's short-lived. It would be the same as, let's say, a guy who came in with his fiancée and you started asking about the relationship and they both smiled and said, 'We just met last week, but from the beginning we knew this was it.' Now, it could be and I hope it is, but we got to make sure that this has sunk in and that this is mature and that it is sincere and that it's not just this burst of enthusiasm. This is what we tell the guys: this has to be borne out in fidelity for a half century. So we have to make sure it's not just a momentary luster, that it wasn't just a momentary thunderbolt that drove you to the seminary."

There's even a rule book: the 109-page Program of Priestly Formation put out by the American Bishops' Conference. It goes over in exacting detail the expectations and goals of becoming a member of the Roman Catholic clergy. What it doesn't spell out are the pressures weighing on the seminarian sent to Rome.

The spot is highly coveted. They are the chosen ones. Usually a bishop or archbishop sends just one seminarian a year from his territory to the North American College. Some dioceses rarely send anyone—trying to save money and get more mileage out of their own seminaries. In some eyes—tinged often with jealousy—the nod to go to Rome is a ticket to stardom in the Church. "They think we're over here having dinner and drinks with the bishops every night," groaned Scot Landry. "What a joke." But it's still the top address for an American studying for the priesthood. For each seminarian at the college, there are others looking longingly from the States. To bail out after arriving in Rome has rumblings beyond the personal turmoil. It can be considered a slap at the bishop who bestowed his confidence and, perhaps even more important, the diocese's money. Tuition and board run about $12,000 a year.

The seminary—especially for the New Men—can be a numbing dash from dawn to dusk. Morning mass begins at 6:30 sharp. Everyone is expected to be there. It's possible to sleep in a few times, but missing mass too often will bring an invitation to talk to the rector for an explanation. Then it's breakfast, the walk to class in central Rome, walk back for lunch. The afternoon is seminars, study, meetings with formation and spiritual directors. Dinner is at seven—astonishingly early by Italian standards but stomach-grumblingly exotic for many New Men.

Up in the green room on the top floor, the seminarians can let it out. "I think green's a relaxing color, don't you?" asked the house psychiatrist, Rev. Jon O'Brien. Seminarians come and cross out an hour on his schedule outside the door of his office—green rug, overstuffed green leather chairs. They drop their names in a box to let O'Brien know who's coming. Before arriving in Rome in 1994, O'Brien counseled medical students at Georgetown.

"The basic question that the medical students struggled with is the same as with the seminarians: 'What shall I do with my life?'"

O'Brien stopped to collect his thoughts. He speaks slowly and precisely, just the way a psychiatrist is expected to speak. He nods often while listening and cups his hands, thin and brittle with age.

The seminarians often talk about sex. "No doubt, it's really something to give up," says O'Brien. But, surprisingly, more often the struggles are about the metamorphosis demanded by the seminary, the letting-go of who they thought they were.

"These guys are signing up for life to an individual diocese. In a way it's like signing up for an individual company for life," said O'Brien. "This is something that is constraining on the type of freedom that Americans value very highly."

"Here the bishops have invested millions and millions of dollars in what we think is one of the finest programs of priestly formation anywhere," said Rector Dolan.

"But you can only lead the horse to water. We can force them to see their spiritual director every other week. We force them to see their formation adviser at least once a month. We force them to go to classes. We look at their grades. We put up a lot of hurdles. But it's for nothing unless those things are internal things and unless a man uses these things as efficiently, honestly, and sincerely as possible. And how can we be sure that they are?"

The morning after Dolan's speech, Gary Benz took a walk. He sat down under one of the umbrella pines on a far edge of the convent grounds. Although the nights were cool, the days were still warm and sticky and it was nice to be in the shade. His back was to the city. A patchwork of fields stretched out before him. Neat blocks of yellow, deep green, and brown all the way to a creamy horizon of land and sky. For most people, it would be an impressive panorama. To Gary, it was cramped and puny.

He thought of another vista—wheat fields and grasslands lapping the base of the ridge at the back of a Benedictine monastery about an hour's drive from his hometown. He recalled their church, built in 1908 in a solid Bavarian Romanesque style familiar to the area's German pioneers. The monks gather for the Liturgy of the Hours in old oak stalls on either side of the altar and sing the psalm tones—the melodies swelling and retreating like the sound of the prairie wind gusts. Gary's great-grandfather, Ignatz Benz, helped build the abbey with the bricks hand-made by the monks. Ignatz and his wife are buried in the abbey cemetery. Their graves are in the old section with lines of iron crosses tilted by the wind. The prayers are written in German.

This is where I belong, he thought. "The desert of southwest North Dakota needs to be replenished."

Gary did not want to be here anymore—not in Rome, not studying for the North Dakota diocese. Homesickness is common for New

Men, especially the younger ones and those unfamiliar with big cities. But Gary's melancholy was much more profound. He felt deeply, tragically, out of place. He didn't show it or talk about it. That just wasn't his way. He just thought about it all the time, suffering in the stoic manner he learned back home. How did it happen? How it usually happened with Gary. He listened to others instead of his heart. He put off joining the seminary because a friend in high school mocked the priesthood. This time, he had allowed himself to be pushed—by the good intentions of his parents, friends, and the diocese—far away from where he believed he should be: a big brick monastery on the bluff in the prairie.

His pastors agreed with the sentiment, but not with his interest in the Benedictines. They saw Benz wearing the collar of a parish priest rather than the black robe of a monk. Benz was being squeezed by the numbers. With fewer and fewer vocations, each new one becomes a prized catch jealously guarded by the diocese. A new seminarian is seen as an investment, a kind of junior executive being groomed for bigger things. They will be the parish priests—some even bishops or cardinals—vital to sustain the structure of the Church.

When a man drops out of the priesthood, a diocese moans. But when they join an order or a monastery, they howl. There was a real vocation that got away. Benz was especially coveted. Here was a young man whose calling seemed solid and who actually aspired to work in the hinterlands. North Dakota has about five dozen priests for its 150,000 Catholics, but most of the clergy is concentrated in Bismarck and Fargo.

When Benz tried to tell his diocese vocation recruiter about his desire to join the Benedictines, the subject was always veered in another direction.

"It's like he didn't hear me," he complained. "Or maybe he didn't want to.

"They think like: 'Well, you have a vocation and now he wants to be idealistic. He not only wants to be a priest, he wants to go for it all.' Like going into the French Foreign Legion or something."

His parents also started to get nervous. They had envisioned their son in a comfortable parish rectory, doted over by his secretary and able to come over for dinner after mass on Sundays. They pleaded with Benz to give the seminary a chance. The full-court press from home and Church was too much. Benz relented—but reluctantly.

"I don't know how to say it nicely, but in the Church they need to fill positions, and I think they looked at me like someone who could fill a position. Because I told them I really felt called to the Benedictines and I'd like to try it out. It's like they don't hear me and they'd go, 'You really have a strong vocation to the diocese.' And I'd go, 'Hear me, please.' So I've kind of been going along really torn. I should have tried it before I came."

Gary enjoyed watching the nuns. They were a part of home. His earliest memories were all interwoven with the School Sisters of Notre Dame, who ran the convent where the seminarians spent their retreat. He recalled being back in first grade at the parish school in his hometown, tagging along like a puppy after the priest at the school run by the sisters. He was the youngest boarder—a frail child with asthma. The school was just fourteen miles from his parents' farm but too time consuming a drive during planting and harvest. In the winter, it was often cut off by ten-foot snow drifts from the high plains gales. The school was very quiet at night. Silence made so much sense, even to the smallest like Gary. The land, the eternal land, welcomed peace.

The monks Gary knows understand.

"I love that idea of not owning anything—true poverty in the sense that everything you have belongs to the community, to all the monks at the abbey. In the diocese, the priests have to worry about debt, administration, and so much of their time is consumed by this.

"This kind of simplicity appeals to me: to come into the world with nothing and to leave the same way."

Gary tried to read. He'd look at the page but couldn't concentrate. Over and over, he would read the same lines. He was too confused. Am I a coward? he thought. Why don't I just walk out the gate and get on the first plane back home? If only it was that simple. His family, the diocese, and whole priest-making system in Rome seemed to stand in his way. If only he hadn't come to Rome in the first place, he thought. It would be so much easier to make the break if he was in a seminary back home.

He recalled what Rector Dolan had told them the night before. Be honest with yourself. Don't drift to ordination.

Gary knew he had a decision to make. And he knew where he might find the heart to make it: Benedict's cave in Subiaco.

CHAPTER III

DEACONS

You may for a time have to suffer the distress of many trials.

—EVENING READING FOR THURSDAYS (1 PETER 1:6)

Time in the seminary can push especially rudely. It's fixed and definite when so much else is not. All seminarians, in different ways, must take the disorienting steps from the familiar ways of secular life to the different precepts and values of religious dedication. For a while, particularly with the New Men, their lives can seem a confusing scramble—pieces, some old and worn and some sharp-edged and strange, are cast about in no set order. Their job is to rearrange them in a form befitting their goal of becoming a priest. There's the piece for unquestioning faith. Others are for acceptance of Church rules and the feeling of holiness—often the hardest piece of all to fit. There also are the old pieces to wedge in somewhere: ego, empathy, humor. Dolan tells them to always think of Christ. What piece—what virtue—would he place above another? It's the most difficult puzzle they will ever tackle. And there is a deadline.

It's always there: a reminder that the seminary is not an open-ended proposition. There are three years of study—equivalent to getting a master's degree in theology. Then, at the beginning of the fourth year, comes ordination as deacons. Later that year, deacons typically take the final vows for the priesthood. It's a shorter time than most students take to get a bachelor's degree.

There is so much to sort out and the clock never stops ticking. The pressure bears down hard on the seminarians having trouble making the pieces fit.

It was only October, but Chris Nalty was already getting worried. He was used to quick action and resolution. "It's like one of those kids' punching bags here," Chris told me. "You hit it square and you think you have a problem licked, then it bobs rights back up in your face." About a month had gone by and he still felt sorely out of sync with the seminary. He couldn't wait any longer.

One night, Nalty waited until the floor was quiet. He left his room and went next door to use the telephone. There was one phone on each wing of the seminary and privacy always was at a premium. The hall lights were usually off, making the long corridors of scuffed linoleum tile dark even during the day. He closed the door of the phone room, turned on the lights, and, before he lost his nerve, dialed his parents' number.

He had been smoking more than usual since arriving in Rome. He lit a Marlboro Light while the phone rang.

"Mom," he said, trying to keep his voice down. "Hi. It's Chris."

"Christopher," his mother exclaimed, a bit startled by the unexpected call. "Is everything OK?"

He hesitated. He knew his mother would sense the edge to his voice. His mother always did. Chris was not one to call home just to chat. Since college, he was always an independent type: close to his family but accustomed to taking care of things on his own. That was then. Times, and pressures, had changed.

"Hey," Chris said, "where have ya'll been? I haven't gotten any letters. You forget I'm over here or something?"

"No, Chris, we've just been a little busy. Sure, we'll write. We'll get a letter out right away. But tell me: how are you doing? Is there anything we can do?"

"I'm just looking for a little support here, that's all," he said. "It's not easy."

"What do you mean?"

"I mean that I can promise you one thing: if I finish here and I get ordained, I'm going to be one hell of a priest. You know why? Because it's trial by fire. There are no bones about it."

"You sound stressed," she said.

"I do? Well, that's probably because I am. In a big way. Listen, remember the stories I told you about law school? It was hard. But here it's really hard. In a different way. I mean, it's hard because you have tremendous constraints on your time. You just don't have time to do things. Pray. Catch your breath. Whatever. I feel I'm under a lot of pressure here."

"Pressure? How?"

"To start getting with the program. To start feeling like a seminarian. To start feeling like I'm understanding what's going on spiritually instead of feeling like I'm some guy who's just trying to stay afloat."

"You're not thinking of leaving?" she asked softly.

"No, no. Things haven't gotten to that point yet. I just need some more support, that's all. Write once in a while, will ya'll? Promise?"

"Promise."

Nalty was stuck. The headstrong dash to the seminary had suddenly bogged down. The scope, the utter completeness of the change being asked suddenly seemed incredibly daunting. Nalty wasn't used to feeling humbled. Or whatever it was he felt. He was having trouble trying to identify precisely what he was going through. It was far deeper than just lamenting the possibility of the end of his sex life. He felt unsure of himself for the first time in his privileged life. What kind of ill-defined place do I occupy now, he thought? I'm no longer my old self. I can't go back to the silly party chatter and killer hours at a big law firm. That's gone forever. But I'm not yet convinced of my vocation. There was so little to grasp at for balance. Who, he ultimately asked himself, am I?

Celibacy was definitely forcing a new self-image. He was ill-prepared for the void left by the possibility of lifelong celibacy. This wasn't just downtime between relationships; it was supposed to be permanent. What an unfamiliar concept. What *is* really permanent in the culture he was raised in, he thought? Jobs, homes, marriage, even names are easily discarded. Cosmetic surgery can take care of physical imperfections. What cannot be undone? An amputation came to mind. Nalty laughed to himself in a wry way. That's a good description of what it was like cutting off from his past.

At first, Nalty felt diminished. He mourned something precious, intimate, that was gone. Now, more than a month in the seminary, it wasn't getting any easier. But at least there where some milestones. A few mornings in the Blessed Sacrament Chapel under the main church, Nalty found himself staring into the single red candle on the altar and believing—really believing—that this was where he was meant to be. They were fleeting but incredibly important moments. It was a shot of pure hope: the most potent antidote to the long stretches of depression and desperation setting in along with the autumn.

"I cry," said Nalty. "You know what I used to be like? A tough lawyer. I made other people cry, but not me. And now I have these spontaneous tears. It's blown my mind."

Dolan advises all the New Men not to exult too much in the highs or dwell on the lows. New Men like Nalty have to be particularly careful, he says. "Going through this—coming to Rome, realizing what the priesthood is really all about—can be incredibly emotionally draining. If we can do anything as experienced priests, we can show them that there is an equilibrium. If there's a true vocation, it eventually evens out."

"How do you show them?" I asked him.

"How? That's easy. By being content and comfortable as priests. I consider celibacy an honor. My gift to the Church. It doesn't prevent me from being, in a priestly way, sexual. I enjoy women. I like to be around them."

"And what about those who cross the line?"

"Unfortunately, we have too many of those. That's why we press this celibacy thing so hard now in the seminary. This is the place to figure out if you can do it or not. Don't wait until you're in the parish."

A few nights after Nalty called home, he asked the seminarian living on the other side of the phone room over for a drink. He needed to unwind after studying ancient Greek. A basic grasp of the language is a requirement for the New Men. He had been plowing through some verb conjugations.

Nalty was becoming quickly famous for his blender-whipped margaritas. But that night, he was in the mood for scotch. He poured himself a double.

Eric Berns, a fourth-year seminarian, opened a beer. Superficially, the two men were as different as their drinks of choice. Nalty's idea of the perfect evening had been dinner with a few other couples in a private dining room at one of New Orleans's best restaurants. Berns daydreamed of taking his rifle and hunting along in the gray and white winter mornings in the Wisconsin woods he had explored since he was a boy. He was delightedly stunned when Chris told him the story about losing his ring while hunting deer in Alabama. Berns is an easy friend—open, relaxed, never judgmental—but he took an especially quick liking to Nalty. They both knew the solitude and patience of hunting—and that palpable reality of sighting the game in the scope, holding your breath and pulling a trigger and making the kill. They could trust each other.

Berns pulled a chair in from one of his two rooms. After the first year, seminarians can usually grab a second room for a study or a living room. It's one of the benefits of not having a full house. The North American College could easily accommodate a few dozen more seminarians. Berns turned his extra room into the famed Carnivor: the last stop for countless steaks, slabs of ribs, and just about any kind of meat cooked up in the student kitchen on the top floor.

Berns was just about a week from becoming a deacon. The diaconate ceremony is undoubtedly the most important event of the year at the seminary. The seminarians return home for final ordination. But they are made deacons in St. Peter's. It is the most binding step before they take their full priestly vows.

After three full years in the seminary, they are finally making a formal, public pledge of fidelity to the Church. A seminarian has the latitude—some would call it luxury—to waver and question. They can simply say they've changed their minds and head home. There may be grumbling from their bishop and explanations to the seminary rector, but, in the end, it's in the seminarians' hands. After they become deacons, it grows much more complicated. One deacon described it as the way it must feel to wed after a long engagement.

The Church leadership must approve any dispensation from a deacon's vows and duties, which include the authority to administer the sacraments of marriage and baptism and preside at funerals. The rest of the priestly functions are bestowed with final ordination.

"So, Eric, ya'll set for the diaconate?" Nalty asked, sitting at his desk chair with its four legs stuck into four spliced tennis balls. It's a trick all the seminarians learn to stop the annoying screech of wood scraping against tile floor.

"You bet," Berns said. "But, you know, time has really flown. I feel like just yesterday I was a New Man. You'll see how fast it goes."

"Man, I'm just trying to think about getting through next week, let alone think about years down the line."

"It will get easier, Chris. I guarantee it. The worst thing you can do is to think that you are alone in this. We've all gone through it one way or the other."

"Did you ever feel like dropping out?"

"Well, I can say this. I was one of those who was thinking about becoming a priest from way back when I was a kid. There's still some of us around, believe it or not. You remember I told you the story about how I confided this to my girlfriend in seventh grade and then she blabbed in the bus and all the kids were yelling, 'Father Berns, Father Berns'? OK. So I've pretty much always known my vocation. But you always have to test it, make sure it's real. You have to make sure that it is God that's calling you to the priesthood and you're just not doing it to prove something to yourself or someone else or whatever. Believe me, there were times I wasn't sure that I'd go all the way to the diaconate. The seminary is here so we can test ourselves. We shouldn't take anything for granted."

"Listen, Eric, I don't. I'm just kind of confused. I feel I'm supposed to be here. But at the same time, why can't I shake off my old life and move on? I want to be looking forward, not in my rearview mirror."

"You're talking about celibacy?"

"Of course. That's the big thing. That's no secret. But a lot of other little things, too. For instance, I feel like I'm in a kind of no-man's-land. We're trying to become holy and grow spiritually, right? But at the same time we have to be open to the temptations that would take you away from the priesthood. You have to think: if I'm so torn over whether I can honestly commit to lifelong celibacy, then maybe—and I stress maybe—that's God's way of telling me I should serve Him by getting out of here and raising a family."

"There's nothing wrong with that," said Berns. "But don't rush to quick conclusions. Promise me that. We all have temptations. I'm not just talking about sex, either. It could be to make a mean comment behind someone's back. It could be to think of yourself rather than go out of your way to help someone. A million things that you'd call unfit for a good Christian, let alone a priest. We're always going to face them. It's life. But, Chris, let me ask you a question."

"Shoot," said Nalty.

"Do you feel you're less of a man because you're celibate? I mean, right now. Do you feel in any way lessened?"

"I used to in some way. I wouldn't say less of a man. I would say that it's just hard to accept. Like, you know, this is it. It's over. But that's fading a little. Just a little. In fact, sometimes it makes me feel good. Like I'm doing something for the Lord. Something like: He's given me so much, this is one sacrifice I can give Him in return. Does that make any sense? I just wonder if God is going to want me to go all the way to ordination. At this point, I just don't know."

"Chris, look, if you honestly believe that God is calling you to leave the seminary, you won't be the first for sure. But don't let the normal trial of being a New Man make you think you won't be a good priest."

"Do you think I'd be a good priest?" Nalty asked.

"Definitely."

Nalty smiled. "Why?"

"Because you're sitting here asking the hard questions. A bad priest is someone who went along and got ordained, then all of a sudden goes, 'Hey, this isn't for me. This isn't what I expected.'"

"We'll see," said Chris. "The jury's still out. I feel like God has definitely called me this far. But, you know, I also feel that He could turn around tomorrow and say, 'That's enough, Chris. It's time to go home.'"

"Chris," said Berns, "it could happen to any of us."

Nalty was pushing for answers. He followed his spiritual director's advice and tried to step deeper in prayer. Those times, kneeling alone in the chapel, became the most important element holding him—at least for the moment—in Rome. It was comfort and inspiration laced together so intricately that each emotion overlapped, layer over layer. He listened for God. He tried, as his spiritual director urged, to be open to the voice. "I know it's not some thing booming down from heaven," Nalty said, "It's my voice. God will speak to me from inside. I just have to know how to hear Him." One of Nalty's most beloved religious figures, Mother Teresa, described her calling to religious life as hearing a "voice within a voice." The message Chris Nalty thought he heard from time to time was: Don't give up. It's not yet time to decide.

The New Men grope for ways to describe what prayer means to them. Some depict it as an anchor. Or the glue holding their faith together. One, a young New Man from the Midwest, came up with perhaps one of the best images. It's like thumbing through an encyclopedia, he said. One passage leads to the other. You learn and grow and crave even more. But at the same time you recognize how much you don't know, how much mystery is out there.

One morning, Nalty went to the tiny Blessed Sacrament Chapel to pray as usual. But he stayed. For almost two hours he was alone. He stared at the simple pine tabernacle holding the Eucharist. Nothing, for Chris, held him more in awe than that core element of his faith: the wine and bread transubstantiated into the Body and Blood of Christ. The uncertainty he found as a seminarian was put aside, for these moments at least, by the pure belief in what lay inside the tabernacle. The summer before coming to Rome, Nalty worked in a parish where he sometimes would bring communion to nursing-home patients unable to rise from their beds. Each time he felt alone in the seminary, he tried to think of the lonely people he met in the homes and how they would often cry as he offered them the host. "Don't ever underestimate its power," Chris told me.

In the chapel, he read the Liturgy of the Hours to start that day.

The psalm beings: "Turn your ear, O Lord, and give answer, for I am poor and needy." It ends: "Console me and give me strength."

When he was done, he buried his face in his palms.

"Is this where I belong?" he whispered.

"Is it? Is it?"

A question changed Nalty's life.

"Have you ever thought of the priesthood?" asked a priest, an old family friend.

Nalty blinked and stammered. "The priesthood?" he laughed. "You're kidding, right?"

The priest was, indeed, serious. Nalty had come to him in 1986 to talk about his breakup with his college girlfriend, who dumped him for a guy in her study group at Georgetown Medical School. Chris had thought he was headed for marriage. It wasn't out of any deep religious reasons he sought out the priest. He was just looking for a friendly shoulder.

They met twice in the span of a week while Nalty was back in New Orleans after his romance fell apart. Right before he was to head back to Washington, the priest told Nalty he had a crazy thought. It may sound bizarre, he said, but try to keep an open mind. Then he asked the question. What about the priesthood?

"It was wild because I know I never thought about it, but when he said it, it was like everything got real bright," said Nalty. "And all of a sudden the idea was planted in my mind right then."

But it's absurd, he told himself. Me? A priest? He didn't even know what a seminary really was. He had to look it up.

The idea, however, just wouldn't leave him alone. Sometimes he wouldn't think about it for months, then all of a sudden it was there as inviting as an unwrapped present. Tear into it, he'd think. Then, just as abruptly, he'd pull himself back—hard. "Come on, get a grip," he'd shake his head. "You are definitely no priest."

Dolan would disagree—at least up to the point of following the call as far as the seminary. Nalty's story—the priesthood question stopping him in his tracks—is told in thousands of variations among new seminarians everywhere. Men with careers, romances, responsibilities suddenly find themselves pulled toward a different light. And all it took, when they look back at the amazing transformation, was someone to point them in that direction.

The reasons for the decline in the priesthood are numerous and difficult to prioritize. Such significant trends rarely can be traced to one distinct cause. But Dolan believes there is a factor in the collapsing clergy that is often overlooked or undervalued: many people, including parents and parish priests, have stopped looking for new priests.

"You would love to think that there are some great philosophical reasons, like secularism, materialism, blah, blah, blah," said Dolan. "It's not so grand.

"It used to be if a son became a priest you'd say, 'Oh, this is great. This is going to bring honor to the family. You know, my son is going to happy. He's going to be cared for for the rest of his life. There's going to be a chance for him to exercise a position of prestige and leadership within the community.' A lot of that is still true, but some of that isn't. So you have mothers who aren't so overt in encouraging sons to be priests. And you have . . ."

Dolan stopped for a thoughtful puff on his cigar.

"OK, is it because we're embarrassed about the scandals that are going on? Is it because we don't want to imply that the priesthood is a more sacred or a special way of life than, say, marriage or even the single life? I don't know what it is, but priests are a little hoarse in encouraging vocations.

"What can you say? There's a decline in a sort of Catholic culture—a lack of respect for the sacred, a lack of faith in many quarters. So that lack of something would perhaps make a young man deaf to hear the call. Plus, there's a presence of some things that might drown out that call: a consumerism, a secularism, a materialism in society that, at times, can make us deaf to the call. Another thing we can never forget: Catholics believe very much in mediation. In other words, the voice of God rarely comes to us directly. More often than not, it comes mediated through other people: family, friends, Church. That's been dulled. That mediation has been dulled because, unfortunately, tragically, other people are not so encouraging today concerning the priesthood."

One day, Dolan was walking by the music room in the seminary and heard a hymn being sung in Latin—the sole language of the mass before Vatican II. It was hard to believe this was the same place he studied, where seminarians in the seventies raced from the past as if it were diseased. Dolan went away humming.

"It's very interesting," he said, "to watch the pendulum go."

Chris Nalty knows how wide it can swing.

Coming out of law school, he had the credentials and the connections. It all fell into place so easily.

The most prestigious law firm in New Orleans—a powerhouse built by some of the city's premier families: Jones, Walker, Waechter, Poitevent, Carrere & Denegre—made an offer to Nalty in 1988 when he was fresh out of Georgetown. Nalty had earned a double-barreled calling card: law degree and MBA. They put him to work overseeing business deals and real-estate transactions. He started at $50,000—"fat money" as some say in New Orleans—and the path to partnership was wide and clear. The firm knew well the dividends of adding the Nalty name to the letterhead. In the conservative and clannish network of New Orleans business, the Nalty family had an upstanding pedigree. Nalty's father, Paul, is a semi-retired business lawyer and permanent deacon at New Orleans's St. Louis Cathedral, with a special focus on divorced and remarried Catholics. His mother, who has a master's degree in French, used to have a local television show on Catholic sex education and hopes someday to put together a retreat for married Catholics.

Nalty did not disappoint the law firm. He showed he knew how to bring in cash. He had some of the highest billable hours: around 2,800 a year. "For the first two years I just plowed into it. I just cranked," he said. Time away from work was time to have fun. Out in the Old Metairie section, he bought a fifty-year-old house and filled it with nice antiques, including an eighteenth-century armoire he used for his stereo system. There was a front yard for his black Labrador and a driveway for his BMW 325i, which went to the car wash every few days. The giant live oak trees made a leafy canopy down his street. Nalty joined some men's social clubs—leather-and-wood places to enjoy his passion of smoking good cigars. The graying older guys, long out of their prime, liked having peacocks like Nalty around.

"I wish I could say that I've never been a sinner, but you know, I was dating and you know what happens," he said. "What can I say? I had lots of gorgeous girlfriends."

But, slowly, almost without anyone noticing, something else was percolating. He'd still throw his catered parties at his house and puff away on smuggled Cuban cigars. He didn't stop renting rooms at the top New Orleans restaurants for parties with other couples or hanging out drinking wine in his buddy's Jacuzzi. Sometimes, though, when things got real mellow after some drinks, he'd pull someone aside and start talking about religion and the priesthood.

"I never really took him that seriously," said his hot tub–owning friend, John Rowland, who also became Nalty's business partner in a catering and party planning business. "I could see something was eating away at his insides, but I thought it was just one of the normal down periods we all have.

"Chris was a ladies' man. I mean, a real ladies' man. So what are you going to think when a guy like that is talking about becoming a priest. It was just like, 'OK, Chris, whatever you say,' type of thing."

The talk of the priesthood was especially discounted by women. They thought they knew Chris or guys like him—religious so long as it doesn't interfere with their other pursuits.

"I was saying to myself, 'Yeah, I'll believe it when I see it,'" said a former paralegal at his firm and old girlfriend, Stacey West Williams. "I mean, he was going out with me. He was just a normal guy. On our first date we went to see a movie about mobsters. What's the name? Oh, yeah: *Miller's Crossing*. It was really bloody. I'm thinking, 'Do people thinking about the priesthood go see things like this?'"

But Nalty was indeed making changes. He began throttling back on his hours at the firm in order to devote more time to civil causes and some pro bono work. He quit at the end of 1991 and started working at Rowland's special events company, which put on concerts, catered bashes. He bought a fax and cellular phone and moved his office into his house. He was co-founder of a courier business downtown and his old contacts paid off and he began picking up some legal work on the side. "I'd be working in the office in my home in boxers and a t-shirt and I'd be practicing law," he said. With the pressures of the law firm gone, the idea of the priesthood had more room to maneuver.

He started reading about seminaries and religious conversions. This can't be me, he'd say to himself. Impossible. It'll pass. Only it didn't.

It all came slamming down in Alabama's pine woods when he plucked his lost ring from the edge of the logging road.

"There isn't a person in the world that can tell me it's a coincidence," he said. "I mean, there's no way. There's thousands and thousands of acres and I just happened to walk in the same spot, and it just happened to have rained that day and I happened to stop at one spot on a road that trucks have been up and down all summer."

A few months after finding the ring—and the courage to test his vocation—Nalty and his family came to Rome for the unveiling of the Last Judgment restoration. At the pope's weekly audience on Wednesday, Nalty ran into a North American College seminarian who was a friend of a friend. It was the guy who used to be called Drench.

Nalty's sister leaned over during the audience and asked her brother: "Why do they call him 'Drench'?"

"Jennifer," Nalty said, "far be it from me to reveal the past life of a future priest."

"Well, I know all kinds of stories about you," she said.

"I hope you will also learn by my good example."

Nalty's other sister, Ariane, kept up the harangue long after everyone else accepted his decision to join the seminary. She refused to contribute to Nalty's monthly newsletter, an elaborate four-color job with pictures and biblical quotations and Italian recipes, done on his laptop. "Notes from the wacko," she called it. Ariane was unmovable in her contention that her brother was stumbling in the wrong direction.

"I'm just trying to save him embarrassment and save our family embarrassment," she said. "I mean, what if he becomes a priest, then drops out? It's a big deal. It's embarrassing for everybody. I think ten years from now we'll all look back on this with a big laugh."

Nalty smirks at his sister's doubts, but there's no laughter. She may, after all, be right.

"I know I had a choice, but then again I'm not really sure that I did. Because in some ways I really felt like I knew that that's what God wanted me to do—come to the seminary. Now I still don't know if God is going to want me to become a priest or not. . . . The only thing I know is that He got me here and all I can do is listen to Him every day. The other day I was walking back to the penitentiary . . . ahh, I mean seminary. Yipes, was that a Freudian slip or what?"

Nalty said his prayers quickly that morning. He had an invitation to join the pope for mass in the papal chapel.

He and a priest from New Orleans hurried down the hill to St. Peter's Square. They were told not, at any cost, to be late. But when they arrived at the Bronze Door leading to the wing with the papal residence, Swiss Guards blocked their way. The door was never opened from 1870 to 1929, when the Lateran Treaty with Italy formed the sovereign Vatican city-state.

"Your names are not here," one of the Guards said, looking over a list on creamy Vatican stationery.

"Please, could you call?" begged Rev. Jose Lavastida, a priest at the seminary's graduate school. "There should be two names: mine and a Christopher H. Nalty."

The guard dialed the number for the pope's private chapel. He nodded and made a quick note on a piece of paper. A fall wind had arrived finally and was blowing hard from the mountains that run down Italy's spine. It swirled and looped through the colonnades in St. Peter's Square. It was chilly, but Nalty felt warm. A nervous heat.

"OK," the guard said in his Italian thickened by a Swiss-German accent. "It's all right."

Nalty and the priest hurried up the steps behind the Swiss Guard dressed in the purple and gold striped uniform that has changed little since the Renaissance. The mass was to begin at 7:15 A.M. Papal masses were always prompt. They were just going to make it in time.

"Chris, hurry up. Come on," Lavastida urged. They were the last ones to arrive. Lavastida went into a side room to put on vestments for mass and Nalty was directed to the audience room outside the chapel. A monsignor came up to Nalty and asked in Italian if he would do the reading.

"Certainly," Nalty replied in the same language. "But in English, if you don't mind."

"Of course," the monsignor laughed. "You're American, aren't you?"

The pope was already praying when they entered the chapel. Nalty sat in the last row behind about twenty-five others. He felt a little queasy and his mouth went cottony. Two months in Rome and he was about to share the altar with the pope. Too bad it was Wednesday, Nalty thought. It was his day for a bread and water fast—part of his personal rigors to reinforce the commitment to celibacy. His stomach felt queasy and empty.

The monsignor gave Nalty a nod. He rose and went to the altar. The others at the mass looked him over. Who was this guy? Did he have some special connection with the Holy Father? The Vatican is always insular and often catty. When someone gets special attention from the pope, the inner circle wants to know why. This case was just a matter of timing. The monsignor wanted a seminarian to do the reading that day. Nalty was the only one on the list.

Nalty brushed past the pope on his way to the lectern. The pope didn't notice. His eyes were closed in prayer. He was moaning, mumbling. He's praying in tongues, Nalty thought. He then turned to the reading, Romans 6:12–18. He didn't smile but wanted to. "It was pretty ironic," Nalty said later. "God sends you these messages sometimes." The passage was about the pleasures of the flesh.

With the pope groaning his own prayers to the side, Nalty began to read:

Do not, therefore, let sin rule your mortal body and make it obey its lusts; no more shall you offer the members of your body to sin as weapons for evil. Rather, offer yourselves to God as men who have come back from the dead to life, and your bodies to God as weapons for justice. Sin will no longer have power over you; you are now under grace, not under the law. What does all this lead to? Just because we are not under law but under grace, are we free to sin? By no means! You must realize that, when you offer yourselves to someone as obedient slaves, you are the slave of the one you obey, whether yours is the slavery of sin, which leads to death, or of obedience, which leads to justice. Thanks be to God, though once you were slaves to sin, you sincerely obeyed that rule of teaching which was imparted to you; freed from your sin, you became slaves of justice.

The pope rose and finished the rest of the mass in Latin. Afterwards, the pontiff walked into the audience room alongside the monsignor who asked Nalty to read. Nalty watched the pope greet others. How clever, he thought, as he watched the deft way the pope distributes rosaries in boxes with the papal seal. The pope palms the box, then slips it to the recipient in a half-handshake. Very dignified, Nalty thought, and, at the same time, so much like a kindly grandfather sneaking a dollar to a beaming youngster. The pope moved down the line—steadily but not in a hurry. He chatted briefly with each person in their own language. He arrived at Nalty.

"I'm a seminarian in Rome and I'm from New Orleans," Nalty said, taking the rosary in both hands. He noticed what many others have remarked about the pope's hands—how smooth and soft. Like the hands of a young man. Not someone who once worked in a stone quarry.

As Nalty walked away, the monsignor passed by. The reading, he said, was *"benissimo."* Nalty tried not to let his satisfaction show.

Then as the pope was leaving the room, he turned. *"Au revoir,* New Orleans."

Nalty and Lavastida were dumbstruck. The pope took a few more steps, then turned again, with a thin smile, and said: *"Auf wiedersein."*

Nalty laughed and said, as courtly as he could: *"Au revoir."*

The day before Berns and the others would become deacons, Chris Nalty ran into the former Drench. He had been made a deacon the year before and was coming back for one more year at the seminary before going back for ordination. Some dioceses pull their seminarians back from Rome after four years. Others, with less pressing demands to fill parish slots, allow a fifth year.

They walked a bit around the grounds—out into the big field used for soccer and football. Some seminarians were playing tennis on the courts built on a small rise at the far end of the seminary's twelve acres. The New Man and the deacon made small talk—How are classes? How was summer? Do any traveling? Then Nalty got serious. He didn't want to lose this opportunity.

"When did you know?"

The deacon knew exactly what Nalty was asking: when did his vocation fall into place? "Chris, I can't put a definite date on it," he said, "but I think it was when I found my prayers changing. It wasn't any longer: show me a sign that this is right. It became: let me do something to show you that I'm worthy. That's when I knew there was no going back."

"I'm finding something else."

"What?"

"I'm finding that I'm crying sometimes. Do you believe it? Just praying and crying. I am not a weepy type of guy."

"Out of joy or frustration?"

"That's what I don't know. Joy, I think. I just don't know yet."

"Don't worry about it, Chris. I know what you're saying. You feel sometimes like you've landed on a different planet. Am I right? The seminary is so counterculture to us in America. We glorify the person, the ability to control and shape our situation. You tell someone that you're surrendering yourself to the will of the Holy Spirit. I'm not talking directly about the Church here. I'm talking about the Holy Spirit—what motivates us to do the right thing. Well, I've seen many eyes rolling. People think I've gone off the deep end or something. It's not something that many Americans are capable of grasping."

"I'm trying," said Nalty. "Believe me, I'm trying."

They walked for a while. Nalty stopped.

"You know something? There's got to be a reason I gave up everything that I was doing beforehand to do what I'm doing now. Logically, especially in our day and age and culture, it doesn't make any sense. Why would you give up a successful career, girlfriends, making money, to give up the chance of marriage, to be without real luxuries, to give up control of your life? Why would you do that?"

"What do you think?" asked Drench.

"Really the only answer that makes any sense is that it's got to be a sign to make you believe in God. That would be the only answer. Why else would I do this? It wouldn't make any sense if I didn't think that God wanted me to do it. I'm not a flaky person. I don't say things like, you know, 'Oh, I got a sign from heaven to do something.' That's the only explanation I can give for doing it."

The day of the diaconate was warm and clear. The guards outside St. Peter's were grumbling about the good weather. Usually, by early October it was cool enough that they didn't have to keep watch for the miniskirts, tank tops, and other flesh-exposing clothes that are prohibited in the basilica.

The fat raindrops that finally douse summer were weeks overdue. The statues around Rome looked tired. Every line and hollow was filled with the sooty powder of the dry months. The cats that live along the backside of the seminary grounds stayed deep in the bushes. You could hear them walking on the crisp underbrush.

The New Men, in the clerics, took their place with the other seminarians in the basilica's curved apse. Some were in the choir. The others found places facing forward toward the raised throne of St. Peter, an ancient wooden chair encased in bronze and ivory. Rows of empty chairs across from the choir awaited the seminarians about to become deacons.

For three years, the seminarians preparing for the diaconate had heard the rector and faculty say it hundreds of times in hundreds of ways: isn't a seminarian just a direct descendant of the original disciples under Christ—coming together to learn, then scattering to work and teach? "It's such a wonderful and appropriate parallel," said Dolan. "I can't emphasize this enough. They are in St. Peter's, standing above the tomb of one of Christ's apostles, and taking vows to carry on the very same mission."

It's Dolan's patented reverse recipe. Put the sweet icing on first. The other layers are grittier. The Bible is graphic: Christ was mocked, misunderstood, and suffered terrible pain and indignation. You need to be braced to face this as well, the seminarians are told. The Church still has its martyrs—whether from past anti-cleric fevers like the French Revolution or in contemporary backlashes in Latin America or Algeria. Italian mobsters have silenced defiant priests with bullets. The United States is much safer ground for the Catholic clergy, but perhaps emotionally shakier. Taunts rain down with bruising intensity. Pick a group—feminists, gays, birth-control proponents, whatever—and there's bound to be a well-articulated gripe against the Church. Dolan warns: a thick skin is part of the clerical garb.

Chris Nalty turned his head toward the side entrance where the diaconate candidates would enter. He didn't want to miss anything. After all, this is what it's all about. Here are guys who had gone the distance. Chris's thought raced: Did they still have any doubts? Is it possible they all could be lock-solid certain in their vocation like his friend Eric Berns? And, most of all, when exactly did they know it was right?

Right on time, the seminarians entered the basilica. Ropes were set up to clear a path through the tourists and pilgrims, most having no clue what was taking place. They took pictures anyway.

Behind candle bearers and censers puffing incense, the deacon candidates took their places in the half-dome apse. They wore spotless white robes called albs that seemed to pulse in the barrage of camera flashes.

Nalty thought about the letter he received from his friend in Washington, Allie, asking for a photograph. They had spent a lot of time together in New Orleans the year before Nalty went to Catholic University. It wasn't quite a relationship, but also not entirely innocent. The flirting was heavy. He wrapped up some legal work and caught up on philosophy and theology credits needed to continue seminary studies in Rome. He even paid his own tuition so he wouldn't feel indebted to the New Orleans archdiocese if he dropped out.

Allie, who moved to Washington after Nalty left for Rome, was counting on that. She believed Nalty would finally come to his senses and return home. She didn't see him as a prospective priest but rather a prospective boyfriend. "Send me a picture," she wrote. "But, please, no priest clothes." Nalty cut out a tie and pasted it over his Roman collar in a snapshot. "Now I know how the lepers felt," he said.

In the apse, Cardinal Edward Iris Cassidy sat on a red velvet chair and waited until all the fourth-year seminarians were assembled. The names of those to be ordained deacons were read out loud. Each rose and bowed to the cardinal.

"Do you judge these men to be worthy?" Cassidy asked Rector Dolan in his Australian twang.

"I testify that they have been found worthy," Dolan answered.

The cardinal turned to the group. "It's not easy, especially in these times, for young people like you to make a lifelong commitment.

"All those born into this world are destined to serve. We have no choice in that. We do have a choice in who we are to serve: the Lord or an idol of our own making. . . . There are no neutral choices.

"Up until now you have listened to God's word," he continued. "Now you are to preach God's word."

Cassidy drew in a breath.

"I ask you, in the presence of God and the Church, are you resolved to remain celibate in the service of God and mankind?"

"I am," the group replied in unison.

"May the Lord help you in this commitment."

They came forward one by one and the cardinal placed his hands on their heads. They were now deacons.

For Halloween, Nalty was a saint. At the seminary's party in the student lounge, Nalty came as St. Sebastian, whose legend of martyrdom at the hands of Romans includes first being pierced by arrows, then being pummeled to death. Nalty spent hours taping fake arrows to a bed sheet toga stained with stage blood sent by his mother. Nalty strode into the party in the ground-floor lounge. He loves a party—especially now. It was a relief to tuck away, for a while anyway, this showdown with celibacy and the nerve-straining transition into seminary life. He gave a thumbs-up to some of the other costume-clad seminarians. "Looking good," he winked at two other New Men dressed as annoyingly folksy Knights of Columbus patrons. "Skokie, Illinois, chapter," one of them added.

"I love this Eye-tal-yan food, but it gives me a little problem with the digestion, don't you know," one of the Knights said to a group of seminarians. "I haven't felt this bad since I had my spastic colon back in seventy-four."

Nalty roared. His arrows shook.

Gary Benz leaned against the back wall and watched the party. When he left North Dakota, this was not what he had in mind.

CHAPTER IV

BENEDICT'S CAVE

I trusted even when I said: "I am sorely afflicted."

—EVENING PRAYER
FOR ALL SAINTS' DAY, NOVEMBER 1 (PSALM 116)

Gary's last steps up the path were the coldest.

It was late morning, but the sun had only just crested the mountain tops. The season's first frost glazed the neat rows of olive trees and, higher up on the slopes, made the clumps of spidery brush shine like reeds of blown glass. It all glistened wet and bright for a moment as the climbing sun pushed the sharp shadow line down deeper into the valley. Then the silver sheen melted away, leaving the browns and greens of the mountains outside Rome.

Gary Benz turned his face to the warming rays. His cheeks were flushed from the chill and the two-mile walk from Subiaco up the mountain road that rises in hairpin curves to the Benedictine abbey about twenty miles east of Rome. He hadn't expected to be so winded and made a vow to try to get back into shape. The sedentary routine of seminary life was making him feel more sluggish than someone in their mid-twenties should feel. He had put on some weight but didn't really know how much. It showed in his face. Once lean angles were now rounded and soft. How he missed working with his hands, feeling the soil churn up under a hoe or a log splitting cleanly in two with a smooth ax blow. He took a deep gulp of air—like drinking from a cool stream after Rome's sour smog. Benz thought about how it would be in

North Dakota today, the first day of November, All Saints' Day. The air would certainly snap with the nostril-burning promise of the deep freeze ahead. But back in your throat there also lingers the mellowness of fall: the sweetness of late-season squash or maybe the musk of cut wheat. These craggy old mountains outside Rome confound him and his rigid sense of seasons. The wind hints of winter but the trees around the monastery stay dark green and lush.

Many of the other New Men planned to go over to the Vatican for a mass by Pope John Paul II, who was ordained on this same day in 1946. The Vatican—especially on a crowded holiday—was the last place Gary wanted to be.

He had looked forward to this trip to Subiaco since coming to Rome, but especially since the retreat. Coming here, he hoped, would end his indecision. He needed strength. Not a lot more. Just enough to help him cut his ties with the seminary and take up his life with the Benedictines.

The long path to the monastery was shaded by thick branches of holm oak and laurel. It was cold as night in the mossy hollow. A priest and another seminarian who joined Benz on the day-trip from Rome looked over at their companion. Benz's head was bowed, staring down at his Rockport loafers.

Benz hurried up the path. Maybe he could outrun all the upsetting memories of his brief time in Rome—just as Benedict did when he fled the city's corruption and vice for these mountains fifteen hundred years ago? But Gary's distress was too big to flee. Being here in Subiaco—a place he had always dreamed of visiting—made it even worse. He wanted the trip to ring with perfection. This was, after all, the saint who spoke with most clarity to Gary's soul. Instead, he kept thinking about another trip some weeks before. It was with the other New Men to see the pope.

The New Men had dressed in their clerics and were on a bus for the pope's villa in Castel Gandolfo in the "castelli" hills southeast of Rome—named after the dozens of medieval castles built to protect the papal kingdom. The seminarians had gotten a late start out of the city and Saturday evening traffic was typically heavy. Then on the two-lane road into Castel Gandolfo, the bus was clogged again in a bottleneck of pilgrims and tourists.

"We're going to be late," grumbled Rector Dolan.

The faculty hustled the New Men through the villa's huge doors. "Let's go, fellas," Dolan urged the seminarians who stopped to watch the sunset reflect into Lake Alban five hundred feet below the town. "Fellas, fellas." Benz was near the front of the group, which came to a halt at the edge of the rectangle-shaped courtyard. It was packed with the faithful to join the pope in praying the rosary, which he does in public on the first Saturday of each month. The New Men shuffled around, trying to get a good spot to see the balcony where the pope would stand.

"No, *prego, prego,*" said a guard, looking uncomfortably hot in a black suit and tie.

Four papal security men began pushing back the crowd for the New Men to pass. Benz nervously fingered his Mexican rosary of black beads linked by a double chain, a gift from a priest back home. Some foreigners muttered and shot cold looks at the New Men. The Italians just stepped back. They are accustomed to being pushed around by dignitaries at papal appearances. An ultra-conservative order reputedly favored by the pope, the Legionaries of Christ, always try to stake out front positions at papal events. Gary hated that type of arrogance. And now the crowd was parting to allow the New Men to advance closer.

Gary was too ashamed to look anyone in the eye as they moved up.

The pope looked down on the New Men, now front and center, and switched from Italian to English.

"Happy new year," he said. An awkward silence and a few uncomfortable titters followed. "I mean, happy new academic year."

Only a few of the better-traveled New Men—Chris Nalty and Roger Landry among them—had seen the pope in person before. Benz studied the pontiff: the thinning silver hair, a slight tan from his annual trip to the Italian Alps, the way he holds papers with the right hand and keeps his trembling left hand at his side. Benz had hoped for a decisive moment, an illumination on the righteousness of his decision to come to the seminary. Instead, all he could think about were the ordinary folks muscled aside so his class could be closer to John Paul. Gary was deeply upset.

On the path to the Subiaco monastery, Gary felt a different kind of embarrassment: a feeling he had let himself and the entire Benedictine community down. He considered his spirituality so perfectly suited for the monastic life of the Benedictines, whose search for God and spiritual peace is guided by the order's Rule on community, communal work, and prayer. As a boy, Benz read and reread the life of Saint Benedict—first in a pocket-size picture book, then in any biography or religious text he could find. He especially loved the part about Benedict's disgust for the corruption and vice of early sixth-century Rome. When it grew too much to bear, Benedict fled to the hills above Subiaco and lived in isolation for three years in a cave near an artificial lake built centuries before by the Roman Emperor Nero. Benz became engrossed by the Benedictines' simple spirituality: quiet contemplation and prayer but also a dedication to physical labor. For a farm boy dreaming of a religious life, it all fit so nicely. His father was named after the saint. His mother, Irene, was born on one of the saint's feast days, July 11.

As Benz grew, so did his devotion for the Benedictines. He learned that the first bishop of North Dakota, Vincent DePaul Wehrle, came from the order's Assumption Abbey in 1910. He began to visit the abbey on the edge of a sloping bluff in Richardton about an hour's drive from his home. He'd listen to the chants and rolling psalm tones sung by the monks during their daily liturgies. It was mesmerizing, comforting. Many of the monks wore flannel shirts and jeans stained with dirt from the abbey farm. Other members of the community went off to pastor in the remote little parishes—off dirt roads that run as straight as surveyor lines along the old homestead grids. This, he thought, is where I belong, with monks whose fingernails are dirty with the land I love.

But he had made a promise to give the seminary a try and, as always, was true to his word. He buried his yearning for the Benedictines for the first two months. Even when his spiritual director would ask how things were going, Benz would fib in his cotton-soft voice: "Fine, just fine. It's getting better." Like a white-knuckle attempt to kick an addiction, Benz figured he needed to go cold turkey. If he immersed himself in the seminary routine, perhaps he could quench the fire for the monastery? He constantly looked for signs that he was doing the right thing. On good days, he felt the bonds with the other New Men growing stronger. Benz got special attention from the new deacon, Tom Richter. "Gary, come on, us North Dakota boys gotta stick together," he'd say.

Sometimes while walking along the shady crest of the Janiculum, Benz would look over the ancient sprawl of Rome. There are no skyscrapers or highways cutting into the center, which spreads out like a jumble of blocks around both sides of the Tiber. On sunny days, the city shines with white marble and faded pastels. So different, Gary thought, from the tans and dirty yellows of the fields at home. Benz liked to look over the church domes and pick out the ones he had already visited. Then, on days when the haze was light, his eyes would drift to the blue-gray outline of the mountains where St. Benedict had retreated. Maybe, Benz wondered, the vocation director back home was right and his calling was really for the diocese. Was he being too selfish in wanting to turn his back on the parish in the same way Benedict abandoned Rome? Benz muddled on. Yet it was becoming clearer to Benz that he and the seminary were an imperfect match.

The go-go environment left him desperate for solitude and quiet prayer. Some nights when the cocktails started to flow and the seminary took on a frat-house rumble, Benz would simply close his door and read. Some of the seminars he found almost comically irrelevant to his faith. He slumped in his chair one evening as a faculty member described the various techniques of how to stand at the pulpit and which gestures seem to work best during the homily. Please, he thought, it's not a show.

This is what Rector Tim Dolan calls the "cookbook" stuff: what you must know in order to perform the functions of a Catholic priest.

"That's fine. I understand that," Gary said several days before his trip to Subiaco. "But all this business scares me. Priests are so occupied with so many things: running the parish and stuff like that. When is there time to do what we should be doing: trying every day to glorify and understand the mystery of God? When would there be time just to take a walk in the woods and think about God. It seems there are so many things in the parish that would pull you away from that.

"I never would want to close myself off from people. I don't want to leave the world. I don't feel turned off by the world. I just feel that we can get too bogged down in the world at the expense of our own soul. Priests are expected to fill up other people's lives. You know, we have to help them with their spiritual quest. But who's helping us?"

Benz occupied a particular niche in the seminary. He didn't cocoon himself in study and prayer like his friend Tam Tran. Yet he held himself in check, preferring to remain always just on the edge: a smile, a kind word, but never a back-slapping hello or a loud joke. "This is a tough place for a contemplative person because we are so busy," said Scot Landry, wiping off his sweaty neck after an afternoon basketball game.

Gary tried often to catalog his indecision, compiling lists of pros and cons. Sure, being in Rome was a glorious sojourn for any seminarian. These are places he read about as a boy. And the education was superb and deftly presented at the Angelicum, the English-speaking college that Gary and some other seminarians attended. But the scales tipped sharply in the other direction when he piled on his worries. City life in general grated on his nerves. There were more people within one hundred yards of the seminary than in his entire county in North Dakota. It was suffocating: such a small sky, so many noises. But, he admitted, that wasn't truly the problem, was it? No, he'd say. It's the step-lively approach of the seminary, its hints of arrogance—partly the homegrown American swagger and partly from being a pretty big fish in the ecclesiastical food chain. The Church always needs to be fed: jobs to be filled, dioceses needing to be run, reports, budget figures.

"Simplicity," Gary sighed softly, as if recalling a faraway lover.

"What?" asked the priest walking alongside Gary toward the monastery. "What did you say?"

"Nothing. I was just thinking how good it is to get out of the city."

"No kidding. It's a beautiful day, isn't it? Gary, you said you want to go straight down to the grotto, right? Well, we'll join you later if you don't mind. We want to just look around for a while."

"No problem," said Gary, relieved that he could be alone. "We'll meet up later."

In the shadows around the monastery, there were still puddles from the heavy rains a few days before. Paper-thin ice decorated the edges.

Gary Benz paused on the small terrace outside the monastery. He listened for the faint hiss of the fast-flowing Anio River, too far down in the valley to see. Behind him, the tentacles of a huge and ancient aloe plant sprouted from the cream-colored stone. He admired how the monastery seems also to grow right from the mountainside. A fifteenth-century pope, Pius II, called it "a real swallow's nest." Deep inside lies the cave where St. Benedict spent three years in total solitude and was fed by a monk who lowered down meager rations by rope.

Benz walked through the single doorway leading to the upper church. Old graffiti pocked the door frame. "BM" from New York passed this same way in 1815. Benz lingered for just a moment in the church to look over the fourteenth-century frescoes. One, stained and faded by humidity, shows St. Benedict whacking monks with a rod—the "Cure for the Lazy Monk."

Down two levels, Benz stood at the opening of the grotto. Foreign tourists and Italian pilgrims—off from work on the holy day—elbowed past like the way the New Men did at the papal villa. Benz waited until the grotto was almost empty before stepping inside, crossing under twelve hanging lanterns. Soot stained the rocks in swirling black lines. The priest and the seminarian who came with Benz whispered a bit, then went on to explore the monastery. Benz stayed silent in the cave, kneeling before a marble statue of the saint as a young man—about the same age as Benz. The gaze of the statue looks upward. Benz did the same. What he saw made him draw in his breath: scenes of the saint's life painted directly onto the raw rock. No attempt was made to smooth the stone. The pictures were distorted by the sharp edges and rough surface. Gary's loves—faith and nature—bonded together. "It's so beautiful to see a synthesis like this," Gary said.

He reached out to touch the rock. Maybe Benedict himself placed his hand on this exact spot. Finally, Gary felt ready to make a decision. He would leave the seminary.

"Gary, there you are," the other seminarian said. "You've been here the whole time? Come on outside, the scenery is just spectacular. Plus it's getting warmer."

Gary got up from his knees. He shivered. He hadn't realized until now how cold it was in the grotto. "OK," he said. "I'm ready. Let's go."

Back in the sun, Gary was chatting nonstop: about Benedict, the order, the Rule of Benedict that directs them. "What's gotten into you?" the priest joked. "You're not thinking of joining are you?"

Gary pulled him aside. He didn't want the other seminarians to hear. "Can you keep a secret?" Gary asked.

"Of course."

"Well," he said slowly, "yes, I am thinking about it." Gary left it at that. He felt he shouldn't go any further in disclosing his feelings—at least not until he told the rector.

"Interesting," the priest said, trying to remain as neutral as possible. "I'll pray for you."

"Thank you," Gary smiled—sincerely for the first time that day. "That's nice."

That night, he began composing four letters: to the Benedictines, to his vocation director back in North Dakota, to Dolan, and, the hardest of all, to his parents. "They think they are losing me," he said.

Dolan knew for weeks that Gary was in turmoil. The grapevine at the seminary is well fertilized. Just about every tidbit eventually works its way to the rector's attention. Gary's devotion to the Benedictines was obvious. What Gary told his spiritual director about his struggle remained, as always, confidential. But his formation adviser, who reports directly to Dolan, is under no such restrictions.

A few hours after receiving Gary's letter, the adviser called him to a meeting. He was on the phone when Gary arrived. Gary waited in the small secretary's office. He looked over the collection of cartoon clippings. One of his latest depicted the pope as a gunslinger on a Wild West street. The body of a Protestant minister lies in the dust. "OK," the caption reads, "does anybody else want to discuss which is the one, true religion?"

"Gary?" the adviser called from his office.

Dolan came around from his desk and sat in one of the two easy chairs on either side of a glass-top coffee table. He didn't like to talk to people across his big desk. He liked to put everyone, especially confused New Men, at ease. Gary sat in the other chair. He was stiff and nervous and did not lean back. He folded his hands over his lap.

"Gary," he said, "it seems you are thinking of leaving us?"

"That's right," Gary said softly. Then he added quickly, "But, you know, for the Benedictines."

"Of course. But, Gary, it's perfectly all right to enter an order. We'll miss you, but it's perfectly fine. So don't worry about it on that score. Just do me one favor if you could."

"Yes."

"Stay around for the semester. Why not see Christmas in Rome? You haven't sent the letter to the diocese, I take it?"

"No, not yet."

"Good. Good. There's a reason I'm asking this, you know. It's for your own peace of mind. You know as well as I that lots of New Men get first-semester jitters. The bishops know this and they'll probably try to talk you into staying. They'll try to tell you, 'Gary, it's too early to make a decision like this. Give it more time.' So, Gary, if your mind is made up to join the order, then there's nothing we can do. But do you think we can finish out the semester? It's only a couple months. Then after Christmas we can have this discussion again. Is that OK?"

"I've waited this long," said Gary. "I guess a little while longer would be all right."

"Excellent. There's a lot worse places to be stuck than Rome, you know."

"I know. There's a lot of places I'd like to see. Father, have you ever been out to Subiaco?"

"Sure, but not in quite a while. I should go back again one of these days."

"You should," said Gary. "It's absolutely wonderful."

Benz put the letters away and pulled out his photo album. Half of the pictures are landscapes—all different seasons. Sometimes the sky is clear and almost purple above the shadeless prairie. Sometimes it's swirling madly in grays and blacks.

Gary ran his hand over the photos.

"People think I sound harsh, but I miss North Dakota more than my family. But let me explain. My family, I can write and call and I know what they're up to. I hear their voices, I see pictures. They send video tapes and it's like I never left sometimes. It's like being away at college in Fargo. I know that I can always be in touch. But I can't touch the land. I can't feel the winter coming. I can't see the galaxy of stars. I can't see the harvest that I miss.

"The land. I've lost that contact."

To Dolan, a vocation is simply an invitation. It's all linguistically mapped out from the Latin *vocare:* voice, vocation, calling, summons. The hard part—the real work—begins at the seminary. It's there the little deaths start, conforming to the new rules. The most painful step for many is letting go of the old self. Now, the Church is the boss. It will set their schedule, their duties, whether they will one day wear the sashes of bishop or cardinal. Someone is always watching, evaluating. And someone else, higher up the clerical pyramid, is watching the watchers. The seminarians are told to put aside the belief in mastery over destiny. According to dogma, the progression goes: the priests follow the orders of the Church and the Church is guided by the pope and Holy Spirit.

"Let's not be foolishly innocent and say this is one big divinely inspired utopia. That doesn't work anymore. People just don't buy it. To be honest, I'm not sure they ever really did," said Rector Dolan. "What we do stress is that the Church and its priests can have a powerful and positive effect if it's handled correctly; if we get priests who aren't always seeing what they can squeeze out of the Church or what they can get away with without being caught.

"Is that too much to ask? Maybe that's why I'm called old-fashioned sometimes."

The night after Benz met with his adviser, Dolan gathered the seminarians in the auditorium for his monthly lecture. Each time it's a different topic. In November, he wanted to reinforce that only going through the motions—learning just his "cookbook" priesthood—is pure folly. He hoped Gary Benz, especially, was listening closely.

"Perhaps you have heard of Baroness Catherine Van de Hueck, founder of the Friendship House Movement, whose cause for canonization has been introduced. She was once called to one of her famous houses that served the poor. The house was experiencing internal strife. Her staff there was fighting and arguing and she was called in to referee. After listening to a couple hours of bickering, she finally concluded the meeting and said, 'I have reached a decision. I am closing down this house.' Well, shocked gasps went up all over. 'But, baroness, who will feed the poor and shelter the homeless?' she was asked. 'The government can ladle soup and make a bed as efficiently as we can,' she replied. 'We are called to do it with love, and if we can't do it with love, we're not doing it.'"

"Gentlemen," he said, "we are in the business of priestly formation, and if we cannot do it with love, there's no use doing it. All the theology, all the pastoral competence, all the preaching ability, all the liturgical style, all the Roman training in the world won't amount to a plate of gnocchi if we do not have love when we're doing it.

"You have seen priests who are men of love . . . who radiate the joy, compassion, and conviction that flow from such a furnace of love. You would not be here had you not been blessed with such examples. And you have seen priests who have either never loved or have fallen out of love—cold, mean, crabby, petty, lazy, selfish. Oh, he loves all right. He loves himself, not in the sense of self-respect spoken of by Jesus but in a narcissistic, selfish way. His convenience, his time, his assignment, his career, his image, his wants—they become supreme in his life.

"The last thing the Church needs is another such priest."

Gary left the lecture and went back to his room. Christmas was less than two months away. Why rush? He was glad his adviser suggested he stay around a while.

CHAPTER V

THE RECTOR

It is better to take refuge in the Lord
than to trust in princes.

—PSALM 118 FOR SUNDAY MORNINGS

Am I getting through? Dolan mumbled to himself.

He was at the desk in his apartment finishing up the script for his weekly three-minute segment on Vatican Radio's shortwave service. It's called *Think About It This Way*. He tries to get his listeners to see the spiritual dimension in the ordinary routine. Usually, he can write the spots in a few minutes—in his flowing cursive with very few mistakes or cross-outs. He was having trouble today, however.

He put down his fountain pen and rubbed his eyes. His thoughts were on a much smaller audience than Vatican Radio: his own New Men.

"I always have to ask, 'Am I getting through to them?'" he told me. "Am I challenging them spiritually? Am I getting them to take a hard look at their vocation?"

As far back as any of the faculty could remember, at least one New Man had dropped out during the first semester. Now it was well into November and still the class was together. Gary Benz, of course, had made his desire to leave clear. But Dolan wasn't entirely convinced he would follow through. "Call it a hunch," said Dolan. There must be a reason behind Gary's indecision. With most New Men who leave, their

mind is made up by the time word reaches Dolan. Gary seemed unsure, as if he was almost hoping someone would talk him into delaying
his decision. "I think he's not fully determined," said Dolan. "If I was a
betting man, I wouldn't bet the farm on it."

There were a few hints from the formation advisers of other New
Men struggling a bit, but that's natural. What wasn't normal was that
everyone was still in Rome. "I should be celebrating, right?" said
Dolan. But why, then, am I worried? he thought.

It must be the trends. Definitely, the trends in the Church make
him a little cautious.

"Does this sound like I'm out of my mind? I'm concerned because
no one has left the seminary," he said. "You might hear otherwise from
some people, but I can guarantee you I am not crazy."

Dolan believes nothing comes without a price. If, as Dolan hopes,
an era of spirituality is arriving, then it could likely be dragging with it
something less agreeable. For Dolan, this could be a strict conservatism
he's noticed gaining ground. Not the pre–Vatican II fish-on-Friday orthodoxy he grew up with. This is a more macho brand, leaning ever
more to the right. The type of religion-ideology hybrid that brings people to attack abortion clinics or get involved in heavy-handed political
movements.

Some New Men openly express their sympathies.

At a prayer meeting in a seminarian's room, they bowed their
heads for "those who protect the unborn." On his desk were newspaper clippings about John Salvi III, who killed two women in back-to-
back attacks on abortion clinics in Brookline, Massachusetts, in
December 1994. Salvi hanged himself in his prison cell nearly two
years later.

Dolan disdains abortion as well—just as he derides most devia-
tions from Catholic teaching. But becoming militant or malicious—or
just focused on one issue no matter how personally distressing—can be
just as distasteful, he says.

He's seen those kinds of attitudes trickle into the seminary: guys
whose identity as priests and Catholics are staked so closely to pushing
one point of view or objective. That's their right. "But if it starts to

overwhelm them—if it makes them unable to see whether or not they should be priests in the first place—then it becomes my business," Dolan said.

"Part of our job here is to challenge guys to make sure they are not floating into the priesthood, to make sure they are asking the tough questions. So sometimes we say—as much as we hate to see a guy leave—when a guy leaves the seminary thoughtfully and prayerfully, you rejoice. If the seminarian has decided it's right to leave, we say, 'Bravo. Thanks for letting us help you make the right choice.'

"That's not happening now and that could be because the New Men are indeed called and thinking about it and probing and are at peace with their vocations. But I'm always thinking, 'I hope there is no malaise here. I hope there are no zealots disguising themselves as prayerful and compassionate seminarians.'

"If anyone said to me, 'Yes, I've heard the voice of Christ directly telling me to be a priest,' well, he might as well not even unpack. I'd put him on the next plane home."

Dolan finished his radio script. He cleared his throat for a rehearsal. "Have you ever heard of the Witness Protection Program?"

He's a natural: all the right pauses, the proper punch to deliver a point. The more he smokes his Macanudos, the more his voice soaks in a smoky bite that doesn't quite fit his round and plump body. There is more peach fuzz than stubble on Dolan's cheeks.

He likes to set up his radio spots the way he smokes. Never manic puffing. Just ease into it.

He starts off describing an article he read about a cocaine dealer who agreed to testify against the main traffickers in exchange for government protection. The dealer and his family started fresh: plastic surgery, new identities, new city.

"Now, it sounds pretty good, doesn't it?" Dolan said, reading from the script. "Sure better than going to jail."

But then he gets to the point. The family has trouble adjusting. "Never could they return home, contact family or friends or even mention anything to anyone about their past life. New faces, new names, new address—a whole new life. They reported a loss of identity, a tragic uprootedness, a haunting disconnectedness, a constant questioning of who they were," Dolan continued.

"All this got me thinking about identity," he continued. "Just who are we?"

He didn't mention his seminarians. He didn't need to. For them, the analogy was obvious. They constantly hear this type of thing from Dolan. It can hurt to become a priest. Stepping out of one's identity into another can be wrenching—like the family blinking in the new daylight of federal protection.

Dolan does not speak from experience when he talks to the New Men about the disorienting changes a vocation can bring.

"I'm what they call a lifer," he says.

From his earliest memory—way back when the Irish nuns in elementary school were pounding in the catechism—he always wanted to be a priest. Sure, there were a few pangs. Watching fire trucks roar by in their St. Louis suburb and aching to be aboard. Flirting at a school dance but always stopping short of going for a sloppy kiss.

"I know, I know," he said. "It sounds almost storybook."

He laughs about it, sometimes incredulous at how seamless it all was. He never felt torn by celibacy like Chris Nalty or dazzled by corporate efficiency like Scot Landry. The Church was always an ideal. The Vatican II ideological battles and the stories of degenerate priests rarely pierced the suburban bubble of his childhood. Maybe a few people grumbled about losing the altar rails and the Latin mass—both done in by the council's modernizing push—but they were quickly hushed up. Scandal and dissent happened somewhere else—places with dirty streets and where people protected themselves with cynicism and window grates. Not in Ballwin, Missouri, where the lawns were watered and trimmed and the collection plate at church was always brimming.

"Lots of people call me naive." Dolan laughed. "I don't know. I wouldn't call naive dedicating your life to something you think is crucial, essential: trying to address the spiritual hunger of people. No one would use naive for an actor or a painter, for example. They'd say,

'What dedication, what commitment.' With religion—and especially the Catholic Church—people say often now, 'How naive.' Well if that's the new definition of naive, then call me naive."

There's that laugh again: a deep St. Nick bellow—ho, ho, ho. Almost a stage laugh. It's genuine, though. It helps break the ice when he's trying to nudge bishops into footing the bill to send more seminarians to the North American College. It echoes through seminary parties and dinners. He jams one of his fat cigars over to the side of his mouth before letting loose a giant cone of smoke the color of Rome's sky on a smoggy day. "The guy's like Mt. Vesuvius," whispered a seminarian after the rector steamed by.

Then there's Dolan's other laugh. It's a discount version of the real thing. It's a diplomatic chortle perfected by years with the Vatican embassy in Washington and then glad-handing deep-pocket American Catholics in search of a cut for the seminary. "How are ya?" Dolan chuckles. "Great to see ya." He can work the room faster than the hors d'oeuvre guys.

Dolan's family was pure apple pie, a case study in the postwar American rush: hit the suburbs, fill up the house with kids.

Tim Dolan was born in 1950, almost nine months to the day after his parents were married. Two brothers and two sisters would follow in the next fourteen years. "One of the early baby boomers I was," he said. He was actually near ground zero. The person considered by demographers as the first boomer—James Otis Stickler, Jr.—arrived a half second into 1946 at Missouri Baptist Hospital in St. Louis, just a few blocks from where Dolan was born.

His father, Robert, had enlisted in the Navy on his eighteenth birthday and came back from the war almost totally deaf in his left ear from a bomb that just missed the ship where he served as a radio operator in the Pacific. He landed a good job on a factory line cranking out Defense Department orders for the Cold War. On Saturday night, he tended bar at a beer-and-shot joint called Charlie's in the Maplewood neighborhood on the edge of the St. Louis city limits. It was the classic

Irish Catholic enclave. Saturday night was for drinking. Sunday morning was for praying. The parish hall—Bingo, raffles, dances—was always packed. Dolan's father loved pouring out draughts and listening to neighbors pour out their troubles. His only gripe was that the work rules said he couldn't drink a few himself until he locked up. Mom took care of the cramped two-story duplex.

But the good-life promise of a Valhalla called suburbia was slowly pulling the neighborhood apart. The easy money of GI loans greased the exodus. When Dolan was four, the family set out for Ballwin—a distant subdivision taking shape on the northern edge of the Missouri Bible Belt. For $11,000, they got a new three-bedroom job on a three-quarter-acre corner lot and part of a little creek with no name. When Dolan arrived at the North American College as rector, one of the first things he did was call his mother from his airy apartment. "Mom," he gushed, "you're not going to believe this, but it's bigger than the house where you and Dad raised five kids." Dolan's bedroom window in Ballwin looked out onto corn fields and thick woods, where they would play army or build rafts for the pond. It's now all lawns and driveways.

There were ten families on the block—six of them Catholic. "Everyone was in pretty much the same boat," said Dolan. "They were all very young families who were struggling financially." The same year the Dolans arrived, the parish was founded and some Irish nuns were brought in to run the school. One day, Tim told one of the nuns he wanted to become a priest. He immediately was lavished with extra attention. "The religion," Dolan recalls, "was presented so positively, so attractively, so holistically as—perhaps only someone from Europe, someone from Ireland, could do—something that animated your whole life."

With cardboard boxes and sheets, Dolan set up a play altar in the basement. A couple times a week, he'd come home from elementary school and drag his mother and siblings down for "service."

"You can't image how many times we had to eat those dry bread communions," said Dolan's mother, Shirley.

"I have to admit, we did think it was a bit odd. But, hey, we figured it's no different than a kid pretending to be a doctor or teacher."

At home, Dolan's puppy love for the faith was encouraged but not demanded. The family was follow-the-rules Catholic. They said grace just long enough to make it count before diving into dinner—which was never meat on Fridays. The kids were sent to the parochial school and they filled half a pew each Sunday. But that was it. There was no family rosary praying or attendance at daily mass. "We weren't what you'd call pillars of the church," said Dolan.

They did, however, become the lords of the backyard barbecue. Dolan's father loved to fire up the coals and ice down the beers—Budweiser if there was a little extra money around, but usually the standby, Busch Bavarian. It was his domain. Work? He could take it or leave it. His new job, foreman at a McDonnell Douglas Corp. plant making parts for the space program, was just something to pay the bills. He looked forward all week to tending bar at Charlie's and getting out the grill after church. His specialty was barbecued pork steaks. "It was like an art," said Dolan. He'd coat them in brown sugar and grill them slowly. The barbecue sauce—homemade, of course—would be slapped on just at the end. The process was long enough for a couple games of horseshoes or Wiffle ball. Afterwards, the Dolan kids could toast marshmallows if the mosquitoes weren't on the rampage.

"Tim," his dad would ask when some new visitors were around, "tell me: what do you want to be when you grow up?"

"Dad, you know, a priest."

"See," his father would boast to the guests. "I told you."

Dolan enrolled in a high-school seminary in St. Louis. That meant leaving with his father at 5:45 A.M. for the half-hour ride into the city, then waiting for the bus that went by the school. The rules were clear: if you want to date, go to another school. Authority was meant to be obeyed. But something was going on in Rome that the high-school students were just dimly aware of. They prayed for the success of the Vatican II council, unclear, really, of the nature of their appeals. They gleaned it was something to do with change and challenging the status quo—a perfect fit for the grooves of the adolescent mind. They read about the civil rights marches in the South and the early stirrings of campus protests. Almost reflexively, the children who wanted to be priests began asking for explanations.

It began to sink in at the college seminary, where Dolan arrived in August 1968. The freshmen lived in military-style austerity with a chair, a small table, a sink, and a metal locker that fit under their hard bunks. That was about the only tradition not being whisked away.

For teenagers like Dolan who reveled in the Church's majesty and mystery, it was a punishing experience. First, the students stopped wearing their clerical collars. Then they started attacking the old mass as something outdated, even quasi-magical. Dolan did not fully support all the clamor, but he went along. No one, not even a seminarian, likes to be branded as a slave to tradition—especially in the late 1960s. So Dolan became a kind of wincing radical. "All of a sudden we found ourselves in church holding hands and singing anti-war songs," he said.

"I thought that the truth of Catholicism is something immutable and that will sustain you and give you a lot of hope and purpose and direction for your entire life, which, by the way, I still believe," said Dolan. "But more or less that was called into question and sometimes downright ridiculed in those four years of college seminary."

When Dolan returned home for visits, he was like a soldier returning from the front. The parishioners all wanted to know what was really happening. Why did they get rid of Friday abstinence? Why did they scrap the Latin mass? Dolan had no idea. He bluffed a few answers with a lot of school-book clichés and pensive nods. He realized, with a bit of quiet satisfaction, that people were just as confused as the seminarians.

When he graduated Cardinal Glennon Seminary in 1972, the enrollment was half of what it was when he began. The decline of priesthood ranks in the United States was already evident. Dolan, however, was heading out. His straight-A grades were rewarded. He and his boyhood friend Dennis Delaney were asked to study at the North

American College. The top-ranked student had already turned down Rome. Dolan and Delaney were the runners-up. Dolan had never been out of the country. In fact, the farthest from St. Louis for him was a senior year trip to Washington, D.C., and the only link with Rome was his uncle's brother-in-law who studied there. Dolan remembers staring for hours at the Vatican stamps on his ordination invitation.

"Our family always lived from paycheck to paycheck. And here I was planning to go to Europe. To Rome! It was a very big deal," Dolan said.

Then came the knock on Dolan's door. Delaney heard it, too, from his room across the hall. Instinctively, Delaney knew it wasn't good news. It was late and the rap on the door was just too quiet, too hesitant. Delaney heard the rector's voice and then the door closed. Delaney put his books down. He was too nervous to study. Did something happen to Tim's parents? Could it be something to do with Rome?

The door opened. "This will be like going to a funeral," Delaney heard the rector tell Dolan. A second later, the rector tapped on Delaney's door. The rector started talking about budget changes, the bishop's new policies. He spoke softly, the way priests do in the confessional. Delaney wasn't listening anymore. He got the message: Dolan was going to Rome and he was staying home.

"Then right after the rector left, there was another knock," said Delaney, now a monsignor in St. Louis. "Tim came in and said right out, 'If you want to go to Rome, I will stay.' From some people you'd know it wasn't a genuine offer. From Tim, I knew he meant it."

"I said, 'No, they want you. You go.'"

So a few months later Dolan was in Rome: homesick, awestruck, and knowing there was no way his parents could afford to visit. That was the worst part. He missed his family terribly. That first Sunday in Rome, he just sat for a while at his window and listened to the Vatican bells and the more distant rings from churches on the other side of the Tiber.

"I remember all of it so well," Dolan told me. "Seeing Pope Paul VI at Castel Gandolfo, my first glass of wine with cannelloni."

A little while later, he was out running around the seminary's soccer field, sweating in his blue nylon track suit zipped tight. "That pasta just stays on me," the rector puffed. "Gotta drop some pounds."

Dolan sometimes calls himself a living dinosaur. It's one of his well-traveled jokes. Not too many guys these days plow straight from boyhood into the seminary system. His was the old way, the dinosaur way. The pun, though unintentionally, confers something else: a last gasp, a stumble toward extinction. An outmoded point of view. Are Americans—the dinosaurs like Dolan are asked—still capable of really believing?

Crunch the numbers and the bits fall on both sides of the question.

More than 325,000 people turned out for the pope's four outdoor masses on an early October visit in 1995. They stood in driving rain in Giants Stadium as the pope told them America's civil rights laws must extend to unborn children. They huddled in fierce winds at New York's Aqueduct Racetrack, where the pope stood between tote boards and denounced the nation's tin gods: money, success, power. In Camden Yards in Baltimore, he preached against the dangers of freedom without restraints. The finale, in Central Park, was the ultimate blur of sanctity and celebrity. The pope was serenaded by Natalie Cole and Roberta Flack. Tenor Placido Domingo sang at communion. The pontiff, his shoulders stooped and his walk now a careful shuffle, stood on the edge of the raised altar and waved to the crowd on the Great Lawn. People were cheering long after he was gone, like they wanted an encore.

He left them with the provocative query: "In the midst of the magnificent scientific and technological civilization of which America is proud. . . . Is there room for the mystery of God?"

Polls routinely reinforce the contention that a vast majority of Americans believe in God.

But other figures cast a far different light. A fall 1995 survey of nearly 324,000 college freshmen at 641 campuses found a ten-year high in the sense of powerlessness and disengagement—the building blocks for apathy about religion and community. More than a third of the freshmen questioned believed a person "can do little" to change society.

What the pollsters' numbers can't describe is the ache: the yearning for a spiritual side. Some theologians argue it's becoming more acute as society becomes more rootless. The New Men say they feel it themselves and sense it pulsing back home: a craving for faith—or whatever it is that gives that lovely serenity coming from conviction, from being certain you know what's out there.

The work-play-work-play routine is wearing thin on some veteran corporate warriors. And the technology bulldozer shoving them to the future turns out to have lots of rough edges. No computer code can cope with the simple appeal: why? It's asked when a homeless man freezes to death over a sidewalk grate, when a crack baby shivers and cries no more, when gang bangers pull the trigger, then celebrate their revenge as they drive away.

"Gravity," said a Benedictine monk at the North Dakota monastery which Gary Benz is considering joining. "Faith is gravity. Eventually everything comes back down to it."

Even Madonna—whose stage name parodies her Catholic upbringing—gave the faith a plug during an MTV interview. "As sexist and patriarchal as Catholicism is, I think it still has a good effect on me in many ways, and it made me ask a lot of questions." She named her daughter Lourdes—the name of the French shrine where believers say the Virgin Mary appeared in an apparition in the nineteenth century.

"The three A.M. questions," as moral theologian Richard McCormick calls them. The times to mull the essence of guilt, love, responsibility, and God.

But are they genuinely being asked? Could introspection in the nineties just be the faddish counterbalance to the extroverted Reagan years?

"Of course, everything along these lines would be anecdotal, but there seems to be definitely a movement back toward traditional religion," said Fordham University theologian Rev. Avery Dulles. "Why? Well, there's the obvious reason of people looking for more stability in an unstable world. But I'm not sure the religious beliefs ever really go away completely. They just get supplanted by something else. Those layers that were covering up religious feelings seem to be wearing off."

It's been totally scrubbed off in South Barrington, Illinois, at the Willow Creek Community Church's nondenominational services. An average of fifteen thousand suburbanites—including a large bloc of disenchanted Catholics—attend the stylized Christian extravaganzas each weekend. It's faith tailored for the short attention span: laser-show Sunday school for teens, hymnal lyrics flash by on a video screen. Still, it's a vibrant and generous congregation—what many Catholic parishes would envy.

In a more conventional setting, the rector of the Pope John XXIII seminary in Weston, Massachusetts, welcomed a 1996 first-year class of twenty-three men—the largest in decades. The seminary is exclusively for older men, at least over thirty and sometimes into their sixties and seventies.

"I remember one guy saying to me, 'I have everything. I have a tremendous income. I can do anything I want," said the rector, Monsignor Francis D. Kelly.

"So I say to him, 'Then what are you doing studying to become a priest?' " And you know what he says? 'Because nothing else I could do would be more fulfilling in my life. I can do anything and the thing I want to do is become a priest.'

"Now we're not talking like people are banging down the door to get in seminaries," said Kelly. "But you can say that there's something stirring out there. The people who have money want something more. The people who don't have money know there is something more. That something more, they are deciding, is found inside a church, temple, or whatever."

At the far end, some of the most orthodox groups have a remarkable attraction among younger and highly conservative Catholics. One of the most organized groups, the Legionaries of Christ, has grown from thirteen seminarians when it was founded in Mexico in 1941 to more than two thousand—including a sizable number of American Hispanics. Their credo is discipline and conformity: a strict adherence to Vatican teachings that has earned the group the open favor of the pope. Legionaries wear identical double-breasted black jackets—leading to some private Vatican jokes about goose-stepping seminarians.

Yet trends in the priesthood—whether heading more conservative or less—won't necessarily reverse the growing divide in the American Church.

Just before the pope's trip to the East Coast, a Time-CNN survey found 83 percent of American Catholics were satisfied with the pope's leadership, but only 15 percent believe it's necessary to always obey the Church's ban on birth control and abortion. Another poll, by *U.S. News & World Report,* found overwhelming support for ending priestly celibacy and allowing the ordination of women. Two-thirds said divorce and contraception are not always morally wrong.

AIDS-prevention groups call the Church a killer. To gay activists, it is a citadel of intolerance. Sex-abuse allegations against priests—once shocking—now seem almost as routine as a politician caught in a lie.

Dulles sees a tug-of-war tearing at the center of the American Church. One faction insists on an entirely liberalized dogma: women's ordination, end bans on birth control. Their counterpoint is a return to lock-step orthodoxy, curiously appealing to some young people in search of a type of obedience even more rigid than demanded by the pope. "It could be very divisive," Dulles said.

"We're in danger of what I would call a practical schism," Dulles continued. "One side is going ultra-conservative and the other side is staking out a kind of inclusive Catholicism—outside the Vatican, of course—with women performing masses and married people being ordained. The priests—and especially those in the seminary these days—would have to make a choice about what way to go, which side to support."

Dolan—one of the youngest rectors ever at the North American College—clearly relishes his job. Helping form priests out of seminarians has never been more important to the Church. Among the many obscure niches and drone jobs in the Church, the rewards of being rector can be clearly measured in the number of New Men who go all the way to ordination.

"You see these New Men come in sometimes with a very vague understanding of themselves and their vocation," Dolan told me. "Then you see them emerge. Some, obviously, discover the priesthood is not for them. Many more, though, find themselves—eventually, not always easily—meshing with the faith. What could be a more valuable job for the Church, especially in these times?"

Dolan likes to quote a saying he heard once from an Irish priest. "These scandals and the publicity given these scandals have brought the Church to its knees. And that's where the Church is most effective.

"The past three decades have been a crucible for the Church," he said. "Now that can do one of two things. That can kind of quiet the Church and make her shut up and become very timid and climb under a rock. Throughout history the opposite has happened. The tougher the Church has had it, the stronger it usually is, you see."

CHAPTER VI

SCOT AND ROGER

The kingdom of heaven is like a merchant in search of fine pearls.

—ANTIPHON FOR THE CANTICLE OF MARY
FOR SUNDAY EVENINGS

"Where's Christensen?" Scot Landry yelled. "Anyone seen him?"

New Men shrugged and continued tossing around footballs.

"Great," Scot growled. "We're down a couple guys and people aren't showing up for practice." Scot—now in the demanding persona of Coach Landry—jotted down something in the playbook folder. It was difficult to write with a right pinkie fractured in practice.

Two other New Men had hamstring pulls. But they told Scot: "If you need us for the Spaghetti Bowl, we'll play."

"We just may," Scot said, whose baseball cap was pulled low so that the brim touched his wire-rimmed glasses. Brian Christensen decided to skip practice to take a walk around the Vatican walls—a towering brick barrier that slopes down to the street. It was too nice a day to waste it running through a football practice, Brian decided. He'd deal with Scot's barbs later.

It was only natural for the New Men to pick Scot as the coach to prepare their team for the Spaghetti Bowl, the flag-football game between the New Men and the other seminarians played each year around Thanksgiving. Confidence and leadership radiate from Scot like an aura. He's just twenty-five and looks his age: a full-moon face still without even a hint of age lines or crow's feet. But his self-discipline and ability to motivate others made him seem much more experienced. His employers noticed his take-charge qualities and rewarded him with supervisor jobs that normally went to older colleagues. The New Men, too, willingly let Scot take the lead. Image, even in the seminary, matters. Scot was quickly perceived as a model seminarian—a guy destined to make his mark whether it was in the Bridgeport, Connecticut, diocese back home or perhaps even on a bigger stage.

"Guys like Scot, as long as they don't step on too many toes early on, can go far," one faculty member told me.

Scot's white-hot intensity was—in the afternoons, at least—poured full strength onto Spaghetti Bowl preparations. He was dedicated to winning this game—something the New Men have done only a handful of times since the 1950s. Scot was far too smart to siphon the fun out of the most carefree weekend of the seminary year. He couldn't, however, approach the game in any other way except to win. Scot always appreciated sports because of their clarity. There are winners and there are losers. About the only time Scot would temper his natural competitiveness was when he was playing tennis or one-on-one basketball with his twin brother. "It's like I'd rather have him win than me," Scot said. "He would say the same thing about wanting me to win. It's a strange thing. We'd rather see the other one succeed."

Scot had been turning to Roger often in these first months in Rome. As always, Scot was pushing hard. He was trying, through sheer will, to make himself conform. Only Roger could see just how hard his twin was battling. Roger could separate Scot the scrappy challenger from his budding reputation as the seminarian most likely to succeed.

As much as some New Men envied Scot for his apparent composure, Scot, in turn, secretly envied others. He saw a serenity in some of the New Men that made him feel so incomplete. Their spirituality seemed to be constantly fueled and replenished. These New Men— Roger and Tran were included in this bunch—were clearly meant to be priests, Scot believed. He was desperate to catch up. It was fundamental for Scot. Never lag behind no matter what the circumstances. Only the seminary was not like a football game or grade-point averages in school. Where was the measure of holiness? Who defined the elements that make a good priest?

Scot wanted reassurance that his late and sudden vocation was valid. Yet the seminary formation to Scot was often like handling a soggy sponge. The harder he squeezed, the more the doubts and questions poured out. Can he wring it dry and get to the pure essence of his own spirituality? Can he find what his calling truly was? This time, he couldn't do it alone. He needed Roger's help, the help of his spiritual director—and especially the help that comes from prayer.

But these discussions would have to wait for a while at least. There's a Spaghetti Bowl to win. The doctor warned Scot he should stay on the sidelines to avoid aggravating his healing pinkie. He had no such plans. They had practiced too hard during the past weeks. "We will not be denied," he cried to the other New Men at practice. Chris Nalty was with the other big guys as linebackers. Roger, an agile and clever player, was used wherever they would need him. Gary Benz and Tam Tran, as expected, didn't want to take part.

Scot was fuming about Christensen. He didn't need one of his best players skipping practice.

"OK, guys," Scot shouted. "Let's run through the plays again."

Scot was in his element. Making plans, setting goals. Preparing for the game was a welcome flashback for Scot. For a couple hours, he didn't have to think about the infuriatingly obtuse principles that now dominated his life. On the field, no one cared about incremental progress in his prayer life or how well he grasped Aquinas's philosophy on the interrelation between body and soul. Out there, he didn't feel pressured to try to match his spiritual progress with the other New Men.

The Spaghetti Bowl was wonderfully direct. It scared him a little how much he missed that life, delineated by hard-edged rules: projects, deadlines, performance reports. He had hoped that would have faded after a while in Rome. If only, he wished, the seminary were more like the office. That's the kind of vocation Scot had envisioned for himself: active, building up the parish, working with children. "The Bible never says, 'Jesus sat down and studied,'" he said. Let the thinkers think and the doers do.

"OK," Scot shouted to the New Men at practice. "Let's run through a few pass drills. Ready? Let's go. Watch the rush! Watch the rush!"

The New Men's quarterback—a professional triathlete-turned-seminarian—rocketed a pass through the flailing arms of the defense. It was caught.

The more Scot dwelled on his vocation, the more fitting it seemed that he be in the same diocese as his twin. They were still just in the first months of being New Men, but Scot already was projecting himself into the future after ordination. The Landry brothers would be separated once again. Scot was sponsored in Rome by the Bridgeport diocese, which covers southwestern Connecticut from the gasping old ports on Long Island Sound to leafy commuter towns with colonial squares and weekend soccer leagues. Roger was with the gritty Fall River diocese up the coast in Massachusetts, hard against the sea and the Rhode Island border. They would be less than a three-hour drive apart on busy Route 95. Scot, however, could only see the gap and not the proximity.

But before he made any move, Scot had to talk to his brother. Roger could sense Scot wanted to discuss something important but as usual held off. He knew better than to try to pressure Scot before he was ready. One afternoon, Scot stopped by his brother's room. Roger was studying at his desk, which he had placed in the center facing the door as if it were an office. Roger's bed was pushed into one corner. On the pillow was a heavy bronze crucifix given to each of the New Men. Roger laid it on the pillow every day as inspiration to keep him from taking naps. Roger can't remember the last time he had an uninterrupted night of sleep. He always wakes several times—sometimes dozens of times—for just a moment. He sleeps with the crucifix at his side. When he wakes, he fumbles in the dark until he finds it.

Scot sat on the perfectly made bed. He didn't have to make small talk with Roger. He got straight to the point.

"Roger, I've been thinking about something about the future. It has to do with us being apart. Or, rather, what I mean is that it has to do with maybe keeping us together."

Roger turned to his twin. He was not surprised Scot was moving toward some unavoidable decisions. He knew something was troubling Scot. However, he assumed all along it was something to do with the seminary grind or the natural doubts about his own priestly qualities. He did not expect this. "What's up?" Roger blurted.

"Well, you know what the faculty and seminarians keep saying to me? 'It's strange,' they say, 'that you and Roger, being twins, are in different dioceses.'"

"They've said the same thing to me, Scot. I just tell them our stories: I applied in Fall River and your vocation hit you in Bridgeport. So what? It's not too hard to grasp."

"Well, it's got me thinking," Scot said. "Maybe they are right, in a way. Maybe it doesn't make sense for us to be in different dioceses like this."

"You're thinking of coming to Fall River?" Roger asked, clearly excited. He, too, had been seriously thinking along the same lines but didn't want to bring it up first. "That would be fantastic. But what do you think would be Bridgeport's reaction?"

"I'm not really sure, to be honest," said Scot. "But I don't expect there will be a big problem. Remember when I first approached Bridgeport when I started thinking about the priesthood? Well, I said to the vocation director, 'I'm not sure I even have a calling and, if I do, it may lead me to another diocese.' And he said it wouldn't be a problem. So I've been thinking about it for a while. I wanted to bounce it off you, though. If you think it's a good idea, then I'll consider it."

"You definitely have my blessing," said Roger.

"That's a big relief to hear you say that. I'm not sure what I'm going to do. I just wanted you to know which way I may be leaning."

Scot wanted to feel whole again. Ever since his rapid decision to join the priesthood, he had a bothersome sense of being only partially rooted. At first, he thought it was just the discernment turmoil common to most delayed vocations. Most of his time before coming to

Rome was dedicated to praying about whether he was cut out for the priesthood and not whether it was right to be separated from his brother. But, gradually, it became obvious how much he needed his twin.

Scot had raced through pre-seminary classes to catch up with Roger. Scot presumed that if God was calling him to the priesthood, then it also meant that he and Roger should be ordained together. "It just seemed to make sense in a cosmic way," said Scot. The scramble paid off. Fall River sent Roger to Rome and Bridgeport sponsored Scot. They were reunited as New Men, and Scot, for a while, felt as if it was going to work out perfectly.

But then Scot started looking ahead. He had no deep connection to the Bridgeport diocese. He had lived there less than a year. Should I be back in Massachusetts? he started asking himself. Other questions naturally followed: shouldn't a priest work among the people he feels most connected with? Wouldn't I be a better priest being in the same diocese as my brother and nearer my family?

It all converged on a single, inescapable point for Scot. If God wants me to be a priest, then it would be fitting that Roger and I should be ordained together. And that must mean, Scot reasoned, that we should not be separated—even only by one hundred miles or so?

Scot's spiritual director, the eloquent Bostonian Father McRae, saw something else in the logic; something that worried him. He wondered if Scot was able to see his calling as something distinct from his brother's. He would have to decide if it was strong enough to live on its own. McRae had been holding off from forcing Scot to make his hard, and potentially decisive, judgment. He was hoping Scot would bring it up on his own. If he didn't, McRae knew he had to push.

Scot, meanwhile, was boiling down the arguments he would use on Bridgeport. He knew marketing. He was trained at knowing what pitch would work best. But this time it wasn't just relying on the old schmooze line—not even close. Scot was, for the first time in his life, engaged in intense prayer to guide his moves. The same themes kept returning to him like reassuring friends. This, he told himself, must be the right path, leading always toward Fall River. It was the type of place he felt naturally drawn to—old red-brick mill towns just like his home city in the Merrimack Valley. He knew those types of city parishes so well: built on Sunday collections placed carefully in the baskets by hands that earned it doing real work. The type of place that another Lowell-born French-Canadian, Jack Kerouac, found claustrophobic and stifling as a young man, but later realized how much it defined him. True, Fairfield County has its rough spots. To Scot, they just felt too different. The pockets of need in Fairfield are not the same as the working-class toil—generation after generation—in the gritty cities up the New England coast.

With each long session of prayer, with every meeting with McRae, the idea of transferring to Fall River seemed to take on added depth. McRae had constantly warned Scot that asking to move simply to be with his brother was the wrong reason. It's too selfish, too short-sighted. He told Scot to pray hard about whether Fall River was the place he would serve best as a priest, not be most comfortable alongside his twin brother. Make sure it's the first reason, McRae insisted. Scot was closer and closer to being able to say it was.

"Rog, do you really think Fall River is right for me?" Scot asked his brother.

"Of course. I was always hoping we could be in the same diocese."

"I know."

"Yes, but do you know why?" Roger said. "You may think I'm fully secure in my vocation. And in the broad sense, I am. Very clear. But in another way. There's something I need that I think God might do only through you. That's where you come in. I'm not going to get all mushy about it, but I think you know what I mean. Honesty. We all know that the priesthood—if it's to be pure—demands honesty. True?"

"Definitely," said Scot.

"So who can keep you more honest than your twin? You're like having an external conscience who can let me know if I ever get too full of myself or veer off in some wrong direction. You know what I mean? I would do the same for you, of course. Wouldn't every priest benefit by having that?"

"Sure would," said Scot, relieved that his brother was so enthusiastic about the transfer idea. "So it's possible? Maybe together in Fall River?"

"Let's hope," said Roger.

Scot knew, however, how fragile plans can be.

This is how Scot used to lay it out years ago: Roger, no doubt, would become a priest. So that's settled, Scot would say to himself, and add to the mental checklists he was constantly compiling. Roger will try to save souls. I will save money.

Just out of Harvard, Scot already saw himself as a sort of patriarch in the making. He'd work hard, harder than anyone out there. Then he'd buy a house—a majestic homestead maybe up on the North Shore where folks from Lowell usually just passed by on their way to the honky-tonk New Hampshire coast. This house would be big enough for his parents. His dad could quit his janitor's job, leave their half of the Lowell duplex, and move in. There'd be rooms for Roger and their younger brother and sister. And plenty of space to fill with children. "Ten, fifteen kids maybe," said Scot. "Basically as many as possible."

He wanted to be married by twenty-seven with a couple of job promotions already under his belt. This was his way: set goals, daily, monthly, yearly. Two months before graduation, Scot picked up the motivational book *Awaken the Giant Within*. He had seen the infomercial by its author, Tony Robbins, and was amazed that this prophet of positive thinking could pack arenas. Scot was enraptured by Robbins's vocabulary and optimism. Scot became a disciple of the go-for-it philosophy. He felt he had always come up just short. It was nothing serious. Just a little pang that he shuffled when he should have dashed. "I always achieved things in my life, but I took every shortcut in the book academically. And I always thought—and this is completely different than Rog—that I never achieved my true potential."

Scot finished Robbins's book on the plane to Cincinnati for an interview at Procter & Gamble. He memorized some of the catch phrases—cheerful, optimistic, go-get-'em stuff. This is just the right tone for P&G's chirpy corporate environment. Scot was offered a job: assistant products manager for Comet cleanser. He knew nothing about marketing and even less about the company. The only reason he sought an interview at P&G was because it was automatic. All you needed was to submit a resume with the Harvard Office of Career Services and, if you passed two evaluation rounds, you were on your way to Cincinnati. Scot felt like seeing another part of the country. But why not take the job? As Tony Robbins would implore: seize the moment, be dynamic.

"Up through the whole college experience and even through the job-hunting process I kind of looked at myself and saw that I was just in a boat and floating down the river," he said. So fresh out of Harvard, Scot was learning how to pitch blue-green cleaning powder. His job included analyzing Comet's market share compared to the competition and leading the promotion campaigns for print and coupons. He also got an education in the strange psychology of rumors. Before joining the company, he had no clue about the odd urban folktale linking P&G's star-and-moon logo with satanic worship. Soon, however, he started a tradition of posting the ten most outlandish customer comments of the week—some distraught over their discovery of the devil behind the detergent. "Very weird," Scot said.

In Tony Robbins–inspired fashion, Scot started setting meticulous five-year goals. The question always: what situation would I like to be in? There was nothing overwhelmingly religious in his plan at first. He always included spiritual development, but never any plans for a religious life. It was, in essence, the cult of success: feed a bank account, get ahead, find the right career, pay off college loans, get married, raise a family. It was a beeline to the adult responsibilities that Scot craved.

But Scot sensed some peril in racing ahead. He was worried about his expansive obsessive streak. Without balance, he knew he could easily become a one-dimensional corporate drone.

Scot started attending a weekly Bible study group at P&G—the only Catholic among a collection of Protestants. And then he began attending daily mass at a Jesuit-run church across the street from P&G headquarters. He got his roommate, a Harvard buddy, to come along.

"I didn't want to get so absorbed in the fast track that I messed up my priorities in life," he said. "I just knew that I needed to center myself every day and do something that wasn't just thinking about myself." Still, he was firmly anchored in the young executive world. "Faith," he said, "was not the driving force in my life."

It began to change along with the scenery. After fifteen months in Cincinnati, Scot took a job at James River Corp., best known as the makers of Dixie brand cups and plates. He felt like heading back to New England and getting a little more responsibility as an associate brand manager. Then he was hugged by the nun on his first day in Norwalk. He couldn't forget her words: "You're sent by God." He thought of the way she embraced him—so tightly and sincerely—and how she stammered on about God.

Something had started. The day before Thanksgiving, Roger was driving home from the pre-theology seminary in Emmitsburg, Maryland, and stopped at Scot's apartment, a two-floor condominium he was sharing with a colleague from Texas. Scot waited for a quiet moment.

"Rog, this may surprise you. It may surprise you a lot. I'm starting to think about the priesthood."

Roger gave his half-smile—his attempt at modesty. "I kind of figured you'd come along."

"You're kidding me. What do you mean?"

"I'll tell you later. I just felt that it was coming." Scot knew better than to press his twin for details. Roger would explain in his own time. The story he kept private began about a year before when Roger was praying for his brother in a chapel in Washington, D.C. "All of a sudden there was a burst of great clarity," Roger said. He knew Scot was going to become a priest and cried for joy for fifteen minutes. It was a feeling close to the experience in a Cambridge chapel the day he decided on the priesthood. "Haven't you ever just known something was going to happen? I mean, just know. That's about the closest way to describe it," said Roger. "It's just a very clear 'I want you,' without hearing the word."

Twins understand this better than anyone, he said. It happens all the time. They kept Scot's news from their family during the holidays.

Then, on the third day of February, they were back in Lowell for a party before their younger brother's wedding.

"I have something to tell you," Scot told his parents.

Immediately they sat down at the kitchen table, the place where anything important was dealt with. His parents were in their usual chairs. His father sat straight back. His mother leaned forward, her hands nervously rubbing her cheeks.

"Mom, Dad. I've decided something. I'm going to enter the seminary. I want to be a priest, too. Is that OK with you?" he said.

His father nodded. "Whatever you want to do, guy, your mother and I will always support that," he said. He always called the twins "guy."

His mother wept.

"What's wrong? If you're upset . . ."

"No! I couldn't be happier," she said, then she told him a story. When the twins were about eight weeks old an old nun who was her fifth-grade teacher asked if she could bring the boys to church for a little ceremony. Of course, she said. The nun brought the babies to the altar.

"I have to tell you," she told Midge Landry. "If a baby's bootie falls off that means they will have a religious vocation."

"Um, OK," she said.

First, the nun held up Roger. "Dear Lord," she said. "I offer this baby to you." He kicked his leg and off came the booty. The nun drew in her breath.

"Ahhh. Congratulations. You are going to have a priest in your family."

Then it was Scot's turn. He fidgeted a bit, then just before the nun put him down, the bootie dropped. The nun was shaking with excitement. "So I always thought that your vocation would come later because your bootie dropped off later," Scot's mother told him.

The next months were a blur. Scot decided to join the pre-theology seminary immediately to try to catch up to Roger in preparation for the major seminary. His colleagues crowded around his desk. Some were simply curious—the way people scrutinize serial killers to try to find the glimmer of what made him do it. He was approached by many non-practicing Catholics. This was his greatest pleasure. Having a co-worker—a "regular guy"—seek the priesthood put a whole new spin on their faith.

"Oh, gosh, not again," said Melissa Lloyd when Scot told her the news. "I'm not going to lose another 'brother.'"

Her real brother, who would have been about Scot's age, skied off a cliff in Washington State in 1979 and died instantly. She had adopted her younger co-worker as a kind of symbol of what she hoped her brother would have been like.

"What's wrong?" Scot asked. "You're not happy, right?"

"Oh, no. It's not that. It's just that I'll miss you, that's all."

"I'll be back, you know."

"I know, but . . ."

"But what?" he asked.

"But it just won't be the same."

"Can't argue with that," Scot said.

She smiled. Armchair matchmakers at work had already started wondering about romantic sparks between Scot and married Melissa, who left James River to promote board games at Mattel. "Before," she said, "I could be very cold and critical of people. Now I'm pretty much an optimist. I really credit it all to Scot."

Scot's farewell pizza party at James River was standing room only—from janitors to vice presidents. People were actually crying.

His boss—who gave him the nickname "pit bull"—pulled Scot aside.

"I want you to know, if you ever feel that it was the wrong move, I will always take you back," she said. "You can look me up, wherever I might be, and you'll have a job."

"Thanks," said Scot. "But I don't think that will be necessary."

On a fall afternoon in Rome, he wondered if he was wrong. The old paycheck world with its Monday-through-Friday certainty was looking comforting.

Returning to full-time study was hard enough for Scot. But sitting through lectures in Italian—which he barely grasped—pressed hard on his tolerance. Some days he couldn't even open a book. He started skipping classes, just for some free time to think and try to catch up on the course material. First it was one. Then sometimes two or three. His prayer schedule was dry. "I felt like no growth was happening," he said.

Scot, though, still pressed ahead even harder. Just as he would on any office assignment with an impossible deadline or if his basketball team was down in the final minutes. He'd try to focus on his prayer with the concentration of a safe cracker waiting to feel the tumblers fall into place. But there were just too many distractions at once. What to do about Fall River? Why is it so difficult to adjust to the seminary?

At first, he felt a tad guilty about skipping classes. It smacked of irresponsibility and, even worse for Scot, indifference. Other New Men at the Greg felt it, too. Their Italian was so weak that they could barely follow the lectures, which were exactly the same year after year. An elaborate system of translated notes at the seminary allowed the New Men to keep up with the classes without having to be there. So the New Men soon come to the conclusion—part rationalization, part reality—that there's often more to be gained by not going to class.

"Attending class in a language you don't understand well, initially at least, is a difficult way to learn theology—the reason we're in the seminary," said Scot.

That is, if you actually spent your class-skipping time in study and contemplation. Not everyone did. Often, catching up on sleep or breaking into a sweat in the gym was just too tempting. Scot was lured by a different seduction that's almost impossible to find in the seminary: quick and tangible accomplishments. He wanted to settle the diocese situation but still was torn about how, when—or even if—to ask for the transfer. His prayer life, too, wasn't paying the rapid dividends he wanted, "I'm giving it 100 percent effort, you know, but sometimes it's just like nothing is moving forward. I'm stalled."

Before entering the seminary, Scot was never stuck in neutral.

"I desperately want real-life experiences," complained Scot.

A seminarian across the table in the dining hall stopped in mid-bite.

"This isn't real enough for you?"

"No, of course it's real. It's just that we're in a preparatory thing here. We all know that we are trying to be priests in a parish, but at this point we are living theoretically, I would say."

"Why rush it? Scot. You think you're ready for ordination? I don't."

Scot didn't answer right away. He swallowed: "You're right. You're right."

"So? Slow down."

"The reason I really like working rather than the student environment is that when I was working I was able to leave my work at the office and go home," said Scot. "I knew I could have a good day's work, see the results at the end of the day, come home, and focus on something else. It's much easier for me to wake up and say: 'Here are the things I need to do. I'll try to do them to the best of my ability.' Here, I found the same things that bugged me in college: the assignments just hanging over your head for so long, knowing that you are studying for an exam two months down the road instead of just waking up that day and getting something done.

"I know a lot of seminarians here may disagree, but what I long for is a regular, real-world life experience. This is something else."

CHAPTER VII

THE SPAGHETTI BOWL

I do not run like a man
who loses sight of the finish line.
I do not fight as if I were shadowboxing.

—EVENING READING FOR THE FIRST SUNDAY OF LENT
(I CORINTHIANS 9:26)

Chris Nalty took the makeshift stage in the lounge, walking slowly and regally. The crowd mellowed. Nalty is the type who can set the tempo in a room. If he's wild, then it's fine to let loose. If he's thoughtful and subdued, then others tend to follow along.

This night before the Spaghetti Bowl no one was quite sure what to expect. So far the seminarians' annual talent show had been typically manic. There were skits poking fun at the faculties, ditties about the Church, and an imitation of two dogs battling over a half-eaten cheese steak sandwich. Nalty had kept his act a secret. He waited until the clamor eased, then sat in an easy chair with a cigar box at his side. He was dressed in a shirt and tie.

"You know, there are good women and there are bad women." Some applause from the seminarians.

"There are bad women like . . . Hillary Clinton," (lots of boos) ". . . Lorena Bobbitt," (hisses) ". . . or Princess Di" (a couple cheers).

"And there are good women: Mother Teresa . . . my mom."

Someone yelled: "Kim Basinger."

"And Kim Basinger."

"But do you think they can match a good cigar?"

Nalty began reading Rudyard Kipling's *The Betrothed*. There was silence until he reached the twenty-fifth and last stanza. "And a woman is only a woman, but a good cigar is a smoke."

He ripped off his shirt. He was wearing his clerics underneath. The seminarians loved it. The dozen or so women—Americans studying in Rome—razzed him with loud boos. Nalty blew a puff of hand-rolled Cuban cigar smoke in their direction.

The evening closed with song. "The NAC-son Five" tweaked every seminarians' sore spot: the endless parade of guests from the home diocese. A cappella to the tune of the 1950s Chordettes' chart-climber "Mr. Sandman":

"Oh, Mr. NAC man?"

"Whaaaat?"

"Could you spare me some time and book a banquet for two thousand and nine?"

Some seminarians shouted, "Maildrop, maildrop"—the code word for being shipped back to the States since America-bound seminarians are loaded with letters to send.

Many went away humming an irreverent ditty to the Rodgers and Hammerstein toe-tapper "My Favorite Things."

Mitres and croziers and pectoral crosses,
Incense and candles adorning high altars,
Rubrics, zucchetos, episcopal rings.
These are a few of my favorite things.

Cassocks with piping and watered silk sashes,
Plenty of vestments for priests at our masses,
Lengthy processions and bells that go ding.
These are a few of my favorite things.

When the gypsy swipes,
When the bus stinks,
When I'm feeling sad.
I simply remember my favorite things, and then I don't feel so bad.

At dawn the next day, a New Man slipped a tape into the PA system and turned the volume up loud. Copland's "Fanfare for the Common Man" blared across the gridiron, empty except for one person sleeping at midfield. The kicker for the New Men team spent a soggy night outdoors in a "tradition" dating back to 1994. "Something happens here once, and all of a sudden it's tradition," said Robert Panke, the safety of the Old Men team. They wore black. The New Men were in white.

The Spaghetti Bowl is much more momentous than just a late November game of flag football. Like most aspects of seminary life, the contest is more than what's evident on first impressions. For the New Men, the Spaghetti Bowl is an especially important landmark. The game is familiar and fun: an antidote to homesickness and the sometimes grinding seminary routine. It's relief disguised as football.

Dolan encourages the frenetic buildup to the game, which has been played every year since the college moved to the Janiculum Hill from central Rome in 1953. The rector sat in for a while at the talent show— and watched himself be skewered in a sketch about the relentless seminary fund-raising among bishops and Catholic patrons. He laughed when his face was pasted over an old *Sports Illustrated* photo showing "crazy legs" Dolan in his Spaghetti Bowl prime. "The fellas need to let off some steam," he said. "This is the perfect way to do it."

The New Men usually take the game extremely seriously. Scot Landry's stormtrooper coaching pushed it up a few notches. The Spaghetti Bowl is a chance to actually accomplish something. The seminary is so full of intangibles. The game is win or lose. The New Men succeed or are defeated. After weeks of trying to advance their prayer life or grappling with self-doubt about their vocation, the Spaghetti Bowl is a captivating diversion. There is an out of bounds, goal lines, and a clock. All perfectly understandable.

Game day was gloomy. Dark ropes of clouds spit a little rain. The field—eighty yards on the hill above the parking lot—was neatly marked off in lime. White-painted water bottles stood on the corners of the end zone. The line crew used a regulation 10-yard chain to mark off first downs.

The New Men marched together off the field for the pregame meeting. Two large wooden crosses leaned against the basement hall they filed through. The walls were crumbling like an old catacomb.

"I think St. Cecilia wrote her name around here somewhere," joked Brian Christensen.

They gathered in the laundry room at the end of the hall. It smelled of detergent. They lined up for their "game face"—black lines under their eyes from either burnt cork or Vaseline mixed with shoe polish. The cheering grew until it was a deafening locker-room growl.

Scot Landry held up his hands for quiet. "Heart, head, and hustle. Heart, head, and hustle. The heart to win. Hustle: chase them all over the place and throw your body around if you have to save a touchdown. And head. Let's execute and run the play we are supposed to.

"Let's go out and kick some . . . um, tail today."

Directly above, the Old Men's spikes clicked on the skylight glass. "Let's put our hands together," said Landry. "To our Lady, Queen of Victory, pray for us."

"Let's go out there and win," cried one of the New Men, who had wrapped a blue bandanna around his head. "It's fun. It's Christian. OK?"

The youngest New Men showed their age—roaring out with fists pumping. Their older teammates trailed behind. Chris Nalty carried a pair of expensive Diadora spikes, walking out onto the same field where he and Drench had discussed their vocations a few weeks before. The New Men's quarterback, Mike Woods, who spent three seasons on the professional triathlon circuit, was the last out.

The pregame foolery was already going strong. The Old Men played around with a skit about their advancing years and ailments. Bryan Hersey, who was flattened and temporarily lost his memory the year before, staggered around aimlessly. The "pope"—actually an astonishingly good portrayal by the college psychiatrist—appeared from a fourth-story window with a papal banner hanging from the sill. The imitation was complete down to the Polish accent.

"This game of football from Am-ay-ree-ica is a dangerous one. It is one of violence, violence like I have never seen . . . in Bosnia or Sara-ya-vo or even to my native Poland. Of course, my people have harder heads than someone like your Bryan Hersey. This game is dangerous. It has already claimed the life of your O. J. Simpson and now it has damaged many of the seminarians. It separates your hearts into Old Men and New Men. Now, with my recent birthday, I am an old man . . ."

The Old Men cheered.

"An old man," O'Brien continued, "but as you know I think like a New Man."

"Right," yelled Nalty.

"So I take no sides," the "pontiff" continued. "I remind you of the words of the apostle: 'It is not against human enemies that we have to struggle, but against the principality and the ruling forces who are masters of darkness in this world'—like the Legionaries. Oops, that last part was not the holy apostle."

The game started badly for the New Men. They were burned on a 40-yard touchdown pass on the second play.

The announcer, Pete Harman, tried to keep his New Men sympathies in check. But it was already time for a drink. "This game is brought to you by Heineken," he boomed over the loudspeakers. "Come to think of it, I'll have a Heineken. I mean it. Really. Could someone bring me one?"

The Old Men scored again, but failed on the point after. Old Men: 13. New Men: 0.

The Heineken arrived. Harman took a sip and cringed. It was water. "Is this out of the toilet? Guys, come on."

The New Men clawed back. A touchdown with six minutes to the half tied the game. Then the Old Men strike with two quick scores. At halftime it's 26–13. It started to rain.

"We are sorry to report that the halftime show will be changed," Harman solemnly quipped. "The 'Up With People' bus broke down. So will we not be able to put on their 'Say No to Drugs' halftime show. We hope you understand."

"Hey, check it out," one of the New Men said as they left the field. He pointed to the cupola of the Ukrainian rite seminary next to the

North American College. Some Ukrainian seminarians were watching the strange American sport through binoculars.

A few New Men waved. One Ukrainian returned the gesture.

Back in the laundry room, Scot Landry waved his finger cast. "We had a couple of stupid errors. We can take these guys."

Quarterback Woods outlined plays for shorter passes. He was their not-so-secret weapon. Woods's football roots run through Penn Hills, a serious high-school football school in the serious football turf around Pittsburgh. This is the land of Joe Montana, Dan Marino, Joe Namath. Woods was the senior year QB—with all the studly perks—but was only scouted by Division III schools. "When you're five-foot-seven, one hundred fifty pounds you don't get the big boys interested," he said. Instead, he went to a state college in Pennsylvania and became a high-school chemistry teacher. In 1991, he broke up with his girlfriend and tried to make it full-time as a professional triathlete. Mostly, he competed in the shorter events. But he tried one Iron Man: a 2½-mile swim, 120 miles on bicycle, and a marathon run. He finished the 1991 Hawaiian Iron Man in 10 hours, 25 minutes—number 400 out of about 1,700 starters.

In June 1993, his vocation barged into his way. The Saturday night before a race in Memphis, Woods and one of the top senior triathletes were at mass. They had never discussed the priesthood, or much of religion for that matter. Yet that night, the guy turned to Woods and asked: "Did you ever consider being a priest?"

"I mean, it was like I was hit with a left hook," Woods said. "I had never thought about it really before and we had never talked about it. It was like—wham." By August 1993, he had cut ties with his racing sponsors and entered a pre-theology seminary.

Brian Christensen, looking hair-trigger intense, leaned against the laundry room's tile wall and listened to Woods urging the team on. Christensen was covered with dirt and lime. He didn't get up when the team joined hands.

Touchdowns were traded during the third quarter until Christensen caught a touchdown pass right before the end. The referee threw a penalty flag. The New Men on the sideline groaned. But it was against the Old Men. High-fives all around on the New Men sidelines.

"We're cheering for a personal foul," shouted Roger Landry in mock dismay. "What kind of team are we?"

New Men trailed 32–26. Then the defense took over. Nalty came up with play after play at the line of scrimmage.

A New Man videotaping on the sideline handed his umbrella to another seminarian in order to pan for better shots. "Someday you'll be keeping the rain off a bishop," the cameraman says. "Today it's just me."

The New Men intercepted the ball with 1:08 left, but the play was canceled by a holding penalty.

"Shit . . . I mean heck," a New Man spit.

"No, you mean shit," another said standing nearby.

The New Men got the ball back with seventeen seconds left. All of Woods's passes fell short.

Walking off the field, Nalty put his muddy arm around Roger Landry.

"Good game," he said.

"Bullshit," he snapped. "That last penalty call was bullshit!"

Dolan smoked a Macanudo and applauded: *"Bravo, bravissimo."* He watched the New Men pass by, one by one. They left a trail of mud and little clumps of grass across the nice terra-cotta tile.

CHAPTER VIII

ROME

A strong city have we; he sets up walls and ramparts to protect us.

—CANTICLE FOR TUESDAY MORNINGS (ISAIAH 26:1)

In ways the New Men can't even yet appreciate, Rome is their most persistent instructor. Its antiquity helps them think beyond the immediate. Its many-layered contradictions force them to add new shades to the quintessential color scheme of American logic: black and white. Italians aren't troubled by the many hues of gray. The seminarians must learn to accept it, and some maybe grow to understand it. How a crucifix, for example, hangs in pharmacies that dispense any form of birth control. How a particular strain of Catholic forgiveness courses through a meandering judicial system that seems constructed to avoid definitive decisions; or how Italians almost universally despise American capital punishment but refuse to admit the reason is more an instinctive distrust of any state rather than some noble compassion.

Some young Italian women like to linger outside the two main schools in central Rome where the seminarians study. They flirt with some of the best-looking seminarians—being particularly attentive to the New Men. The women rate the seminarians' looks as they walk by. Sometimes, they get a seminarian into conversation and may even go out for coffee. No one really expects it to go farther. It's a game. The seminarians have to learn a whole new set of rules.

Being a stranger—a spiritual immigrant of sorts—opens the seminarians to the self-reflection and insights that come from feeling separate from their surroundings. The less you blend in, the starker the relief. Many New Men cocoon themselves in the American familiarity of the seminary. A curious evolution takes place at the North American College—one of the few U.S. seminaries that takes men from all around the country. In the first days in Rome, the New Men swap stories about their home dioceses and joke about regional quirks. Then, just as the initial excitement of their new surrounding wears off, they begin to take on a generic American quality. Differences melt away. Suddenly, everything American is celebrated. Every Tuesday is hot dog and hamburger night in the dining hall.

A few seminarians, however, are insatiably curious. They want to know Rome not just as the adornment around the Vatican but as their real home for maybe up to five years. Brian Christensen walks. He likes to head out with a vague idea of a destination, then let whatever notion take him in any direction. Christensen is no innocent abroad. He was an exchange student in France during high school and later served in a special visiting pilot program with the French Air Force. But nothing—not travel, not the military—ever sapped his wonder. His bluemarble eyes open wide as he tells stories about the places he's been. It could just be watching a grandmother in Trastevere hang her laundry or the way the *baristi* can steam the milk for a cappuccino while packing in the coffee for two more *espressi* in a single movement of elegance and economy. Christensen tries to see the beauty in the most common acts or articles. A woman he met in the minor seminary before coming to Rome taught him how to do that.

So he takes his walks—like the one that kept him from the Spaghetti Bowl practice. That day, he wandered first down by the infamous former papal fortress of Castel Sant'Angelo, whose round walls and turrets look out over the Tiber and Ponte Sant'Angelo lined with statues from Bernini's workshop. In the other direction is the approach to Vatican City along the wide and straight Via della Conciliazione started in 1937 as part of the Fascist building frenzy in Rome. Renaissance popes once enjoyed private baths heated by a wood-fueled cauldron, and securely stashed the Vatican's jewels and treasures in huge chests in the Castel Sant'Angelo.

Brian turned onto Conciliazione, lined on each side by thirteen towering obelisk-like street lamps, and headed toward the Vatican. He constantly marveled at the variety of pilgrims streaming into St. Peter's Square each day through the wooden crowd-control barriers and around the vendors peddling trinkets and religious cards. Rector Dolan urged the New Men just to spend time in the square and play tourist. The lesson was not lost on Brian. He saw what Dolan said they would: the Church universal on display. In the diversity, Brian saw unity. An array of languages and customs brought together under the rubric of Roman Catholicism and its nearly one billion followers. He thought about the little farm parishes in his Rapid City diocese—a place where money is always tight. Few of the folks there could ever afford the time or plane fare to stand where he was now: looking at the white dome of St. Peter's Basilica and how, after a late fall rain if the afternoon sun is just right, it reflects in the rectangle-shaped cobblestones of black basalt in the square. He wanted to bring this feeling back to them. He couldn't speak for the motives of the Curia and the minions inside the Vatican. But he did know that this place made him feel part of something big and good.

"How can I say this?" Brian told me while we walked away from the seminary. "I see the face of the Church as all the millions of people who come here to Rome just to be at the Vatican. The Church is not the pope or the cardinals. They are just part of it. Rome, in a way, made the Church more human for me."

In Piazza Pius XII, just in front of St. Peter's Square, Brian stopped to scan the Italian newspaper headlines. The latest crises: a stumbling lire and a vote of confidence facing the fifty-fourth postwar government led by an unassuming former central banker, Lamberto Dini, whose droopy features led political cartoonists to depict him as a toad. It frustrated him that he still knew so little of the language and the country. His French helped him figure out some of the words, but he was desperate to learn Italian and not just fumble through.

"Why do bishops send seminarians here?" Dolan often says. "It's the address."

Having a seminary in Rome is considered a cornerstone of any important national Catholic congregation. New Men from France, Ireland, Germany, and other countries attend their respective counterparts to the North American College. The seminary is an indispensable location to register the views and subtleties of the Vatican. Most cardinals and bishops visiting Rome stay at the North American College. The list of visitors—a Who's Who of the American Church—sits under a glass table in the seminary's foyer. During conclaves to elect a new pope, the American cardinals first stop at the seminary to share their thoughts and prepare their strategies for the inevitable politicking before the white smokes rises from the Sistine Chapel. The collective memories of hundreds of influential Roman Catholic clerics run deeply through the seminary.

"Sometimes there is a false perception the men are sent to the NAC to kind of tighten them up and to train them to become very disciplined, rigid people," said Dolan. "The opposite happens. A man from Rome tends to have a tremendous sense of the universality of the Church. He also imbibes—which can only happen in Rome—a great sense of patience. *Pazienza*. They use that old cliché: Rome thinks in centuries. And isn't that true? You learn to put things in perspective."

The danger is a cookie-cutter clergy: seasoned with the same ingredients and stamped out in the same form. Firebrands tend not to emerge from the North American College. They quickly learn that pulpit pounding wins you no points at the Vatican unless your target is preapproved. Communism was one back in the Cold War. Now abortion and urban poverty are among the top of the list. Some New Men may want to jab in those directions. But joining the ecclesiastic fringe—pushing for women's ordination, easing of birth control bans, for example—is an unlikely tack for North American College alumni. Although Dolan disdains the comparisons with West Point, it's close to the mark. The brass—the play-by-the-rules guys—often get their start at the seminary.

The North American College has mirrored Catholic history in the United States since the first twelve seminarians walked up narrow Via Dell'Umiltà—Humility Street—in December 1859.

Without their four-cornered caps, they looked almost military. Four white stripes decorated the high collars of their cassocks, fastened with ivory buttons lined in a rakish curve from the neck. A red sash and blue trim were added in a patriotic gesture. Even the seminarians from the East Coast cities had never felt the type of urban crush of central Rome. Everyone seemed to be out. Horse carriages and vendors were thick on the main Via Corso. Chairs from a coffee bar were arranged under the slivers of afternoon sunlight that made it through the buildings.

Not everyone back home was pleased by the dozen men sent to Rome. Some bishops felt the whole plan was outrageous. They saw the Vatican's sometimes heavy hand once again at work. What does Rome know about the reality of Catholics in this new immigrant nation? These seminarians, they complained, would become papal foot soldiers but not American clergymen. They heaped scorn on the archbishop of New York, who had written a letter to Pope Pius IX in 1855 asking for consideration for an American seminary in Rome.

Pius, a plump man who swept his silver hair forward in ancient Rome style, seized on the idea. He would not be deterred by some grousing bishops in an upstart country. He had been through too much already. In 1848, he was spirited out of Rome dressed as a simple priest after anti-Vatican riots broke out over the question of unifying the various kingdoms on the Italian peninsula—including the vast Papal States under Vatican control.

Despite the turbulence around them, the Vatican could not ignore for too long what was happening in America. The Curia wasn't pleased to see the independent streak that was growing among American Catholics along with their nation. Clergymen were starting to challenge the notion that the faraway pope should have all the clout. The duty was to the parishioners, many being ground down by relentless poverty and low-wage purgatory in the reputed land of opportunity.

Pius's decision to donate the building on 30 Via Dell'Umilità to the American bishops carried a double blessing. It acknowledged the coming of age of the Catholic Church in America—at least in the Vatican's eyes. It was no longer a missionary country but a place with its own character and ideas. Pius also wanted to keep a short leash on the Americans.

On a sunny late fall day—December 7, 1859—the twelve seminarians marched from the Piazza di Spagna to take possession of a sixteenth-century convent building. They were greeted by the first rector, Bernard Smith. They knelt and sang a hymn before a statue of Mary Immaculate.

Back home, their nation was lurching toward the Civil War. Around them, warfare was creeping toward Rome. The Papal States—areas controlled by the pontiffs since the eighth century— were shrinking and under pressure from forces of Italian unification. In 1860, troops of King Victor Emmanuel II defeated the papal guards and took control of papal territory outside Rome, which was protected by French forces. For a decade, the noose tightened around the Eternal City even as rival bands battled for the privilege of storming the walls.

Two days before Emmanuel made the final assault on Rome in September 1870, thirteen American seminarians wrote a letter to Pius IX volunteering their services to the papal forces. The signatures bear their adopted Italian names: Patrizio Cassidy, Giuseppe O'Keefe, and so on. The pontiff declined the order but was impressed by their loyalty. Rome fell and Pius retreated into the Vatican and refused to acknowledge the new order. When he died eight years later, a mob tried to grab his coffin and hurl it into the Tiber.

Literally barricaded in the Vatican by their refusal to accept the new Italian nation, the pope and his close advisers assembled legions of envoys. The North American College was closely watched—often for some needed amusement. Vatican lore says the Italian cardinals demanded a full report from their proxies sent to watch Buffalo Bill's "Wild West" show at the college in 1890 and to listen to Mark Twain's homespun tales a few years later. The seminarians received special dispensation to take off their cassocks for afternoon baseball games in the vacant lot near the seminary.

By the turn of the century, however, the Vatican's view of Americans took a sharp turn. No longer were they curious but generally harmless provincials. The Vatican felt under attack from the other side of the Atlantic. The flashpoint was a movement that had become known as Modernism. It was a simple, if somewhat arrogant, concept: make the Church reflect the age. And the age that was dawning was led by America. The Church, said the hard-core Modernists, must break clean from its single-minded past and embrace the prevailing culture of the time. This called for an activist-minded clergy who celebrated, rather than condemned, the constitutional separation of Church and State.

The seminary's rector, Dennis Joseph O'Connell, was caught in the middle. His friends back home, including many progressive bishops, demanded he act as their liaison with the pope. Explain our views, they asked him. Smooth things out. The opposite happened. Pope Leo XIII, a slim scholar of Dante who spoke impeccable Latin, quietly but firmly asked O'Connell to resign in 1895.

Four years later, Leo fired a more blistering shot: a letter denouncing the concept of "false" Modernism and attacking any notion that the Church in America could be "different from that which is in the rest of the world." It was the first serious tussle between American Catholics and the Vatican—one that remained the core for future spats large and small.

The North American College remained opened during World War I. Indoor plumbing and heating arrived at the seminary while Europe itself regrouped from warfare. The tract on the Janiculum Hill was purchased in 1924, with the Vatican breathing a sigh of relief since some Protestant groups were shopping around for a Rome base. The site remained undeveloped while the American bishops looked to raise money for a new seminary in Rome. War put their plans on hold. Mussolini's Fascists came down hard on the college. The seminarians raced to Genoa and left for New York by steamer just eight days before Italy declared war on the United States. The seminary on Via Dell'Umilità was taken over by an orphanage for boys separated from Italian parents living abroad. The American seminarians were gone for eight years.

The war would change everything. Not least of all the way Catholics were perceived and how they lived in the States. The GI bill opened up college education to huge numbers of people who couldn't have gone before. The green hills of suburbia beckoned.

The new North American College grounds were dedicated on October 14, 1953. Every important American cleric made the trip to Rome. Diplomats from forty nations joined them in the chapel for the dedication mass celebrated by Pius XII, who came to the city from the summer residence at Castel Gandolfo. The pope squinted behind his wire-rimmed glasses as he got out of the black sedan. An honor guard of students flanked his way into the chapel. The pope walked briskly inside, his white cassock cut short at ankle length as he preferred. The organist played Ravenello's "Tu es Petrus."

He said he had watched the construction of the new seminary from the Vatican down the hill. The buildings, he said, "reflected the morning sun like a city on a mountain."

By the time Kennedy was elected, Catholic America had reached a kind of zenith. Gunshots in Dallas brought it to an end. Camelot was sacked. In a few years, the Church would feel its own gates being rattled. The Second Vatican Council, which opened on an October day in 1962, sought to catapult the Church out of its imperious past.

The council produced sixteen documents—most dealing with liturgical reforms, emphasizing the pastoral role of bishops, urging improved ties with other faiths, and dealing with the Church in the modern world, among others. Reformers were encouraged and hungry for more, especially in the area of birth control. In 1968, the word came from the Vatican: no. An encyclical, *Humanae Vitae,* by Pope Paul VI touched off tremors that are still quivering.

Back in the States, the council's message was being implemented at a dizzying pace. European Catholics, with inbred patience on religious matters, let Vatican II slowly seep in. Americans tend to take the Vatican much more literally. The orders were there. The American psyche says: let's get it done. The old, familiar Catholic way of doing things was given the swift boot. Catholics were left without a good, new road map. "When the gate was opened," said the North American College vice rector for development, Monsignor Bernard Yarrish, "everyone scampered outside."

The American seminarians in Rome were sent into terra incognita along with everyone else. Before the question was: What does it take to be a priest? Now it was: what does it mean? Rev. Daniel Kampschneider recalls walking to class through Rome in the late 1970s wearing jeans and a flannel shirt. The cassocks and clerics were abandoned years before. "And I'm thinking, 'I look just like any other young guy here.' The collar is a strange thing. I distinctly remember wearing it for the first time and the first time someone called me 'Father' or 'Padre.' Now I was here in Rome without that identity. It was hard."

There were no more scheduled morning prayers at the seminary. "There wasn't much sense of dedication," said Yarrish, who became Dolan's friend at the seminary. Dolan was dismayed. He was a kid in love with the traditions of the Church. He enjoyed opening up his cheese sandwich on Fridays in school and letting the other kids see that he didn't eat meat. "I liked people knowing I was Catholic," he said.

But even Dolan eventually joined in the stampede for change.

"The seminary people kind of capitulated in a way," he recalled. "So when we told them, 'We really think Latin is stupid and we shouldn't have to study it,' they said, 'Oh, OK.' Or: 'What's this bit about philosophy? Why don't we get to learn psychology or sociology? That's a lot more relevant!' 'Oh, OK.'"

An important showdown occurred about the same time Woodstock was getting under way. A consistory was being held to elevate a group of bishops to the rank of cardinal. The seminarians made a manifesto declaring the ceremony a medieval throwback and contrary to the Vatican II principles. They did not want to welcome the new American cardinals or host the guests coming to Rome for the event.

The rector took the paper from a committee of seminarians. He pretended to read it and sat back as if he were trying to come up with a response. He had already made up his mind.

"Anyone," said Bishop-rector James Hickey, "who shows any disrespect to the consistory or makes any protest will be immediately expelled. There is no room for debate on this matter."

Hickey—now the cardinal archbishop of Washington—tried to reassert some controls, but there were just too many holes in the dike. Priests were leaving the religious life in droves and fewer and fewer young men were entering the seminary.

By the time Rev. Edwin O'Brien arrived as rector in 1990, the seminary was a tangle of loose ends. There were few restrictions or obligations on the seminarians, who generally set their own schedules and drifted in and out at any hour. O'Brien immediately convened a caucus of seminarians and began laying down some rules: a curfew, obligatory attendance at morning mass. The protests were loud, yet O'Brien—a steely-eyed New Yorker—refused to budge on trying to rein in the seminarians.

"Look, any changes like that have some symbolic value. They get in their minds that this is not some sort of hotel setup—a do-it-yourself formation program in that as long as they see their spiritual director, for instance, and go to classes and say their prayers the way they want to say them, they should be ordained," he said. "That's not the way it should work."

But perhaps O'Brien came down the hardest on a group coming— ever so carefully—out of the closet. There were no openly gay proclamations, but the perception was that a clique of seminarians were pushing things too far. It's no secret that there are gay seminarians, yet they are expected to show the same degree of respect for their celibacy commitment. "We don't have centerfolds on our walls," said one priest who studied at the North American College, "but it's OK if someone else marks the Stonewall raid? I don't think so." O'Brien didn't either and worked to persuade several seminarians to leave.

"There was no blood on the walls, but the message was clear: you respect the seminary and what it's about or get out," he said.

Are the 1990s a time of spiritual renewal, as many New Men believe?

"History does move in cycles," said Yarrish. "We had the 'God is dead' era and tried to root ourselves in something other than these spiritual and ethereal absolutes. Once we played that out to the hilt we discovered that, well, maybe there is some truth, and began to return to these roots and examined whether there was something the human spirit innately longed for, desired."

In one of the basement classrooms at the seminary, a second-year seminarian took a piece of chalk and began to sketch out salvation for the New Men.

"It's worth all the effort," he said as he plotted a flow chart on the blackboard. He stopped for a moment as Chris Nalty slipped in late. Chris took a chair in the front row. The seminarian at the blackboard made a few more strokes with the chalk.

"There you have it, gentlemen," he said. "The note system. Any questions?"

There were many. This was their future they were talking about. The note system is the seminary's venerable conspiracy against the demands of bilingualism. Essentially, it's a translation and synopsis of the theological lectures at the Pontifical Gregorian University—the Greg—where the sole language is Italian. Native-speaking Italians serve it up too fast even for the few New Men who arrive with even a rudimentary grasp of the language. Foreign instructors can render the dialect of Dante a hobbling facsimile battered beyond recognition. "I can't even tell when one sentence ends and another begins," groaned one New Man.

"You ever hear the Australian, Father O'Collins?" another seminarian asked.

"Yeah, it's like Crocodile Dundee with a mouthful of spaghetti: Bon-ge-are-no, mate."

Some Greg professors consider the note system an outrage. They want the students to think for themselves, not recite the template answer during the two oral exam periods. A perennial story around the

North American College is that a professor once intercepted a seminarian with the notes and threatened to fail him unless he coughed up details and names. The seminarian stood his ground and passed, but just barely. The seminarian—whose name no one can seem to remember—has reached something like anonymous sainthood in the seminary.

The system, however, is more than just an elaborate study guide. It's the seminarians first test of cohesiveness; a challenge of organization and cooperation. Grades—and egos—are riding on how well it comes together. "There will be arguments. There will be frayed nerves," said the second-year seminarian, Bryan Hersey, who spoke with the conviction of one who knows. He was picked last year to sit on the uncomfortable point of his class's note system pyramid. The *capo generale*. The godfather of the note system.

It was time to pick another. "Nominees?" said Hersey. The New Men tossed out names. They were jotted on the board. "Don't forget they should be very organized," Hersey added. A few names were erased.

"Chris Nalty," a seminarian shouted.

"Good idea. He was a lawyer," someone seconded. "And he has an MBA," another yelled. Nalty slid lower in his chair.

"I shouldn't have sat in front," Nalty mumbled.

More names, more erasing. Finally, it was down to two names. They were asked to leave the room for the vote. It was Nalty by acclamation. He received a standing ovation when he returned. "I will never sit in this chair again," he smirked.

The *capo generale*'s job is expansive: cajole, berate, motivate. Do whatever it takes to get the notes in order by mid-terms and finals. The flow begins with note takers, hopefully the best Italian speakers in the class, who translate and condense the lectures. Typists punch it into laptop computers and print it out. The *capo* for each subject makes sure it's working for their division. The *capo generale* lords over the entire process.

"You're going to get mad at him sometimes," said Hersey. "He'll be bugging you to get the work done and you'll be thinking, 'Man, I'm doing all this and he's just sitting back and bothering me.'"

"Can't wait," Nalty drawled. "One more thing to do."

Brian Christensen was the only New Man going to the Greg not taking part in the note system. He decided to tackle Italian alone. If he could master French, Italian should be relatively easy to wrestle down, he assumed. His plan was for one long study session of Italian at least once a week. Then, of course, whatever he picked up in Rome. Only time and tradition were not on his side.

His Italian text book lay unopened on his desk. The only locals he had talked with at any length so far were the kitchen help and the seminary doorman behind the glass window at the main gate. *"Buon giorno,"* Brian would say as he returned each morning from the Greg. *"Giorno,"* the doorman would shoot back, but obviously not anxious to expand his job description into language tutor.

"And that's basically it," grumbled Christensen. "We're supposed to be learning the language, soaking up the culture, right? I can barely keep up with all the stuff they have us doing. I was strung out at the Air Force Academy and now I'm strung out here. And I wonder if that's what we're supposed to be doing. People always say, 'When you're a priest you're going to be strung out and busy and you're going to have to manage time. So start learning now.'

"That's the thing about his place," he added. "People look and say, 'Rome must be so wonderful. You immerse yourself in the culture.' Well, you don't. You come through those gates and you're in fortress America."

Christensen tries to listen to the news on the radio each day, picking up more of the buzzwords of Italian journalism. *Sciopero* is a strike. *Rinviare a giudizio* an indictment. *Tangenti* equal bribes. "Hammamet"—the Tunisian resort where former Premier Bettino Craxi fled in 1993 just ahead of the reach of anti-corruption magistrates. Craxi sends his comments on political and diplomatic developments to reporters by fax. The labyrinth of Italian politics fascinates Brian.

Down in the television lounge, he tried to strike up a conversation about bits he's gleaned from the papers or picked up on the radio.

"So what do you think? Will Dini survive?" Brian asked a group of New Men.

"Who?" one replied.

"Dini, man. The prime minister. There's going to be a vote of confidence."

"You serious?" The New Man groaned. "What is this? Italy's five hundredth government or something? Excuse my language, but who gives a shit?"

"Forget it," said Brian.

"It's forgotten."

But Christensen wasn't through. "I mean, don't you think . . ."

"Shhhh," someone from a few rows back hissed.

The news was starting. American evening news pulled in by satellite dishes on the roof. They get sports courtesy of the Armed Forces Network, which the U.S. ambassador to the Holy See pulled some strings to arrange.

"A possible step forward in the fight against AIDS today," Peter Jennings began. Italian politics, naturally, didn't merit a mention. Christensen once proposed alternating between American and Italian news. He was soundly rejected.

"It's the craziest thing, we live in Italy now but we still feel like perpetual tourists," he said as he walked back up the hill toward the seminary. He headed down to dinner. It was Tuesday: hot dog and hamburger night as usual.

Brian's education in the language was also training in the nuances of the Vatican, whose ecclesiastical and diplomatic tongue is Italian. The official newspaper, *L'Osservatore Romano,* is often the compass to which way the wind is blowing from the Holy See. The meat of the pope's weekly addresses is always in Italian before the polyglot salutations to various groups of pilgrims. Any student of the Vatican—as seminarians must be—needs also to understand the language that flows through its veins.

But the refined Vatican watchers also take notice of what's not there. The subtleties are worthy of the old Soviet machine: Who was mentioned or omitted from an article in *L'Osservatore?* Who helped serve mass with the pope? The Vatican spin doctors are illustrious.

Victories—real or exaggerated—are prodigiously trumpeted. Defeats can be re-engineered into something honorable. When the Vatican withdrew its $2,000 annual gift to UNICEF in November 1996 because it claimed the U.N. agency encouraged contraception use, it used Vatican media to hammer home its point of view. Being in complete control of its media allows the Vatican the luxury of conveniently ignoring any embarrassments, like the university student who used his moment before the pope to stomp one of the Vatican's old stalwarts, Giulio Andreotti—the gnomelike political patriarch whose Christian Democrat stronghold was torn apart brick by brick by corruption investigators and who was left defending himself and his party's past in court. Brian Christensen read about the student in the next morning's Italian papers. Some of the other seminarians did their daily computer login and found a wire service item on one of the networks.

But from the Vatican's point of view, it never happened.

Any mention of the college student's outburst in St. Peter's Basilica before the pope was censored or scrubbed from official Vatican records. *L'Osservatore Romano* never carried the story. Vatican Radio—which records all papal events and masses—snipped the section from its archive tape. Vatican scandal-squashers seized the cassette of Telepace, a television service that closely covers the pope. Only one word filtered out to reporters demanding reaction to the student's action.

"Disconcerting," said Cardinal Camillo Riuni, a powerful Italian cleric. That was it.

Some of the seminarians were astounded by the brash reality-bending of the Vatican. One of them suggested a new confessional opening for surreptitious tape erasers: "Bless me, Father, for I have Nixoned."

Christensen was catching on. In Italy, the Church is buried under a deep sediment of cynicism. There have been too many unholy papacies and expedient Vatican-political alliances over the centuries. It all piles up. Mass attendance is among the lowest in Europe and many couples are opting for city-hall marriages rather than taking the vows before a priest. Fellini reveled in it. His 1960 commentary on frivolity and decadence, *La Dolce Vita,* opens with a helicopter carrying a lonely statue of Christ over Rome.

Giulio Andreotti, who claims to attend daily mass, is a convenient and well-pummeled target for anyone with gripes about the Church, Italy's political morass or basically anything that went on in the country from the World War II armistice to 1993. Andreotti's shredded Christian Democrat party long enjoyed the Vatican's favor as well as Washington's support as an anti-Communist buffer. In November 1995, Andreotti attended a Vatican conference on health care and was introduced as a "good Samaritan." Andreotti and the pope grasped hands and nearly 6,500 people in the hall gave the fallen political lord a long ovation.

What a shy political science student, Maurizio Anastasi, did the following month was atypically blunt. Many Italians may grumble privately about the Church and its sometimes extra-religious forays into politics, but they rarely make a scene.

Anastasi, the son of a factory worker and housewife, did just that. Standing just five feet from the pope during a special mass for students, Anastasi was supposed to read a prayer. Instead, he launched into a diatribe about the Vatican and its warm feelings for Andreotti, a seven-time premier indicted in 1995 after magistrates accused him of being the Sicilian Mafia's political godfather.

"You," said Anastasi referring to Andreotti, "will pass into the sad history appropriate for you." John Paul was slouched low on his thronelike chair in St. Peter's. The mass was at the end of a long day. Anastasi finished the speech, then proceeded to read the prayer. The pope never flinched.

On the other side of Italy, a priest in rumpled clerics put down his glass of wine and maneuvered toward the pornstar. She was decked out in black lace lingerie, stockings flecked with glitter, and silver fox coat. A ring of people three-deep gathered around for Jessica Rizzo's autograph or to pose together for a snapshot. *"Bra-va, bra-va,"* a group of twenty-something guys chanted. Father Valerio Pieralisi had already given his blessing at the opening of a clothing store just outside Falconara on Italy's Adriatic coast. Rizzo, however, was the main attraction.

"Ciao," she breathed at the priest with graying temples and a sagging double chin. They hugged. They kissed. Not a continental cheekpeck. This was a lip-to-lip grind. Rizzo tilted her head to the side. Pieralisi's right hand brushed her neck. *"Bravo,"* the guys yelled. The local photographers knew they had a front-page shot. "But where's the scandal?" Pieralisi pleaded. "Who has ever said that a religious man can't enjoy a woman?"

His bosses in the diocese felt otherwise. The archbishop asked for Pieralisi's parishioners and other clerics to help him "in this difficult time." Pieralisi was sent on "vacation" to Switzerland for fifteen days. When he returned, his parishioners gave him a party. "Don Pieralisi was a bit naive," said the press officer for Falconara, Avio Turchi. "He did it as a joke, but he let himself get carried away. . . . Obviously, he is not the ideal model of seriousness."

It was all so unabashedly Italian. There was nothing particularly odd about a grand-opening bash that included a man of the cloth and a woman of the sack. The smooch was just a little too passionate, just a bit too much of a slobbering reminder of the nation's odd-couple rapport between, as the painter Titian coined it more than four hundred years ago, the sacred and the profane.

But the shock was mostly for the courtesy of the press and the incident was just a little whirlwind that quickly passed. Italians are a tough audience to startle, especially in matters of religion. "Italy," said the ubiquitous television showman-shill Pippo Baudo, "lives on *spettacoli.*" The show. The triumph of sensuality over subtlety. The cushion for life's hard edges. Italy needed this whimsy as it struggled to reinvent itself from poverty to prosperity after World War II. It stayed around.

Brian takes it all in. But why did it irritate him so much that others didn't? Normally, Brian would be content to head his own way and let the others extract as much—or as little—out of Rome as they wanted. The difficulties in moving ahead with his prayer life was a bother. He wanted, more than anything at this moment, to feel that sense of God, that connection, that his spiritual director constantly talked about. But it will come, he told himself. Give it time.

No, it had to be something else. Maybe, he thought, it's because being around the seminary reminded him so much of home? His inability to make that one final cut had left him dangling, still not prepared to admit that he was fully committed to his vocation. Her name was Kristin, a dark-haired woman he met while getting his philosophy credits in Minnesota before coming to Rome. Why didn't we define our relationship there? Brian kept asking himself. Should I be with her instead of here? It was a question he couldn't honestly answer. Not yet.

Back in his room that night, he started two letters. One was to the woman he left in Rapid City when he first felt the calling while in the Air Force. She cried and called him names. She never really understood. "Please write," Brian urged.

The second letter was to Kristin. Their relationship was left in mid-step, somewhere between a friendly hug and a heated embrace. He had to see her to find out where it would lead.

"You still planning to come to Ireland after Christmas?" he wrote. "We can meet there, I really need to see you."

Dolan was still waiting for the stone cutters to deliver the new plaque. In Italy, you learn how to wait.

The old one chiseled with the seminary's name was taken down in the mid-1970s during anti-American protests led by Italy's Communists. The American bishops didn't want any more trouble than could be helped at perhaps their most important beachhead in Rome. There's always enough regular flak to go around.

The signals from the Holy See and the volleys shot back from Americans pass right through its corridors. The Janiculum Hill is named for the Roman god Janus, the two-faced deity of gates and doors. The seminary, too, needs to have its attention riveted two ways. The vantage point offers a nice, broad panorama on the relationship between two colossi: the American Catholic Church and the Vatican.

For the seminarians in Rome, the Americans' tantrums for reforms or insistence on fidelity to the Church can seem kind of touching in their idealism compared with the indifference from many European Catholics—especially in Italy. The Vatican, in turn, exerts a strong aura on the North American College. The seminarians see cardinals and bishops continually pass through on their way to be rewarded or reprimanded at the Vatican. Yet they also see the remarkable array of other pilgrims and clergy. The pope can go weeks without even meeting a group of Americans or mentioning some trend in the American Church. The United States is an important part of the Vatican's realm, but the seminarians see it's still just a part.

There are clues all around of the seminary's weighty position. A plaque marks the spot where John F. Kennedy—the nation's first Catholic president—visited less than five months before his assassination.

More than a generation later, another president, Bill Clinton, told the North American College seminarians about a friend from law school who became a Jesuit priest.

"And one of my most treasured possessions that I ever received from a personal friend was a letter he wrote to us after he had been a priest for twenty years, explaining, without being at all self-righteous, what it had meant to him to have kept his vows for two decades and why he thought in a way he had lived a selfish life because he has achieved a measure of peace and comfort and energy that he could have found in no other way."

Clinton won sincere applause from the seminarians for the 1994 speech. It had been an odd reception. Clinton is no hero at the seminary. The wall outside Chris Nalty's room was a gallery of cartoons, many aimed at Clinton. One of his favorites is from the *Seattle Post-Intelligencer* of Clinton drawn as an early Christian being questioned by a grim-faced centurion. "Jesus?" the Clinton character stammers. "I don't know him. . . . That is, I met him once. . . . Well, OK, I do know him, but I never really agreed with him about the poor and all that liberal stuff."

"Perfect, right?" laughed Nalty, who never misses a chance to needle a Democrat.

But Clinton also is one of them: an American who intrinsically shares connections that no foreign bishop, indeed no pope, can truly fathom. A nation conveniently bashed as the grand infidel is actually a religious hotbed. Religion is part of the prism through which Americans see themselves. It's always there. "What are you?" children innocently quiz each other, waiting for an answer like Catholic, Methodist, or Jewish. Adults proclaim themselves non-practicing, agnostic, or atheist—itself an acknowledgment of religion's identity-shaping power.

If demographic predictions are reached, the United States may have more than 66 million Catholics going into the new millennium—bolstering its place as one of the world's most populous Catholic nations.

But, at the same time, the clergy is growing smaller. Priests, particularly in rural areas, are being forced to be one-man dynamos, racing from parish to parish while trying to keep their niche financially afloat. It's hard to be a sympathetic ear and spiritual counselor when your schedule is chock full.

The timeless and timely intersect at the seminary.

The New Men's call to the seminary shares chords stretching back past their own religion, past the gods of the ancient imperial capital around them, and back to the earliest stirrings to try to fathom immortality. When the New Men stepped off the bus from the airport on their first day in Rome, they walked directly through the courtyard of the seminary's chapel to mass. The arches outside are decorated with mosaics of the zodiac—some of the earliest attempts to piece together the beyond.

But the future resonates clearly among the seminarians. They know what's happening.

The total number of priests in the United States has fallen from 58,161 in 1971 to slightly less than 50,000—while nearly 1,500 new parishes were created, according to the Center for Applied Research in the Apostolate at Georgetown University. The shortage is offset a bit by lay deacons, whose ranks have more than doubled to about 11,500 since 1980, but their sacramental and administrative roles are limited.

Worldwide, the number of seminarians has risen from about 73,000 in 1970 to more than 105,000 today, the Vatican says. But the increase has been driven by vocations outside North America and Europe. European seminary enrollment has dropped from about 34,000 in 1970 to around 29,000. The decline in North America was even greater: from 14,365 in 1970 to about 5,700 at the present in all types of seminaries: high school, college, and post-graduate.

The number of advanced-degree American seminarians—like those at the North American College—dropped from 8,325 in 1966 to 3,300 in 1996, the Georgetown research group reported. The decline, however, has leveled off since 1990.

"The good news is that it doesn't seem to be dramatically decreasing," said Rector Dolan. "The bad news is that the increase is hardly noticeable yet."

The New Men's vocation blossomed as their faith took a pounding: priests defrocked because of sexual abuses; anti-abortion militants pulling the trigger in the name of religion; a society whose me-first code makes ordinary acts of charity worthy of space in the morning paper or the well-how-about-that? spot on the television news. Is there room for "Thou Shalt Not Kill" when the other guy could care less?

At least Dolan thinks so. He tries to see the cleansing power of the tempest. The Church, he believes, can emerge stronger and more relevant. Taboos, such as discussions about sexuality, also have been washed aside.

"I tell the guys, 'If there is anything internally that is eating at you or bothering you or if there are inclinations that you think are not right, for God's sake, admit them to yourself, to your God, and to someone who can help you.'"

At Harvard University, the senior chaplain at the Catholic Student Center sees a potentially calamitous intersection ahead: fewer priests with more everyday burdens tending congregations swelling with people seeking attention to long-ignored spiritual lives. Baby boomers suddenly wondering about the mortality that lies on the other side of

2000, which once seemed so distant and full of utopian promise: organized, sanitary, safe.

"The American Church by empirical standards may very well be the most well educated congregation that the Roman Catholic Church has ever faced," said Rev. J. Bryan Hehir. "This brings a whole set of expectations. The priest can't just drone on. He needs to engage the people intellectually. He has to make the Church credible but not condescending.

"Look, the external pressures to be Catholic are very, very, very eroded. Not many people are going to come to church because they feel they have to. They are going to go to church because they want to. Being a priest these days is by no means an easy job."

Brian Christensen often writes in his diary about the overlapping pursuits of trying to understand the vocation within him and the city around him. His thoughts often loop back to Rome's antiquity. "Sometimes," he wrote, "when touching the old marble or when visiting the early Christian catacombs, I feel drawn in two directions. There's a touch of the infinite combined with a reminder of how brief our lives are. This, to me, is the feeling of Rome. Isn't this also the feeling of religion?"

PART TWO

INTER

CHAPTER IX

BRIAN

My sacrifice, a contrite spirit.

—PSALM 51 FOR FRIDAY MORNINGS

Brian didn't have to look at the return address. He knew instantly it was from Meredith. The dusty pink stationery was a giveaway. It was her color: wallpaper, sheets, clothes. She never outgrew pastels. His name tumbled over the paper in her looping script speckled with circles instead of dots and big fish-hook curves in place of commas. She always wrote that way. Big, bouncy letters. It could be a love note or a shopping list. It didn't matter.

Brian turned the square envelope over and over. He had forgotten how lavishly feminine Meredith's writing looked. It was so familiar but, at the same time, surprising—the way the regular route home seems if you ever bother to stop to look closely. Christensen had been so long among men: high school, the Air Force Academy, then active duty. Now the seminary. All were places of accomplishment, evolution. He shook hands with the principal and got his diploma. He saluted his superiors and got his wings and promotions. He now was working toward the day when he would lie flat on his stomach before his bishop and become a priest. All these were places of tight, herky-jerky writing. Men's writing. The message mattered, the aesthetics didn't. Brian never was entirely like that. He was careful to keep his printing clean and the letters round and distinct. It was a small habit but important to him. It was one of the ways Brian kept himself apart; part of his personal fight against conformity.

Brian was no rebel. In fact, he listened intently to Dolan and his spiritual director and tried diligently to follow their advice. What he resisted was complacency. He was like that in the Air Force: personally demanding, intent on improving his skills because he wanted to and not because some higher-up told him to make the grade.

"The way I look at it is either you push yourself or stagnate," said Christensen, whose lips go thin and pale when he starts focusing on a task. When his spiritual director told him to expand his prayer life, Brian attacked head on. He'd sit in the chapel contemplating his own shortcomings as a seminarian over and over. The list was short: spinning always back to what he considered his incomplete grasp of his own spiritual potential. There has got to be something more profound than what's happening now? he'd tell himself. To believe in God is one thing. To understand Him, feel a force guiding you, is something entirely different. Brian wanted so much, so quickly. His spiritual director kept telling him to slow down, don't become too ambitious in your expectations. For some people, it takes years to break through the crust.

Sometimes, he felt it. It was like being in a deep daydream: only realizing you were mesmerized after you snapped out of it. "You're praying—or more like meditation really—and then you're in this state where you're like outside yourself looking in. Only you're not outside your body. You're outside your normal, regular self and looking down—I mean really looking down—into your soul. Then you pop out of it and say, 'Whoa, where have I been?' Am I describing this well?" Honesty, Brian said later. Getting close to God requires harsh, uncompromising honesty. He wanted, more than anything ever before, to become a priest. But not if there is any shred of hesitation; anything left unresolved. And it always returned to Kristin. He couldn't go forward without settling their relationship. Maybe, Brian thought, that's what's holding back my prayers.

Kristin was the world. Not in the poetic or romantic sense. At least, not right now, Brian admitted. But she represented the sum total of all he must leave in order to be fully at home in the seminary. Kristin was the world of emotional commitments and obligations. That was what Rector Dolan was talking about all along: the death of the old life and old values. A seminarian who can't fully leave the world he knew is destined for trouble. Remember, Dolan warns, you are not renouncing the world, just leaving it for a time. The seminarian must think of himself in a way as an epic traveler: a modern-day Ulysses. The time spent in the seminary cannot compete with distractions from the past. All the work, all the old aspirations, must be left behind. Keeping a relationship with a woman alive, even faintly, is inviting the Siren call from the rocks, Dolan says. You're on a journey to turn yourself into a priest. "Become," he urges, "something so different and so radical from your former self—a part of Christ's legacy on earth." And when you return to the world—your diocese, your old friends—they will no longer see you as you were, Dolan promises. "They will see a priest: part of the old way merged with the new you configured to Jesus Christ."

Maybe that's exactly the problem? Brian thought. He was scared to change. Kristin knew Brian as he was. When they met, he had just made the decision to give the seminary a try. Minnesota was a first, careful step. Actually, it was more like college for Brian than seminary preparation. He studied for the credits he needed to enter a full-time seminary but was still not convinced he would even take that step.

Brian walked through the streets of Rome and wondered: is the force to keep myself the same for Kristin greater than the change demanded by my vocation?

Brian was one of the most concise New Men on the subject of importance of the priesthood. And even with Kristin he could sharply summarize the situation. "Two choices," he said. "The calling I feel for the Church or the love I feel for her."

And now—to complicate matters—comes this letter from Meredith. Brian was worried. What could she want? Is she going to lay on more guilt for leaving her? He held the envelope, not sure if this was the right time to open it.

The swirls of Meredith's handwriting wrapped around his memory and pulled: back to a two-story townhouse in a public housing block near the air base; Sunday mornings in bed downstairs while the kids watched cartoons up in their room. He smelled the envelope but there was nothing there. No perfume, no hint of anything. Just a grainy paper scent; the smell of old romance.

He slid the letter into his pocket, the pink paper swallowed by the black cloth. He'd read it later.

Brian Christensen had made some fast decisions after giving up the Air Force for the priesthood. It was impossible not to leave behind some bruised feelings. Meredith, however, was blindsided. Brian had tried to give her hints he was considering entering the seminary. She didn't pick up on the cues, or didn't want to. Brian knew he was being coy and felt a bit ashamed. But he was hesitating, and opening up to Meredith would only complicate it all.

On a Sunday afternoon at his apartment, Meredith couldn't hold back. It was impossible to ignore anymore how distant Brian had grown.

"What is it? We have to talk now," she demanded. "It can't keep going on like this."

She asked for it, he thought. So he spit it all out. It wasn't the smooth logic he had rehearsed for weeks. The words gushed out. You know I'll always care about you, he started. She instinctively recoiled. But I'm troubled by something, Brian continued. It could be nothing. But I need to see. She closed her eyes as he started talking about the seminary.

"No!" she screamed. "I, I . . ." Then she cried. For a long time.

"But, Meredith, don't you see? I need to follow this. At least try," Brian pleaded. She didn't hear him. So much had unraveled so quickly. Emotionally, it was a divorce.

"No, I don't see," she sobbed. "What I see is someone leaving me. That's all I see."

Brian had been like a father—a real, involved father—to the two children she brought west from a collapsing life in Massachusetts. He threw parties for them. Some things they had never had: balloons, big cakes with sweet, colored frosting. He watched them while Meredith attended a nursing assistance program after obtaining her high-school equivalency. They even started going to mass together. Meredith, raised without religion, was cautious at first but with Brian it felt like the right thing to do. He was so generous and attentive. Meredith needed a new car so Brian bought her one: a four-door Mazda.

She wanted Brian around all the time, and he was too in love—or so he thought—to disappoint her. Any time not on the base was spent with Meredith. Brian was being wrung dry. He could feel it and so could others. He was stumbling through his obligations to the local church—choir, Sunday school. Without warning, he'd sometimes slip into a depression of self-doubt. Why do I feel stuck? What do I want? Is it Meredith? Then he'd lash back. He refused to yell at the children, so Meredith got it full force. The more it seemed the relationship was slipping, the harder she'd hold on.

"Meredith? Meredith?" Brian pleaded after he told her he was leaving for the seminary.

She just cried. "Leave, then," she moaned. "Go."

He tried to hug her, but she pulled away. She rushed out. He wanted their eyes to meet one last time. They didn't. Just the sight of her running away. Brian looked around his apartment. It was time to think about moving.

Driving over to the minor seminary in Winona, Minnesota, to get his philosophy and theology credits, Brian thought many times about pulling over and giving Meredith a call. He decided it was better to press on. Tears always sounded extra mournful over the phone.

He carried it all to Rome. He prayed Meredith would understand. "Lord," he would say, "let her see that it had to be like this." He trusted she would—maybe not right away but eventually. But the kids, he was not so sure. He hated to think that he didn't get a chance to explain to them. He imagined them looking out the window for his pickup truck or getting ready for church, then wondering why he never came. Would Meredith even take them to church anymore? The youngest one—just two when he left—had probably already forgotten him. That was good. Maybe Meredith will keep some photos and someday perhaps he'll ask about the tall blond man next to Mom. What would she say? An old friend? A priest? His sister would remember. That was the man we used to call Bri-guy who flew planes.

Christensen knew Meredith was now married to an Army missile maintenance technician out in southern California. They had a baby. He didn't know much more.

Finally, it was time to open the letter. He laid it flat on his desk. Out his window, the pointy cypress trees were like gentle brush strokes against the evening sky. He opened the letter carefully, slowly pealing up the backflap. Everything he does is precise. His shirt is always tucked neatly in his sweater, his shoes are placed side by side in military fashion at the side of his bed at night. The pages of the letter were folded in thirds. She got right to the point.

"Can I tell you something I used to do when I lived on Curtis Street? Now don't laugh. I used to sit upstairs in Jamie's bedroom and stare out the window waiting for you to drive up the street.... Then you would knock on the door. I remember watching and waiting. Oh, what a wonderful feeling."

He read on quickly. At the end of the second page, he relaxed.

"One thing that has not changed is my feelings and love for you. I'm still deeply in love with you, for you have never hurt me intentionally. I finally came to that realization that we broke up for reasons that were beyond your control. I do not blame anyone or anything anymore. I just know that it is this way, and this is the way it ought to be. Knowing that your long struggle with your emotions has finally come to a place where you belong makes me as happy for you as it was painful to let you go."

He folded the letter and put it in the top drawer of his desk. Often, back in his room after dinner, Christensen would take it out to reread. It was late fall and it was dark by early evening. The pink pages seemed even brighter under the fluorescent desk lamp. He'd linger on the middle of that long sentence—"A place where you belong." How could she be so sure? Christensen looked out his window. It was dark now. He was on the side of the seminary looking away from the Vatican. Lights outlined the street zigzagging away from the Janiculum.

The church domes—unlike the illuminated St. Peter's—were barely visible, just a darker shade of charcoal in the night.

"So there's always this question: why me? I'm here looking around and looking at the world and looking at myself and saying, 'Why me?'" Brian said a few days later. "Why did I get this incredible gift known as a calling? And why do I believe it's real? Why did God pick me even though in my life I tried to cast my lot with others and include myself with others? Do we ever really know why?"

His plans had once been so tidy, so logical. Squadron officers' school, rising in the Air Force ranks with an early retirement and nice pension, fatherhood, fly a little Cessna just for fun. "I mean, I started to see this very clearly," he said. "It all made so much sense."

Yet another, parallel image was taking form. He'd try to swat it away, but it kept returning—each time brighter and more substantial. The picture was of dedication to religion, sacrifice, the mysteries of faith rather than the certainties of the military. He considered himself a good Catholic—"whatever that really means," he added. He enjoyed mass and tried—sometimes seriously, other times less so—to follow his vision of being a Christian. Flying a bomber capable of dropping 42,000 pounds of explosive power didn't fit so neatly in the equation. But, hey, he'd remind himself, this is not a perfect world by any stretch. And I'm no religious fanatic.

"Sometimes I'd go, 'Yeah, that's right: the Church, religion. That's what it's all about.' Then I'd sort of slap myself and say, 'What are you thinking, Brian? You're talking yourself into this. I got to get back to work.'"

Religion always had been part of Brian's life, yet hanging on the edge. The crazyquilt of Long Island suburbia didn't support anything too heavy. Masses were kept short and breezy—a little guitar strumming maybe. The village of Green Lawn ran to the supercharged energy of children. Lots of them. The Christensen's side yard became the neighborhood baseball sandlot. In winter, they'd flood the patio for hockey games or bruising attempts at figure skating. Brian was an altar boy—because his mother demanded it. His favorite moment was just before communion when he and the other altar boy would pull back the twelve-foot tabernacle gates for the priest to take out the hosts. It was appropriately grand for his boyish imagination.

Or like when he'd sit on his grandmother Kelly's sofa and look up at the oil painting of her uncle, Archbishop Edward Hoban of Cleveland. To think: someone in their family was important enough for a portrait. Each Good Friday, grandmother Kelly would pray one thousand Hail Marys. Brian wondered how she kept count.

Christensen went to a high school run by Franciscan Brothers, but only because they had a good hockey team. His father, a Presbyterian, wasn't happy about the idea of a Catholic education but agreed after one of the brothers told him: "We have discipline, then discipline, and more discipline." It appealed to his sense of order instilled by the Merchant Marine. He came home from sea to take charge of a money-churning plumbing contractor business with a giant Yellow Pages ad and work all over Long Island. The firm was onto its third generation in the Christensen family and the owner's seat was being warmed for first-born Brian.

Christensen saw his future in diplomacy, not pipes and faucets. Four months as a high-school exchange student in France stoked his interest in the State Department foreign service. The Bordeaux coast also led him back to church. On the way home—sometimes by bike, sometimes hitchhiking—he often stopped at a little chapel set back in a field of coarse grass on the edge of a village.

"I didn't know why exactly. It was a familiar place. It looked almost the same as at home. Everything was there. And, in fact, I'd be exhausted some afternoons. It would be five o'clock and I'd be lying in the back pew and go to sleep. And there, I just felt at home in the church. In this cold, stone church in the middle of southern France. It was able to bring me home."

His application for Georgetown's foreign service program was turned down. He was, however, accepted in the business school and hoped to transfer. The trouble was family money was tight for the first time. A restaurant venture went sour and drained the bank account—college fund and all. Christensen applied for an ROTC scholarship and his guidance counselor suggested the Air Force Academy. "I didn't even know where the place was," said Christensen. A couple months later, a guy with a buzzing hair clipper yelled "next" and Christensen watched his yellow-blond hair drop away in wispy clumps. Welcome to the military. Christensen's only family war stories were hazy references to an Irish immigrant descendant in Illinois who fought in obscure battles for the Union army. Basic training ended on Christensen's eighteenth birthday. That just meant a new kind of harassment begins.

Upperclassmen heap abuse on the first-year guys—Doolies—spitting criticism about their uniform or quizzing them on arcane military facts. The brickbats came down particularly heavy at dawn, when the cranky upperclassmen have to march the new cadets to breakfast. Christensen quickly figured out the chapel was a sanctuary. The academy allowed cadets to go to morning prayer and meet the others at breakfast. "My motives for going to church were not necessarily the most pure," he said, "But it kept me from getting screamed at."

He liked the routine of daily prayer. Nothing too serious. Sometimes he would just sit and think. But soon it became a vital part of the day. As Christensen rose in the academy, so did his devotion to religion. He joined prayer groups, talked to his girlfriends about God to the point where they'd have to kiss him just to quiet him down.

After being assigned to the B-1 squadron in Rapid City, Christensen became more involved in the diocese. He started to ask some questions about vocations. Not directly, just nibbling. A priest who studied at the North American College told him his own story: how he fought the urge and felt even a bit ashamed, like he couldn't find a niche in the secular world.

"Why are you so curious, Brian?" the priest said. "You interested?"

"Me?" Christensen jumped. "Me? No, um, I got a, um, friend who's been talking about it."

"I see," said the priest, who didn't push the point. He knew what was up.

In the summer of 1993, just before the pope's visit to Denver, Christensen learned about a friend who was leaving the Air Force to do missionary work with the Russian military in St. Petersburg. Christensen asked him to lunch. The friend wanted to talk about this grand experience he was undertaking, but Christensen kept steering the conversation back to what it took to hang up the Air Force wings. "I'm thinking about doing it, you know," Christensen said. "I mean, it's getting serious now."

The B-1 training circuit usually is a large loop over the western Great Plains and the foothills of the Rockies. On a flight in August 1993, the bomber banked to the left over Montana. Its bearing was now in the direction of Denver, where hundreds of thousands of people gathered to see the pontiff for World Youth Day. Just north of Denver, the B-1 turned back toward Rapid City. That night, Christensen watched the coverage of the pope's visit on television in his apartment. He decided that night—lying on the couch in his t-shirt and shorts—that he'd have to give the seminary a try. But not, he thought, right now. He just didn't know if he was ready to ask for a discharge.

Success forced the showdown. Christensen got word he was selected to be on the first B-1 crew in Gunsmoke, the aerial war games and flight competition held every two years. Then he was picked to fly the B-1 in an air show in Nova Scotia. You need to settle this, he told himself. His stock in the Air Force was rising. If he didn't cut it off now, it could wrap up his life for years.

He finally asked for an early discharge. The door surprisingly swung open. With military cutbacks accelerating, his request got immediate attention. Within three hours, it had shot up the chain of command and was stamped approved. He even got his parting wishes: fly in Gunsmoke and the Canadian air show.

"Sure I would have felt good about becoming an aircraft commander and becoming squadron officer. But if I would have had to go home every night and live with myself wondering, it wouldn't have been any accomplishment at all."

Six weeks after Meredith slammed his front door, Christensen was at a seminary in Minnesota. To his bishop, it was a place for Christensen to take some philosophy courses before the full seminary training. For Christensen, it was a chance to seek his bearings. For the first time, he had the time and encouragement to face down this nagging religious call. He'd read the Liturgy of the Hours. He'd try long periods of prayer. Some days it felt right. "Then sometimes I'd be saying, 'Give me a break. What do I think I'm doing here?' " And temptation sat right next to him: a black-haired student getting her bachelor's degree in philosophy. Kristin Peters was part of the Catholic Worker Movement. Brian sometimes watched her counsel battered women. She'd listen to them pour out their stories. She could sit for hours just listening. Ever so gently, Kristin would touch the black eye or yellowing bruise.

"She was very attractive. Very holy. I think she's like St. Francis reincarnated," said Christensen. He started thinking he could have it all: a life dedicated to religious work and a wife who wanted to do the same.

"She was a cross I had to bear—a cross that came in the most beautiful package that it could," he said.

They parted with an awkward hug at the end of the school year.

"We'll see each other again?" Kristin asked.

"Definitely," Brian said. But he knew it would be tough. He was planning to bounce between Long Island and Rapid City several times. "We have to stay in touch."

"I know," she said simply.

They hugged again. Brian didn't like how it felt to hold Kristin. It felt too nice.

In Rome, Christensen lay in bed and watched the gray night shadows on the white walls of his room—Spartan quarters without pictures or a rug over the tile floor. It would be close to dinner time back in the Midwest. He wondered what Kristin was doing. Maybe she was just leaving the Catholic aid center where she volunteered.

He just received a letter from her. She said she would definitely be in Ireland after Christmas for her cousin's wedding.

Brian bought a ticket to Dublin the next morning.

"Brian, what's wrong?"

The other seminarian knew instantly Christensen was upset. Brian was walking back from the Greg with his head down, his hands folded over his notebooks. Normally, he's looking around—studying building facades and translating every poster to try to improve his Italian.

"What is it?" the seminarian pressed.

"Nothing, really," Brian lied. "I'm just a little tired. You know, studying for exams and everything."

"Tell me about it. OK, see ya."

"Sure. *Ciao.*"

Christensen walked for a long time. He thought for a moment about going to see his spiritual director, but he wouldn't even know how to clearly describe what was torturing him. "Frustration is about as close as I could come," he said. He felt his vocation was stalled. There was the question of Kristin, of course. It scared him how much he wanted to see her.

He had been praying hard for guidance. Maybe too hard, he thought. "Listen to the inner voice," urged Brian's spiritual director. "Prayer is not just rattling away, 'Give me this, I want that.'" The dervish inside rarely slowed down. And the closer it was to Christmas break, the faster the doubts spun. Brian wondered: will I see Kristin again and realize this was all one big mistake?

"I'm frustrated like I've never been in my life," he told me. "I want to know and love God right now. This is when I need Him. How do I get there? How do you grow? And what should I see? How do you measure it? In a business meeting you say, 'Yeah, I got a lot of stuff done. I accomplished something.' This is different. How do you know you're making progress at all?"

The question was becoming all-consuming. He cut back on nights with other seminarians in the lounge—Christensen's roost during the early weeks. In page after page of his journal, he tried to sort out his confusion. "I don't feel in touch," he wrote. "I know God is there, but I wish I had more of a grasp. I feel like I'm blocking it. What am I not letting happen?"

Alone in the chapel after mass one morning, Christensen knelt with his eyes closed. His right hand moved. He couldn't tell whether it was voluntary or not. He didn't notice it until his hand was hovering over the back of the next pew. He felt like he wanted to hold onto something.

"And I'm thinking, 'What am I grasping for?' God has already reached out to me. What am I groping for in return?"

A few days after Meredith's pink pages arrived, another letter arrived from another old girlfriend. This was one typed in slanted script. The return address: Our Lady of the Angels Monastery in Birmingham, Alabama. They had met in Paris, where they both were studying in 1989. She returned to San Diego and Christensen went to pilot training in the Arizona desert. They kept in touch for a while, then the phone calls and letters trailed off. Years later, a mutual friend contacted Brian while he was studying in Minnesota. Remember Meghan Campbell? the friend asked. Give her a call, but he didn't say why. You should just do it, the friend said. Brian put off the call for weeks.

Christensen decided to call her—completely by chance—the night before she was about to become Sister Marie Andre, a cloistered nun whose commitment, if she keeps it, means never again leaving the convent grounds.

"I'm so glad you got me," she said. "Did you hear? I'm entering the convent tomorrow."

Brian was startled. "What? Really? A cloister?"

It was odd, being on the other end of a vocation story. He listened as she described her resistance, then recognition of her desire for the convent cloister. She felt—in some fundamental way she couldn't quite describe to Brian at the time—that she must dedicate herself to prayer. It had to be total, all-consuming. Nothing else. It was a much more radical break than even the priesthood. Brian suddenly felt lighter, like he wasn't such an unusual specimen after all.

In her letter to Brian in Rome, she calls outside the cloister "the world." A place she is no longer part of. Many of the sentences in the letter end with two exclamation points. When she mentions her struggles, she underlines them with a flat line or a downward curve. The effect looks like little faces grimacing or frowning.

"With the receiving of the habit, I feel I am 'digging in for the fight' . . . buckling down for the long haul," she wrote. "The life I lead is by no means easy (as you well know as a seminarian). The transition can be painful at times!! The Lord's stripping of 'self' can seem to be a little rough in spots!!

"Believe you me, I've questioned the Lord a few times on His wisdom in calling me to a religious vocation!! Especially when I see how little in common I have with some of these women. . . . If it weren't for God's graces, one couldn't live in the community for ten minutes."

She wrote that she missed her mother "something fierce at times." Mother Angelica, the convent's superior, is blunt. She likes to remind the sisters of what Jesus told St. Therese:

"Courage, my daughter, it only gets worse."

CHAPTER X

PRAYER

In the Lord's eyes, one day is like a thousand years
and a thousand years are as a day.

—EVENING READING FOR DECEMBER 23
(2 PETER 3:8B)

It almost snowed. The raindrops were thick with slush. The last time snow stuck to the ground in Rome was nearly a decade before. The seminarians waited—some maybe even prayed a bit—for the changeover to snow. But, instead, the horrible half-sleet continued to pour down. Some New Men had to head down into Rome to buy gloves. They didn't realize Rome could get this cold.

The heat in the seminarians' rooms is generally good—a distinct difference from the typically frigid Rome apartments. But the halls and chapel at the seminary can be teeth-chattering cold.

Brian Christensen was wearing a heavy black sweater for his appointment with his spiritual director. The weather made him feel even more forlorn.

"It's not working," Brian huffed almost as soon as he closed the door to Father Cornelius McRae's office. "I'm just not feeling it."

"Feeling what?" asked the priest.

"Whatever it is that I'm supposed to be getting from prayer. A closeness to God, serenity. Whatever. Actually, it's even more confusing than when I first arrived. It's . . . I don't know."

"Go on," McRae urged.

"It's like I'm trying to push everything aside for a while when I'm praying. That's how you said to do it, wasn't it? Try to clear your mind. But it seems the harder I push, the more it all stays rooted. Do you know what I mean?"

"Yes."

"Well, what am I doing wrong? Am I praying the wrong way?"

"What are these thoughts? These ones so hard to move?"

"You know, the usual: the strength of my vocation, my relationship—or whatever you call it—with my friend from home. You remember? I've told you about her. Mostly, though, I'm worried about this prayer thing. If I'm not making progress, what is this telling me? Is it saying that I don't belong here?"

"Brian, listen. You are making progress. Just recognizing your turmoil is progress."

"There's something else, Father. I'm very nervous about this. I told you I'm going to Ireland over Christmas. Well, the reason is Kristin will be there."

"So?" McRae said, trying hard to make it sound as flat and neutral as possible.

"I don't know what it's going to be like. What if there's still some strong romantic feelings left? I really think there might be. It could be a disaster."

"A disaster?" McRae smiled. "On the contrary, Brian. It would be a disaster if you didn't go and left these feelings unsettled. And what if you do find you'd rather be with her than in the seminary? Where's the disaster? I can't see it. As long as you honestly follow where you believe God is leading, then so be it. If it's to love a woman, hallelujah. I wish a lot more priests would have tried to settle this very question while they were still in the seminary."

"But can you understand why I'm nervous?" Brian asked.

"Making a choice is always nerve-wracking. Some people get nervous picking out what tie to wear. Your situation is completely understandable. I ask you one thing, Brian. Don't let your prayer life slip, especially during this trip."

"But that's what I'm worried about. I don't think . . ."

McRae cut him off. "Wait a moment," he said. "A lot of people have this idea of emptying yourself out in prayer. I have a feeling that's what you are trying to do. But you can't empty yourself out, you know. It's impossible. You are filled with thoughts and desires. I mean, look at you now. They just don't disappear because you want to pray."

The priest told Brian to imagine a glass of water churning with sediment. This, he said, was everyday life. The bits of sand and silt and stone represent the tasks and emotions we all face or, sometimes, try to avoid. You can't remove the sediment. Try, though, to let it settle. Let it all drift to the bottom.

"Then when it's all settled, just sit and try to feel God's presence," McRae said. "Don't push, Brian. Let everything settle. This is what we're after at this stage in prayer. Learn to let things sink. Let the water clear."

It's perhaps the ultimate quandary of the seminary, the grand transformation. Taking the tests, wearing the clerics, cutting the ties with the secular life—are all subordinate to something as seemingly basic as prayer. It is the lead in the stained glass. It can elevate or frustrate. But without it, the seminarians say there is nothing. A journey with no compass.

"It probably would seem so silly to lots of Americans in the so-called 'real world': a bunch of grown men on their knees just praying," McRae told me. "They'll say, 'Great, but what are they doing? What are they accomplishing? Why aren't they out helping someone or righting some wrong?'

"But they are doing something that most people try at all costs to avoid: steadying themselves, looking for the hand of God in the world. Would you really want a priest who didn't take prayer seriously? We're in a curious position in America. America has been labeled a very religious country compared to some European countries, for example. But the question is: are we a spiritual country? There's a difference."

The type of prayer encouraged for the seminarians is a distant kin to the familiar recitations at mass. The faculty comes up with any number of metaphors for the process: dissolving self, illuminating tranquillity. The goal is something transcendental in its most unadorned definition—trying to slip outside ordinary experience. Try to sense the infinity and wisdom of God, the seminarians are told. It's there. Be open and, above all, listen. They say: let God pray you.

This is the breach between ordinary petition—the give-me-this-and-I'll-be-good praying started in childhood—and the union of contemplation and meditation the seminarians are told to seek. It's a hazy goal, especially for many of the New Men. This new state—called infused prayer by some theologians—has no rules, no well-marked path to achieve it. Each seminarian struggles alone to reach the moment the saints and spiritual scholars exalt: a serene oblivion to everything but you and God; a tangible feeling of God's existence. It's the first level to the ultimate state for Catholic mystics, a transforming bond in which someone feels their entire soul is attuned to God, and the line between free will and God's will merges.

"I'm not promising everyone will reach this state. You progress as far as God wants you to," Rev. Thomas Radloff told the New Men at a meeting to discuss progress in their prayer lives. "But if you seriously try to advance in prayer, there is one thing certain. You will be in for some rough times."

He handed them a nine-page copy from the Handbook for Spiritual Growth. It's as close to a written guide of how to pray as they will get. There are tips on how to best ease into spiritual contemplation. How to sit to best relax, for example, or the value of starting off meditation on a reading from Scripture to clear the mind of the ordinary buzz from the day. "Why are so few Christians really committed to spending time with God daily?" the New Men read in the handbook. "The answer is the false self system. Prayer spells death to the false self, and the false self exists to control our lives according to its own fearful values."

In essence, serious prayer is being able to let go. St. Augustine called it purgation. It's the first of the torments as one moves deeper into spiritual contemplation. Augustine—once a first-rate hedonist—says that breaking the mirror of narcissism is the first step. The shards often cut and the wounds take a long time to heal.

The New Men flail about in the pile of apparent contradictions. Give yourself up to God's will, they hear. But then they see Dolan and the faculty fawning over the visiting American cardinals and bishops, who did not reach these positions without employing the same mix of cunning, wit, and politicking that leads to election victories or corner offices in the corporate world. Follow what you perceive as God's call, they are told, even if it means leaving the seminary. Back home in their diocese, however, the message is sent: lots of other seminarians would love to study in Rome, so consider yourself honored. The bishops would never say it, but it's clearly implied to the seminarians: we are investing in you.

Brian Christensen had seen something like this before. "When you join the Air Force, they try to break you down, then form you in their image. It seems the same thing goes on in the seminary. God is breaking you down and forming you. It's not easy to go through this again."

Yet, in spite of the difficulties in grasping how to approach their new prayer lives, most seminarians, somehow, inexorably make headway. There's something addictive, urgent, about it. It's the time when being in the seminary tends to make the most sense. Prayer recharges, focuses. The New Men may not even fully comprehend what's happening. They just feel—on some instinctive level—the need to pray. There's a seduction they can't logically explain.

Even Chris Nalty was at a loss for words. Prayer was somehow keeping him rooted. His secular reflexes were telling him to leave the seminary. Many times—behind his smile and jokes—Chris was terribly insecure. He compared himself to some of the others. Roger Landry. Tran. They seemed so content in the seminary and well suited to religious life, Chris thought. He knew it was silly, even self-destructive, to make these types of seminarian-versus-seminarian contrasts. Everyone moves at his own pace. But Chris was not in the same safe terrain as back home. His anxiety fed on itself. Being uncomfortable was making him more uncomfortable and so on.

"I can't say much about my vocation and being here in the seminary with absolute conviction," Nalty told me one night over dinner.

"But I know this. If I didn't have my prayer life, I'd be home by now. That is a given."

Why? I asked him. What is it like?

"In your prayer, I think you get glimpses of heaven or what heaven's like. Sometimes when I'm praying I can get a feeling—a sense—of God that is so strong that tears just start streaming down my face. It's this feeling, this love that the world doesn't have to give, that's not in this world.

"When I think about heaven, I'm not thinking: 'Is my dog going to be there? Is my family going to be there? Is there going to be really good scotch?' I just get this feeling like the love is so intense—nothing separating you from the love of God. When you feel that on earth, it's really intense."

A friend from home sent Chris an E-mail asking about how he was doing on the celibacy front. "Praying about it," Nalty typed back.

"Huh?" the friend replied. "You must be on your millionth Hail Mary."

Chris laughed it off.

"Telling people about praying is like telling them how to swim. Unless they go out there and try it, they're never going to know what it's like."

Under an alabaster sky just before dawn, Chris Nalty arrived at the Blessed Sacrament Chapel. A cold wind slicing down from the mountains shook the shoulder-high palms outside the seminary. It was just before Christmas: clammy weeks when Rome's shutters are clamped tight and coffee bars put up signs for hot chocolate with fresh cream. The stubby palms flapped with a whisper-hiss sound, almost like deep sighs, as the gusts came in waves. The cats out back were huddled under a car. On the steps leading down to the chapel below the main church the walls were damp and cold.

Nalty pulled open the chapel doors slowly in case someone else was already there. No one was. The small chapel, no bigger than a living room, was below the main church. Bare concrete steps. It felt far away from the rest of the seminary.

The chapel was dark except for a single vigil candle burning in a red glass cylinder. The little flame is enough to light the tabernacle decorated with a woodcut of a shepherd carrying a lamb. Nalty squinted for a second then moved down the chapel aisle. Even in the darkness, he moved without hesitation. He knew the way. In a chair by the wall, Chris Nalty buried his face in his hands. It was so quiet, he could hear the sound of the candle sputtering as it melted down the wick.

Chris tugged at one of the five page-mark ribbons in his breviary. He meticulously keeps them up to date on the proper pages. He read the morning Liturgy of the Hours. Then he closed the book and prayed. For more than a half-hour, Chris sat very still. Sometimes he closed his eyes. But more often he would stare at the tabernacle.

"You can't express the feeling I get from being near the Eucharist," Chris told me. "It's pure peace."

After a while, two other seminarians arrived. They scattered to different edges of the room. These quiet hours are precious. Before the classes and seminars and lectures—and just the normal turbulence of grown men living in a dormitory—this time of peaceful prayer and contemplation before the morning mass is a safety valve for many seminarians.

Along the dark corridors at 5:30 A.M., little half moons of light spill out from under the doors. Most seminarians stay in their rooms, reading or praying. Only a few—no more than a dozen—normally spend the time in the basement chapel. Chris Nalty has been coming every morning without fail. His prayers for his family and friends may change, but his personal plea never wavers: give me the strength to stay celibate.

He has no idea exactly what's allowed him to remain faithful to his vocation for this long: nearly four months in Rome. It didn't matter, really, how much was God's intervention, the dedication that comes from his prayer routine, or just the lack of opportunities to meet women in Rome. The desire for women wasn't fading, but his ability to tap into self-control was gaining an upper hand.

Chris kept promising to call Allie, the woman in Washington. Even if he wasn't going to stay in the seminary, he had to cut things off with her. He couldn't stand the idea of her waiting for him—whether in vain or not.

Then there was another woman, an Italian who lived just a few miles from the seminary. They met in 1982 when Nalty was in London at a college semester abroad. They had a few dates; nothing too intense. They had kept in touch for a while, but they drifted apart as acquaintances often do. Chris found her last name in the Rome phone book. It's a common surname, but the address seemed correct to him.

"She'll freak out when she finds out I'm a seminarian," Nalty told a newly ordained priest back in the seminary for a final year.

"When are you going to call her?"

"I don't know. One of these days." Nalty later decided it was best to write a letter. Then he felt it was best to wait a while. A note with her name and the address he found in the phone book was shoved to a corner of his desk, near the packs of cigarettes he used to burn through in a day. Nalty was down to just a few smokes a day now.

"Some days I walk out of the chapel knowing that I can do it," Nalty said. "Celibacy, anything. I feel like I'm invincible. Prayer does that for me. And believe me, if I didn't think that was pretty cool I wouldn't be sitting here."

Just before Christmas, Nalty went out to dinner with the priest who knew Chris was poking through the phone book for the woman's number. It was a nice little trattoria recommended by some people at the Greg. The windows were steamy from the ovens. Chris never realized how damp and bone-chilling a Roman winter could be. The conversation turned to Allie and why Chris was hesitating making a clean break from her.

"So what you're saying is get it over with, right?" Chris asked.

"Sure, why not? Unless you're thinking of leaving, that is."

"No!" Chris said, a little too passionately to be believable. "Nothing like that."

"Are you sure?"

"I'm not going to lie and say I'm rock-solid in my vocation. But something's been going on. Something I'd call positive. I have to say it's finally getting a little easier. I can see why celibacy is such a trial for me.

I was only looking at it from my point of view, what I was losing. I'm talking about the physical pleasure. I'm talking about intimacy. I'm trying now to follow what my spiritual director is suggesting. I'm trying to look at it from a different side."

"The spiritual side," the priest said.

"Exactly. I'm seeing it now as a test of my faith. That makes it a lot easier to fight it. Look, this may sound nuts, but I still believe in God and the devil and the devil being around."

"Interesting. Go on."

"I think when you're moving toward holiness you have the tendency to get attacked more because the devil doesn't want you to get there. So you're struggling with your own niche and trying to reach higher to holiness. If you lead a life of hanging around and drinking beers, you don't really think about holiness, and that's just where the devil wants you to be. But when you start to reach for holiness, you start to get attacked in very subtle ways. I mean, the devil doesn't appear in a tail and horns, you know. If the devil appears to me, he will be a babe."

"Well," the priest asked, "are you going to call her?"

"You don't let up, do you? I'll do it. I'm just waiting for the right moment."

Chris Nalty arrived late at St. Peter's Basilica for Christmas Midnight Mass, barely giving a glance over to the one-hundred-foot Christmas tree in the square as part of the northern European traditions started in Rome by Pope John Paul II.

Nalty had a special pass to allow him in, but the only room was far in the back with the tourists, who had waited more than three hours in line. Chris had never seen the basilica so full—more than ten thousand people—and so expectant. Sometimes papal masses can seem more like a show for tourists, with all the cameras and tour groups and talking in the pews. This time, the mood was different. For once, it was much more quiet than he expected. The importance of the mass seemed to penetrate even into the back pews. The basilica felt entirely altered at night—somehow more intimate, more ancient. The small chapels to either side of the main corridor appeared darker because of the strong overhead lights needed for the worldwide television broadcast. The lights reflected off the gold band of Latin and Greek inscriptions that rings the basilica. The statues of saints and popes looked eerie under the harsh lights. There is no stained glass in the basilica save the gold starburst dove in the apse—the same pattern looking down upon the papal altar from the underside of the baldacchino. The other windows are ordinary glass squares with black panes. They were like eyes looking down on the basilica on this muggy Christmas Eve.

The Landry twins—Scot and Roger—were in the second row as guests of the president of Assumption College in Worcester, Massachusetts. The weather had turned warm and humid. Inside the basilica, it was already uncomfortably steamy. But not a single woman in the VIP section removed her fur coat.

The choir sang Handel's *Messiah*. The papal procession entered the basilica. The pope, once so young and robust, looked shrunken. His yellow and white vestments hung loosely off his shoulders. His pointed mitre bobbed with each hesitant step. He broke his hip the year before and needed hip replacement surgery. He was healing slowly. It was a shock to those who hadn't seen the pope in a while. Always so robust and active, the pope for the first time seemed older than his years.

From where the pope enters the basilica, it's about one hundred steps to the papal altar—ringed with red poinsettias and pale yellow forsythia. It took the pope a full minute to walk up the aisle, stopping only a few times to acknowledge the outstretched hands of people on either side. The Landrys were close enough to see the pope's pain. He drew his breath in sharply with each step up to the altar.

The mass is elaborately choreographed. Twelve children from different parts of the world placed orchids at the foot of a statue of the baby Jesus, which will be laid in the life-size Nativity scene below the Vatican Christmas tree.

The pope, his voice sometimes wavering, wiped sweat from his forehead.

"This hour when the Son of God is born in the stable in Bethlehem, is the hour in which God's holiness breaks into the history of the world," he said in his homily. "It is the holy night, as a well-known Christmas carol proclaims.

"On this night of the Lord's birth," he continued from the marble altar, "we sense renewed hope for peace for all individuals and for all peoples afflicted by war: in the Balkans, in Africa, and wherever there is no peace."

The pope held up the host, the wheat wafer the faithful believe is changed into the Body of Christ. He grasped the host with his right hand. The fingertips of his trembling and weaker left hand just brushed its edges. The pope gave communion to more than fifty specially selected people who walked up to his seat in front of the altar. Tim Dolan and about a dozen other priests and deacons from the seminary helped distribute communion to the rest of the congregation.

Dolan was off to the pope's left—by chance near a group of American servicemen who came to the mass from their bases around Naples. "I loved that," Dolan said later. "To give communion to Americans in St. Peter's is particularly special for me." Dolan never tires of giving communion: the symbolic re-creation of the Last Supper. It's the faith stripped of all the politics and all the extraneous trappings. It's saying, in a simple gesture, that the teachings and sacrifice of Jesus still resonate among the faithful two thousand years later.

"And to give communion in St. Peter's Basilica with the Holy Father is a staggering experience," Dolan said later. "There are no rankings, no pecking order. We all for a moment become just priests giving the Body of Christ. Nothing I can think of can equal that."

As the mass ended, Roger said he saw the pope's wince as he descended from the altar. "His leg buckled a bit and he grabbed onto the railing," he whispered to his brother. The pope regained his balance and blessed the congregation again.

By Christmas morning, the pope was too sick to celebrate mass in the basilica. Word filtered out through the pilgrims, and throngs left in disappointment before the beginning of the service, led by an Italian cardinal, Virgilio Noe. Chris Nalty took advantage of the thinning crowd and grabbed a pew near the front.

After mass, he joined the gathering in St. Peter's Square for the papal *Urbi et Orbi*—to the city and world—Christmas message. No one was sure John Paul would make it. But then, right on schedule, he appeared. Chris strained to see whether he could detect any sign of illness. It's too far though. For those in the square, the pope is a postage stamp–size figure. For Christmas and other important dates, the pope uses the balcony of the basilica to speak to the square rather than the window of his study as he does for his Sunday addresses. Nalty tried to follow as much as he could of the pope's Italian. His mind was also on getting out of town. He was leaving for the Canary Islands and still hadn't really packed.

Suddenly, it was quiet. The pope was on the second of his fifty-four Christmas greetings in different languages when he leaned to the side. Then he moaned, a deep humming moan that was picked up by the microphones. The instant seemed to stretch on and on. The bishops around him on the balcony were frozen in indecision. No one, it seemed, wanted to be the first to assume the worst and rush to the pope's side. Finally, John Paul leaned toward the microphone and mumbled quickly in Italian: "I cannot go on. Merry Christmas." Then he was gone. Vatican television services quickly cut the feed to networks serving millions of viewers around the world. Vatican Radio did not break its rules about discussing the pope's health. "The pope," they said simply, "wished the world a Merry Christmas."

Inside the Vatican press room, journalists were barking out urgent updates or rapping out the news to their stories on laptops. The pope's speech is handed out hours in advance and almost all the journalists had their pieces prewritten, waiting for the moment when the pope started speaking to send them off. After that, it was just a matter of listening to make sure the pope kept to the prepared text and then head home. A radio journalist who brought her newborn daughter to the press room to pick up the speech was forced to wedge her behind an old typewriter while she called New York.

All around St. Peter's Square there was that gasping instant—like before a mishandled glass shatters on the floor. For a second in the square, everyone just stopped and looked at the vacant window. It was cold and very quiet. A group of Croatians who didn't seem to notice what had happened waved their checkerboard national flag.

"What do you think?" Scot Landry asked his brother.

"I really don't know," said Roger.

They hurried back up the hill to the seminary. Roger tapped into his computer and began pulling up wire stories about the pope. The Vatican spokesman had earlier said that a slight fever kept the pope from celebrating Christmas Mass in the basilica for the first time in his papacy. But there was still no word on what happened on the balcony. Finally, an update: a wave of nausea, the spokesman said. About fifteen minutes after he had ducked behind the heavy curtains, the pope reappeared briefly on the balcony. He knows very well the value of images in a media-driven world. He waved a few times and managed a halfway smile.

All afternoon, seminarians stopped by Roger's room for any news on the pope's condition. "Better, I think," he told them. "I don't think there's cause for alarm."

But reporters covering the Vatican—known as *Vaticanisti*—were on high alert and papal obits were quickly updated. Among the high Vatican officials or the Curia, any talk of the pope's frailties borders on heresy. But Vatican Radio has to be ready. Quietly, almost clandestinely, they assemble the sound bites and copy for their obits—oddly called "crocodiles," which shed their insincere tears, according to the expression. Rector Dolan is on double call. He's been asked to be a commentator for the radio's English language service in case of the pope's death. The North American College is also the first stop for many of the American cardinals and their contingents arriving for a conclave to elect a new pontiff. A former rector, Cardinal James Hickey of Washington, keeps a full wardrobe in the top-floor suite that bears his name.

During the secret gathering, the pope-electing cardinals, those under eighty years old, will stay in new quarters with private baths and reading rooms, mostly funded from a donation by Pittsburgh entrepreneur John Connelly, a close friend of Pope John Paul II, who generously bankrolls dozens of Catholic causes. The Vatican willingly accepts the cash, but is careful to edit Connelly's biography to bypass any mention of one of his ventures: river boat gambling. "Profit is not an evil word," he's fond of saying. Connelly later was given exclusive worldwide rights to distribute reproductions of Vatican art—the first time the Church had authorized an outside vendor. Connelly plans to start peddling the Vatican memorabilia in Pittsburgh parochial schools and then expand.

The new lodgings he funded just outside the Vatican walls end the necessity to squeeze up to 120 grumbling clerics into cubicles—and sometimes corridors—around the Sistine Chapel meeting site. There's one thing that won't change, John Paul insisted, and that's airtight secrecy. Updated rules issued by the pope take note of the new technology available—from cellular phones to high-powered eavesdropping dishes—and warn Catholics that divulging any details of a conclave will result in summary excommunication.

At the top of the stairwell leading to the choir gallery above the seminary chapel, the wall is covered in a timeline of graffiti. "November 2, 1973: European Premier of *Godspell* in the auditorium. February 1974: First European showing (private) of *The Exorcist*. Generally disappointing, only one person got sick." Then in fat letters: "10–16–78. First Polish pope. This is no joke."

"The pope's death is the taboo subject to end all taboo subjects around the Vatican," said Dolan. "The strange thing is everybody thinks about it, everybody talks about it privately, but you'll never hear the Curia breathe a word about it—in public, that is."

Out of earshot of the Vatican, however, Dolan is one of the few who will discuss the inevitable. Before the pope went in for surgery in October 1996 to remove an inflamed appendix—the cause of a "feverish syndrome," the Vatican said—Dolan was trying to put off negotiations with television stations battling for the rights to broadcast from the North American College roof during the next conclave.

A former American ambassador to the Holy See, Raymond Flynn, liked to repeat a quip he heard back when he was mayor of Boston. "Everyone wants to go to heaven, but no one wants to die. It's true over at the Vatican, too. Lots of cardinals want to be pope, but no one wants to talk about the present pope dying."

On Christmas night, a special intention for the pope was read at vespers at the seminary. Chris Nalty couldn't make it. He and another New Man, Rob, were on their way to the Canary Islands. He caught up with the papal news from a *USA Today* he bought at the airport. The Landrys left the next day for France to visit religious sites.

The seminary emptied. In the quiet, the building's own voice emerged. The glassy rattles from the wind; the metallic groans. All were clear. A hall phone rang for a long time, unanswered.

CHAPTER XI

TRAN

I have swallowed up my enemies;
I rejoice in my victory.

—CANTICLE FOR WEDNESDAY MORNINGS
(1 SAMUEL 2:1)

Tam Tran listened to the seminary grow still during the Christmas break. Tran was one of the few seminarians who didn't leave. He had sent a letter to a priest friend in Paris wondering if he would be there for Christmas. There was no reply.

"It doesn't bother me to be alone with myself," he said. "Some people need company all the time. I don't need that."

If the sun was out, he'd sometimes take a walk alone. The solitude was a pleasant gift after the hectic first months in the seminary. It was nice just to think without the pressure of conversation, especially the small talk with seminarians he barely knew or wanted to know. Their mutual interests—besides prayer and discussions of faith—rarely overlapped. Tran never bothered to buy a guidebook of Rome.

"I'm not interested in going around to see the new, special, wonderful things in the world—either religious or secular things," he said. "Maybe sometime in the future. Now, I need to look inside me."

Tran is so thin his neck muscles ripple like bits of plucked wire when he tosses back his black hair, carefully parted to one side. He moves through the seminary like a wisp. He's a stranger to the hyper-American energy of the seminary; a foreigner living among foreigners.

Tran's separateness, however, does not mean loneliness. He is solitary by choice, enjoying the barrier that the seminary walls can offer. The landmarks of his faith—the churches in Rome, the centuries of art— hold very little interest. Even the Vatican and the papal audiences seem extraneous. Tran at first politely declined to join other seminarians for their sightseeing trips around Rome. Soon, the invitations stopped coming.

"You go out to see things because you have a desire to see things," he said, sometimes falling into a stutter while looking for the English word. "I have no desire like that. Right now, at this stage of life, I'm interested in something more internal."

The walls of his room are bare except for prayer cards of some saints. His favorite is St. Theresa of Lisieux, a nineteenth-century French nun whose "Little Way" to holiness stressed simplicity and ordinary acts of charity. St. Theresa is one of Chris Nalty's favorites as well. "She rules," he roars. Tran quietly says: "She is goodness."

Tran's room is extra chilly without a rug. He decided he didn't need one. He doesn't require much. It's been that way as far back as he can remember. Spirit, inner strength count. "Things," he says, "are just something that—how do you say?—come and go."

Tran, his mother, grandmother, and his two brothers and sister left Saigon on a creaky bus carrying refugees out of the city. His mother's stoic facade broke down as the bus groaned north. She buried her face in her palms and cried the tears of a woman fearing she may never feel her husband's embrace again. The growling bus engine drowned out her sobs. Diesel fumes leaked out of rusty bus exhaust. The nauseating smell—sometimes strong on Rome's narrow streets—still makes Tran recall the trip.

The Communists ordered Tran's father to remain in Saigon along with the other South Vietnamese officials and police. The family couldn't stay, they said. No, Tran's mother demanded, I'm staying with my husband. But she realized it was impossible. Tran's father was being herded off to a camp. "Re-education" was the word they used. She knew what it really meant: work, torture, starvation. A death sentence most likely, but not quick like a bullet in the head. This was worse.

She couldn't stay in Saigon. There were too many informers. Too much danger for the children of a South Vietnamese police officer who used to have American officers over for dinner now and then. At least back in Da Nang, she knew the neighbors and could better sense if danger was closing in. At least she used to.

"We'll see your father soon," she told Tran, leading him by the hand to the bus. He saw she had been crying. He wanted to as well, but even his eight-year-old senses told him it would only make everything worse.

"It was the first time in my life I was really suffering," Tran recalled. "It was just the beginning. The worst thing was thinking: 'What's going to happen next?'"

They found out two days later when the bus rattled into Da Nang. Their house was looted bare. The Vietcong forces took everything except a heavy wooden bed too cumbersome to drag away. The other rooms were stripped clean. Tran looked out in the gutters and their small garden for any of his toys and books—the historic tales and fables that his parents pieced together for the children. Nothing but some broken glass and spent bullet cartridges. That night it rained—a drumroll on the tin roof that echoed in the empty home. They were fortunate the house was listed under a relative's name. If the Communists knew it belonged to a South Vietnamese policeman, it would certainly have been taken over or burned down.

"Mother?" Tran asked, lying down on one of the few mats they could scrounge from neighbors. "Will father be all right?"

"Yes."

"You know?" he blinked. "You do?"

"Don't you have faith?" she said.

Tran nodded and listened to the rain. He couldn't decide whether it was scary or comforting.

Weeks later, word arrived. Tran's father was at a camp near Saigon, about four hundred miles south of Da Nang. They needed police permission to make the visit. Free travel was banned under the new regime. Tran's mother, thin and tired, knew what awaited her at police headquarters. "Why do you want to go see a criminal?" the officers taunted. "You are better without him." She took the abuse and kept coming back. Finally, she had travel papers. The Communists allowed Tran's mother to keep her public-school teaching job, but the pay now was almost nothing. It took every bit of money they had to buy the bus tickets for the family to head south again.

They carried several kilos of rice, dried fruit, and clothes for Tran's father. The camp guards allowed families to bring food to prisoners who didn't make trouble. "Otherwise," Tran said, "they would starve." The camp diet of rice and unclean water withered those with no help coming from outside. Tran begged his father not to make trouble in the camp. Any infraction would mean an end of visiting privileges— almost a certain death sentence.

"Don't worry," he said, hugging Tran. "I'll be fine."

But Tran could feel how thin his father had become. Some bruises were on his cheek. Tran was too afraid to ask how they got there.

The family was given a half-hour together in a stuffy room. The children wanted to climb all over their father. Tran had to explain to his younger brothers that, no, their father couldn't come home just yet. This was really all he knew himself: the Communists won the war and their father's side lost. He was too young to fully understand why. "Dad, Dad," the younger boys yelled, "come home." He settled them down with a quick stare, then went off to the side with his wife. They hugged and whispered encouragement to each other until the guards said it was time to go.

Tran's family was marked. They were petite bourgeoisie of the losing side. They were unapologetically religious. Tran's uncle, a priest with the Redemptorist order, denounced the Communists long and loud enough to end up under house arrest for three years. The police harassed Tran and his family relentlessly. Tran's mother was mocked each time she went to ask for permission to travel to the camp to see her husband. Trouble getting money and the travel papers meant they could only go twice a year at most.

Their refuge became the church, a small wooden building built in the simple missionary style. Communists had a strict warning: keep it inside the four walls of the church. Any missionary work, any charitable group, and the church was at risk of being padlocked. For a little while inside, however, they could forget about the way their lives had been shredded by war. Tran learned the hymns and memorized every word of the mass, celebrated in Vietnamese. He watched every move of the priest—who once seemed so ordinary. But now, to the skinny boy who the Communists mocked as an "American," the priest seemed heroic and unafraid. He was rooted in something bigger than any baton-swinging policeman or revolutionary slogan, no matter how loud and long it was chanted. Tran thought, just maybe, he was looking at his own future up there at the altar draped with white linen. He prayed for his father's freedom. His prayed for an end to his mother's tears, which she held back until she was alone. He prayed because it was the one thing no one could control.

"When you push someone to the corner, this person naturally has to react. It has to defend itself," Tran said. "When you publicly denounce, attack the religion and identity of a person, you force this person to make an act on behalf of the things he loves and respects."

"For faith to be mature and to be perfect, it needs to spend time in the hard soil of trouble."

During the Christmas holiday, Tran sometimes picked a single flower. It reminded him of the "Little Flower," St. Therese. Little acts are important to him, contemplating a single bud or stopping everything just to savor the sound of the wind. This is how he copes. Concentrate on the small things, the ordinary pleasures. The mountain of problems in the United States does not blot out the sun. Believe it can change, he says, and anything is possible. "Faith," he says, "makes things happen.

"Confronting between good and evil—between dark and light— you make an act of faith. Even people in a crisis of morality, they can make an act of faith. Something even little can do it. It can just be one tiny act. To say no to a drug one time, make a prayer rather than make an act of aggression.

"With this act, then they can convert to the light. It can be a dramatic conversion. It can happen like that." Tran clicks his thin fingers.

With the new year still hours away, the explosions began. Italians welcome the new year with bottle rockets, fire crackers, and just about anything else that makes noise. About twenty minutes into 1996, the clouds drifted away from Rome. Glittering bursts dissolved into a sky of stars. Tran lay in the darkness of his room and listened to the city grow still.

CHAPTER XII

IRELAND

Dispel the mists around us.

—INTERCESSION FOR MONDAY EVENING
OF THE FIRST WEEK OF ADVENT

Brian Christensen's year arrived in fits.

"OK, here we go," shouted a guy pointing to his watch. The rest of the pub crowd joined in: "Three . . . two . . . one. Happy New Year!"

Brian raised his pint of coal-black Guinness stout and gave Kristin a kiss on the cheek.

"Happy New Year," he whispered. "God bless."

"And you, too," she said.

They started looking around for a quieter corner to talk when someone else yelled over the celebrations: "Wait, wait. My watch says we have thirty seconds to go." They all counted down again. Another toast. Another kiss in the smoky County Mayo pub with no clock on the wall.

A minute later, another second hand on another wristwatch swept toward twelve. "Now," its owner promised, "it's really New Year's."

A fresh calendar. Resolutions. "Auld lang syne." All the cozy images of newborn January seemed less hackneyed to Brian this time around. This time, it was true. This was one of those rare times when everything was in play. Life, for a while, was intoxicatingly immediate. It would pivot one direction or another: away from the seminary or back to the fold. Brian knew it had to go one way or another. He just didn't know which direction. His past relationships—even the decision to join the priesthood—unfolded slowly. The crucial moments never had the heart-pounding urgency he now felt in Ireland. He had a few days with Kristin. Everything had significance: each word, an inflection, a touch. Was it accidental or meaningful? Was there something worth following at any cost? They were there to find out.

Yet now, in the first minutes of the new year, it was still as murky as Christensen's half-empty Guinness.

Their cautious flirting and the long talks about religion had grown into a bond that quaked with something that seemed dangerously close to love. They each sought advice from priests and received the same answer: patience. Maybe God really wants you together. That is certainly possible. Then again, maybe He is truly calling Brian to the priesthood and this is a test—the kind of temptation He often lobs in the way of priestly vocations. Pray about it, the priests said.

When Brian first heard priests encourage prayer for problem solving, he was disappointed. A cop-out, he thought. No wonder the Church has problems. The time in the seminary, however, had radically changed his view. Brian was now deeply committed to prayer. It stabilized his life. It was like his daily run when he was in training for hockey. If he didn't do it, he felt uneasy and antsy. He was experiencing what the priests were talking about: let the serenity of prayer open you up to yourself. "It all comes back to being honest with yourself," Brian told me. "Once you do that, the solution to any problem just shows itself like a big beacon." He believed he was making some real progress with his prayer life in the seminary. Except one obstacle remained. He could not avoid the question of Kristin.

She, too, found no epiphany. "Is this what He wants? For us to be together?" she asked before coming to Ireland. "It's so easy to say, 'Yes, we see it.' It's so much harder to say, 'Let's wait and really decide what road we should follow.'"

The pub was crowded with people toasting the new year and trying to get in one last beer before closing. Brian and Kristin were forced to stand close. Too close for real conversation—at least the type they wanted. They kept the banter light. Kristin told him about her plans to continue her aid work with the diocese in Joliet, Illinois, where she moved after getting her degree in Minnesota. Brian answered the predictable questions about Rome. Have you seen the pope? Yes, several times. How are the other seminarians? Interesting. Very diverse. Do you feel stronger about your calling? On this one, Brian paused.

"You know," he said, "there are many different types of callings. A calling to a marriage and a relationship can be just as valid as one to the priesthood."

"I know that," she said, keeping her eyes down. Brian waited for her to add something—anything—to give him a clue. She changed the subject. They safely reminisced. "Remember the Sun Dance?" he asked. He had thought often about it—the last time they were together.

Kristin was on the back of his red Harley riding through the ancient weather-worn buttes outside Rapid City. The gullies and ravines collect water and allow things to grow. "It's like riding on top of the trees," he said. She squeezed his chest as he punched the bike into full throttle. The speedometer on his Sportster 1200 licked 100. Everything was moving fast, faster. Then he eased back to 70. She still squeezed tight. "Real romantic sparks," Christensen recalled. "I could feel them."

Just three weeks before he was to leave for Rome, they agreed to meet in South Dakota. Brian wanted to see a few friends and take care of some details—like selling his cherished motorcycle that every year he'd scrub clean for the annual fest of rumbling bikes and tattooed bikers in Sturgis, South Dakota. Kristin's Ireland trip was not yet definite. They assumed this could be the last time together for at least a year.

One night they drove out to the Rosebud Reservation to watch the bloody ending of the Sioux Sun Dance. For four days, young men from the tribe danced inside a ceremonial medicine lodge created by poles surrounding a central cottonwood tree. The annual event has been practiced in slightly different variations among the Plains tribes since the eighteenth century, when the widespread domestication of horses speeded long-distance travel and allowed various traditions to spread and intermingle. It was a chance to collectively seek supernatural favors and insights. Today, the dynamics of the rituals remain generally unchanged except that pickup trucks have replaced the horses ringing the site. But now there are also new deities to appease: the sun-reddened tourists and their money.

Brian brought Kristin to the final hours, when the dancers pierce the skin of their chest with skewers attached by rope to the cottonwood. They continue to dance. The skewers are ripped out, leaving shallow flesh wounds. The blood represents the sincerity of their petitions to the spirits.

Out of respect, Kristin wore a head scarf and long peasant skirt. No one asked her to dress modestly. It was a religious ceremony and it seemed appropriate. Her empathy—the acute consciousness of her surroundings—always so impressed Brian. He came out to the reservation to learn a bit about the culture he hoped to serve if he becomes a priest. But he was distracted. He kept turning to look at Kristin's face. He could tell she saw something else.

"There's beauty in their suffering," she said. "Can't you see it?"

Brian wanted to. He always was trying to see what she saw, feel what she felt. It was a frustrating endeavor. Brian imagined her senses and perceptions were so much more acute than his. He had always believed in different levels of spiritual dexterity: the ability to perceive and comprehend the web of the greater cosmos; to appreciate the connections and intersections that everything possesses. Brian never considered there was a sort of caste system of the soul, in which you were bound to one stratum. Being open—listening, learning, praying—could enlighten even the most self-absorbed bore. But some people were simply born holy, he was convinced. He counted Kristin among them. "She is," he admitted later, "close to perfection for me."

She repeated her question. "Can't you see it?"

He looked over but said nothing. Their faces were in chiaroscuro, stark in purple shadows and red-orange fire light. "What? See what?" he asked.

"The surrender," she said simply. "Their bodies, their flesh—they are all given over. They know there will be suffering, but it's done willingly, almost joyfully. To watch someone else in pain is always painful. But it is so powerful and raw, this kind of spirituality."

Brian was pleased. For once, he felt he could offer something to her spiritual outlook. He knew she would never forget the Sun Dance. Everything that night had an edge. They walked slowly, trying to wring more time before they parted. Brian drove at an easy pace back to Rapid City under the late summer shooting stars.

As their reunion in Ireland neared, Brian found all the old feelings for Kristin were suddenly uncorked—either coming as a stab of longing or a butterfly tickle that suggested love.

What surprised Brian was not the persistence of the yearning but its depth. It ran like a fracture—down into the foundation of his calling. Abandoning his vocation had once seemed the radical option. It seemed less and less outlandish a few days before the North American College closed for Christmas break. His plans: visit some friends in Paris, then fly to Ireland on the last day of the year.

"When I first came to Rome I felt very confident that I was in the right place. I mean, very confident. But it was like I was fooling myself," he said before leaving Rome. "I knew my feelings—my love—for Kristin were not settled. In the back of my mind, I was wondering, 'Why does God have this very special friend in my life right now?' It doesn't make sense. I don't get it.

"I had a struggle where I didn't think I had a struggle," he said.

In Dublin, Kristin waited for Christensen's plane in an airport growing quiet for the holiday night. December 31 is a light travel day. The bus she took from her cousin's hometown of Carlow—down in the spearmint-green hills and earthy-smelling peat of Mayo—arrived early. She always was amused by how the Irish bundle themselves so heavily in the winter. To her, the penetrating Irish dampness was a relief from the icy deadness in the Midwest. She wondered if Brian would be shivering with his Mediterranean-thinned blood. She wondered about a lot. Was this New Year's a beginning or an end?

"I'm here waiting for a seminarian I love," she said to herself. "A peculiar situation, I would say."

Then there he was, wearing jeans and ski jacket. Just like before. If Rome had changed him, it wasn't superficial. She really didn't know what to expect but found herself overjoyed to see nothing obviously different. She thought again as they hugged and Brian gave her a kiss. It wasn't a polite kiss between friends nor was it the intimate kiss of lovers. It was somewhere in between.

They took a bus to Carlow, arriving just in time to reach the pub for the elusive stroke of midnight.

Brian wanted to stay up and talk. He had gone over so many of the lines on the plane. He was bursting to get them out. And they all intersected at one point: what should we do? He was plowing toward a resolution between them with the same intensity he searched for a breakthrough in his prayers. Not everything, though, fits snugly in the framework of identify the problem, fix it, and move on. Love—whether religious or romantic—moves to its own slippery tempo.

"Kristin, listen. I've been doing a lot of praying about this and . . ."

She cut him off. "Take it easy, Brian. We have all week."

But she already had a feeling where they were headed. As usual, she was a few jumps ahead. She noticed the strain first. Time apart had severed something vital and it wasn't reconnecting. The physical attraction survived, no doubt. Something soulful was absent. "There wasn't that comfort anymore," she confided to someone asking about Brian. "I don't know how best to describe it. We just weren't clicking."

They circled for days, moving by degrees toward the point where there's no more room to spin away from the question. Gradually, Brian was sensing that the emotional distance between them was unlikely to shrink. Each time he'd hunt for that romantic singe he felt so distinctly on the Harley in South Dakota, Kristin would parry. She would either deftly change the subject or grow silent, which at first didn't seem unusual to Brian. When they first met they would often spend time walking or sitting without feeling the need to talk—a contented silence they both relished. But Kristin's hush in Ireland was pulling inward, too personal to share.

"Are you all right?" Brian kept asking.

She'd snap back from her thoughts. "Sure," she'd say. "Absolutely fine."

One day they set out early on a walk. They had an ambitious plan: a nearly twenty-mile circuit along the back roads of Mayo. Brian's visit was nearing its end and still the question of their relationship was not definitively settled. Brian kept recalling the analogy used by his spiritual director. Let the puzzle work itself out. Allow the water to clear. All the hints said they were not heading for the transforming union, with Brian abandoning the seminary and Kristin putting aside her consideration of joining a religious order. Neither of them, however, was ready to formally declare their flirtation over. Brian was especially reluctant to say they had no chance. He knew that once the statement was made, they would start immediately drifting apart. Maybe his old passions were not dying, as Rector Dolan urged. Being around Kristin was still captivating.

Along a small road, just wide enough for them to walk side by side, Kristin bent down to look at a little grove of smooth stones blanketed by a fuzzy moss.

"Brian, come here," she said. "Look at this." She ran her hand over the green strands soft as a baby's hair. "It's beautiful, isn't it?"

Again, Brian tried to see what she was seeing—just a quick glance through her very different perspective that can draw out complexity and fascination in the most ordinary places. He rubbed the moss and waited for an insight that never came.

"Kristin?" he asked. She anticipated the question.

"You know, Brian, I am very happy for you."

"You are? I have been trying to tell you all week how much I've missed you."

"I know. And I've missed you, too. But I can be happy for you at the same time, can't I? The seminary fits you. I can see it."

"I wish I could," said Brian, getting up and rubbing his wet hands on his jeans. "I mean, I do feel like I belong in the seminary. It's just, just . . . I want to be sure that my calling isn't someplace else."

"You mean whether God is calling you to me. I know He is, Brian, in some way. But I can see now that it's to be friends, to encourage each other along."

"And what about, you know, something deeper?" Brian asked.

Kristin took his hand. "You know we could drop everything and just be together if we wanted. We could do it. But is that right? I know it's not. I know you are where you are supposed to be. Your calling is to be a priest. Can't you see it?"

"I can. Most times, that is," Brian said. "But it was always there: why did God put you in my way at this time?"

"Don't think so much, Brian," she said. "Maybe it was just to have a special friend to take a walk together with like this. Priests need friends, too."

"You better believe it."

"You know, Brian, I'm kind of envious of you."

Brian laughed. It seemed such a surprising statement from the person he considered almost saintlike. "Envious of me? Why?"

"It's not obvious? Because you've found your way. I'm still looking."

"For what, Kristin?"

"For exactly what you've found: my calling."

Brian's instinct was to keep talking it out. But, surprisingly, he was speechless. She was right. He knew it. What could he add? He felt relief as anyone does when a difficult decision seems resolved. There was something else though.

Regret maybe? Or perhaps a pang of sentimental sorrow? It wasn't the wrenching parting like he had with Meredith. He and Kristin had been careful not to push themselves into a place where the choice would be everything or nothing. No, Brian mourned something else: his vision of a perfect relationship that he had held onto as long as possible—all the way to a skinny road in Ireland that he found leads back to Rome.

They walked a while. Brian said softly: "Love you."

"Love you too," Kristin answered.

They both knew exactly what they meant.

The ride to the airport was quiet.

Everything had been said. The visit ended just as it began a week before: a long hug. This one, however, was not between two people wondering how hot the flame will grow.

"There's incredible love between us. It's obvious. I'm very attracted to her," said Christensen a few weeks after he returned to Rome. "She's just my . . . my call, my desire. But also the call to do what I'm doing is so strong. I think it's so right after spending time with her and sharing exactly these same thoughts with her. Now, finally, I feel solid—I guess whole is the better word—in my vocation."

Kristin went home and joined a program in the Joliet diocese to assist homeless and unemployed people in a hard-luck area where troubles just seem to pile deeper and deeper.

"It's hard now to see us in a different light—him there, me here. But that's the way it is. We have to accept it," she said.

"Brian, to me, is a gift I couldn't keep. He's a gift from God."

CHAPTER XIII

MONKS

My eyes grow weak gazing heavenward:
O Lord, I am in straits, be my surety.

—CANTICLE FOR TUESDAY MORNINGS
(ISAIAH 38:14)

The monk listened patiently while Gary Benz tried to describe his anguish.

More than a month had gone by since he came within a heartbeat of writing the letters that would have sealed his decision to leave the seminary and join the Benedictines. Since then, it has been purgatory. How could he best explain this to this gentle monk sitting so patiently on an old wooden chair?

Gary didn't want to appear like he was wavering. That would lead to another open-ended chat just like with Dolan and the seminary advisers. Gary didn't want the monk to tell him to wait, think it over. He was looking for a push. Anything to confirm his desire to return to North Dakota and join the monastery. So be careful what you tell the monk, Gary told himself. Edit yourself. Keep the conversation focused. This could be the clarity he needed.

What should I say? Gary thought. Quickly. How do I answer?

"A dangling feeling," Gary told him. Something like a suspended step. Going back offered no promise of comfort, but the ground ahead seemed somehow craggy and unsteady.

"You're not happy, Gary," the monk said. He was also from North Dakota. He knew how to read faces.

"No," Gary said. "Not really."

After his adviser persuaded him to stick out the semester, Gary thought there would be a nice respite; a breather before confronting his vocation again. Only it grew worse. He watched the other New Men evolve. Their discussions about prayer and faith were incisive and vital. Their friendships tightened. They started talking about their own diaconate ceremony and ordination—still years away but becoming a clearer and more tangible goal. In Gary's eyes, it was almost as if they were swelling to fit the ideal Rector Dolan constantly implores: sane, stable, spiritual priests. He felt himself shrinking—more and more disconnected from the seminary and the other New Men. Gary stayed on the fringe, listening to seminarians he may leave behind and listlessly watching the preparations for Christmas at the Vatican. Gary thought: the next time I see the square the pope's Christmas tree will be down and my mind will be made up.

"I'm struggling," he told the monk. "I'm really struggling."

Gary visited the monk just before leaving to spend the Christmas break at a Benedictine monastery in southern Germany. The monk had been sent by Assumption Abbey to study at San Anselmo College in Rome. Perfect, Gary thought. If anyone can understand this dangling feeling, it will be this monk. He'll remind me why I need to become a Benedictine. It all gets so drowned out in the seminary. The monk, Gary told himself, will bring me back to simplicity.

Only the monk just sat there while Gary spoke. Gary was getting nervous. Say something, anything, he was thinking. Why won't he help me? But the monk was quiet, almost impassive, as Gary rattled on. There were no "welcome home, brother" embraces that Gary anticipated.

"The seminary isn't right for me," Gary continued, growing bolder in his declarations and trying to push the monk to respond. "I'm called to the Benedictines. I believe that sincerely. I should have joined right after high school and saved myself all this pain."

"Why didn't you?" the monk finally said.

"Well, I have to say it was a friend. My best friend, actually. When I told him I wanted to become a priest, he said to me, 'Gary, why are you throwing away your life? You can do so much more than that.' You know what? That really shook me up and got me second-guessing my vocation. 'Maybe he's right,' I thought. So I just thrashed about during college. I couldn't decide on a major and felt out of place. It was only after graduation that I knew my vocation was real."

The monk waited to see if Gary was finished. Gary was rubbing his hands together—something he does when he's anxious. Then the monk asked: "So then, what is your vocation?"

Gary sighed. Was he not listening? This was no different from the vocations director at the diocese. Gary rubbed his hands harder. He's not listening to me.

"I've been trying to tell you," Gary said. "I can't make it any more plain. My calling is to be a Benedictine, live at the monastery, and serve the people of North Dakota. It's very clear."

"It's not so clear to me," the monk said.

"What do you mean?" Gary pleaded.

"What I'm saying is this: you say you have a vocation to the Benedictine order. Fine. But then you tell me you feel a vocation to be a pastor to the farmers. Where does the monastery fit in, Gary? What about the community of brothers there?"

Gary blurted: "That would be my home, my base, my spiritual center even if I was out in the parish. There are many who do that, right? You can have both. Others have both."

Gary was correct. Over the decades, dozens of monks from Assumption Abbey have become ordained and worked in parishes around North Dakota to help offset the shortage of diocesan priests. They run some of the far-flung parishes that may have only a few Catholic families.

"But, Gary, you're not hearing my question. Listen to what I'm asking: What is your true calling? Is it the priesthood or the monastic life? You can have both, as you know. But your first and only real vocation must be to the monastery and the community of monks. You can't think of yourself as a part-time monk. We don't need monks like that."

Benz swallowed hard. How ironic. That's what Dolan says, too: we don't need halfway priests.

The monk's tone softened. "Look, Gary, I don't mean to be harsh. It's just that sometimes you have to be blunt to get people to really assess the truth. There's nothing saying you can't join the order. God knows we'd love to have you if your vocation is there. And you could become ordained and go out into a parish. It's all possible. But you have to realize it's not in your hands. It's the community of monks that decides. The community takes precedence. Listen, it may be that we need your talents in the monastery. You must be fully ready to accept anything and everything for the good of the community—even if it means not working with parishioners right away or maybe never. So I'll ask you again: where does your true calling lie?"

"I . . . I just don't know if you put it that way. I feel so torn apart by this. Why is it so hard to serve God? Why?"

"It's not hard at all, Gary. What's hard, if you ask me, is trying to really decide how God wants you to serve. Don't do something like join the monastery because you think it's right. Wait until you know it's right."

"And when will that be?" Gary said. "Look, I'm on track here to be a diocesan priest. If I wait one or two more years, I'm going to be staring at ordination and maybe still unsure about my calling. Tell me, please, what am I going to do?"

"Gary, Gary," the monk urged. "Don't beat yourself up over this. Take your time. There's no rush. We'd take you in the monastery at any time. We just want you to be certain that's where you want to be."

"But do you think it's fair to keep going in the seminary if I'm not sure this is right?"

"Do you think it's fair to the monastery to enter the community if you're not sure it's right for you?"

Honesty is like an antiseptic on a wound, Dolan sometimes tells the seminarians. It can sting, but it cleans and heals. A vocation is nothing more than an honest choice. He makes sure the New Men understand: don't trap yourself into believing that a priestly vocation is some-how more noble than the other options. Look at men who become wonderful fathers. Isn't that also a vocation? Look at teachers. How can that work be less important in God's eyes? "Sure, the priesthood demands perhaps a special dedication and self-understanding," Dolan told a group of New Men at dinner one night. "But everyone can't be called to the priesthood. Just like everyone can't play Major League baseball. Some got it, some don't." One of the New Men at the table de-scribed the moment he knew his vocation was right as a feeling similar to coming up from deep underwater. The water gets brighter until the sunbeams reflect all around like silver confetti. Then you break the surface and gulp in the air.

Dolan was keeping out of Gary's way. He wanted Gary to work it out on his own as best as possible. Every vocation has a crossroads. Most are clear: bail out or stick with the seminary. Gary's, however, was more subtle, more interior. "This type of thing maybe takes even more honesty," said the rector.

After leaving the monk, Gary walked back to the seminary, pulling his coat tight around his neck. Back in North Dakota, winter drizzle would be considered a nice break from the icy clamp. Gary shivered. Rome's back streets can seem so dank and empty on foul win-ter days. Everything and everyone is pulled inside.

The monk says: pray about it. The seminary says: pray about it. He was starting to be a little irritated by their catch-all answer. Of course I've been praying about it, he wanted to shout. What I'm waiting for is an answer.

The Christmas break had come just in time—a chance to get out of the seminary and try to straighten things out. Gary walked along the Tiber, stepping carefully so not to slip on the slick leaves on the uneven sidewalk. Gary was planning to spend early January at a Benedictine monastery near the birthplace of his paternal grandparents. Gary's par-ents spoke German at home when they were children. Gary and the others picked up enough to get by. Maybe this will be the place—in the solitude of the monastery—where he can answer the monk's defining question?

Life can turn on a word. Gary knew it well. He thought about how the old priest's stories of the Bible whetted his interest in the faith as a young student boarding at school; how his friend's comments estranged him from his vocation for four years in college. Now, the monk ambushed him with demands he had never considered.

"You never know how one small word, a tiny gesture, is going to affect someone," Gary told me that night. "It has to be always on your mind that every action has a consequence."

When he got back to the seminary—wet and chilled—a present was waiting. The vocations director of the North Dakota diocese sent him a book for Christmas. It was a typically thoughtful act from the monsignor who helped Gary reconsider his calling to the priesthood during college. He was one of the few people who had the patience to listen to Gary, to help rebuild his confidence in his calling. It made a difference. "Other priests I talked to would just kind of give me their card and say, 'Call me if you feel a calling.' It's like some sort of hotline or something," Benz said.

He unwrapped the heavy brown mailing paper around the book. Normally, he would stick a new book on the shelf until he finished what he was reading at the time. But this one intrigued him: *Abandonment to Divine Providence,* attributed to an eighteenth-century Jesuit, Jean-Pierre de Caussade. The book was actually published more than one hundred years after de Caussade's death and is a compilation of letters between spiritual directors and nuns who followed de Caussade's doctrine of inner peace as the essential ingredient for all spirituality. Gary thumbed through the first few pages. He sat down and continued reading. He finished after midnight.

"It's about basically turning everything over to Him," said Benz. "Not doing something irrational, but letting the Holy Spirit work in your life. Things may happen slowly and maybe not on the time schedule you want, but it will happen."

The message was like cooling salve for Benz. What was the rush to join the monastery? he thought. He could always stay in the seminary at least until the end of the first year. There was no point in making any move until he sorted his own mind. Was he a monk or a priest? Was his home the monastery or seminary?

"Wouldn't you sometimes just love a big sign to drop out of heaven saying: this way?" he sighed.

He was glad when the train pulled out of Rome's squat Termini station. He needed new surroundings. He wanted to be around the Benedictines again.

Gary arrived in time for vespers. The monks sang in Latin and Gary followed along as best he could. It felt wonderful to let the psalm tones wash over him. The way they swell, round and whole, bigger and bigger, then recede. Like breathing. The sounds echoed to every corner of the old stone church in the Bavarian lowlands. For a while, there was just the psalms and the voices and no room for anything else: jealousies, impatience are crowded out. It's just the rolling sounds of the psalms. Gary closed his eyes and imagined the music flowing right through him like a cleansing bath.

The evening chill had set in. Gary liked the feeling of real winter after the damp ambiguity of Rome. He tried to identify all the familiar smells: candle wax, pine, fireplace smoke. The stained-glass images of St. Benedict looked muted and stern at night. Darkness came earlier north of the Alps. It all reminded Benz so much of winter evenings at Assumption Abbey back home.

"When is morning mass?" Gary asked as they left the church.

The abbot looked startled. "Gary, you're on vacation," he said. "Sleep in. There's a later mass that's open to the public. Come then if you want. Please, relax while you're here."

Benz didn't argue. He'd been getting up at dawn since late August and some extra sleep—even an hour or so—would seem a luxury. "Fine," he said, then headed to his room. It was the archetypal monastery guest quarters: desk, simple bed, and a Bible. Gary had planned to read a bit. But, finally alone, he realized how terribly exhausted he was. December had been a blur—an emotional tug-of-war with no clear winner. He hadn't really decompressed from it all yet.

In the little monastery room, Gary sat on the edge of the bed. There were scuffles and creaks outside the door as the monks went off to their rooms. Gary tried to imagine he was one of them; that his world was defined by the monastery and its needs.

Is this what I want? he wondered. Do those footsteps outside the door sound like mine? He fell asleep thinking these things. Sometime later, he woke. For an instant, as it often happens to travelers, he didn't know where he was.

The next morning, Gary thought he missed mass. The church was empty. He checked his watch. No, he still had fifteen minutes. He sat down in a pew and waited, letting himself slip into contemplative prayer. He tried to blank everything out. Feel your heartbeat, your breath. Try to sense God, his spiritual director told him. Gary never had the trouble of the other seminarians to grasp these deeper levels of prayer. It seemed natural. Gary is restrained in most aspects of his life, but with prayer he is uninhibited: always seeking ways to enhance the experience.

An old woman came in and kicked off the snow from her boots. It had snowed lightly the night before. Gary couldn't wait to get outside and take a long walk. Soon, a few other people arrived—mostly women, the anchor of Church congregations worldwide. There were a couple of men who looked like pensioners. Mass began.

Gary glanced over the thin congregation. It made him smile. After these months with seminarians and monks and tourist-packed Vatican events, it was nice to be back with ordinary people at an ordinary mass. Gary waited in the short communion line and opened his mouth for the host. He didn't like taking it in his palm.

Each day it was the same: Gary attending the regular morning mass, then praying the Liturgy of the Hours with the monks at midday, afternoon, and vespers. Oddly, he found himself looking most forward to the mornings. "I can't really explain it," said Benz, "but being around the people was, like, giving me energy, revitalizing me. So I'm thinking: 'What does this mean?' "

Just before he was to return to Rome, Gary approached one of the monks. They had shared some meals together and Gary enjoyed his company.

"Brother? Do you have a minute?"

Out in the monastery yard, they walked side by side. Gary recounted what the Benedictine in Rome told him.

"He's right, you know," the monk said.

"I know. But I've given the seminary a try. Don't you think it would be wise to do the same thing with the monastery? I could spend a year with the Benedictines before I make up my mind."

"You could do that," the monk replied. "But be clear about your motives. The monastery is not a place to run for escape."

Gary frowned—about as openly angry as he ever shows. "I've been going back and forth on this for a long time. This isn't some rash move, you know."

"I know, I know," the monk said, touching Gary's shoulder. "What I'm saying is that entering a monastery may be harder than you think."

"Harder?" Gary asked.

"In the sense that you'll find yourself always peering right down into your soul in the monastery. It can be a raw experience. On top of that, there is all the work that needs to be done around the place. If you are not sure of your calling to the order, Gary, it can be even tougher. It may make you even more confused."

"So what do you suggest?"

"Prayer, of course. The answer will come."

"Please," he said in exasperation. "Everyone says that. But I've been praying about it. All the time I pray about it. Yet I still don't know what to do."

"Maybe God's given you the answer already and you don't recognize it. Possible?"

Gary stopped walking and turned to the monk. "You think so?"

"I don't know. I'm just saying, don't force a decision. That's when you get yourself into trouble."

On the train back to Rome, Gary watched the Italian peninsula scroll past through his second-class coach window, the alpine snow giving way to the brown winter fields and bare trees of the Po Valley, then back up to the gray-rock mountains rising over olive groves and terraced fields scratched out long ago by farmers. The train passed through tunnels and into the depressing concrete-and-steel apartment blocks on the outskirts of Rome.

At least he had made one decision: don't stay so distant from the other New Men. Why just look at them with envy or frustration? Maybe they can help. Gary was never like this growing up. He always considered himself tolerant, very generous in his opinions of others. Even his older sister, who became a hardline Baptist and trashed the Catholic Church, was not judged harshly. Lately, however, Gary was picking at the perceived faults of others. Maybe wrestling with his vocation made him yearn for some perfect place that just doesn't exist? That could be it, he guessed. Anyway, it's got to stop. He didn't like who he was becoming.

"I realize that when I was looking at other people or seeing seminarians . . . there were some people who didn't do nice things," he said after coming back from Germany. "But I'm realizing I can't criticize them for what they've done, because at some point I don't know the good that they've done. They may have touched people in a profound way. I'm going to try actively to see the good.

"Have you ever heard of St. Therese? Well, she was known as 'Little Flower.' She was always so concerned about what she was doing in life. She always saw other people who were big flowers blooming and doing well and successful and so holy and alive with the Spirit. She was just a little flower compared to all these other giant flowers. Well, that's how I want to start looking at my life. I say, 'Imagine that I'm a little flower and God is going to water me and I'll get to the height that God wants me to and, maybe, I'll be a big, beautiful flower.'"

Gary had just finished his last exam, taken several weeks after the seminarians returned from Christmas break. It was the new and nerve-jangling experience of the oral testing system. All the North American College seminarians—either at the Greg or the Ang—have to make the adjustment to the Italian-style system. It all comes down to two oral finals a year: the first in January and the others ending in June.

The question could be anything. Explain the theological views of pope such and such? Tell me the roots for the schism between Rome and the Orthodox churches? Anything from the material covered. Gary felt good. He didn't nail the questions as well as he could, but he knew his stuff. He also knew his limitations. He wasn't going to be able to slide through the orals on the strength of a smoke screen of eloquence. Few, if any, can. The professors have no problem in failing a seminarian, especially a New Man. "Come back," they would say at the winter exams, "when the leaves are green." All Gary got was stony stares and a curt "thank you" at the end of each oral.

Gary really hadn't expected to even go this far. He once thought he'd be out of the seminary well before midterms. But there he was in Rome along with the other New Men—all of them. No one had left. Gary wondered if he'd be the first.

CHAPTER XIV

MARDI GRAS

When you fast, do not put on a gloomy face like the hypocrites.

—ANTIPHON FOR THE CANTICLE OF ZECHARIAH
FOR ASH WEDNESDAY

The day of decadence came with a delicate perfume.

A rain storm had scrubbed the sky to a steel blue. Then a full day of sun coaxed out the flowers. Tiny white daisies opened on the seminary lawn and the field where they played the Spaghetti Bowl the past fall. Spring suddenly seemed very close.

A Mardi Gras party was Chris Nalty's idea and was months in the planning—the traditional New Orleans blow-out party before the forty days of Lenten fasting and self-sacrifice beginning with Ash Wednesday and ending with Easter. His choice of the Mardi Gras king was super secret. "The King and I," grinned Nalty. "We're the only ones who know." Nothing could chip off even a hint. He was impenetrable.

"Here," Nalty said, "taste this."

The victim's face spasmed like he was swallowing cinders. "Wa, wa, wa," he quivered. "Hee, hee, hee."

"Almost there," Nalty tsked. A little more pepper should do it. This was the jambalaya for risk takers—extra pepper, extra tabasco, extra anything to make it sear.

The finished product was labeled *"Pericolo di Morte"*—Danger of Death. Milder versions were laid out for lesser mortals, Nalty pointed out. The seminarians grabbed paper plates and lined up. Nalty hovered behind his killer concoction like a guardian angel.

"You sure?" he said to everyone reaching for the big spoon. More than a few were scared off.

The rector passed by in a trail of Macanudo smoke. "This is it," he said. "I'm giving up cigars for Lent."

Like the Spaghetti Bowl, Dolan encourages the seminarians to stage these bashes. There are few failings that irk Dolan more than a socially inept priest. It's part of your job to be comfortable with people, he tells them. "If you put yourself in an ivory tower, soon you'll find yourself very alone," he said. Dolan wouldn't say it directly to the seminarians, but personality may mean a lot in your ecclesiastical career. Few bishops were ever given the job because they were shy and unassuming.

Nalty lit up a Monte Cristo No. 4; rolled in Cuba. He planned on finally giving up cigarettes. Chris ducked out of the lounge.

Scot Landry nursed a beer by the bar. Usually, he'd be at the center of the festivities. But he no longer felt as he usually did. He had hoped by now to have the transfer process to Fall River under way. But it was still a secret to everyone but Roger and Father McRae, his spiritual director. They had decided it would be best to hold off making any decision until summer. He didn't want to be distracted from his study—either now or next fall—and it would still give Bridgeport a chance to send someone to Rome if they wanted.

It felt good for a while to slow down the transfer question. But Scot kept returning to the question that made him truly uneasy: could his vocation have run its course? Scot didn't even like to entertain the thought. But why, he asked himself, do I still feel uneasy? Why can't I let go? Scot looked over at Nalty. Chris seemed, with each passing month, to grow more comfortable with his decision to enter the seminary. Scot didn't like what he was feeling. It seemed dangerously close to envy.

"I would love to be a priest," Scot told me. "But I would hate to be a priest who felt like his heart wasn't in it. What a shame for both the Church and also for the priest."

At 8 P.M. sharp, Nalty reappeared wearing a red-and-black Harlequin costume that his parents shipped from home. The suit's gold trim sparkled as he put on an eerie flesh-tone mask and unrolled the proclamation.

"The king," he bellowed.

Side doors flapped open and two seminarians in bed-sheet togas entered pulling a luggage cart chariot. On top rode rex, a pudgy new priest named Nicholas Cirillo, sitting on a paisley print chair tied to the float.

On looks alone, Nalty's selection was superb. Cirillo had the overstuffed regal quality down cold. A nonchalant wave. A condescending half-smile. His plastic crown was jauntily askew.

"Stand or kneel," he yawned, "whatever is more comfortable."

His six-foot scroll unfurled. There were decrees to read.

"We, the king, declare the Pontifical North American College to be my palace, the Janiculum Hill is my throne, and the Pontifical Gregorian University my footstool." The seminarians roared. Few, however, noticed the biblical plagiarism.

The band broke into "When the Saints Come Marching In" and King Cirillo I was rolled through the lounge. Other seminarians in masks blew in through the side doors and started throwing confetti, plastic bead necklaces, and souvenir coins.

Brian Christensen, wearing a red Lone Ranger mask with fringe, was firing handfuls of necklaces over his shoulder. One hit Dolan square in the chest. He didn't notice. He was enjoying his last cigar for forty days.

PART THREE

PRING

HOME

Every shower and dew, bless the Lord.
All you winds, bless the Lord.
Fire and heat, bless the Lord.
Cold and chill, bless the Lord.

—CANTICLE FOR SUNDAY MORNING
(DANIEL 3:64–67)

They arrived in the dead hours.

Gary Benz had been in Italy for more than a half year but still often forgot about the sacrosanct afternoon siesta. There was no post-lunch repose at the seminary unless you decided on your own. Few seminarians did. The Benedictines at Subiaco, however, were closed tight. The doors wouldn't reopen for two more hours.

Gary and his friend, a seminarian from Washington, D.C., were alone in the terrace of broad gray stones warmed by early March sunshine—still not strong enough, though, to dry the puddles in the corners from a week of chilly gloom in the mountains. Gary's friend picked up a pebble and tossed it across the patio. The little stone ricocheted off a wall and dribbled to a stop. The rattling jarred Gary from his thoughts. He looked up.

"Shhh," Gary said to his friend. "Just be still for a while."

The friend shrugged. "Whatever," he said. This was tourism to him; a nice afternoon trip out of Rome. But he knew how important this was to Gary. Together, they had combed every inch of Gary's vocation. It was a true dilemma. Each point in favor of the seminary was nullified by something boosting the Benedictines. In the end, Benz's friend could do no better than the old chestnut: "follow your heart."

"That's the trouble," Gary said. "My heart is lonely for home and tells me, 'Gary, act now. Join the Benedictines.' My head reminds me of what the monks told me, 'Take your time. Be sure your vocation to the monastery is real.' And my soul just weeps."

The return to the seminary didn't help much. The second semester was even busier than the first for the New Men with the added duties of apostolic work. Gary was counseling students planning for their confirmation at Marymount Academy, an English-language school run by nuns. Soon, he and the other New Men would have to begin plans for the summer. The North American College insists seminarians do not return to the States until after their second year unless there is some compelling personal reason or the diocese demands their help. The logic goes that a quick immersion into their old lives and old friends could cancel out some of their vocational training as New Men. "This is an especially fragile time for the seminarians," said Rector Dolan. "Too much of homecoming hoopla and not enough prayerful reflection is not a good idea. What I'm trying to say is that we'd rather have them thinking about their vocation than knocking back beers with buddies back home. You should see 'em when they come back after that first summer away. They are energized."

The rector, for example, encourages staying in Italy for Italian study or heading to the Third World for mission work—although some bishops hold a cautious leash over their seminarians and forbid them from work in developing countries. They don't want to see their Rome-trained protégés snared in unrest or ravaged by some tropical malady.

Gary was holding off even thinking about the summer. He tried to get out of the seminary as much as possible—sitting alone in churches around Rome or spending time just walking back the long way from class. He had always planned to return to Subiaco at some point, and his friend's visit was a well-timed opportunity. Gary's thirst was getting unbearable. He wanted—no, needed—to drink in that head-clearing draught he first sampled in Subiaco back on the first day of November.

"Gary?" his friend asked. "You're not upset we came, are you?"

He smiled—for the first time in hours. "Oh, gosh, no. I'm fine. I'm just looking at the mountains. Think about it: Benedict looked up and saw the same thing."

They watched the mountain tops and the cubist patterns of inky shadows and sun-shimmering rock. Did Benedict, too, wonder about some long dead shepherd who stood on the same site and surveyed the same peaks? And did that shepherd mull over the generations before him who also watched the landscape? Gary tried to feel the ghosts. He knows they are there. They are everywhere, and especially in places like ancient Subiaco. Gary's ghosts are not the kind from spook lore. His dwell in the rocks and soil and trees. The ghosts float out in a belly laugh or contented yawn; swim in a tear or drop of sweat—it's all absorbed by the land and waiting there to be dredged up like the contents of a thick soup. Gary thinks often of the universal connections, the ghosts that bind us together and hum on the invisible sinew of time.

"I stand at places sometimes and think of all of the people who stopped in that spot before. I can feel these people," he said. "How better to praise the land than to reflect on our mortality and its immortality?" The centuries, decades, hours that connect him and St. Benedict are just a little half-note to the land. Maybe not even that. Gary always feels the forever in nature, even though he understands it's all in flux. The elements will eventually tear down these mountains around Subiaco, then take the grains elsewhere to start all over again. "It's beautiful to think about it, really: nothing gone, only changed," he said. "I think of our souls that way."

Gary started his time-traveling as a boy. He'd climb the butte behind his family farm and try to feel the pulse of the pioneers who looked out on the same wavy horizons and the Sioux before them who left behind their arrowheads and footpaths before being driven away.

Leaning on the stone wall outside Subiaco, Gary Benz closed his eyes and prayed. He prayed in thanks for the beauty of the land and the wisdom he knew it held. "Man can be wrong," he said. "Nature, never. Our job is to see God's hand."

But was He pushing me away from the seminary? Gary asked himself. Was this second trip to Subiaco a homecoming like it felt back in November?

"Gary," his seminarian friend said. "Look, they are opening." A monk pulled open the doors to the passageway leading to the grotto.

"Wait a second," said Gary, who had been looking through his breviary for the February 10 memorial to Scholastica, the sister of Benedict who followed his example and dedicated her life to religious works and contemplation.

"I just wanted to find this," he said.

The responsory repeats: "My heart is ever pleading, show me your face . . . Show me your face."

At the grotto, Gary stood very still for a very long time. His friend had left to explore other rooms. Everything was the same in the grotto—the candles, the statue, the fresco on the bumpy rock. It was all there except the passion he felt in November. He ran his hand over the stone entrance arch. It felt cold. Colder than he remembered.

Gary turned and walked up the stairs toward the sunlight and the long walk down the hill for the bus back to Rome.

"So?" his friend finally asked.

"Well, it wasn't there like before. The certainty, I mean," said Gary. "Looks like I'll be staying at the seminary—at least to the end of the year."

"You don't seem so happy about it."

"I'm relieved, that's for sure. Happy? I don't know."

"Why not?"

"I just never thought everything would be so tough. I guess God sometimes doesn't want to make it easy. I just wish I could do one thing, though."

"What's that?"

"I wish I could be home. I'd give anything for just a few days there. It would much easier to figure things out."

"What do you miss the most?"

Gary stopped. "The most? Feeling I belong."

Irene Benz, Gary's mother, carefully unfolded the latest letter from her son. His cramped script ran down a full page of North American College stationery. As always, his capital letters were textbook perfect—habits burned in during penmanship drills at Catholic school. He wrote briefly about attending mass with the Benedictines at San Anselmo's on the Aventine Hill, where the side streets are quiet and lined with crimson bougainvilleas and deep green vines. Irene ran her finger over the line. She knew he was struggling with his vocation. But the letter held no suggestion—not a word—of a decision reached.

"I worry about him," said Irene, a large, solid woman whose hair is always carefully collected in a mini-beehive. "He's so far away. I wonder all the time if he's happy, if he's happy way over there in Rome."

Benedict Benz looked up sharply from his cup of coffee—black, no sugar, as is proper west of Bismarck. The cup looked small in his beefy hands. The great dome of his belly began below his armpits and swept well below his belt. On either side were log-sized arms, built muscle by muscle and scar by scar, during a lifetime of farm work.

"Do you, Mother? Do you really worry so about Gary? He'll be fine, just fine. We all come to those points when you have to go one way or the other. It's natural. This is one of them times for Gary."

They sat at the kitchen table for a while and said nothing. It was very still. After ten children—the youngest now off to college—it was a novelty to be able to hear the creaks and ticking clocks in the one-story home at the end of a long dirt road. They didn't know quite whether to welcome solitude or try to drive it away. Benny cleared his throat and read Gary's letter again. So much had changed in the past few years: closing down the farm, weddings, grandchildren. At least the wind was there as always, familiar and relentless. It shakes the windows like an intruder trying to get in. It pries back the tan coat of their mutt, Cinnamon, hunkered down outside the little alcove packed with a washing machine and the names of Irene, Benedict, and all their children burnt into little blocks of decorative wood. The wind pushes the buildings ever so slightly off center as a reminder that nothing is permanent except the elements. The wind was in the faces of the first settlers from Vermont—trying to push them back to where they came from. Expansively worded handbills back East called the area a "poor man's paradise."

Although it was the first week of spring, the wind still carried its cold bite. The bare ash trees along the dirt road out front quivered in the gusts as if they were shivering. Benny Benz poured himself another cup of black coffee and wrapped both hands around the mug. He let the steam drift over his chin. Spring was late. But Benny sees the coming warmth rather than cursing the present chill. Farmers have to be optimists. You couldn't bear all the disappointments any other way.

Above the farm house, the first purple crocuses of the season grew in clumps on the slope of West Rainy Butte. The red buds of the prairie roses were closed tight. There was still some dirty snow in the folds of the buttes closer to town.

It was one of the two moments of high anticipation on the farms. Just before harvest was one. Please, they would pray, no surprise hail storms or tornadoes until the crops are in. Early spring was another. When to plant? Being early might lead to the first harvest and the best prices. But a late frost could wipe you out. The rule goes: no spring planting until the snow is off the buttes. Only the foolish or desperate go against the rules.

It took leaving North Dakota to show Gary the intensely primitive side of his own spirituality. Gary had always perfectly understood the Sioux and Lakota and the other tribes he studied when he was a boy. The land, the weather—how it gives and claims life—is the indelible backdrop for everything Gary feels about God and how he should serve Him. When he's at summer mass, Gary wants to feel the sunburn lingering on his neck. In December, when all the farms are still and the livestock is penned, Gary savors the warmth and protection of home as part of his meditations on Christmas. He needs the land he was raised in—craves it in a way the other New Men from the cities and bland suburbs just can't appreciate. This is why St. Benedict speaks so clearly to him. Reverence for the eternal land and eternal soul cannot be separated for Gary. This is what is pulling him back to the wind-scarred ridge where Assumption Abbey sits.

"Gary sees things that I can't," his father told me. "I see a farm and, to me, it's a farm. Nothing more, nothing less. Gary will look at it and see the colors of the sky in the panes of glass or how the crops push up toward the sun. Sometimes I really think, just maybe, he sees a part of heaven."

The Benzes called it quits on their farm after their youngest daughter graduated from high school in 1992. They sold off the wheat fields and hogs. The price wasn't bad—enough of a cushion to splurge on platter-size steaks at the restaurant over in Amidon and consider cracking open the nest egg for a trip to Rome. Benny had been to Europe as a soldier after the war. In Germany, he found his family: cousins and uncles in his grandfather's hometown of Renchen in the Black Forest. He spent the night in his grandfather's old bed. "Only I couldn't sleep," he said. "It was like I was surrounded by centuries of spirits from my family." A woman gave him a medal she received from the Third Reich to promote motherhood. The more children, the bigger the medal. Benny thought about throwing it away but decided to keep it in a little cardboard box. He hates to get rid of anything. The prairie makes you thrifty. It's so hard to tear down the unused barn.

Benny went outside and walked the worn paths around the idle buildings. The chicken coop, the root cellar—which also doubled as a storm shelter for the occasional twister—where it's always 38 degrees. And then over to the barn. He touched its sides, lumpy from coat after coat of the cheapest white paint. Old calluses sat like big pearls under his skin, crisscrossed by so many little scars. None of them carried a story the way old wounds do for people in the city. They're just scars. "Farming takes a little blood and a lot of patience," said Benny, whose right middle finger is bent at a sharp angle. He has a grab bag of different stories about how it was broken and healed crooked. Sometimes he'll say that he whacked his finger on a table edge after he missed in an attempt to slap some sense into Gary when he was up to his chore-dodging mischief as a boy. Irene will quickly add in a whisper: not true, he hurt it on a machine.

"Maybe I could sell some of the wood," Benny said, walking around the barn. "We can keep some for firewood. I don't know. It's got to get done sooner or later, I guess." Bits of dry grass kicked up by the wind ricocheted off the side of the barn.

The top of West Rainy Butte above the Benz farm used to be considered the highest point in North Dakota. A cone-shaped copper monument was erected, but it was stolen and sold for scrap metal during World War II. Years later, pilots on training missions out of Ellsworth—Brian Christensen's old base—discovered that a nondescript rise near the South Dakota border was actually higher than the butte.

It was somehow fitting. Recent decades have not been kind to little New England.

Driving the rolling stretch of Route 21 into town, Benny Benz can find little good news. On both sides of the road—as far as the horizon—is the evidence of the two forces most unforgiving for farmers: the weather and the economy.

"Hailed out," he said, pointing to a field of ankle-high stubble that was, for a time last summer, a thriving wheat crop.

"There, too. Hailed out. Hailed-out crops."

The North Dakota hail beats down like a gavel. Season over. Case closed. Fists of ice from the purple storm clouds can wipe out a crop in minutes. Good wheat these days can surpass five dollars a bushel. There are about 40 bushels in an acre and 640 acres in a section, the basic unit for the large wheat tracts. Benny Benz doesn't even have to do the math. He knows it by heart. "We're talking like 128,000, 130,000 dollars a section," he said.

There is nothing anyone can do except hope your land is somehow spared. The devastation is maddeningly selective. One tract of land is untouched while the neighbor's wheat is pummeled to oblivion. The Benz farm was hit about a third of the years since he started on his own in 1957. Benny ticks them off the way he does his children's birthdays: "'64, hailed out, '67 hailed out. '72 hailed out. '78, partially hailed out. Mother, what about '80? Hailed out, right?"

"Yes, hailed out."

Hail leaves you with nothing but some melting ice. An entire season's income and its plans—the Catholic school tuition, the new shoes—gone. When farm equipment was cheaper and credit freer, getting hailed out was an inconvenience but not always a tragedy. Maybe the kids ate more peanut butter and jelly and shared presents on Christmas. But families pulled through. Now, they are pulling out. A good combine costs about $175,000; a serviceable used one is at least $70,000. Insurance takes a bigger bite each year. The easiest thing is to sell out to one of the mega-farmers and move to Bismarck or Fargo. Or get out of North Dakota altogether.

"When the hail is pounding down on the roof and bashing in the windows and the family is huddled together and you know that all your work with the wheat was for nothing—you know, those are special times," said Benny. "I don't mean they are good. They are special—'specially powerful. About the only thing you can think about at that moment is how nice it feels to be surrounded by your family. It's a feeling that God is right there with us. You know you are going to pull through somehow, so you don't worry. It's funny to think about those bad times so kindly, I guess."

"I don't think you can work the land and not believe in God," Irene cut in. "That's what he's trying to say. Right, Benny?"

"Exactly, Mother."

"That's why I can't see Gary in the monastery," Benny continued. "We're farm folk. We help each other in the good times and the bad."

"Especially in the bad," Irene added.

"Yes, 'specially then. It's in Gary's blood. Nothing against the monks—they are good, holy men—but Gary can't be separated from his people. People like us. He'd wilt. Anyway, that's what I think. He'll make up his own mind, but I think he'll eventually see that he needs to be the type of priest living out among the farmers. He needs them and they need him—more than the monastery needs him. But he's a man now and will make up his own mind. I'll say no more. It's just my opinion. What about you, Mother?"

"You forgot one thing, Benny."

"What's that?"

"That Gary never liked his chores. Remember how he used to hide around the side of the house. Well, there's lots of chores to do around the monastery."

"You're right, Mother," he laughed. "He's got to become a regular priest."

Benny slowed his '81 Buick to funeral speed in front of the abandoned homesteads. In many, the houses are gone, but the places are marked by the old silos and the little groves of pine, ash, and American elm planted as windbreaks.

"Over there used to be a farm," he said, gesturing off to the silhouette of trees on a small ridge.

"And over there. That used to be a big farm. Big family."

"You know, it used to be that Sunday mornings you could look in your rearview mirror and see a line of cars with families going to church. Now, it's nothing. You're out on the road alone."

It's the equation draining so many breadbasket towns: fewer family farms means fewer families means fewer stores and so on. It's a spiral toward extinction or, at best, irrelevance. The rule of thumb in New England is for every seven farms that close, one business dies. There's not much left to padlock. The demographic downturn coincided with the closing of the rail spur into New England. It was the lifeline. Spare parts for farm equipment would come in by rail. Folks would make an order from the Montgomery Ward catalog and two or three days later it would be on the loading dock. Benny Benz began the biggest trip of his life—boot camp, then duty in Europe—leaving on the train in 1954 and watching the tawny wheat fields wave goodbye.

In this world of planting, harvesting, and praying for the hail to hit elsewhere, New England was once a giant. More wheat moved out of its grain elevators than in any single point anywhere in the world. *National Geographic* once did a story on the North Dakota wheat belt and ran a full-page picture of the elevator row bathed in warm sunset light. It was a shining moment for the town as well.

But then, without the railroad, the trucks filled with harvested wheat took the bypass road over the Cannon Ball—a river with steep banks of rich brown soil marbled with clay—and then up the state road up to Dickerson. That's where the drivers stop to fuel up and chow down. Oil was discovered in the 1950s in the deep coal deposits. Only recently, however, have the drillers and speculators returned. Dickerson boomed into a neon forest on Interstate 94. There's a Walmart, every variation of fast food, and even some low-stakes blackjack and Bingo at the motels. The people from the dying towns out in the prairie are drawn like pilgrims. They have no choice.

A weekly newspaper manages to survive in New England, almost exclusively on ads from Dickerson.

"You might think we are silly little folks for sticking out here on the prairie," said its lone reporter and columnist Walt Jacobs, whose house is surrounded by an astonishing collection of petrified wood, some chunks as big as a trash can. "But what I consider silly is pulling up stakes and leaving. This is their town. How can you just turn your back on it? People from the outside might call it a dying town with no future. I don't see it that way at all. We are tough old birds out here and know that hard times come. They always do. But then good times may follow. Maybe someday Gary Benz is going to come back from Rome and be our pastor. It could happen. That's reason enough right there to keep going."

The town's hub these days is off Main Street, around the corner from the shuttered State movie house. A small bowling alley with a restaurant and video rentals. The daily specials are written on a blackboard.

"The chicken soup and the roast beef sandwich," said Rev. Robert Williams, who heeded a recruitment call for priests in 1954 and came west from Boston.

"Can I cut that up for you, Father?" the waitress asked.

"No, that's OK. I'll do it," offered Irene Benz.

Father Williams nodded. "That would be nice."

The priest was still winded from the short walk from the car. It's not often he leaves his wheelchair. Severe diabetes and kidney problems have left him feeble and on three-times-a-week dialysis to stay alive. His right arm is paralyzed, forcing him to offer mass with his left hand. A special low altar was built to allow him to remain in his wheel-chair. Yet retirement—or even cutting back on duties—was not an option for years. The diocese is so short on priests that dwindling rural parishes are low on the priority for extra help. It's an irony not lost on the parishioners in New England, which has produced twelve priests and twenty-seven nuns.

Gary Benz, who would be number thirteen, sometimes listens to other seminarians at the North American College daydream out loud about someday returning as priests to their hometown parish. "With me," he says, "I wonder if it will even exist."

A few months later, Father Williams said his last mass as pastor. A young priest—a product of the North American College—took his place.

"It was a sign for us that the Church had not forgotten us," said Benny. The day before, a summer hail storm leveled the fields on the other side of the butte.

Behind the chapel, an entire wing of the squat St. Mary's School is perpetually dark. It was no longer possible to keep the high school open for a handful of students. In 1992, the last twenty-one graduating seniors received their diplomas, including Gary Benz's sister. The darkened halls, classrooms, and cavernous gym throb with a desperate melancholy—like a widow who keeps two place settings at the kitchen table. Nothing is disturbed in the school. The books and desks are just where they were left. Someone wrote on a green chalkboard: Bye. The Notre Dame Sisters—only three left now for the elementary classes—refused to dismantle anything. That means defeat.

One of the sisters likes to walk just south of the school and meditate on the land. In early spring the grass is the color of buckskin with a faint wash of yellow. A meadow lark skims over the grass.

"In the quiet of the prairie," she said, "you can hear God."

A monk recounts: "Sometimes there is a minute or less just before the Office begins when everyone is in place. There is no creaking, coughing, clearing of throats; no blowing of noses, sniffling, shuffling books. There is just quiet."

Strange, isn't it, how something so benign as silence can be so frightening? he asked. Then he quickly answered his own question: It's because it's so alien. The din reaches everywhere. A cellular phone ringing on a mountainside. A television droning on in a corner of an empty room.

"How timid," the monk scoffed. "How timid we are, afraid of something as harmless as silence."

At the monastery tugging at Gary Benz's heart, silence is cultivated and its power respected. Early each morning, the monks assemble in their dark oak prayer stalls on either side of the altar for the Office of Readings. This is the first of four times the community will get together for prayer. The monks are dressed for their work: some wearing overalls for the farm; others in black cloaks for inside duty at the brick abbey built in the sturdy Bavarian style of the area's German-speaking homesteaders. When prayers are done, they head to breakfast. It's eaten in silence before big picture windows offering a panorama of wide prairie sky and the land rippling below. Millions of years ago, this was a vast and shallow inland sea. Its character seeped into the land. It sculpted the land in its graceful image. From the abbey refectory, it's easy to imagine: a big sea with its groaning sea noises.

The monks eat quickly, efficiently. They take just enough. Almost nothing is left on their plates when they carry their trays back. It happens just like this—season passing into season, year melting into year. An unwavering cycle like a remnant of the tides of the ancient sea.

One of the rules of St. Benedict calls for complete silence to surround a monk who dishonors the community. The monk would be ostracized by the others and forced to do his work and take his meals alone. The monk, says Benedict, must not only confront his infraction but something of far greater consequence: himself. To understand the monastery, the monks say, is to understand the joy and terror of facing yourself in the naked terrain of silence.

And what is there at the bottom of it all, after so many decades of contemplation?

"How to listen," said one of the oldest monks at Assumption Abbey. "How to listen to God, how to listen to yourself and then listen—really listen—to the others around you. This is as close to grace as I think you can get."

"Try something," he continued.

"Have you ever just tried to listen to your own heart beat or the sound of your breathing? I bet not. Try it. This is God saying, 'Pay attention.'"

The old monk has seen Gary Benz on his visits to the monastery in Richardton, an old rail stop town about fifty miles from New England. The monk has kept his distance, eyeing Gary at prayers and meals. He's seen dozens of young men like him: pious, searching, testing. He was one of them himself. That was long ago. It's different now. He's so different now. The monk prays for new members. It's so obvious that the community was growing collectively older. He worried, though, about reckless recruitment.

He rubbed his bony hands together under the sleeves of his robe. In the back of the church, he spoke softly so no one would overhear.

"After all these centuries, it's hard to be pessimistic for the order. Strange, though, I am pessimistic.

"I just don't know if I would encourage vocations these days. I mean, I'm not telling people they shouldn't think about the monastic life. What I'm saying is that there are so many people with so little grounding in the faith in what it takes to lead a religious life. They may feel a call, but it could be just a desire to escape. The monastery is no place to escape. Everywhere you turn you bump into your conscience."

That night, another monk stood outside and watched the sky. Brother Placid had just finished his chores at the farm down the hill. The stars were hard and bright. Placid looked west for the comet.

He has spotted the faint tail of Hyakutake a few nights before. Now, it was gone.

"I love comets. I mean the idea of them, really," he said. "The continuity."

He closed the abbey door quietly behind him and turned off the light.

CHAPTER XVI

LENT

Declare your sins to one another.

—EVENING READING FOR FRIDAY
OF THE SECOND WEEK OF LENT (JAMES 5:16)

They walked in a tight, silent pack toward a fat crescent moon. It was low in the sky and, from their vantage point, it just brushed the stalks of countless television antennas poking like scarecrows from Rome's rooftops. The seminarians looked down to make sure they didn't clip the heels of the one in front of them. There was no reason to stay this close. It was primal. In the darkness, in the unfamiliar, claustrophobic streets, they herded together.

Some of the seminarians wore their clerics. They didn't have to for this early mass, but it was an easy routine to fall into: throw on the black suit. After all these months, it felt odd to some of the New Men to be at mass without it, in "civvies" as they say. The seminarians in black melted into the shadows on the side streets on the other side of the Tiber, then materialized again under a street light or the glow from the window of an early riser. Page-mark ribbons sticking from their breviaries fluttered like tiny flags.

The group entered the oval piazza of Campo dei Fiori, where the vendors were already setting up their stalls. A few shoppers—mostly old women with rumpled shopping bags—were already there to pick through the crates. "Artichokes," a vendor shouted trying to get an early jump. "Fresh Roman artichokes. Fresh, fresh."

It was mid-Lent. In Rome, that is the best time for artichokes.

"Still so much to learn here," a seminarian said.

"About what?"

"Food," he said, rubbing his stomach. Breakfast wouldn't be for a couple hours. A draft of wind carried the scent of baking bread from an alley. Everyone slowed a half-step to breathe in the warm and doughy smell.

Each morning during the forty days of Lent, the seminarians travel to a different church for 7 A.M. mass. Most walk together in a group that gathers for a prayer in the seminary lobby. The farther away the church, the earlier they set off. This time of year, it's always before dawn, though.

The group walking past the market vendors that morning was smaller than usual. Dozens of seminarians were hit with a nasty flu virus tearing through the city. The pope, too, was sick again with a fever of about 100 degrees and was forced to cancel his weekly Wednesday audience. The Vatican—always stingy with information on the pope's health—broad-stroked it as a "feverish syndrome of a digestive nature." *Vaticanisti* groped for details, anything to give a hint on whether it was serious or another blip on the papal health vigil.

Since the pope's Christmas bug, the *Vaticanisti* had been extra keen for any sign of decline. A grimace by the pope—common since his 1994 hip replacement surgery—was analyzed and quantified. Was it longer than others? How much was he relying on his cane, which the pope later abandoned to the surprise of the doomsayers. Even a cough reverberated like a warning bell. Could this be another retching episode like Christmas?

The pope was in a particularly bad humor in an audience for Rome's diocesan priests to mark the beginning of Lent that year. Normally, the encounter is a somber affair dwelling on the period of contemplation before Easter. This year, the pope was squinting. Not a good sign. He slapped the priests of the Eternal city with a wake-up call. The city, he admonished, is slipping away from you. The problem is priests who refuse to rub elbows with parishioners. You are pastors, the pope said, so go out and tend the flock. Not just the prayerful widows in opaque stockings, but also the skinheads in jackboots.

"The Church has to know how to respond to the many demands in the search for God from all quarters," the pope said. During the address, an ancient priest in the first row collapsed. The pope read a prayer for the sick as the first-aid people took away the wheezing priest. The pope didn't look good himself.

"He's a tough old guy," said Brian Christensen while walking through Campo dei Fiori on his way to the morning Lenten mass. "You have to be to run the show over at the Vatican." He laughed and then realized he was talking a little too loud too early. Shhhh, Brian, he told himself.

Brian was in a stellar mood these days. The trip to Ireland was a catharsis. It was a clean and—thankfully—reasonably comfortable break. He finally could let go of the questions about a romance with Kristin. And he believed they could remain close friends. What a cliché, he thought. So many couples say it, and so few carry through. But, this time, he thought it was truly possible. "It's not going to be because I find another girlfriend—at least I hope not," he joked. He couldn't turn it off. He was happy: to be back in Rome and, finally, settled about his vocation.

What irritated him before about the seminary—the time constraints, the circle-the-wagons Americana—barely were noticed anymore. He was going to be a priest. He could say it, for the first time really, and sincerely believe it. "Father Christensen," he said, trying it on. "The Reverend Brian P. Christensen. Not bad, huh?" So keep the eye on the prize, he told himself. Get yourself mentally ready. Learning the theology and the intricacies of the Vatican were fine, but Brian more and more considered the seminary as a personal trial. Not unlike the sweaty Air Force Academy boot camp. "You don't learn to be a priest in a classroom," he said. "It has to come from inside and seep out your pores. The seminary, I'm learning, is not a priest factory. They can't build you. You have to build yourself."

He took a couple long strides to stretch his legs. He and Nalty and one other New Man had been the only ones to complete on foot the annual seven churches walk to seven basilicas, starting at St. Peter's. The tradition, begun by St. Philip Neri in the sixteenth century and started in the late sixties at the seminary, entails a single-day, eighteen-mile trek all the way out to St. Paul's Outside the Walls on the Via Ostiense heading out of the city toward the sea. While they were in the church— the second biggest in Rome after St. Peter's—they heard something tap at the windows. They looked out into a spring downpour.

"Come on," said Nalty. "If you run a marathon, you don't give up right before the end. No, you just freaking finish it. Let's go."

Everyone balked at first but Brian. "You really going to do it?"

"Damn right. I'll do it alone if I have to."

"If you do it, I'll do it."

"Then let's go." One other New Man came along.

Two hours later, soaked and limping from blisters, they stood dripping in the seminary lobby—shivering but satisfied.

Christensen's new purposefulness earned him some unexpected needling. Some of the New Men who carried their convictions about the priesthood for years had little patience for guys like Brian—latecomers who suddenly seem so certain of their vocations.

"It irritates some people. Why? I don't know," said Brian. "But I can tell you that I feel it. It's like a certain coldness that says, 'What makes you so sure of yourself all of a sudden?' It seems to bug them that we led a very different life before."

The knot of seminarians was stretching out a bit as the day grew lighter. They were in a line about two blocks long as they threaded through the old Jewish ghetto and into the cyclone of Piazza Venezia, the frenetic crossroads of traffic and tourists capped by the audacious white monstrosity to memorialize the unification of Italy and its papal-scorned king, Victor Emmanuel II. The house where Michelangelo died was destroyed in order to provide a better view of the gaudy behemoth. Tour buses—the first of hundreds—were already growling their way around the looping course of the piazza. Around the corner was the open wound of Via dei Fori Imperiali, a straight-line boulevard Mussolini ordered built so he could have a view of the Coliseum from his office window and, conveniently, also a grand parade route. His bulldozers leveled churches, medieval buildings, and parts of the ancient Roman Forum.

The Coliseum shone bone white in the first dawn rays. Part of the crescent moon was just visible over its uneven lip.

"Incredible," gasped Christensen. "It's times like this that open your eyes. You know what I mean? You can walk around with your eyes open but really closed. It doesn't matter if it's Rome or Rapid City. It shouldn't take scenes like this to remind us to open our eyes to what's around us. We should see it all the time."

He entered the Church of Cosmas and Damian, the first Christian structure appropriated from the Forum. Mass was just beginning under the sixth-century mosaic.

Chris Nalty was already there, standing next to a column on the far side of the church. He had been up since 4:45 A.M. to get in his daily Holy Hour. Gary Benz took a seat in a back pew. Tran stayed back in the seminary for a small morning mass held in a basement chapel.

The Landrys walked in, one right after the other, carrying their helmets. They had recently bought motor scooters.

The twins, so close for so long, were having their relationship redrawn by the seminary. Superficially, very little had changed. They still confided in each other, planned trips together, and played tennis. Roger kept a racket-stringing machine in his room. It was pretty much like it always was—as far back as their memory would allow. Their stories are almost always in the plural: when we were at Harvard; when we were living in the duplex in Lowell; when we won the Little League playoff game. They especially loved that baseball story. It's the type that makes boys drool and men remember when you could go home to dinner covered in dirt and glory.

"It was gettin' dark," Roger recalls. The less serious the subject, the more Roger's accent turns the consistency of Boston clam chowder. "I was throwing kinda wild, so that was good. It gave me an advantage."

Scot Landry held out his catcher's mitt. Roger had already fanned eight Yankees in a row in extra innings, including the league's best player and coach's son—a beefy piece of work named Russ who already had one homer that game. And the Yanks were swinging away trying to seal the first game of a best-of-three playoff series.

Scot gave his mitt a quick jiggle. The signal meant: right here. Right in the pocket. Roger heaved the ball, which skimmed the top edge of the strike zone. It had some heat though. Russ swung. And missed. Inning over.

It was almost too dark to play, but the umpire let the Athletics have the bottom half of the inning. The first two batters were out quickly. Russ was pitching his specialty: fastballs that scared the pants off most Little Leaguers. Scot came to the plate. The first pitch was a hard strike down the middle. Scot took a deep breath to relax. Russ then gave him something inside and about belt high. Scot crushed it into the June dusk. It flew over the left fielder's head about 250 feet out. Since the diamond didn't have a fence, home runs had to be run out. Scot had just crossed second when he saw the ball coming in. Both teams were screaming in the soprano shriek of preadolescence. The third base coach was yelling for a slide into home. "Hard and down, Scotty," he said. "Hard and down." Scot saw the catcher move to his left. He knew the throw was coming in wide. He crossed the plate running.

Roger was the first to mob the twelve-year-old hero. Even the manager got his 350-pound bulk into a jog. The coach tossed over the game ball. "You did it again, Scotty," he said. Back at home that night, Scot presented the ball to his brother. He said it should be shared. Roger took the ball and held it for a while without saying anything.

"Good story, isn't it?" Roger asked. "I mean, there's Scot motorin' around the bases, and we're yellin'. I'm tellin' ya, it was beautiful. To see your brother—your twin brother, I should say—being a hero is even a greater feeling than it happening to you."

The Landrys are bound in an impenetrable way that maybe only twins can truly fathom. They literally see the world the same way: suffering from complete color blindness. They even have what should have been each other's names.

Scot was born about five minutes ahead of his brother. His parents decided the first born would be named after their father, Roger. But they mixed them up in the nursery and the number-two twin was placed in the "Roger" bassinet. "You know how emotional you are after giving birth. Well, I just started bawling. I thought everything was messed up," said their mother, Midge. "But my husband knew just what to say. 'It doesn't matter,' he says. So Roger was supposed to be Scot and Scot was supposed to be Roger. So they are that close. They have the other one's name."

Yet the vocations that brought them to Rome were pushing them in different directions.

Scot had stopped talking about ordination. In the early months in Rome, Scot's passion for his vocation was in full blaze. He mentioned the type of parish he would like to run, sketched out the ideas for youth programs. Now, with Easter coming, he was quiet. The times he mentioned his vocation at all, it was often in the context of doubts and nostalgia. Or he'd mention how transferring to Fall River could be just the thing to seal his calling. He was slipping back always to the question he wanted to answer but could not: was there a calling to the priesthood?

His spiritual director knew it was time to act. Scot, he felt, could be an exceptional priest, especially in a parish that needed a dynamic leader. But Father McRae didn't feel Scot was looking squarely at his vocation and trying to figure out if, without Roger around, it could survive.

McRae gave Scot a lot to think about during Lent. Try, he asked, to separate your vocation from your brother's. Is this priestly calling you believe you have being nourished by God or, just maybe, Roger? Why must you go to Fall River when you are still unsure of your vocation?

"Think about this," McRae told Scot. "There can be nothing—absolutely nothing—more important to you than this question at this time."

Roger—always the more intense one—was burrowing deeper into the faith. If there were any doubts about his calling, they were settled years ago back at Harvard. He was onto another level. His prayers had evolved into contemplation on what it meant to be a Christian, a servant of the faith. He had spent so many years devouring and memorizing the lives of the saints. Now, he believed it was his time. "It's our job to try to become saints," he said. "I'm not saying we're going to be canonized. What I'm saying is that it's our job—no, our obligation—to try to be holy twenty-four hours a day."

For Roger, part of this meant trying to mellow. He'd tell himself: this is not Harvard, this is not a contest to see which one of us rises highest in the Church. But, then again, isn't that competitive spark always there—sometimes a sharp flare but always warm enough to be a reminder? It could be the secret sneers when one of the seminarians is picked to read at a papal audience. It could be the rural seminarians finding themselves envious of the big-city guys and their automatic contacts at the Curia. Back in the dioceses in the States, North American College alumni bear all the baggage of the favored sons. Some folks, who've only seen Rome through postcards, find the chummy fraternity downright boorish.

"I have to tell you that I've been at some events where I've been totally turned off by the performance of priests who've come through here as seminarians," said a former rector Edwin O'Brien, now the archbishop of the archdiocese for U.S. military personnel. "They get together and talk about the old days, share their jokes, and, if they know it or not, make the other people feel like they are somehow inferior, or at least weren't as fortunate as them to be part of this oh-so-wonderful club. You need to have your head screwed on pretty straight not to let all this Rome stuff go to it."

Roger Landry tries hard to remind himself that he should have checked his ego at the door. But he's not naive enough to deny that he is just the type of guy the Curia is seeking. He's sure of himself, a tad cocky but clever enough to throw in a self-effacing comment at just the right moment.

He's impressive; an intellectual quick-change artist. In the span of five staccato minutes, he can pick apart Red Sox pitching, examine the ramifications of the Council of Ephesus in 431, and quote from the pope, Kierkegaard, and the melancholy middle child Jan from "The Brady Bunch." It somehow all holds together.

But it's really Scot who steps in when a dose of humility is needed. "He's kind of like an external conscience." No, Roger said, he's more.

He's almost like God. "Awe-most like Gawd," he said. "Even when he's not around, you know he's there."

And Roger could feel his twin foundering. At first, it was simply Scot's reminiscing about work; the freedom and the clout he had. Then it was the increasing pull toward Fall River. Roger told him he thought a possible transfer would be a good idea and he was sincere. But what if it doesn't work out? Roger asked him. What then? Scot didn't want to hear such things. He was, just as he was with the Spaghetti Bowl, determined not to fail. One way or the other, he would sort out his indecision over his vocation. If he decided that he must be in Fall River to best serve his faith, then Scot expected the Church to clear the way. Why would they not? he asked. And why was his twin suggesting there could be obstacles?

Roger had no real idea what could happen. Scot hadn't even made up his mind about the transfer. But Roger did know that the Church didn't often respond well to requests that gave any hint of desperation—especially from first-year seminarians. Scot had to be firm in his vocation before making a move on the transfer. Roger advised: it had to be to enhance a solid vocation, not an attempt to rescue a hazy one. Otherwise, Roger feared trouble ahead.

One afternoon on a bus stuck in airport traffic, Scot was staring out the window. They had been talking about the seminary and Roger sensed Scot's frustration. The temperature of Scot's calling was in constant flux: some days warm and inviting and others cool and weak. This wasn't unusual at all for a New Man. But Roger knew his twin's patience was running short. He wanted things settled. His prayers all bore down on the problem. "Don't try to pin it down. It won't happen that way," Roger urged. "Listen more and fight less."

Scot wasn't questioning his love of the faith but whether the framework—the seminary, the bishops, the Vatican—held any sense for him. He remembered how happy he felt as a layman teaching Sunday school in the Bridgeport parish. Could he find that same fulfillment as an obedient cog in the Church's vast clergy?

"Scot?" Roger said. "Scot?" He asked louder.

Scot turned around.

"Scot, listen, it's natural," said Roger. "You've come out of a place where you were calling the shots, where you had responsibility. It's a tough transition. You know that other seminarians are going through it."

"Sure, I know. I'm past weighing the differences between the seminary and work. They are so different. Apples and oranges. What I'm asking myself is: how best do I serve God?"

"By finding your true vocation and following it, whether it's here or whether it means going back and raising a good Catholic family."

"That's the trouble, Rog. What if I think—right now, anyway—that my vocation is to be a priest, but I'm not sure about how the Church will treat my vocation?"

"What are you getting at?"

"I'm trying to get at the nature of obedience—as a priest and also as a plain Catholic. The key question, to me at least, is this: what do you do when, in good conscience, you know you could do more for the faith than you are being asked to do?"

"You're referring to the priesthood, I assume," said Roger.

"Of course. We know that we have to give up substantial control of our lives after ordination. We're already getting a taste of it here. So what I'm saying is: Where is our ultimate obedience? Is it to the priesthood or to the faith? It's tough to give up control if you don't know how you'll be able to use your gifts. I'm guess I'm saying: Will the Church best use our talents? Wouldn't it be worse, let's say, to be sent to study canon law or something when you feel your strength lies in being a hands-on priest in the parish? That could happen, right? So what do you think God would want? Don't you think He would want us to maximize what we can do?"

"But, Scot, you have to have faith that the Church will recognize your talents."

"I know what you are saying and I agree. But imagine if it didn't. It certainly happens. It would be very hard for me to sit by and watch the years slip by knowing I could be doing so much more."

"Scot, there's a word for what you are talking about. It's pride."

"Is it, though?" Scot cut him off. "It seems logical to me."

"Exactly!" Roger said. "That's what it's all about here. We have to see a new kind of logic—the logic of seeing God's hand in what we are doing, in what we will be doing."

"That's not logic, that's faith."

"We're asked to do something very hard: combine the two together," said Roger.

"OK, I know a guy who's not—what can I say?—not overjoyed by his work at the Vatican," Roger continued. "It's not an extremely challenging position. Sometimes he told me that he goes into work and there's no work to do, but he has to stay around."

"I know all this," said Scot.

"So then you also know that he's extremely prayerful. He keeps a very supernatural outlook on the whole thing. He says, 'This is what God wants me to do at this point.' It's not giving up, Scot. He looks for the beauty, the sanctity, in where he is at that particular moment."

"But, Rog, who knows you better than I? You can be impatient and definitely proud."

"Did I say I wasn't? We all struggle. I'm just asking you not to make any rash moves. Try to translate your trust into God. Until you do that—until we all do it—the temptations to our vocations will always be there."

"Rog, you said 'our' vocations. That's interesting. You know what Father McRae asked me to do? He said try to separate my vocation from yours."

"And what did you say?"

"At first, I thought it was strange. You know, especially with us. I was thinking, 'How do you separate what you are as a person from what you are as a twin? Can it be done?' Then, slowly, it started to make sense. I can't count on you to make my vocation grow."

"True," Roger said. "McRae's a prudent man. You can count on me for anything, but in this one you're on your own. It's a tough thing to say, but that's just how it is."

"Rog, I know. Listen, would you be disappointed if someday I discerned that I wasn't called to the priesthood and dropped out? What if it did come down to the fact that my vocation was to go back to work, get married, and that whole bit? How would you feel?"

"I'd only be disappointed if you acted without really praying about your decision. Go where you feel God is leading you. That's all."

"So, Rog, let me ask you one more thing. Aren't you ever afraid of being lonely?"

"Like how?"

"I don't mean like lack of company. I mean, being out there alone, feeling you've lost control of it all; feeling like, 'How did I ever get here?'"

"I do think about it."

"And?"

"And it's a sacrifice. There's no way around it. You know what's out there. We have many priests living alone in the rectory. In some cases we won't have anyone to go back to. And often times the sheep aren't docile. Sometimes they can give you the impression that they could care less if you're there or not. They are just checking in their time card to go to mass because they have to and don't really care who is the priest. I mean, some of the time we won't get the reinforcement you'd get in a family setting. Just by having your child run up to you at the end of the day delighted that you are home, jumping up and down."

Scot sighed. "You're right. So what do we do?"

"Pray to see God's will in it all, Scot. What else is there? And maybe one other thing."

"Which is?" Scot asked.

"Some priests get a dog."

CHAPTER XVII

EASTER

*This is the morning on which the Lord appeared
to men who had begun to lose hope.*

—EVENING PRAYER FOR EASTER

Easter, the fulcrum of the liturgical year, also opens the last phase in the seminary calendar. The fourth-year seminarians, made deacons earlier in the year, now begin to look ahead to ordination to the priesthood in the summer. The other seminarians in the middle years begin to think about going home.

The New Men—who generally are required to spend their first summer abroad—start to image themselves in the various places they will go. Some already had plans. Roger Landry was heading to Portugal to begin language study. Brian Christensen was being called back to the Rapid City diocese, which needed his help more than they thought he needed a summer overseas. Chris Nalty had a secret. He hadn't told anyone yet, but if things worked out he might spend the summer working with Mother Teresa in India. By Easter, religious identities were taking shape among the New Men.

Easter would also probably be the last time the entire North American College would be together for a holy-day mass. The doors of the chapel were left open to allow in some of the cool night breeze. The lights in the chapel are not overpowering as in St. Peter's. There is a nice dusky feel inside.

Dolan would be again helping serve communion at the papal mass on Easter Sunday. But his midnight mass with the students was truly the centerpiece of holiday for him. From the altar, just a few steps higher than the pews, he could see each of the seminarians. They usually sat in the same places. He especially looked for the New Men. Sometimes it amazed him how far some of them had come. Dolan spotted Gary Benz in one of the middle pews. He hadn't heard much more about Gary's pull toward the Benedictines. Probably a good sign. The rector still believed he would stay.

The Paschal mystery of Christian faith—Christ's death and resurrection—and the parallels Dolan makes with joining the seminary all unite in this moment.

"On this day we are all truly new men," Dolan said as midnight neared.

During communion, Dolan looked down at the line of seminarians waiting to receive the sacrament. All of them, brought from every part of America to a chapel on this hill in Rome. He thought just for an instant about the times as a boy playing priest in his basement.

Scot Landry knew what to expect after Easter. Father McRae would be probing even more into his vocation discernment. Scot, for his part, also was anxious to talk to McRae. He was still undecided about his calling but felt he was closer to knowing "how" to make a decision. His prayers were more focused on what he wanted, rather than trying to keep pace with Roger. He hoped to close in on the decision in the spring. Then, if he chose to stay, he could start discussing the possible transfer to Fall River. Time was pushing from behind.

He didn't want to face it all at once. So he did what he does best— stay busy. He immersed himself in his duties as president of the New Men's class: organizing meetings and working with Chris Nalty to make sure the note system was in order in time for the second-semester oral exams. He had become a trusted friend for many New Men. On the surface, he was so organized and confident. His opinion mattered.

One night just after Easter, Scot and three other New Men were in the television area of the lounge. It was getting late and two of them headed for the door. "G'night, you guys," one of them said.

Scot was typically gracious. *"Buona notte a voi."* The other New Men just waved.

They closed the door quietly. It was almost 11 P.M. and many of the other seminarians on the floor were already sleeping—especially those going to the Angelicum, which ran an American-style Monday through Friday schedule. The Greg held classes on Saturday, so Thursday was a day off.

"You tired?" the other seminarian asked Scot.

"Not really. Hey, it's Wednesday night. We can live it up."

"Right," the seminarian said flatly.

"Want a beer?" Scot asked.

"No, thanks. Well, OK, why not? Like you said, TGIW: Thank God it's Wednesday."

Scot handed him a beer and waited for his friend to continue. They like each other's company—sitting together at the same table in the dining hall or walking to class—but they had never had a serious discussion. It was always light: sports, jokes. Everyone liked the guy. He never got heavy or annoyingly righteous like some of the other seminarians. Scot, however, felt his friend stayed around for a reason this night. He seemed edgy, distant.

"How long we've been here? More than seven months, right? Man, sometimes it seems like years. Doesn't it? I mean, they call us New Men but it's really kind of true, don't you think? I feel . . ."

"Like inside out," Scot offered.

"Exactly, like I've been pulled inside out. The demands here are so different from out in the real—I mean, secular—world. What was once important isn't anymore and vice versa. Take prayer. Out there it's something I tried to squeeze in. Here, it's right in your face all the time. All the rules are changed. What's been the hardest thing for you?"

"Me?" Scot said, surprised he was first to have to open up. "Well, letting go of the control I had on my life is definitely the biggest. I was a serious planner before. I had all sorts of goals. And I had plans to meet them. I loved work. I really got a high from getting stuff done. Before I came into the seminary, the work year I had before was—up until this point—the high point of my life. Everything went well. It was all gravy. Here, I don't get that same—what would you call it?—that same buzz. It's different. It's discern your vocation, get ordained, and surrender yourself to God's will. I've talked to my brother about it. He seems to have come to an understanding that I'm still having trouble understanding—putting all your trust in God and sensing His hand in every moment. It's a wonderful concept that I hope to fully appreciate someday. But, boy, it's so different from where I was at before."

"And what about the idea of having a family?" his friend asked. "Was that hard to give up?"

"Maybe even harder," Scot admitted. "I always saw myself as a father. Always. It's hard some days, especially when I see fathers with their children. I'm always thinking, 'How does he feel? What's it like to hold your own child in your arms?'"

"Did you have a girlfriend?"

"I dated, if that's what you mean," said Scot. "Nothing serious."

His friend leaned forward.

"Listen, Scot, I was wondering if we could talk. I didn't want to do it in front of the other guys because you know how things get around here. This has to be secret."

"You got it. My word."

The other seminarian relaxed a bit and turned off the television. He knew he could trust Scot, who took his role as president of the class with almost paternal responsibility. Scot had always dreamed of heading a large family. This might be as close as he gets.

"I was in love. Guess I still am, really. I was seeing this woman at home and, well, you've heard the story: I thought I had a calling and left her to join the seminary. You know, Scot, I could go back right now and marry her."

"Wait a minute," Scot said. "You said you 'thought' you had a calling. You're leaving?"

"I decided last month. Yeah, I'm going."

Scot stumbled over what to say. There were some other guys he thought might cash it in, but not his friend. He had heard about Gary Benz's groping about for his vocation. Even if Nalty or Christensen pulled out, it wouldn't have shocked Scot like this. His friend was always so upbeat. There was never a hint of distress. He was—or rather seemed to be—sailing through the first year. It was odd to have the tables turned like this. It was usually Scot looking for reassurance from his brother. Now, he's the one trying to rescue a sinking vocation. Should he tell his friend about his own doubts?

"Is she the reason—your girlfriend?" said Scot, instantly wondering if he should have said "ex-girlfriend."

"No, that's not really it. It's just that I feel the priesthood isn't for me. I can't really pinpoint it. I still have faith and believe in the Church and all. That's not it. It's more the seminary. I don't feel whatever it is we're supposed to be feeling: more spiritual, better Catholics. I just don't think the priesthood is for me."

Scot rubbed his neck. "You remind me of someone," he said.

"Who?"

"Me."

"What! You? You're kidding."

"Look, you're not the only one going through this. I can't tell how many times I thought, too, that I didn't fit in. Probably about 10 percent of the days in the seminary I've been a lot happier than the happiness I experienced when I was working. The rest of the time, I haven't. The learning for me has been in the 90 percent of the days when I haven't been."

"So," the New Man interrupted, "what have you learned?"

"That a good seminarian doesn't necessarily mean you'll be a good priest and vice versa. Other priests have told me that they never liked the seminary, either. Their calling was to the priesthood, not the seminary. And anyone who feels called just to the seminary, well, they worry about them when they are sent out to the parish.

"It's been a killer roller coaster ever since I entered the seminary. It was particularly bad in the minor seminary, but here as well," Scot continued. "There are times when I've been so certain that it was right I become a priest, but there's been an equal number of times that I knew I wasn't called to the priesthood. Do you know what I mean?"

His friend nodded. "That's me, too. I couldn't agree more. But, Scot, with me it's the times when I don't feel called that are getting more frequent and seem a lot more powerful. Here I am, sitting in a seminary in Rome, wondering about what it would be like to get married and have a family. Is this what I should be thinking about? I mean, really, we're in a seminary."

"It's definitely natural. You think all the other seminarians here just turned off their old lives when they walked through the door? No way. The way I look at it, if we didn't believe we'd be good husbands and fathers, then we probably wouldn't be good priests, either."

Scot wondered for a moment whether he should elaborate about his own doubts—raging when they should be ebbing—that he would go all the way to ordination. No, he decided, it was time to be a listener and adviser. Anyway, it felt good. Scot had gone over this same conversation so many times in his own mind: Am I called? Am I not called? Finally hearing it out loud from someone else was a strange sensation—almost like having your thoughts plucked out and read aloud. It was close to how Scot and his twin brother could communicate eloquently with a simple gesture or a few stray words. They knew what the other was thinking. Scot felt that with his friend—knowing precisely what he was going to say and even how he would express it. "Don't fit in," his friend said. How many times, Scot thought, had I gnawed over those exact same words?

A lot had been bottled up. It was hard enough to talk about vocation troubles with other seminarians, but especially with those who had felt the calling since they were boys. They couldn't understand the rough landing some of the others had after catapulting into the religious life.

"So have you told anyone else? The rector?" Scot asked.

"No, just my parents. And you."

"What did they say?"

"Well, at first they were a little stunned. They told me they didn't think I was giving the seminary a fair shot."

"Well, do you?"

"Man, Scot, you're worse than my parents," he laughed. "The answer is: yes and no. My parents finally told me they'd support me in anything I decide. I knew they'd say that. But I agreed to at least stay until the end of the year. That's the deal."

"Look, I'm not trying to change your mind. No one would criticize you for leaving the seminary if you just feel it's not right. That's what the seminary is here for, you know. But let me tell you something Father McRae told me when I was down. He says being a New Man is all about survival. We go through so many changes the first year and we are trying to absorb so much that our goal should be just to get through. It's not about how we are going to do as priests. It's not about how holy we are. It's about making it through, he says. And, if you want my opinion, we have to be open to seeing God's hand in it. If we accept that we should try to see God in everything, then we should try to see Him right here among the New Men. In all the headaches. The crazy schedule. Everything. They say God works in mysterious ways. Sometimes it's awful mysterious to me here."

His friend laughed again. Scot was pleased. "Scot, you really see God's hand in all of this?"

"I try to. I really do. It helps me a lot."

"Can I ask you something, Scot?"

"Sure, anything. What?"

"Are you going to stay?"

"Right at this moment, right in this room, I have to answer yes. But if you ask me if I'm certain that God won't come tapping on my shoulder someday and say, 'Scot, that's enough. Go back and become a father and husband,' well, I can't say that won't happen. It could most definitely happen."

The other New Man looked at his watch. They had been talking for three hours. They both realized they had been up for almost twenty-one hours straight. "Let me ask you a question," Scot said as they straightened up the room. The glassy rattle of bottles came from the trashcan. "Did this talk help?"

"More than you know. It means so much to know someone is going through the same thing—and it looks like you're on top of it."

"Might look that way, but it's not always true," Scot said.

"Anyway, thanks."

Scot put a hand on his friend's shoulder. "You, too."

They walked down the pitch black corridor.

"Survival, huh?" his friend said.

"Huh?"

"Survival. You said McRae said we should concentrate on surviving."

"Right," Scot said.

They parted by the elevator. "Good advice," he said.

CHAPTER XVIII

CHRIS

*Live in accord with the spirit and you
will not yield to the cravings of the flesh.*

—EVENING READING FOR FRIDAY
OF THE SEVENTH WEEK OF EASTER (GALATIANS 5:16)

Chris Nalty rang the bell, then passed the cigar box to his right hand. He now held one box in each hand.

Monsignor Dolan opened the door to his apartment and rumbled a laugh. "Ah, Chris, I was expecting you," he said, rubbing his smooth, puffy palms together. "Hand 'em over."

Chris passed him the boxes. Dolan looked down and wondered why there were two. "I smoked about half of yours," Nalty confessed, "so here's some of mine. They're Dominican. Just as good, I assure you."

Dolan read the label on the light brown container. "Paul Garmirian, eh," he mumbled. "Hey, sounds good to me."

"Well, monsignor, a happy and blessed Easter and, of course, congratulations. You made it."

"I know," Dolan wailed in mock misery. "The secretaries were complaining I was getting so crabby toward the end. I hope not, but it wasn't the easiest thing I ever did, I can tell you that. You know something? I've always said there's nothing like a good cigar and a Bud after the Easter Vigil."

Just in case temptation came sniffing around during Lent, Dolan asked Nalty to hold his box of Avo, size number 2: the big fat ones. Chris made up for the ones he smoked with a half-box of the Garmirians. Allie, his old sputtering flame back in Washington, sent him two boxes.

"Enjoy, monsignor. I really think you'll like the Garmirians."

"Fantastic. Thanks, Chris."

Nalty turned to leave. "Wait a second, Chris," Dolan said suddenly. "How's everything going? Classes, formation? Anything you want to talk about?"

"The truth, monsignor? No. Not at all. In fact, things are going just fine."

"You sure about that? I'm all ears if you want to talk."

"Honestly, monsignor. I'd tell you if there was a problem. You know that. I have to say, things have been going pretty well lately."

Dolan knew better than to nag a New Man who seemed to be heading toward solid ground. "Um, OK. Well, then, *buona sera.*"

"Buona sera."

Dolan closed the door and lit up. The last cigar he smoked was at Nalty's Mardi Gras party—more than forty days ago. Dolan let the taste of the smoke roll around his mouth longer than usual. It was exquisite. He missed everything: the taste, rolling the warm smoke around his tongue, the smell. He'd notice the odor of old cigars in his clerics and sweaters during Lent. That made it even harder to keep his vow. He wondered if he would give up cigars during the next Lent. Don't rush ahead, he told himself. That's a whole year away and there's still a class of New Men to shepherd through and another to welcome.

He was pleased—and not just a bit surprised—that no one had dropped out yet. Back before Christmas he had the same feeling: am I getting through to these guys? As much as he would hate to admit it, the odds were against having a full class of New Men with firm priestly vocations. It just rarely—if ever—happened that way. It's normal to lose at least one New Man. But, now, with less than two months to go before the summer recess, there didn't seem to be anyone sinking—he hoped.

Dolan knew that the faculty—expect perhaps the spiritual directors—never saw the whole picture. Many things occurred among the seminarians that never filtered out. It was like that when he was here two decades ago and it was like that now. That's why he tries to spend as much time with the New Men as possible. You may hear a grumble or an offhand remark that means a guy is in trouble. You may see a New Man drunk and rowdy—another sign that maybe the vocation isn't there. But he couldn't quite read Scot Landry. Was there trouble behind all that enthusiasm? He just didn't know. And that, to be honest, bothered Dolan even more.

Dolan is usually quite good at assessing the New Men. He particularly likes to watch the older guys such as Nalty. They helped set the tone. A winsome seminarian just out of college is naturally going to look to the guys in their thirties to lead the way. And Dolan was growing to like Nalty's approach: have fun, keep a well-stocked bar, smoke your cigars, but don't let your prayer life slip. He hadn't expected it at the beginning of the year, but Nalty was turning out to be a role model.

A story was going around among the faculty about a New Man who was blowing off morning mass at least a couple times a week. He always had an excuse: alarm didn't go off, wasn't feeling well, drank a little too much the night before. The seminarians generally kept the same spots in the chapel and his was in the second row just behind Nalty, who doesn't like to wear his glasses and needs to be as close as possible. When Nalty would turn around for the handshake of peace near the end of the mass, there would often be an empty space where the sleeping seminarian should be. One day when the New Man did show up, Nalty and a fifth-year priest cornered him with an ultimatum. If you're not happy, then leave, they said, but don't stick around and make a joke of the place. "You're not holding up your weight and that creates a problem for everyone. You got it?" Nalty said. Suddenly, the New Man's alarm started going off on time.

Dolan was impressed. More than anything else, he liked to see the seminarians deal with problems among themselves. It's a good lesson for after they are ordained.

"When a priest is in trouble—drinking, sexually—who is the first to recognize it?" said Dolan, sitting in one of the easy chairs in his study. "It's not usually the bishop. He has a lot of other things to deal with. Is it the parishioners? Not usually. It's other priests. If they don't intervene, then things start to spin out of control."

Nalty had made no secret of his battle with celibacy. The rector kept an eye on him and was happy to see some progress. Chris was much more relaxed lately. He saw him talking to the younger New Men about prayer. Nalty has a bigfoot personality—in a way not unlike Dolan himself. They enter the room and just seem to take over. Dolan thought that if Nalty's on the way to sorting out his vocation, it can only help any others—if there are any others—who may be wondering if they should remain.

Dolan finished the cigar, smoking down to a damp, thumb-size nub in a glass ashtray. He took out his fountain pen and jotted down a few more thoughts for his next rector's conference, his monthly talk to the seminarians. This was the one he wanted to make sure the New Men, in particular, remembered. It was going to be the sex talk.

"We spend a lot of time with the 'cookbook' stuff. You know, showing guys how to 'do' the priesthood: how to baptize, how to offer mass, how to offer pastoral counseling, how to preach. This, we have to do. Seminaries have always done it. But these days we have to go a lot deeper. We have to dig into areas that not so long ago were completely off limits. I'm talking, of course, about sex. Some of these guys have been through relationships with women. Others are totally inexperienced and may have never even thought about themselves in sexual terms."

Dolan underlined two words in his talk with two bold strokes: *self-knowledge.*

"Self-knowledge. That's what it's all about," Dolan told me. "We try to tell the guys: admit who you are and whether you have anything that is eating at you. It's not the end of your vocation to admit you may have trouble sorting out some of the sexual issues. No one says the rules the Church has are easy. But, for God's sake, don't wait until you're ordained to realize you have a problem."

His talk was set for the auditorium next Sunday evening. Word had already leaked that this was to be the sex lecture. The New Men were especially curious about how blunt Dolan would get. The rector doesn't normally shy away from anything. Gary Benz remembers how he almost blushed when Dolan mentioned masturbation before their retreat last fall. "I was thinking, 'Gosh, this is a priest talking like this?' " Gary said.

The seminarians took their places in the chapel. It was still daylight out. The clocks had just been pushed ahead for spring. Dolan began by talking about the historic legacy of priestly celibacy, which took root nine hundred years ago. It's tradition, not dogma. But, as Pope John Paul II has made clear, don't count on any changes.

"If you are expecting it to change in your priestly life," said Dolan, "you are gravely mistaken.

"As the old saying goes, 'A man can do almost anything as long as he knows there is a reason,'" he continued. "Lord knows, if you do not understand the *why* of celibacy, its faithful living-out will be tough."

He went back to 1967 and an encyclical by Pope Paul VI to make his case. A priest's love for Jesus is so strong that it is exclusive, Paul VI wrote. Celibacy reminds Catholics of the bond that transcends the priest's life, and keeps the priest's attention to his duties focused and undiluted, Dolan told the seminarians.

"We are purely His from . . . our brain cells to our sperm cells," he said. A few seminarians smiled. No one laughed.

Dolan couldn't have been more serious. He enunciated each word strongly and clearly. He was in no rush.

"We are acting foolishly if we accept celibacy only because it is required. In other words, you must be confident that you are personally called to celibacy. We don't just say, 'Well, I guess I'll have to be celibate if I want to be ordained' . . . Celibacy is not 'spray painted' on, as something that just happens to come along with the priesthood, like an AM/FM radio might happen to come along with a new car.

"If," Dolan said, pointing his finger out at the pews, "you are unable to live a chaste life here and now, that is a rather clear indication that you cannot embrace celibacy, which means, my brothers, you are not called to the priesthood.

"Can I get specific? I hope I do not offend with this candor:

"If you now find yourself in a genital relationship with a woman or man;

"If you are purchasing pornography or viewing pornographic films;

"If you visit prostitutes, female or male, or are into cruising, that is, frequenting bars, parks, or areas of town in the hopes of making sexual contact of any kind;

"If you bury or ignore questions of sexual behavior or orientation, or cannot even calmly discuss such matters without becoming tongue-tied or snickering like a sophomore in high school."

Dolan went on, ticking off problem after problem:

"If you detect any genital attraction to children;

"If you have an uncontrollable habit of frequent masturbation;

"If you find yourself constantly viewing women—or men—as sex objects, existing to satisfy your lustful desires;

"You should seek the time, space, and counseling necessary to control this before continuing on toward the priesthood. Now, brothers, I'm not talking about periodic falls, ongoing temptations, or the struggles to live chastely that every healthy person faces. I'm speaking about serious, continual, sustained lapses or uncontrollable urges."

The church was totally—almost unnaturally—silent. No one moved. No one sniffled or scratched. Gary Benz didn't blush. No one wanted to draw attention to themselves. They sat and waited. Dolan did his trademark pause—longer than usual. When he began to speak, his voice sounded even louder than before.

"Have any of us been untouched by the tragedy of priests who have been unchaste? We have seen these poor men on TV and, while the cameras rolled, it seemed like their lives were disintegrating right before our eyes. But that disintegration was long in coming. They had kept a compartment of their lives hidden, where the lights of faith and truth were never turned on. Problem is, you can never live your life for long in separate compartments.

"So, no double lives; no 'Sunday celibacy'; no time off for good behavior; no hidden compartment of our behavior. . . . It is possible to live a happy, wholesome, fruitful life faithful to one's commitment to celibate chastity. The world will tell you it is not. They will deny celibacy's value, contend it is unhealthy, unnatural, and impossible. They will tease you and say, 'Come on, you're getting it somewhere.' And, let's face it, enough priests have acted in such a manner to provide them with ammo.

"Is it difficult? You bet it is, at times, but so is the chastity and sacrifice of marriage.

"Is it tough at times? You bet it is—and not just the lack of conjugal love, but the absence of the tender, understanding, affirming companionship of a woman.

"So we embrace celibate chastity sincerely, realistically, sanely, joyfully, freely," Dolan said, pulling back from the lectern. "Fear, holding back, a lack of honesty, has no place in this romance."

Walking out of the chapel, Chris Nalty thought about the last time the rector grilled the seminarians about getting a handle on celibacy. How long ago was that? Seven months. Could that be? Ages ago, it seemed. Nalty tried to remember how he felt when Dolan got to the part about celibacy in the speech before the retreat. Uncomfortable, for sure. He sat there in the retreat prepared to pull out, just waiting for someone to convince him that this was one big mistake and he should hustle back before Allie got tired of waiting. It was like Dolan was reading his mind and bearing down: start deciding where you want to be. But he didn't need the rector—with his lifer vocation—to tell him how hard it was to give up sex. He knew it. He was getting up before dawn and praying about it. That was only seven months ago? Unreal, he thought with a touch of self-congratulation. He was still around, still celibate, and—the surprise of all—reaching some kind of personal truce. Dolan's latest talk simply washed over him. Agreement had replaced frustration. He counted again on his fingers just to make sure. Yes, only seven months.

There had been no grand defining event since he arrived; no sudden rush of fortitude or inspiration. "I was waiting for something like a lightning bolt or a dove to fly in my window," Nalty said the day after Dolan's speech. "I realize now that wasn't going to happen."

Rather, it was the simple formula Dolan urged that helped him most: be honest with yourself. Just a couple nights before the talk, he finally was. Brutally so. He called it his "duel to the death" debate with himself. He told himself: look, Chris, if you can't hack celibacy, if it is too much of a burden, then it is time to pack. Are you fooling yourself, your family, and the diocese? he asked himself. Get on with it. Make a choice.

This showdown was touched off by an article he read in the *National Catholic Reporter,* which criticized a cable television movie about a priest having an affair. "You start to see all the scandals and they really wake you up. You do not—NOT—want to be part of that. If I think that is going to happen to me, well, then, I ought to get my butt out of here," he told me.

"If I was a lawyer and I blew some ethical rule and I was brought up by the bar association, big deal. I don't feel like I owe anything to other lawyers. I don't owe anything to the profession. I would never feel that way. But I really feel I owe something to other priests. If I was to go out there and screw around, I would think the damage that I would do to the priesthood would be terrible. It isn't just about the girl; it isn't just your little parish church; it's all the people who depend on priests all over the world.

"So I sat there, all alone in my room, and told myself: 'Chris, if you can't do this you ought to just freaking go home.'

"It was really the first point where I really said, 'I can do this.' I need God's help to do this, but I can do it."

There was still one thing left undone.

He had to call Allie in Washington and tell her that—for the foreseeable future—they had no chance. For months, Chris had put it off with any excuse he could snatch. His vocation was too unsettled. Why make a scene during Christmas? Let's wait until after she sends the cigars. There was no good reason to postpone it any longer. "If you're going to be honest with yourself, you might as well be with everyone else, right?" Nalty said. Two days after Dolan's lecture on celibacy, it was time. By this time, the seminary had taken a big step and installed private telephones in each of the rooms. Nalty was glad for the privacy, but his bills had gone sky-high.

Allie answered on the second ring. He was half-hoping she would be out and he could leave a message and force her to make the call—an old attorney trick.

"Allie? It's Chris."

"Chris!" she answered. "I wasn't expecting to hear from you. How's everything? Did you get the cigars? The guy said they were just as good as the other ones. What do you call them? The ones the priest there wanted."

"Avos. And, yup, I got the Garmirians you sent. I can't thank you enough, Allie. I hope it wasn't a big problem."

"Not at all, Chris. So what's going on over there?"

"It couldn't be better," he said. "Well, I should say it could always be a little better. But, you know, I'm starting to get the hang of this seminary stuff. It's starting to feel a little like home."

"Home? Chris, come on. Is everything OK?"

"Allie, I'm telling you. I'm really getting into the groove here. It's all starting to make sense."

"The groove? Chris, get real. When are you coming home? Are you still hooked on this priest thing? You coming back this summer? When are you going to get out of there?"

"That's what I wanted to tell you, er, that's part of what I wanted to tell you. Allie, I'm not coming back. I mean, at least for about another year. What I'm trying to say is that I'm staying. I think—no, wait a minute, I know—this is what I want to be doing right now. You know where I might be going this summer? Guess."

"I don't feel like guessing."

"Come on. One guess. OK. Forget it. Me and another seminarian—remember the guy I told you about who went with me to the Canaries after Christmas?—well, he and I are probably going to go to India to work with Mother Teresa's Missionaries of Charity."

"India! You serious?"

"Very serious. My dad knew someone who had connections with the missionaries and . . . Well, it's a long story. But what do you think? Pretty cool, huh?"

"Sure, I guess. I mean, is this like some big-deal commitment? I mean, you're talking about Mother Teresa. What are you telling me?"

"Allie, I'm just telling you what I'm up to. I'm telling you that I'm happy. I'm telling you that I'm going to India to work with a woman who will someday be a saint."

"No, you know what I'm talking about. Is this your way of telling me that you're staying in the seminary? You're going to finish the year, go to India, and come back to Rome. Right? Is that the picture, Chris?"

Nalty thought for a second about making a joke to try to lighten the conversation. Bad idea. "That is pretty much the picture," he said.

She was quiet. Chris waited her out and listened into the receiver. Funny, he thought, there were hardly any of those strange hums and clicks he remembered from his transatlantic calls from London in the early eighties.

"Allie? You still there?" he said.

"I'm here. And you're there. That pretty much sums it up, don't you think?"

"Allie, you knew that this was always a real possibility—that I would stay here. We used to talk a lot about my vocation, remember?"

"I remember. It was just talk, though. I really didn't think you'd go through with anything, ah, permanent. I don't think hardly anyone did. You know that. I'm just a little surprised, that's all. I thought you'd be back in the States by now and you'd be telling me stories about what it was like in the seminary before you realized you weren't cut out to be a priest. Like I said, I'm just a little surprised we're having this conversation."

"Well, to be honest, sometimes I am, too. You want to hear something incredible? I got calluses on my knees. I looked at them and said to myself, 'Dude, what are those? Geez-em, they're calluses.' I got great big calluses from praying so much."

"You're shitting me."

"No way. Would I shit an old friend?"

The conversation trailed off. Chris had said all he wanted to. Allie held out one parting shot: "I don't think we should stay in touch. Good-bye."

Chris was certain they would talk again. It might be a very long time, though. But it felt good to get it over with. He was even relieved Allie asked him not to call any more. It was crisp, final. That's just what he wanted.

"I think that part of the reason that coming to Rome is good is that you have to cut the ropes that may be holding you down," he said after making the call. "But you can still hold on to the ropes if you want. Like me, in a way, with Allie by still talking to her on the phone. Even if it's a little thread. I think the only way you really get the whole picture is if you really cut everything."

It was one of those rare clean slate days. Everything was ahead with nothing nipping from behind. Even the Carnivor next door was showing signs of life. Perfect. Chris wanted company after calling Allie and he enjoyed the Carnivor crowd.

The place had been pretty quiet much of the year. Eric Berns—the founder and guru of the club—had been ordained a deacon and there was lots of new business to attend to with his diocese in La Crosse, Wisconsin. But a rasher of venison jerky was too much to pass up. Tom Richter's brothers smuggled it in from North Dakota. Word got around the seminary that Berns and the boys were holding court at the Carnivor, a spare room dedicated to meat. Stalking it, preparing it, and eating it. Anything that could be put on a grill, they probably grilled it. On the wall is a fading photo of Berns's father next to a giant buck he shot years before Eric was born. Another shot is of a pathetic squirrel Bern stuffed for his father in high school. They had to toss it out after it began to stink.

Seminarians began to trickle into the Carnivor—given its oddly spelled title in an attempt to differentiate it from a wild game restaurant of the same name in Nairobi that is a popular feeding stop for seminarians on missionary assignments. Some seminarians grabbed a beer and lingered around the Carnivor. Others just popped in for a second to look around. One New Man asked about the chicken story. Was it really true?

"You mean, you haven't heard the chicken story?" bellowed Nalty.

"Umm, I guess parts of it," the seminarian said.

"Come on, Eric. Tell it," cried Nalty, definitely in the mood for a laugh. "Come on."

"OK," Berns conceded, getting comfortable in his easy chair. If he was going to tell it again, he wanted to do it right. "I'll be one hundred years old and still telling this.

"It goes like this:

"One day—back when we were New Men—a guy from New York comes in with an article from the *Spectator* magazine talking about how things that are shocking today, like butchering animals, were once commonplace, and how drug use and sexual topics, which were once on the fringe, are now blasé. So I said to him, 'You've never seen an animal killed?' He's a New Yorker, mind you, so the answer was no. But he was interested. It was like a cultural experiment. So we went off to get us some chickens."

They climbed on a motorbike, toting Berns's father's old army duffel bag, and headed to the market at Campo dei Fiori. The meat sellers had nothing live but suggested they go to Piazza Vittorio—a bigger outdoor market with more exotic fare.

"We found this old woman. Man, she robbed us on the price of those chickens, but we had no choice and paid it. I tell you, we got lots of looks heading back—two guys riding a *motorino,* wearing clerics and carrying a duffel bag with two live chickens. They weren't getting too much air in the duffel, so we had to hurry. They were like half-dead by the time we got back.

"So we get to the roof. Richter takes out the first chicken and cuts its neck. He did just like you're supposed to. He stuck it into a bucket of water and it caught all the blood. I cut the second one and Richter held it. He thought it would be kind of funny to freak out all the New England boys, so he held up the chicken while it was squirting blood. It made a perfect circle of blood about twelve feet in diameter. And you should have seen those other guys jump, like they never saw chicken blood before. It was getting late and we had a meeting at eight. So we figured we'd just go clean it up later. That's when it all started to hit the fan."

The music director, who was then a layman who lived just off the roof terrace, was the first to see it: a circle of blood, a bucket filled with bloody water, chicken feathers everywhere, two chicken heads, and Richter's beer bottle.

"Well this guy starts to hyperventilate and runs and gets another faculty member up there, a Jesuit. He takes one look and says, 'Looks like something satanic or some crazy sex thing.' Immediately, the faculty was called together for an emergency meeting. They were going nuts, absolutely nuts. They thought they had some satanic cult in their midst. They got Kampschneider to go up there. And, being a farmboy himself, he goes, 'Well, to me, it looks like somebody just got hungry for chicken and hasn't gotten around to cleaning it up yet." The others just went, 'Come on. It's got to be something weird.'"

But before calling all the seminarians, the faculty wanted to make a few checks. Richter and Berns were the two most likely to have anything to do with cutting up animals. They knocked first on Richter's door.

"I don't know what got into him, but he decided to play along. He goes: 'Chickens? Killed? Sacrifice? What chickens killed? That's pretty strange in the city, don't you think?' Well, they went white. Then he felt sorry for them and started laughing.

"It was terribly embarrassing for the faculty. Here, supposedly a place of God, the first thing they had on their mind was satanism rather than looking for a more logical explanation. It shows how twisted things have become when devil worship is the first thing that comes to mind when you see some slaughtered chickens. It was hilarious, but afterward when we thought about it, it showed a real sad side to our culture."

"So how did the chickens taste?" the New Man asked.

"Oh, yeah. Excellent."

Chris Nalty roared, then went to get himself one of the cigars that Allie had sent over.

While the Carnivor was filling, Scot Landry was out alone shooting baskets. The others he had been playing with had gone back in. Scot stayed and fired long-range shots. He was good. Most went in or at least had a chance. Shooting hoops had always helped him think. His vocation had once been such a simple and pure act: renounce his dreams of a family and take up the priesthood. What had happened along the way? It was all getting so cloudy and complicated.

First, there was the transfer. Scot prayed hard about the decision and he seemed comfortable that being with Roger was the right move. The waiting, however, was unnerving him. Scot was hard-wired for action; staring down problems and doing something about them. He knew it was best not to make any final decision until summer. It just was hard to keep it slow. Also, he told himself, it wouldn't help his case to bring up any of this second-guessing about his calling with anyone back home. You're going to have to work this out with your spiritual director and, of course, with Roger, he thought. "He's the best counselor there is," Scot said. "He can sometimes tell me what I want better than I can myself."

And, he asks, what is that?

"It's like sometimes I don't trust myself or my feelings. It's a brand-new feeling for me. Now, one minute I'm committed one hundred percent to the priesthood, then the next I waver. I start thinking, 'If I'm so bothered by the seminary, maybe the Lord is telling me He doesn't want me to become a priest.' That's the type of rationalization I'm going through."

Scot thought a lot about how he helped talk the other New Man into sticking it out for the rest of the year. He was so passionate about not letting the difficulties of the seminary cloud his calling. "Am I giving myself the same chance?" he asked.

He did a few hard dribbles and stepped back for a long, arching shot. It clanged off the rim and rolled off the court.

CHAPTER XIX

THE CIRCLE

*Speak boastfully no longer, nor let
arrogance issue from your mouths.*

—CANTICLE FOR WEDNESDAY MORNINGS
(1 SAMUEL 2:3)

Scot Landry was the last to arrive and pulled a chair into the circle. To his left was Mike Woods, the quarterback from the Spaghetti Bowl. Six other New Men completed the ring in the student kitchen on the top floor of the seminary for their monthly meeting. A late spring rainstorm had just finished. The mountains outside Rome, normally hidden by haze and smog, were perfectly visible—down to the clay-tile roofs in towns the seminarians would probably never visit.

The leader of the meeting, a thin New Man with blond hair, lit a candle inside a red glass holder. They sang a hymn.

"A rhetorical question," he said when they finished. "Are we really holy?"

He passed around a photocopied page from a book describing the stages of holiness, written by a Franciscan priest in New York. Each seminarian read a paragraph aloud.

"Purgation, the first stage, is the long period of time when an individual escapes from his or her own self-centeredness and narcissism," one of them read.

"Usually, the purgative period is a time of darkness and trial," he continued.

Scot Landry listened intently. He had heard this articulated in so many different ways. From his brother, his spiritual director. It's so conveniently cataloged in books like this, he thought. Like holiness was some recipe and you're home free if you follow the steps and avoid the pitfalls. In a way, he surmised, it was. Nothing will happen unless you want it to. He agreed with the basic premise of the spiritual directors: God doesn't dole out graces to those who aren't at least looking. He chuckled a bit at the irony, though. He used to map out his life in step-by-step goals. Reach one, go for the next. Religious writers thought the same way, it seemed. Only Scot was having some trouble getting off square one.

He looked over the other New Men in the room. He had high hopes for this gathering; more so than the ones before. They had been getting together once a month since the fall. Each New Man who wanted to could join a group like this—a chance to talk freely about the seminary and their personal path toward ordination. The appointed leader for the meeting would bring a topic. But anything could be raised once the discussion got under way. Dolan often talked about honesty as the cornerstone of forming priests. This was as honest as it gets.

The rules of confidentiality were clear: nothing left the room. Without the honesty that comes from confidentiality, the meetings would be worthless. The first few times together were mostly occasions to vent to the obvious complaints about seminary life: the lack of privacy, how their free time just drained away. "Basically, men whining," one of them said. "You could look at it as just a glorified gripe session. But there's much more than that. Once someone is able to put their doubts or temptations into words, it all of a sudden becomes so much more real. It's something they can start dealing with."

In time, however, as their trust grew, they started to veer inward. First they dissected their thoughts on the priesthood. Scot was always firm. The lessons and the theological theory were fine, but he craved the pastoral—the paternal—role. In a way, he looked at the parish as a surrogate family with the priest as the father in name and demeanor. Scot, as he always had, was pressing hard to latch onto new challenges. The seminary was sometimes just too stagnant.

But this meeting, the last of the year, intrigued him the most. Finally, the New Men were starting to talk about what it means to be truly good and how to go about getting there. If God was really beckoning them to the priesthood, why are there so many obstacles? Why do so many New Men feel like they are thrashing, gasping, and sometimes, like now, crying out for help?

"It's that mystery that calls you but repels you," the leader of the group said, passing around some chocolate chip cookies sent by his mother. "The only way to grace is to surrender to the will of the Lord. But isn't that the hardest thing to do because it's so 'other'? Why is the thing that I want more than anything challenging me so much?"

Scot nodded.

"We are so goal driven—most of us, anyway," the leader went on. "I tell my spiritual director, 'Why aren't I farther along? I want to be there, not here.' And what does he say? 'God will only allow you to get as close as He wants you to be.'

"What's that supposed to mean? That's hard for men like myself who can be very inflated and full of themselves. I go down to the chapel and think, 'What am I doing all this for? God will only let me get as close as He wants. It's totally out of my hands.' So I figure that holiness is no more than the desire to be close to God. It's up to Him whether He'll let you near."

Scot cut in. This was precisely what had been bothering him—everyone insisting the key to the priesthood was surrender. How alien this was to his take-charge attitude. He knew it bothered his brother Roger as well. But nowhere near as much. Why? Scot kept asking himself. Does this mean Roger has a vocation and I have some misguided fervor that carried me all the way to Rome for nothing?

The sun had gone down and the only light in the room was the candle on the coffee table in the middle of the circle. Scot leaned forward into the reddish glow.

"We've all heard holiness described as a passive thing, right? Well my question is: where are our hearts? Where are our minds? What happens to Scot Landry and the things that make him Scot Landry? The struggle for me is what to do on a daily basis. Do we just want to be holy? Is feeling that we're holy just enough? It might make us feel good, but what is it accomplishing? It's hard for me to think about it just being totally passive. For me, it's necessary to feel that I've grown. Is my goal God or is it for something personal?"

"Right!" said a New Man sitting across the circle wearing a baggy sweatshirt. "That touches on the ultimate question I've been battling all year. If we're supposed to turn our lives over to God's will, how do you know you are really doing it? I mean, let's say I sense the need to, I don't know, leave the seminary and get married. OK? How much do we trust our own feelings? How do we know when God is talking or if it's just some random feeling taking hold?"

The New Man to his left held up his hand. "Want to hear something? I felt holier before I entered the seminary. I was working and going to daily mass and thinking, 'Wow, I'm holy.' But then you come here and everyone is doing it. There is a danger here. We all go through the motions. Yeah, yeah, yeah—got to go to mass. Yeah, yeah, yeah—got to go to pray. You know what I mean?"

"Definitely," said the sweatshirt seminarian. "We are all learning to be priests, not necessarily how to be holy. We learn all the tricks of how to act like priests, and people on the outside see us act like that and say, 'Wow, isn't he holy.' We can start believing this without really examining our own souls. This compliment—Man, is he holy—can be very seductive and very dangerous."

"Yeah," Scot said. "People on the outside—as we all know—are much freer in a sense. They don't have labels, or at least the type of labels that are put on us so often. Priests are expected to be perfect. Perfect and holy. Sometimes I want to shout: 'We are struggling with holiness just like you.'"

"It really wears me down. It really burns me out sometimes," the leader said. "Every decision we make, we're supposed to be looking for the Lord. I don't care if it's charitable work or a college degree or how you are going to spend your summer or how you are going to spend the afternoon. It's always: OK, where is the Lord in this? Where is the Lord in that? It's that constant forgetting of self—or trying to forget.

It's just brutal. It's good, I guess. But I'm just always left bruised and battered."

"I just had a dirty thought," added Mike Woods, who had been quiet so far. "We were talking about purgation here and a phrase comes to mind: the urge to purge. It's locker-room talk, but it also applies here. There really is an urge to purge. There should be a strong urge to purge what we left behind. That—this urge to get rid of our past—shows that we are on the road to holiness. It's not wrong, however, to say sometimes, 'Hey, I need help.' We are training in holiness. The agony will come. We have to be in shape to deal with it."

"The agony, the struggle, the urge to purge," the leader broke in. "I mean, deep down inside we know that this is where our happiness lies. We wouldn't be here if not. Yet how bizarre when you try to convince people that they are not going to be happy, I'm not going to be happy, this world will not find peace until we all go through it."

"Especially men," said Scot. "It's especially hard with men."

"What do you mean?" the New Man in the sweatshirt asked.

Scot looked around the circle. The others were nodding. "Surely, you must see it. A lot of men see holiness just in terms of piety and they think piety is just for old women. Haven't you ever thought about who fills the congregations on Sundays. It's mostly women—and the children they, for the most part, drag there."

"Right," the leader said. "One of our hardest tasks as priests will be to show men—average guys—what manly holiness is."

Scot clapped his hands together. "Exactly. We've all been weaned on the tough-guy stuff: strong and silent is some sort of ideal for American men. Am I right? I look at my own family. My mom is very pious, but when I was growing up my father never talked about his faith and religion. So I really saw holiness as a kind of feminine thing. Men aren't going to return to the Church until we—I mean the Church, of course—begin to take seriously the job of showing that caring, charity, can be very masculine things. Priests should be role models in this, don't you think?"

"Definitely," the leader said, "but these days it seems each step forward is offset by a step backward. I'm talking about all the scandals; priests who can't keep it zipped up. On some level it shows that we are human. There will always be people who just cannot keep their commitments, be it to the priesthood, marriage, work, whatever. But don't you think it also shows a breakdown inside the Church as well? Being a priest can be extremely lonely. Who can you turn to for help when temptation comes? Other priests mostly. If that support network breaks down, then we're going be facing a lot more problems."

"Into the frying pan," one of the New Men across the circle said.

"Right," Scot said. "We have to rely on ourselves. We can't really turn to the parishioners for help and say, 'Hey, I'm struggling with the priesthood here. I'm not sure of my path to holiness. I'm not sure I can deal with celibacy.' You can't. Priests have to help other priests. We have to talk things out before they become a problem."

To end the meeting, they all sat in silence for a while. Some, like Scot, bowed their heads. Others looked into the candle. The stillness, the intense privacy of silence, was eloquent. No matter how much they confide in each other, no matter how much they admit to their spiritual directors, every New Man is alone with his vocation to accept it, understand it, and, at times, fight with it.

Scot wondered—not for the first time—about what it meant to be holy and whether he would return to Rome.

"Set point," said Roger Landry. He knew that his opponent was aware of the score. It was habit.

The monsignor across the net twirled his racket.

Roger's first serve—hard but not as hard as he could hit—skipped in just in front of the line. Dan Thomas stepped back and returned a nice topspin forehand. Roger slashed back a hard shot into the corner, catching the left-handed monsignor leaning the wrong way. But he recovered and slapped back a two-handed backhand that floated softly about three feet over the net. Roger took two steps forward and swatted the ball cleanly down toward the other corner. The monsignor waved his racket meekly in that direction, but he knew he was beaten. Again.

"Great shot!" he yelled. "Hey, I got two games off you this set. Not bad."

Roger smiled. "Good set. You had me worried there for a while."

"Please," the priest said, wiping the back of his hand across his forehead. "No lying. You'll have to go to confession."

"OK, OK. Let's take a break for a sec. Want some water?"

"Sure. I'm dying. When was spring? Seems like we went right into summer."

At the side of the green concrete courts at the far end of the athletic fields near the dome of the Ukrainian seminary, Roger and the young American monsignor gulped down bottled water. They had been getting together for matches on and off during the year. It was always the same result: a wipeout by Roger. But Roger was impressed by the monsignor's determination. He never gave up on a shot—lunging, sometimes diving. Here was a priest—still in his thirties—called back to work in the Curia in the powerful Congregation for Bishops, which oversees the appointments and coaches the damage-control teams after scandals in the dioceses around the world. Yet there were no outward signs of smugness; no smell of superiority. He sweats like everyone else. "I had the same impression of the Vatican clerics that most Americans have," said Roger. "That they are priests, yes, but they really have cold blood running through their veins. It's somewhere between seventy and eighty degrees or something." His tennis partner was a warm contradiction to the stereotype.

Roger saw something of himself in the contented priest he trounced on the tennis court. Maybe, Roger thought, he, too, would be called back to Rome like the monsignor. And someday—"older, wiser, and ever balder"—he could be playing tennis with a New Man hungry for any scrap of advice to help him deal with the two sides of the North American College: being told to look no farther than the parish but seeing every day the Vatican and its enormous needs.

Every seminarian knew the Vatican could come knocking someday. The North American College makes them prime material to be sent back when the Curia calls. And there is no reasonable way to refuse.

"Once you're a priest, you stop applying for jobs," said Monsignor Thomas. "They call and you come."

"But what about the sense of importance associated with the Vatican; of being at the center of it all?" Roger asked.

"You can't think of this like you're in a company and the pope is the CEO. The closer you get, the brighter you shine in the company. I can tell you the truth: I can't wait to get back to a parish someday. I know that's true with a lot of priests over at the Curia. For some, it's a real sacrifice to be away from preaching, being with a congregation. It's tough."

"But some of us are probably going to be called back to work in some capacity. It can't be all bad. It must be amazing to go to work every day over there."

"Sure, Roger, there are some people who bask in it all. But what is it, really? You can't help but sit there thinking, 'How is this helping save souls? How is this helping me grow spiritually?' It can eat you up if you can't see the wisdom in it."

"Wisdom? Whose wisdom? The Church's wisdom in picking you?"

"Well, not really. Sure, you have to assume the Church knows what she's doing when it assigns people to the Curia. No, what I'm saying is that you have to try to see the wisdom in what you've been asked to do, even if it can seem tedious or maybe you don't see the whole picture. You have to try to sanctify each moment; try to make it holy and extraordinary."

Roger ran his hand over his cropped hair, leaving his palm shiny with sweat. "But how do you handle your expectations? Everyone has some kind of ambition. In their mind's eye there's always some picture of the future."

"And you can let that dominate your life or"—he raised a finger—"you can bask in the beauty of the moment. Look, Roger, have you ever been in a play?"

"Sure."

"OK. We may not think it's such a good idea where the director wants us to stand, or he may ask us to say our lines in a way different from how we think they should be," the monsignor said. "But there has to be one guy in charge or everything falls apart."

"Pandemonium."

"Exactly. If we don't appreciate our roles, we'll be out of the whole play."

"Speaking about play," said Roger, "you want to keep going. One more set, OK?"

"You haven't humbled me enough, I guess," the monsignor said. "Let's just volley for a while. I'm wiped out."

Roger hit an easy forehand.

Thomas lobbed it back. "You know what, Roger? There's nothing wrong with ambition as long as it is properly directed." He batted a slicing backhand. "We all try to pretend it's not there." A forehand. "But it's always there in some form."

A top-spin by Roger fooled him and he bashed the ball into the net.

"What I'm saying," said the monsignor as he hit one back to Roger, "is that let's say if you ever are asked to work over at the Vatican some day, or even let's say you become something important in the Church, you only have to remember one thing."

The monsignor lunged for a forehand. "And if you forget that you're in deep trouble."

His shot landed beyond the baseline. Roger caught it. "What's that?"

"You must never stop seeing the world through the eyes of a priest. You do that and it's all over."

They played a while longer, then ended the way they began, with a quick prayer on the court.

CHAPTER XX

GARY

No servant can obey two masters.

—ANTIPHON FOR THE CANTICLE OF MARY
FOR SUNDAY EVENINGS

Tam Tran jogged up behind Gary Benz.

"Are you sure you know where it is, Gary?" he asked.

Gary looked over an overused Rome street map, ripped along the creases into rectangle pieces. Gary ran his finger up the fat line of Via Nomentana, one of the ancient main thoroughfares out of the city. The church they were looking for was somewhere along the way. They had come by bus—Gary making sure everyone in the group had a proper ticket—but they had gotten off several stops too early.

"OK," he said, tapping his finger on a spot in the unfamiliar zone of northeast Rome—the opposite end of the city from the seminary. "We're here. It should be close."

Tran checked his watch. "Let's go. We're late."

The group of seminarians raced along the access road paralleling the boulevard. Tran was sweating in his wrinkled clerics. He darted into traffic, not waiting for the green *"Avanti"* sign to cross.

"Wait," he shouted back to the others. "There it is, I think."

They ran across Nomentana and under the gateway arch to the compound of the basilica of Saint Agnes, described in Church legend as a young and beautiful martyr. They knew if they were late, they would be shut out. One of their Angelicum professors, an Irish Dominican, had over the years gained special access to tunnels, crypts, and archaeological sites normally closed to the public. His students accompany him several times during the year. Gary looked forward to each one. Being surrounded by the damp stones and cool subterranean air reminded him of St. Benedict's grotto at Subiaco.

They were in luck. The priest was a bit late himself and was just starting his lecture. From a courtyard rung by purple bougainvillea, he pointed out the contours of the original basilica, ordered constructed by Constantina, daughter of Emperor Constantine. It was a huge brick structure, much like the first St. Peter's. All that's left of Constantina's endeavor are some jagged walls—and the circular mausoleum built after her death.

"Let's go inside," the Irish priest said. Tall bronze doors were unlocked and pushed open. Gary went in and, as he always does, touched the stones inside: coarse brick inlaid with white marble worn smooth over the ages.

"Walking in here really gives the impression of what it was like in Constantine's time," the priest said, instinctively lowering his voice because of the sharp echo. "This was what the old St. Peter's was like, what the Church of the Holy Sepulchre in Jerusalem was like.

"Imagine," he added. "Imagine that you are a fourth-century Christian. This was what it felt like; to walk toward a simple brick building like this, then come inside and be overcome by the majesty. The atmosphere, the incense, the play between light and darkness. It must have been an awesome, awesome experience."

Shafts of sunlight angled down from narrow widows above the wall murals in the curving alcove overhead. Gary stepped into the light.

"It must have been something," he said.

"What?" Tran whispered.

"You know, like he said: to come in here as an early Christian and feel how solid and permanent a place like this is. Not too long before they were hiding in catacombs. Think about what it was like to be out in the open."

At the other end of the mausoleum is a copy of Constantina's sarcophagus. "The original," said the Dominican priest, "is in the Vatican museum. As we all know, they like to keep the good stuff under one roof."

The priest pointed his flashlight beam at the ceiling mosaics: mostly images of objects from pagan funerals. "Look," he said, "there's wreaths, drinking urns. It's all pretty typical. But now here's something special."

One of the murals near the entrance is considered an important bridge between imperial iconography and Christian-influenced art. The image of the Roman emperor was often placed in the center of a mural and depicted as dispensing laws or wisdom to the empire. "Here," said the priest, "we see it's the same concept but new characters. There's Christ in the center handing some sort of scroll to Peter. And there's Paul over to the side. The little huts on the edges represent Bethlehem and Jerusalem. Most of this is original, but some parts were ruined by a bad restoration in the last century. Look around their feet how the colors don't match."

"OK?" he finished. "Let's move on."

Gary lingered as the other seminarians followed the priest along the circular gallery. He looked up toward the mural and stepped closer. He just wanted to stand there for a while and study the arched alcove—imagining the artisans, so many centuries ago, baking the clay tiles, then adding the colored glazes. The designer who climbed up into the nook to create the mural had a name, a family, a vision of Christianity. Gary said a small prayer to him—the anonymous artist who decided to make his Christ with warm, almond-shaped eyes. Gary rubbed his own. There was that vertigo feeling again—staring down into the enormity of time. It was the sensation he found standing on the wind-raked grass on top of his butte. Where else? Certainly at Subiaco. But those were places open to the sky. This was different. Someone— maybe a young man just like himself—pieced together this mosaic and countless pilgrims had done just what Gary was doing now: trying to feel the pulse of their shared humanity, trying to hear the perfect pitch of infinity. There was another place he felt this. Where? Yes, of course, he recalled. That first day in St. Peter's while waiting to go down to the tomb. Yes, Gary nodded, that was it.

Tran came back and touched Gary's arm. "Come on," he said. "We're going."

"Tran," Gary said. "This is an incredible place, don't you think?"

"Sure. But every place in Rome is like that. Every church is incredible."

"You're right. But I mean, I really get this feeling here of being connected to the Church. You know, to the early Christians. I can sort of feel them around me. It sounds strange, maybe, but it's a comforting feeling to me to think about how immense it is. I like to feel small like that. It's a good lesson," Gary said.

"In what?" asked another seminarian who was walking alongside.

"Well, humility for one."

"I can agree with that," said the seminarian, who was one of the few who knew of Gary's struggle between the monastic and parish life. "But don't you think you can make too much of it? You can become too passive. The Church doesn't want all its priests on the sidelines just gawking and saying, 'Wow, isn't it wonderful to be so spiritual.'"

Gary stopped. "I'm not saying that at all. You know me. I want more than anything to be out there with the people. It's just that I want the faith to be the important thing, not me. You've seen it, haven't you? I'm not going to get this messiah complex and tack up how many souls I've saved."

Tran went ahead down a flight of wide marble stairs to the cavernous basilica built around the ruins of Constantina's church. Gary and the other seminarian were alone. With each step down, the air grew just a bit damper and cooler.

"So, Gary," he said. "I get the feeling that you're sticking around. True?"

Benz smiled. "I've made a decision if that's what you mean."

"And?"

"You're right. I'm staying."

"I knew it! I could tell! You've given up on the Benedictines?"

"Not entirely. Who knows what will happen. I'm leaving things open. But, right now anyway, I know this is where I should be."

"So what did it? What changed your mind?"

"I can't really say. It's a combination of things, really. I think it took a while to understand my vocation. I had to figure out that I would be lost if I was stuck inside a monastery. I see my calling now as being with people, being with families. I love the Benedictines, but sometimes it's not always the best path to blindly chase the thing you love. Remember I told you about being in the monastery over Christmas?"

"Right."

"Well, that was a real turning point. Watching the people come in for mass each morning was a powerful thing. I felt so connected to them. They reminded me of the people back home in a way."

"How?"

"I don't think it was one thing. But you know what? I'll always remember that they had snow all over their shoes. They walked in the snow to come to church. That really meant a great deal to me."

"I'll tell you the truth. I didn't think you were going to stay. You seemed so down on Rome and the seminary for a while. Well, congratulations."

"For what?"

"Making a decision and reaching some peace about it. Some people spend their life trying to do just that. You *are* comfortable with your decision?"

"For the first time in a long time, I can definitely say, 'Yes, I'm comfortable.' My place is with the people of North Dakota. I've always felt that. It's just taken me time to realize that joining the monastery may not bring me closer to the people. I see myself in a parish—a little one, I hope—with families, old people, everyone."

On the bus ride back to the seminary, Gary was grinning and joking with the others. He made up his mind about staying at the seminary weeks before, but finally talking about it was a tremendous relief. For the first time, Rome seemed friendly. He no longer felt so much like an outsider looking in.

"So I hear you're going back to Washington this summer?" Gary asked Tran.

"That's right. What about you?"

"Turkey."

"Really? On the military base. What's it called?"

"Incirlik. It's in southern Turkey. I'll be doing counseling in with the chaplain."

"Sounds exciting," said Tran. "So you've gotten this Benedictine thing out of your system?"

Gary jerked back. "You knew? Did everyone? There's certainly a pretty good rumor mill around here, isn't there? Well, I think it's safe to say I'll be back next year. Definitely, yes."

"That's really good," he said.

"Why?"

"We need guys like you, you know. Steady guys."

"You know what I think?" the seminarian next to Gary said. "I think it's like we're here"—he pushed his index finger onto the bus window—"and that lots and lots of Catholics are over here." He jabbed the other finger about five inches away from the other. "We know why there is a gap. The job is to figure out how to close it."

"And so how do we do that?" Gary asked.

"By sticking with the program: being prayerful, charitable, and don't forget celibate," he said. "Catholics have to respect the priesthood before they'll start respecting again what we are counseling them to do."

"It's true," said Gary. "Very true. I just hope things don't get any worse before we get ordained and get out there."

The bus pulled into the asphalt expanse in front of Termini, Rome's main train station. Dozens of buses were idling, ready to begin their runs. The seminarians ran toward the 64—called by some the "Heaven to Hell" express for its Vatican to Termini route and its reputation as the preferred line for pickpockets and purse thieves.

"No, no, not that one," Gary yelled. "Over here."

They boarded the 65, which gets them to the base of the Janiculum and close enough to walk the rest of the way to the seminary.

"Hey, country boy," one of the seminarians poked Benz. "You're learning."

That night in the dining hall, the seminarians raised their glasses. The American cleric who oversees the Vatican's finances shook his head as if he were unaccustomed to being toasted.

"To Edmund Cardinal Szoka," said John Riccardo, a deacon heading back to Szoka's Detroit archdiocese for ordination. Szoka had watched Riccardo grow up, son of a mogul in a city where they still existed in the supreme form: a reach that spanned from assembly lines to the White House and, through American Church channels, to the Vatican. The elder John Riccardo retired after a twenty-year chairmanship of Chrysler in 1979 after helping his successor, Lee Iaccoca, create a successful pitch for a federal bail-out for the ailing automaker. He also was a substantial donor to the archdiocese and one of Szoka's selected lay advisers.

Szoka stood up. He was nearing his seventieth birthday but seemed much younger. As always, he has a slightly mischievous smirk. Boyish almost. His nails were immaculately manicured. Szoka already had a long day with celebrations for the twenty-fifty anniversary of his ordination as a bishop. He seemed, however, in no hurry to get the dinner over with.

"Thank you, John," he said. "and thank you for not calling me 'the money man.' I hear that all the time. As you all probably know, John's father was CEO of Chrysler. Often, we talked money and figures and that sort of thing. Now I'm over here doing the books for the Vatican and I'm being toasted by his son. I guess I just can't escape this money-man reputation."

Dolan leaned over and whispered to a faculty member at the head table: "Man, here's a guy who balanced the budget of the Vatican. We should elect him president."

"But," the cardinal continued, "let's not forget that money is just money. It's important, no doubt. But it's not holy—although some might disagree. The essentials of my life have remained the same. The high point of my day is to celebrate mass. Don't lose sight of that.

Never let the external obligations of the Church divert you from the internal beauty of prayer."

The seminarians clapped wildly, even Gary Benz. Back at the beginning of the year, this would have been the type of event that would rile him endlessly. A fancy reception. Dolan all smiles at having a cardinal over to the seminary. Now, he just enjoyed it and even drank a second glass of wine. There is no sense trying to change what Rome—indeed what the seminary—is about, Gary decided. "How can I judge others?" Gary said when the toast was over. "Who am I to say that spirituality can only exist in simplicity? It may work for me, but maybe not for, I don't know, Chris Nalty. I've learned a big lesson here: holiness comes in all types and shapes—maybe in the overalls of a farmer or vestments of a cardinal. Who am I? Just like anyone else, I'm trying to understand God."

For Gary, the year of suffering over his vocation was, in a small way, emblematic of the modern values that he finds so out of synch with his own. It's a question, Gary asks, of how much control we truly have.

"Ever since the first machine—and now especially with computers and virtual reality and all that stuff—there's been this growing idea that man is changing his environment to suit his needs," Gary said. "And in a sense, that's true. Look, we have air-conditioning, pesticides, all sorts of things to make life easier for us. But don't you also think this kind of seeps into our souls, too? I mean, our view of religion and God. That God and the Church—and priests even—should bend to our own will and fulfill our expectations and needs.

"In a way," he continued, "that's what was going on with me and the Benedictines. It was a selfish thing. I wanted the faith to accommodate me and my desires. I wanted it all: the spirituality of the monastery and being with the people like a parish priest. Like I said, it was selfish. I learned that God, if you really listen to Him, forces you to make decisions."

The cardinal was definitely not what the seminarians had expected. A pep talk about the need to keep the collection plates filled, perhaps. But certainly not a plug for prayer from the Vatican's number cruncher.

"What do you think?" one of the seminarians said. "Another outbreak of 'scarlet fever'?"—a reference among the seminarians about daydreams of someday wearing the cardinals' red sash and skull cap.

"Maybe," a New Man said. "He's impressive."

"Boy," said an older seminarian, "we get to have a cardinal for dinner. The pope's meeting with the mother of the guy who shot him. What next?"

"What?" a few seminarians blurted at once.

"You didn't hear? The pope met with her over at the Vatican. I'm serious. She came over to ask Italy to free him. What's his name?"

"Mehmet Ali Agca," a seminarian at the table said.

"Right. Yup, they think Italy is going to let him out."

"Yeah, right," a seminarian laughed. "Stranger than fiction."

And then some. Italy's state broadcaster, Radio-Televisione Italiana, funded the trip from Turkey for the mother and brother of Ali Agca to make an appeal for his release on the anniversary of the May 13, 1981, shooting in St. Peter's Square. Foreign media was aghast, but in Italy the obvious cross currents were barely a ripple: state TV spending state money so the relatives of the would-be assassin could make a plea for compassion from the state during a trip that could become part of a state-funded documentary.

The pope met the bewildered village woman after his weekly general audience the day after the attack anniversary. That was it. There were no further appeals for leniency for Agca, who months later sent the pope a get-well telegram after his appendectomy. "I'm spiritually close to you," Agca reportedly wrote.

A few tables over from the chat about the Turkish gunman, Roger Landry remained riveted on the cardinal. His tennis-court conversations with Monsignor Thomas had reshaped his views about the Curia. And now the cleric they most expected to be crusty and hard-bitten is waxing on about celebrating mass and praying.

"I'm frankly surprised," Roger said to his brother.

"I know what you mean."

"I came over here with this impression that the Curia's some sort of beast that just has to be tamed," said Roger. "I really don't think that way any more. I mean, here's a guy who has every opportunity to be tempted to put away the sacramental side, but he hasn't. That means something to me."

These last few months had been, for Roger, like taking a deep breath. Rome—the *pazienza* of the city—had begun to work. "It was some point, I really can't say when, that I came to understand that the rules we knew before no longer apply. Before, you work, you study, you impress, and you get ahead. You can try that in the Church, too. But will it get you anywhere? No. Not always, anyway. The Church may elevate you to levels of huge prominence. Or it could decide it's best to leave you in the most obscure parish.

"So much time is spent here by seminarians trying to figure out the type of niche they see for themselves. That's not just going to get shattered once, but probably a hundred times by the time they have their fiftieth anniversary as a priest."

"You're starting to sound like me, Rog," Scot cut in.

"Maybe I am. I was—and I guess still am—very competitive. Not too long ago, in fact, I was extremely impatient. I wanted to keep moving, ever higher in everything as quickly as possible. But there's been a noticeable change. I won't say I'm meeker, but let's say more understanding."

"And not so lonely?"

"Yeah, I guess, not so self-absorbed. I hadn't treasured my relationships with others before. Now, I want to see God in others. How He makes His presence felt. I guess the Church has made me more human just as it's trying to strip me of the truly human qualities like pride. It's a paradox, don't you think?"

"Lots of things here don't make sense if you think about them too hard," said Scot.

"It's kind of like a dog chasing its tail," Roger said. "I'm pursuing God, but He is also pursuing me at the same time. It kind of goes around as a circle, but the circle becomes a spiral."

The dinner ended and Cardinal Szoka walked out to his Mercedes sedan along with some of the Detroit seminarians. One of them mentioned a seminarian from Omaha who broke his ankle sliding into third base in a softball game. "He was disappointed he couldn't see you," he said.

"Really?" said Szoka. "Me?"

The cardinal poked his head into the window of his car. "Wait a minute," he told the nuns inside who are on his personal staff. The cardinal went back upstairs to pay a visit to the seminarian in a cast.

CHAPTER XXI

PENTECOST

The Lord delights in those who revere him.

—PSALM 147 FOR THE VIGIL OF PENTECOST

Chris Nalty waved his orange ticket at the Vatican gendarme, one of the ones in the dark suits that patrol the crowds at papal events.

The guard stepped back, but just a bit to make sure no one else slipped past. Chris weaved around. The hem of his black cassock scraped against the heavy wooden barrier. He looked down to make sure there were no marks on the cassock. Chris spent about $300 for it at Gamarelli's, the tailor shop that has made the papal cassocks and vestments for decades. Nalty loved the custom fit—not too snug on top, then flaring nicely down to ankle length. It also conveniently hid his expanding midsection. He had gained a reputation as the seminary kitchen Epicurean. His Cigar Smokers' Dinner before Christmas included fettuccine with porcini mushrooms and grilled veal scaloppini topped with artichokes and mushrooms. The last of three cigars during the meal was 1995 Romeo y Julieta Churchill from Cuba accompanied by Sandeman Original Rich Ruby Port (serial number SW091161). Lately, he had been experimenting with fettuccine and various cream sauces.

He wore the cassock to all the liturgies at St. Peter's. He enjoyed the stares and smiles from the pilgrims. They are always asking if Chris can pose for a photograph. The Japanese particularly loved the old-style image. They would take the shot and bow. Nalty would bow back.

Chris looked behind him to check if the other New Man got through. He was just getting by the guard. Rob hung on to the brim of his hat, the traditional wide-brimmed *cappello romano* he liked to wear. It wasn't too windy, but it only takes a puff to flip the hat away. The two seminarians had been nearly inseparable during the year—traveling to the Canary Islands, Egypt, around Italy. They were in the middle of a regime of inoculations for their summer in Calcutta with Mother Teresa. They particularly wanted to be together for this last time in St. Peter's as New Men. The pope had chosen the holy day of Pentecost to formally launch the preparation for 2000, declared as the Roman Catholic Church's twenty-eighth Jubilee year—a time for special celebrations and pilgrimages. The Holy Door at St. Peter's Basilica will be pushed open.

Pentecost—a day buried deep in the faith of both Christianity and Judaism—was first celebrated as the renewal of the covenant bestowed by God on Mt. Sinai. The Christian roots are in the New Testament story of the Holy Spirit descending in the form of burning flames that hovered over a group of faithful in Jerusalem. Those blessed began to praise God in foreign tongues. The pope always fully exploits the religious imagery. When the Orthodox ecumenical patriarch, Bartholomew I, visited Rome in 1995, the pope chose the feast day of two saints, Peter and Paul, to highlight their meeting. To begin the preparations for the global Roman Catholic Jubilee year, what could be more appropriate than a day that celebrates the reversal of Babel? Pentecost celebrates unity and illumination.

For the New Men who continue to ordination, the year 2000 will be their first full year as priests. Chris and Rob made a vow to return to Rome then, no matter what happens. Nalty also wondered whether the archdiocese may keep him in Rome to study canon law. He finally felt stable enough in the seminary to actually start thinking about ordination and beyond.

"Here we are," said Chris. "Not bad."

"Yeah, look. We're finally ahead of you-know-who," said Rob.

"Yesss," Nalty quietly celebrated.

Their early arrival put them in front of the hyper-conservative Legionaries of Christ, all in their black double-breasted clerics. For once, Nalty thought, they didn't get their favored front-row spots at a papal mass and will have to look at the back of my head. The best places for the Pentecost Mass went to the clerics from Rome and city politicians, who were desperately trying to work out plans to handle the maybe three-fold jump in tourists during 2000. They pay homage to the Vatican, but smolder at its arrogance. The pope declares a Jubilee year. The city coughs up the money to try to make it work. That generally sums up the lop-sided relationship between the Holy See and the mayor's office on the Capitoline Hill in central Rome.

The sun was going down behind salmon clouds when the music started. "What?" Chris thought. "What's that?" He was expecting the Sistine Screamers—the seminarians' dismissive nickname for the Sistine Choir that normally sings at papal masses. "A choir of soloists," went the critique from one faculty member. This night, however, a guitar and piano duet from a Rome parish started up.

Chris leaned over to his friend. "What's going on?"

He shrugged. "I don't know. Hey, go with the flow."

That's exactly what Chris had been thinking about. He had tried in every way to convince himself he should not be in the seminary; that it was some big misunderstanding. Then the prayers for celibacy started to give him comfort, a welcome routine. Then he finally broke off whatever halfway relationship there was with Allie. That was a defining moment. It was as if the umbilical cord to home—to the past—had finally been cut. His identity was clear to all: a seminarian on his way to becoming a priest. Not a wayward lawyer dabbling in religion and looking for some context to his life. He hoped Allie would tell people about the calluses on his knees.

And now, he's here, back in St. Peter's, just a short walk from the tomb where he was a confused and scared New Man during that early morning mass. What did Dolan say to them at the tomb? Nalty never forgot: "Where are you going?" Back then, he wouldn't have bet that he was headed toward a solid footing in the seminary. A quick and painless exit was more what he would have guessed. Why didn't it happen?

"I just don't know," Chris mulled. "I guess, to be selfish, you can call it happiness. I thought I was happy when I was raking in money as a lawyer. I thought I was happy going from party to party, girlfriend to girlfriend. I assumed I was. But I wasn't. It was a hollow thing, but I just didn't recognize it. I wasn't happy until I did the hardest thing I ever did in my life. That was to decide to come to the seminary."

The pope, sitting in a high-back throne in the center of the altar right in front of Nalty, looked out over the square. He did not speak for a few seconds. Instantly, a group of reporters started murmuring. Was he sick again? Then he spoke. He went directly to the point: prepare yourself for the millennium. With both hands, Chris grasped the unlit candle he was carrying.

"Living in this metropolis, that unfortunately cannot escape from the temptations of secularism, there is a subtle threat of weariness, of a spiritual torpor," the pope said.

Nalty was awed. It was as if the pope was speaking right to him—just like the surprise of reading about the sins of hedonism at the private papal mass months before. Chris felt a contentment as never before. It was running through him but at the same time pouring outward. It seemed as if he was unfolding. And at the bottom of all the many folds was the prize: the core of the force that pulled him toward the Church. It was clean and solid. Is this what destiny feels like? Chris was breathing faster. He gave a quick prayer of thanks for not leaving the seminary back in the lowest days in the fall. He couldn't imagine turning back now: back to his BMW, his house, his law practice, clients. All of it. It all seemed like a receding image as he bolted away. This is right. I am meant to be here, he said to himself. Then out loud: "It's perfect."

"What?" Rob turned.

"It's incredible, isn't it?" Nalty said, not taking his eyes off the pope. "Rob, I know you know this already, but I really think I'm going all the way."

Rob leaned over to whisper just as the floodlights came on in the square. "I know," he said. "I could see it happening even if you couldn't. Besides, who would I go on trips with?"

Usually, being stuck in a throng made Chris edgy. But not this night. It was warm and secure. A perfect sync—everyone reciting the prayers, riding the comforting swell as the mass moved toward its conclusion. Then silence and cleansing fire.

Twelve torches were set ablaze to light the pope's candle, symbolizing the biblical tale of the tongues of fire of the Holy Spirit that descended upon each apostle. The flame was then passed from candle to candle, until thousands of candles were glowing in the square. The warm light of the flames was projected on the white stone columns that cradle St. Peter's Square like two cupped hands. There were so many candles that you could feel the warmth, running over your cheek or up the back of your neck. Chris looked into the yellow-and-white flicker atop his candle, then looked into the sky. Imagine, he thought, what it looks like from the top of St. Peter's dome or from a passing plane.

"Or heaven," he said. "Think about what this must look like from heaven."

The pope was on his second loop around the square in the glass-enclosed popemobile. It passed so close to Chris—not more than ten feet away. Close enough to see the reflection of the candles in the pope's eyes under the awning of his heavy brows. "Awesome," Chris said. "I mean, unbelievable." He was content to stand there and watch his candle slowly melt down.

Chris and Rob filed slowly out of the piazza with the crowd of pilgrims and clergy. More than 50,000 of them were going to join a procession through central Rome to the Basilica of Santa Maria Maggiore, where in ancient times candidates for the priesthood were scrutinized by the Curia.

"Fathers, Fathers," shouted a guard toward Chris and Rob, whose cassocks probably fooled him into thinking they were young monsignors. "This way, *prego*. It's easier."

He moved back a barrier for the pathway used by the popemobile. "*Grazie,*" Chris said. The two New Men walked down the center of St. Peter's Square in a clear lane with tens of thousands of people crushed on their side of the barricades.

"Are you coming?" asked Rob.

"No. I just want to go back," Chris said.

"Are you sure? It should be an amazing thing, marching through Rome."

"No doubt. But, thanks anyway, man. I just want to head back. See you back there."

"OK, *ciao,*" said Rob as he joined the column of people streaming down Via della Conciliazione toward the Tiber, now already well on its way toward its low and sluggish summer level. Chris turned right, up the Janiculum. He walked quickly. It was very quiet. He turned back once to watch the river of light from the thousands and thousands of candles flow over the bridge and disappear behind the squat buildings on the other side of the Tiber. It was remarkable how quiet it was. Nearly 50,000 people were in the procession and almost no one was talking. Nalty was glad Rob followed the procession. He wanted to be alone, anyway. This is what he had waited so long for: a real decision. He wanted to relish it, as he would some exotic cigar.

"The question always was: am I going to be tormented by celibacy or am I going to reach the point where I can sort of see it and accept it?" Chris said after walking through the seminary gates. "I think I'm finally ready to accept it now." The sign that Rector Dolan had ordered from the stone cutters had finally arrived.

It was well past midnight when he entered the little Eucharist chapel. He knew he'd be back in a few hours for his morning prayers, but he couldn't wait. He knelt, pressed his face into his palms, and cried. He didn't know why he was too self-conscious to cry back at St. Peter's. But it was better alone. Tears leaked through his fingers and over the ring he once lost and found on a dirt road in Alabama.

Brian wanted to swear. He was losing the class.

Any time he felt he was making some connection, he'd run into a roadblock with his Italian. It just wasn't good enough to make the points he wanted. All the New Men are required to take on an apostolic work during their second semester.

The most coveted are the English-language assignments: conducting the *Scavi* tours of St. Peter's tomb and the warren of chambers and passageways deep below the basilica; or counseling students at the religious-run academies for children of expatriates and wealthy Italians. Brian's request was unusual. He asked to teach religious instruction to adolescents preparing for confirmation, the symbolic passing into adulthood in the Church. Brian wanted to force some big improvements in his Italian and needed something that would put him on the spot.

The children were bored. Children—restless and ruthless after a whole day of regular school—can strike viciously at any weakness. Some of the boys giggled mercilessly over a stumble over a phrase or an off-target pronunciation. Confirmation class was bad enough, but having it with a seminarian who spoke sputtering Italian was simply twisting the knife. And Christensen knew there were few things more volatile than restless twelve-year-olds.

"*Prego, prego,*" he pleaded. "*Un po di silenzio.*" It wasn't working.

He pointed at the class's most obvious agitator, a snide kid who reminded Brian a little bit of how he used to try to shake up the public-school teachers before heading off to no-nonsense Catholic classes.

"OK, that's it," snapped Brian, trying his best to remain stern in Italian. "Just go outside, then, if you can't be quiet."

The boy left, muttering something Christensen knew he probably wouldn't understand even if he could hear it.

"Can you take over the class?" Brian said to another New Man.

"Sure. Why?"

"I just want to go talk to him."

"Well, good luck."

Brian went out in the hall and sat next to the boy. No one else was around.

"So?" Brian asked in Italian. "What's the problem?"

"The problem," the boy shot back, "is that I don't want to be here. I just can't be here. My mother makes me come, but it's just, well, I just hate it."

"What don't you like?"

"Look, everything. It just doesn't make any sense."

"What doesn't? Do you go to mass? You must go to church, right?"

"Yeah, I go. But my mother makes me do that, too. I don't give a damn about it."

"You don't?" Brian asked.

"No, I don't. I don't see what God has to do with anything. He's nothing. He's a story."

"You really believe that?"

"Yeah."

"Well," said Christensen, speaking slowly to make sure he made as few mistakes as possible, "there are other kids in there who don't think that. They believe in God and are trying to get something out of the class."

"Good for them. I don't care."

"Look, it's OK how you feel. But would you make me a deal? Just try to be quiet. You don't have to do anything except that. Deal?"

The boy threw up his palms as if in surrender. "Deal. But can I ask you one thing? You always believe in God?"

Brian smiled. "Yes. I always did. But, you know, I didn't always think I'd want to be a priest. I was a pilot in the American Air Force before this."

The boy looked up. "Really? No joke."

"I thought once I'd probably be in the Air Force for a long time."

"I can't believe it," the boy said. "It's impossible."

"I'm telling you the truth. So you never know. Maybe someday you'll be a priest."

The boy laughed—not the snickers Brian was used to in class. "Good joke."

They talked a while about planes until the class was over. The other New Man came out of the room last.

"Brian, there you are," he said. "I was worried he killed you or something."

"No, in fact, I think I really accomplished something for the first time."

"What's that?"

"There's at least one Italian kid out there who'll look at a priest and wonder about their other lives."

"Lots of people do that nowadays," the other New Man joked.

"Yeah, I know. But that's not what I meant."

They had a good laugh. There was nothing left to do but pack for the summer.

They called him Father Brian wannabe back in the parish. In the seat of Tripp County near the Missouri River flood plain, Brian spent his first summer away from the seminary doing the work of a country pastor: helping vaccinate the hogs on a parishioner's farm; trying to reach out to teenagers desperate to see what's beyond their South Dakota town; feeding the jobless Sioux men, like his friend Xavier, from the reservation down the road from Winner—which took it's name after beating rivals to host the seat of county government. "You can't imagine how many peanut butter and jelly sandwiches I made."

It was full immersion. The Rapid City Diocese asked the North American College to waive the policy of not allowing seminarians to return home after their first year. Christensen understood the larger world but not really the one he was planning to serve as a priest.

"I felt like a real prairie priest," said Christensen. "And you know what? I loved it. I really did—an old Long Island boy like me."

Christensen knew when Xavier had been drinking. He'd knock on the back door of the rectory. His brother, who moved off the reservation into Winner, wouldn't let Xavier in the house if he was drunk. So he'd head over to the church. Many nights, Brian and Xavier would sit on the rectory steps. Xavier would tell him stories about the area and recall he was a student at the parish school. Sometimes, he would ask Brian to unlock the church so he could pray and sober up.

"Here was a guy who probably never went to mass," said Christensen. "To watch him in there, all alone and praying, was very, very powerful."

The steaks were almost done.

"How do you like yours again?" Chris Nalty asked.

"Medium," said Rob.

"Wine?"

"Don't mind if I do."

For their last night in Rome, they bought some fat filet tenderloins to grill on the roof and a bottle of good French Bordeaux. By this time the next day, they would be on their way to Calcutta.

Chris gave a contented groan as he stretched back in one of his lounge chairs that he lugged to the roof on sunny days, when he had the time, for a bit of tanning.

"You gonna miss this place?" he asked.

"Man, I don't know. It might start to look pretty good after a couple days in the Calcutta slums."

The smoke from the grill blew toward the Vatican.

Chris recalled what one of the New Men told him as he watched the fifth-year priests leaving. "It was all so sad and everything," Chris said. "You know what he told me?"

"No."

"He told me, 'When it's my last day, I'm going to go, 'Wuuuuuuu, I'm outta here.' I kind of know what he means. But then again, it's getting a little like home. Don't you think?"

"I don't know, Chris. I'll be happy to get back to the—quote—real world, if you know what I mean. This place can get pretty surreal sometimes."

"Can I tell you a story about the—quote—real world?" Chris said. "I haven't heard a word about what's going on with my house back in

New Orleans. I don't know how my dog is. These things used to drive me up the wall. I needed to be on top of everything—especially anything concerning my stuff. But you know what? I don't really care about it. I know I should be a little preoccupied, but, for some reason, I'm not. It's a great feeling."

They ate their steaks and talked. They used to stare over at the Vatican all the time as they would at a new and curious neighbor. They don't do that so much anymore. There's too much to figure out right there in the seminary.

CHAPTER XXII

LEAVING

To you, O God, I will sing a new song.

—PSALM 144 FOR TUESDAY MORNINGS

A few days before leaving Rome, Scot Landry sat at his desk and stared for a long time at a grove of evergreens in the back of the seminary. They were big, probably more than a century old. Their roots ran deep into the soil, and big heavy pine cones dropped from their branches.

"You know something?" he said. "I've started to see everything around here in terms of what's solid and permanent. I mean, its a psychological thing, I'm sure. I thought by this point, I wouldn't be still questioning my vocation. But God works in mysterious ways.

"I'm still open to the point that the Lord has me in the seminary just so I can know Him more, then I'll do something else. I'm completely open to that."

Scot said goodbye to his brother. Scot was heading for the Italian Alps for some language study and Roger was leaving for Portugal. They usually just shake hands or pat each other on the shoulder. This time, they embraced. They knew Scot was close to unraveling his interwoven predicaments: whether to continue studying for the priesthood, and, if so, whether it should be with his brother in Fall River. The twins felt it might be all sorted out during the summer. Only they would be far apart if it happened. No more chances to talk it out in person. Phone calls and E-mails would have to suffice.

"See you in a couple months," Scot said.

"I'll be praying for you," his brother added quietly.

And they parted.

For Scot, the peace of the Alps was a catharsis. It was like seeing his vocation from a distance: whole, with all its strong parts and flaws. In Rome, he felt as if he was only able to approach it piece by piece—concentrating on one question at a time. The long walks in the mountains gave him a wider scope.

One weekend, Scot and several of his friends from the seminary traveled to the French town of Ars, the home of Scot's most beloved saint, Jean Vianney. One of the passages that helped nudge Scot toward the priesthood was in the saint's autobiography, which describes him striving to meet the spiritual and material needs of his parishioners. The poor, the saint believed, need food and shelter as much as they need nourishment for their souls.

While praying in Ars, Scot kept thinking about what it could be like if he was ordained in the Bridgeport diocese. "Fairfield County, Connecticut"—Scot pronounced each syllable as if it were a new foreign word. "This place," he said, "is one of the wealthiest counties in America. Sure, people need priests there, but not really to help them with material as well as spiritual needs." Then Scot thought of hard-luck Fall River. These people need him more than Bridgeport, he thought. And Scot could have one of the things he craved: being close to his brother. In prayer in a chapel in Ars, Scot decided to make the transfer request.

"I was finally at peace," he said.

During the six-hour drive back to Italy, Scot thought hard about how to the handle the transfer. He asked his friends. They all decided it would be best to make the request during the summer rather than wait until busy September. They advised him, however, to talk to the seminary faculty spending the summer in Rome before letting Bridgeport know. There is precise protocol to follow, especially in matters concerning seminarians.

The next day, Scot returned to Rome. But before leaving, he sent an E-mail to his brother. "It's decided," he wrote. "I'm called to Fall River."

Back in Rome, Scot discussed the situation with two faculty members. They told him it was now time to let Bridgeport know.

Scot called the vocations direction in Bridgeport, braced for a cool—and maybe even angry—reaction. He was surprised.

"Scot, if you truly feel God is calling you to Fall River, then it's our loss, but we'd consider it our service to the universal Church," the vocations director said. "I think you'll make a wonderful priest."

"Thank you," said Scot, smiling he was so relieved.

"But just do me one favor, Scot. Could you do that?"

"Of course."

"Pray about it a little more. Then, if you are sure that Fall River is your decision, get back to me."

Scot hung up the phone. He was relieved. The huge struggle he expected was nothing more than a pleasant phone call. He sent Roger the good news by E-mail. Scot kept his promise to Bridgeport and prayed every day about the decision. But he knew it would always lead back to the same point. It was obvious to him he should be with Roger.

He notified Bridgeport about a week later. They told Scot to write a formal letter of request to transfer and contact Fall River. It was done immediately. All the pieces were falling smoothly into place.

The Fall River diocese made Scot feel immediately welcome. The bishop, who had met Scot during his visits to Rome, asked him to return to Massachusetts to start the paperwork and spend a month working in a parish.

Fall River is in an extremely cautious mode concerning its seminarians after a torturous sex scandal involving a former priest, James Porter, who was considered one of the country's most notorious child molesters. He was convicted in December 1992 of sexually abusing twenty-eight children in several parishes in the 1960s. He was sentenced to eighteen to twenty years in prison, but will be eligible for parole in 1999. Dozens of other people in other states also had accused Porter of abusing them as children. In May 1996, the Fall River Diocese announced plans to run background checks on all its religious educators and require child abuse awareness training for all its employees and volunteers working with children.

The diocese also imposed a rule on all prospective seminarians not raised in the area who transfer to the diocese during the years of study for the priesthood. They would spend a year of volunteer work in a parish. But the bishop told Scot that because of his brother and year in Rome, a month in a parish should be sufficient. Scot canceled a trip to Ireland and caught the next flight to Boston. He expected to be back in Rome in five weeks.

Then the foundation began to crumble.

Scot was in Fall River a few days when he received a message to meet the bishop, who was clearly rattled.

"Scot," he said, handing Scot a piece of paper, "we received this from Bridgeport."

A knot built in Scot's stomach as he read. The letter from the vocations director accused Scot of being "disloyal" and "manipulative" and claimed he was "just using the generosity" of the diocese to get to Rome and then try to join his brother. The letter implied Scot had been working on the transfer "plan" for two years. And, most hurtful of all, it recommended that Scot not return to the North American College until, at least, he completed a year of pastoral work in the diocese. The vocations director, above all, was worried that sliding Scot through could send the wrong message for other seminarians that switching dioceses is a consequence-free proposition. A copy of the letter was sent to Rector Dolan.

"The accusations are completely ridiculous," Scot roared.

The bishop was sympathetic, but now that it was in writing the accusations could not be ignored. The bishop suggested, gently but firmly, that Scot consider enrolling in a local seminary or taking a year of parish work.

Scot felt sick as he left the office. Can this be happening? he asked himself. He ran over the phone conversation from Italy with the vocations director. What did he say? "Our service to the universal Church." And now this?

"I felt," Scot said later, "like a bomb had just been dropped on me that night."

For a few days, Scot went through the motions in Fall River, always hoping that the diocese would come to his defense, disregard the accusations in the letter, and allow him to return to Rome to study. "I can only hope," he E-mailed Roger, "that they just clear this whole mess up."

But it got messier. The Fall River bishop called Scot into his office again.

"Scot, we've decided that the best option would be for you to stay here for a pastoral year."

"I don't understand," Scot said. "I thought there was no reason for that. We had discussed it. If this is because of Bridgeport's letter . . ."

"I haven't even contacted Bridgeport or Monsignor Dolan about this at all. It's our recommendation for you at this point."

"This point? But, I've already bought my ticket to return to Rome. What is going on?"

"Scot, I'm not sure that the NAC will take you back this year."

"Have we tried everything?" Scot pleaded. "What about Bridgeport? Can't we get them to write another letter."

"I think that the harder we push Bridgeport, the harder they are going to push back."

It wasn't losing his place in Rome that bothered Scot as much as the idea of losing touch with his vocation. Working in a busy parish was not the right setting to dig into his soul, Scot thought. "A seminary is a place where it's OK and understood to be working out heavy issues," Scot said later. "But I really didn't think a parish setting is a good place to work out the emotions and to have serious doubts about a calling to the priesthood. The seminarian is a high-profile person in the parish community and the parishioners have certain expectations."

In the mail the day the bishop advised Scot to consider parish work, Scot received a letter from Dolan. Under the circumstances, it was very gentle. Dolan asked for explanations of Scot's reason for waiting until the summer before initiating the transfer process and keeping the seminary faculty in the dark. Scot quickly sent back a reply, stressing how he had discussed the issue with his brother and Father McRae.

Scot waited, all the time growing more disenchanted and confused at the way the Church was working; how letters and accusations were seemingly given more weight than his own explanations. Is this what he was struggling for, he asked himself, to have to deal with missives and power plays? Finally, a reply from Dolan arrived on September 8, the day Scot was scheduled to return to Rome. Dolan seemed satisfied with Scot's explanations, but Scot was worn out. Even if Fall River would have sent him back, Scot had decided that he had enough of the entire process.

He felt returning to Rome with his grave doubts about his vocation would be counterproductive and frustrating. He also refused to go to a parish and "fake that everything was fine with me—when everything was far from fine."

Scot went home to Lowell. At the same kitchen table where he told his parents he was joining the seminary, he let them know he was not going back—at least not that year.

"I need some time away from this," Scot told them. "Maybe I'll go back? I don't know. All I know is I just need a break."

"But what about taking the year in a parish in Fall River?" his mother asked. "That's out of the question?"

"Mom, I don't think it would be good for either the parish or me. It's just not the right setting for someone already unsure about their vocation."

"As a whole," Scot said months later, "the process greatly weakened my desire to serve as a priest and it challenged my faith by weakening my trust in Church leadership to always seek out the truth."

Scot decided to look for his old job. Work, an environment he once thrived in, seemed the perfect medicine. The interview went perfectly. Scot always did well. "It's like playing in a championship tennis match or basketball game," he said. "It's a huge adrenaline rush." He started the next Monday as a senior associate product manager and moved in with a friend in Norwalk—the same Connecticut city where the old nun locked him in a hug years ago and murmured, "You've been sent from God." Scot decided to wait until going back to the parish. He worried about disappointing the congregation. "Many people in the parish only know my face in a clerical collar," he said.

And he wondered whether he would ever wear one again.

"I have a visceral hatred toward politics in the Church," Scot said. "I learned through the process that it is a reality that I would need to cope with as a priest. And I'm not sure if I've been blessed with that 'coping' gift."

After word of Scot's decision reached Rome, he received a stream of letters from others who were New Men with him. He saved them all. All offered their prayers and support. Some joined him in assailing the Church bureaucracy.

"When I read your letter, my first reaction was one of anger," wrote a seminarian who was in Scot's monthly discussion group. "It is my opinion that such mentalities of the powers are squashing vocations instead of nourishing them. You have every right to feel the way you do. We, indeed, see the humanity of the Church in such instances and still we are called to trust in its leadership. What is leadership?"

"Hang in there and keep praying honestly, and I think God's will eventually will become clear," wrote a seminarian who used to play one-on-one basketball with Scot. "I have no explanation for all the other stuff that has happened, but I don't think God would test a soul unless He knew that the soul was a resilient one."

Another wrote in all capital letters: "I feel terribly that you have to endure seeing yourself become a victim of the idiocy and selfishness that has infected parts of our Church. It must be terribly painful to be hurt by the same organization that you're trying to selflessly commit your life to."

One short note was dashed off by a seminarian just before entering the annual retreat. It closed with a thought Scot cannot forget: "God draws straight with crooked lines."

CHAPTER XXIII

NEW MEN

As for man, his days are like grass;
he flowers like the flower in the field;
the wind blows and he is gone
and his place never sees him again.

—PSALM 103 FOR WEDNESDAYS

Monsignor Dolan stayed in the shade. It was a magnificent morning—cobalt sky, not too humid, just a little breeze. A rare combination in August in Rome. From where Dolan stood—just to the left of the entrance to the chapel courtyard—St. Peter's dome was framed by two towering umbrella pines. He thought it was entirely the best view from the seminary. Dolan was in full vestments and didn't want to get out into the sun. He sweats easily and feared looking soggy for the new seminarians.

"So they're gonna drive them by the Vatican?" he asked.

"I think so," said Roger Landry. "But you know the Aurelia Antica is closed now for some construction, so I'm not sure what they're going to do. They'll probably come up and around the Janiculum."

"Sure," said Dolan. "They'll figure it out. I just wish they'd get here. We're going to have to postpone lunch, don't you think?"

"It's all under control," Roger assured him. "We've put it back an hour."

The plane was late. The faculty spent the morning pacing around or watching television reports about the latest findings in the investigation of the explosion aboard a TWA jetliner—the same company carrying the 1996 New Men. No one said anything. It's possible to be both religious and superstitious. Finally, they received a call that the plane had landed. Everyone started to assemble at the front of the chapel, a brooding chunk of Fascist-style architecture equipped with what passed as a far-sighted innovation at the time: electronic bells.

Dolan and the rest of the faculty hung back. The orientation committee—the New Men of the year before—milled about the courtyard. Mostly, they talked about their summers.

Roger was back from Portugal, where he studied the language at the request of his diocese, Fall River, which still has parishes almost completely dominated by Portuguese immigrants and their descendants. Since returning to Rome, he'd been in contact with the diocese about any change in his brother's situation. Even though Scot had told the bishop he would be leaving, Roger still refused to give up without last appeals for his twin. It broke Roger's heart to have his vision of their dual vocations derailed by squabbles between dioceses.

"It's one big mess," said Roger. "It's not supposed to end up this way."

Brian Christensen and Tam Tran weren't due back from the States until early September. The Washington archdiocese asked for Tran to return for the summer and assigned him to the city's northwest section. It was a place in decline. Many of the parishioners were too old or infirm to come to mass. Tran brought them communion and a short bit of companionship. Where are you from? they would inevitably ask. Vietnam, he'd answer, but I'm studying for the priesthood in Rome. "And they always ask if I've seen the pope," Tran said later. "I say, 'Yes, I have,' and they always smile.

"I don't always feel that America is my home," he added. "But when I'm in the parish, bringing communion to people or working with the pastor, I smile to myself because it feels perfectly right. I am not among strangers."

Gary Benz had finished his stint as a U.S. military chaplain at the Incirlik air base in southern Turkey and was now cramming in a couple weeks of intensive Italian in Florence.

He had stopped by the seminary a few weeks before to unpack. Then he heard the bells. They sounded so beautiful to him. He had heard them from St. Peter's hundreds of times before; so often he rarely paid attention. This time, in the quiet and sweltering seminary, he stood at the window and listened.

"To hear them for the first time after being surrounded by the calls to the mosques in Turkey was like an incredible homecoming," said Gary. "I just stopped everything. You know the feeling when you're back around something familiar? I had chills."

Chris Nalty couldn't stop smiling—his big, gleaming grin that looked even more impressive against his leathery tan. It was all too much: being back in Rome after months in India; feeling calm and content to help to greet another crop of New Men, which he knew must include several that would be tested and tempted the same way he was.

"So what was it like?" one of the seminarians asked Chris Nalty, who was wearing an elegant black suit and his Roman collar. He had just returned from Calcutta, where he worked the summer in Mother Teresa's House for the Dying.

"It was a trip. It was mind-blowing," he gushed. "I mean, here I am walking around with Mother Teresa leaning on my arm. At times it was, like, this is unreal. I have a saint on my arm. You know I gave her communion?"

"What?" Roger Landry blurted. "You're kidding."

"It was our second day there—really our first full day at the home. They told us to be there early to help serve mass. The chapel has no pews, just a concrete floor. There are no fans, so we're up there dripping with sweat. Since everyone was sitting on the floor, I couldn't see who was out there. So when it was time for communion, I went off to the side of the altar and I look up and the first person standing in line is Mother Teresa. My knees just went weak."

By this time, Dolan and the others were gathered around listening to Nalty.

"Ya'll know what Mother says, right? She says her mission is serving Jesus in the distressing disguise of the poorest of the poor. There is a total belief that everyone you are helping is Jesus. And the volunteers talk about it. As Americans, so much of what you see is sort of repugnant. You say, 'I can't do that. It's gross. Look at the sores on those people and look how dirty they are.'

"But let me tell ya'll something. It doesn't really register on you until you do it. One day I'm holding this guy while they clean maggots out of his leg. You could see the bone through the sores. And if that's all you thought about and all you focused on, you couldn't do it. It would just be sick and disgusting. But then you think about what Mother's saying and it becomes incredibly beautiful. I was weeping as I was holding this guy. Not because he was sick but because it was beautiful. Here's this guy and he's helpless and he's Jesus."

Chris made two promises to himself during the summer in India: return someday to work with the Missionaries of Charity in Calcutta and ask for an assignment in the poorest parish in New Orleans when he's ordained. "I say 'when I'm ordained' now rather than 'if I'm ordained.' A big change, huh?" he said. "Well, I'm thinking that this is what God really wants me to do. It's something for me to say that with confidence."

Nalty loves to tell stories and one of his new favorites is what happened on July 23, his thirty-fourth birthday. He worked all day taking care of the patients at the House for the Dying—bathing them, holding their hands. Near the end of the day, a Muslim man died. They put him in the ambulance, which was also used to shuttle sisters and volunteers around the city. Chris and Rob got a lift back to the rectory in the ambulance. Ten novices—women preparing to take vows to be missionaries—also climbed aboard. Just as the ambulance was leaving, they picked up a thin and wheezing man covered with sores. Everyone was squeezed together. It was a Hindu festival and the street was clogged with people. The ambulance couldn't move. And suddenly, it started to rain—a monsoon deluge. The rain was coming down in horizontal sheets so they had to close the ambulance windows. Inside, it was like a sauna. They were all drenched in sweat.

"But the sisters did just like they do everyday, they started to pray. They handed us the book and we started to pray the afternoon Liturgy of the Hours along with them," Chris said.

"And who would have imagined that on my birthday, I would be in an ambulance with a dead person, a sick person, ten novices sitting on top of each other, sweating my behind off, stuck in traffic and praying and be this happy?"

Chris suddenly realized he had an audience and this wasn't his show—it was for the incoming seminarians. He quickly shifted gears— "And you can see it's a good weight-loss program."

Nalty came down with malaria and lost about fifteen pounds— some of it regained during a week at the beach resort of Goa.

"I want to try to keep it off," he said, running his hand over his slimmed-down chest. "I started running. It's nice to have your clothes fit nicely again." He suddenly wished he hadn't made a joke about malaria. A few days before, Mother Teresa was in intensive care in a Calcutta hospital with heart and lung problems aggravated by a 100-degree malarial fever.

Dolan looked over. "Chris, you really running? Good for you. I had to give it up, you know. Had lots of problems with my feet. I'm into walking now."

"We'll try to inspire each other, then," Chris said.

"You got it."

"Monsignor!" Father Daniel Kampschneider called out, bounding up the chapel steps.

"Were you in the lead car?" Dolan asked.

Kampschneider nodded. "OK," Dolan said. "Just a few more minutes."

A seminarian, dressed in a white robe, lit incense in a bronze censer swinging at the end of three metal chains. He wafted it around. Smoke the color of heavy cream billowed out over the entrance to the courtyard leading to the chapel doors.

Everyone pulled back to the sides. They wanted the new seminarians' first view of the chapel to be uncluttered. "It gets more choreographed every year," Dolan whispered. Someone hit the switch for the church bells and they started to peal.

"Here they come," said Nalty, peeking around the corner. "Ready?"

Forty New Men climbed the stairs. Just then faculty and seminarians streamed out from the sides and lined the steps. Nalty was near the front, applauding loudly just as seminarians did for him a year before. He watched them pass, trying in the blink of an eye to decide who might face the same troubles he did as a new seminarian. He knew it was impossible to say, but he couldn't resist. He remembered exactly how it felt ascending those stairs for the first time. The fatigue from the flight is momentarily gone. Everything is sweeping at full speed as if your world is being funneled through the seminary gates and up into the chapel. And the Vatican is so close. Right there, over their shoulders.

Nalty guessed that this is what it must feel like on your wedding day: partly exhilarating, partly surreal. The grounds smelled of freshly cut grass. Was it like this on my first day? Nalty asked himself. "I remember when I was going up here I didn't know what the heck I was getting into, I didn't know what this place was going to be like." He also remembered how it felt to look around and see no familiar faces.

Chris had previously met two of the New Men and made sure he waved to them as they passed.

"If someone last year would have told me I'd be glad to be back here, I would have told them they were crazy," Nalty mused. "But, you know, I am—glad to be back, that is, not crazy."

The New Men walked under the courtyard arch decorated with designs of the zodiac—from the medieval concept of the Church guiding all the forces of the universe. Carrying Bibles, cameras, and duty-free bags, they passed through the clouds of incense and entered the green marble chapel.

The seminary's music director began to play the organ up in the balcony. Dolan sat to the side of the altar and watched the New Men enter the pews—four in each, evenly spaced. Just like the year before. And the year before that. This was Dolan's third time greeting a new group of seminarians. It was one of his favorite days. He had tried to memorize their names from the photographs sent by the bishops. Now there they were assembled before him—each New Man absorbed in his own thoughts, his own fears and expectations. The youngest was twenty, the oldest almost fifty. Among them there were two lawyers, a former marketing manager, and a man who ran the family's janitorial services company in Pennsylvania. The entire seminary enrollment was above 140 for the first time in more than twenty-five years.

"It never ceases to amaze me," Dolan whispered to a new member of the faculty—a new spiritual director. "These guys, tired and in need of a shave, are on their first step in a brand-new life. Even if they drop out or go on to become bishops, their faith brought them this far: to this chapel in Rome."

They read two psalms. Dolan then walked slowly from his chair, across the altar to the lectern.

"Your heads are spinning, New Men, your eyes are heavy, your ears may still be blocked from the plane ride, so my remarks will be succinct, only two words: loss and look.

"You, like St. Paul, have just lost many things: the nearness of family and friends, the routine and comfort of home and America, the security of a more predictable way of life, jobs, careers, promotions, money. Oh, the changes that begin today: new faces and names, new language and food, new superiors and schedules, new culture and customs, a new building and home . . .

"And number two," Dolan continued. "Look.

"Look at the men next to you, your brother New Men, whom you will grow to know and fraternally love these next years, and to whom you will refer for the rest of your lives with one of the most affectionate terms a seminarian or priest can use: 'He is my classmate.'

"Look around at brother seminarians here, our orientation committee, who represent the men of the house in receiving you and helping you settle in; who, just a year ago, were as confused, tired, and homesick as you are now.

"Look at this Eternal City, Rome, the most effective of classrooms to teach you about the Church.

"Look over that dome, overshadowing every corner of this Janiculum Hill, reminding us of St. Peter and his successor.

"And, New Men, look within. Look within and see a man who has come to do His will."

The New Men filed out pew by pew. The musical director played the old organ and Roger Landry stood by to turn the pages.

EPILOGUE

Chris Nalty's friend and travel companion, Rob, dropped out of the seminary in late 1996.

A few months later, near the spot where he and Rob attended the Pentecost mass, Chris stood for a long time on a very clear night and watched the Hale-Bopp comet directly over the dome of St. Peter's.

Scot Landry refused to begin dating until he determined whether he will return to study for the priesthood. He believed he would—someday. He just didn't know how long it will take.